Situating Governance
Context, Content, Critique

Antonino Palumbo

ecpr PRESS

Antonino Palumbo

First published by the ECPR Press in 2015

The ECPR Press is the publishing imprint of the European Consortium for Political Research (ECPR), a scholarly association, which supports and encourages the training, research and cross-national co-operation of political scientists in institutions throughout Europe and beyond.

ECPR Press
Harbour House
Hythe Quay
Colchester
CO2 8JF
United Kingdom

Typeset by Lapiz Digital Services

Printed and bound by Lightning Source

British Library Cataloguing in Publication Data

A catalogue record for this book is available from the British Library

ISBN: 978-1-907-301-68-1
PDF ISBN: 978-1-785-521-52-2
EPUB ISBN: 978-1-785-521-53-9
KINDLE ISBN: 978-1-785-521-54-6
www.ecpr.eu/ecprpress

If you are interested in modes of governance, political theory, and globalisation, you may like to explore these other ECPR Press titles

Concepts and Reason in Political Theory
Iain Hampsher-Monk
A selection of Hampsher-Monk's writings on historicity and rationality in political theory.
ISBN 9781907301704

Varieties of Political Experience: Power Phenomena in Modern Society
Gianfranco Poggi
A collection of essays on power – particularly political power – and its institutional embodiments.
ISBN 9781907301759

Choice, Rules and Collective Action: The Ostroms on the Study of Institutions and Governance
Elinor Ostrom & Vincent Ostrom
Edited by Filippo Sabetti and Paul Dragos Aligica
Works representing the main analytical and conceptual vehicles articulated by the Ostroms to create the Bloomington School of public choice and institutional theory.
ISBN 9781910259139

The Modern State Subverted: Risk and the Deconstruction of Solidarity
Giuseppe Di Palma
Democratic states under the yoke of contemporary neoliberalism.
ISBN 9781907301636

Globalisation: An Overview
Danilo Zolo
Analysis of the concepts and theoretical issues.
ISBN 9780955248825

Visit **www.ecpr.eu/ecprpress** for up-to-date information about new and forthcoming publications

Contents

In memory of Lynnette Caicco (1953-2015)

'The morning's work began with a visit to the offices of Control Services, the company which supervised the borough's parking. The contract for parking had been enforced with such lack of sensitivity, such aggressive pursuit of the officially non-existent quotas and bonuses, such a festival of clamped and towed residents, such a bonanza of gotcha! tickets and removals, such an orgy of unjust, malicious, erroneous, and just plain wrong parking tickets, that in local elections it had cost the incumbent council control of the borough not once but twice. And there was nothing the borough could do, because the terms of the contract were set by central government, so that there was no effective control, at local level, of this local service. It was a local government classic: it was a total cock-up, it was completely unfixable, and it was nobody's fault.'

John Lanchester, *Capital*, 413

Table of Figures

Acknowledgements

The present work is an expanded (and highly revised) version of my 2011 Italian book *La Polity Reticolare* (XL Edizioni, Rome). Three new chapters have been added (Chapters One, Two and Five), while others have been omitted; the Introduction and Conclusion have been rewritten. These changes have made it possible to divide the whole work into three main thematic parts, as originally intended. As it turned out, writing the Italian version first was an unnecessary detour that took precious time away from this enterprise, as several chapters were originally written in English. This said, it has allowed me the time to write the missing chapters and revise the rest thoroughly, taking on board feedback on the first version. My hope is that these additions and changes will make the whole enterprise more extensive and comprehensible.

Chapter Three is the oldest part of this manuscript. It was originally drafted in 2007 and published as the Introduction to the first part of an anthology of works on governance I co-edited (and translated) with my colleague Salvo Vaccaro: *Governance: Teorie, principi, modelli, pratiche nell'era globale* (Mimesis, Milan, 2007). That collaboration also yielded a second co-edited volume where a very early draft of what is now Chapter Eight first appeared. However, the version proposed here is a refinement of the revised paper published in 2010 in *Critical Policy Studies* (4, 4, pp. 319–43). Of the other material composing Part II, Chapter Four was presented at two conferences: the European Network for the Philosophy of the Social Sciences (ENPOSS), First joint European/American Conference, held at the University of Venice Ca' Foscari, 3–4 September 2013, and the conference on *Governance and Public Policy in the UK Today*, held at Institut du Monde Anglophone, Université Sorbonne Nouvelle, 5 June 2014. The final part of this chapter has also appeared in the *Observatoire de la société britannique* 16, décembre 2014, pp. 125–141. In a shortened form, Chapter Seven has also appeared in a volume edited by G. Scichilone, *L'era globale: Linguaggi, paradigmi, culture politiche* (FrancoAngeli, Milan, 2012, pp. 65–82), whereas an earlier version of Chapter Nine was used as the Introduction to a 2010 volume of the Ashgate Library of Contemporary Essays in Political Theory and Public Policy which I co-edited with R. Bellamy, *Political Accountability*. Other conferences where parts of this work were presented are: *The Effects of Crisis, New Media and Social Protest on Democracy in Southern Europe*, Die Philosophische Fakultät der Universität Siegen, 25–26 October 2013, and *La politica. Categorie in questione*, Università degli Studi di Sassari, 22–23 April 2015. I would like to take this opportunity to acknowledge the publishers for authorising me to use and revise the material already published and my co-editors for their help and feedback on this material. I also wish to thank all those who attended the above-mentioned conferences and took part in the discussion, and the conference organisers for giving me the opportunity to present my work to a larger public.

A number of other people have, since the publication of the Italian version of this work, helped me to recast part of the arguments advanced here. Francesco Biondo read and commented on that work in its entirety and, thanks to his feedback, I decided not to include the Conclusion to the Italian book in this new version. My more normative work regarding what I call 'principled governance' needs to wait a little longer before being submitted to public scrutiny. Throughout the years, Alan Scott has been a source of permanent support, encouragement and feedback, reading the manuscript of this book in various stages of completion. I have also received useful and extended commentaries from Peter Triantafillou, whom I wish to thank for being very kind and accommodating. A similar thanks needs to be extended to Sigrid Baringhorst, Dario Castiglione, Mitchell Dean, Alessandro Ferrara, Sebastiano Maffettone, Michele Mangini, Alfio Mastropaolo, Virgilio Mura, May Pettigrew and John Schwarzmantel for commenting on various aspects of this work. The legibility of my English prose is due above all to Susie Heyman, complemented by the editorial work of Jacque Woolley and Simon Ward at ECPR Press. An acknowledgment for their patience is due to the rest of the editorial team at ECPR: Laura Pugh, Kate Hawkins and Mark Kench. Throughout, my partner Kate, an old-fashioned erudite, has supplied me with a constant stream of empirical cases, classical references and details of British social and economic history.

Introduction

Governance: What a Difference a Word Makes!

This is a work in political theory dealing with a topic, governance, that has so far been an object of research for mainly empirically-oriented studies in political science. Moreover, it is a study of political theory carried out by someone whose interests are above all normative, rather than descriptive or simply explicative. This means that it is structured and develops in ways which make it distinctive (if not idiosyncratic) from mainstream literature in governance studies. The aim of this introduction is, therefore, to explain these differences and give the reader the means to navigate through it. In fact, its abstract reasoning and complex structure require a proper justification, if only to avoid easy misunderstandings; one that is able to clarify: first, the intentions behind this work, second, the aims it sets out to achieve, and finally, the methodology used throughout. The work is also divided into three main parts which follow their own inner logic. In clarifying the latter, this introduction wishes to suggest ways in which the work can be read so as to satisfy the interests of different audiences: one composed of those who have a general interest in the nature of the dominant neoliberal consensus politics; a more specialist audience concerned with the recent political and institutional changes at the root of the passage from 'government' to 'governance'; the diffused constituency of those wishing to challenge the current state of affairs and move beyond neoliberalism. In proposing a personal interpretation of recent political and institutional change, the work wishes to indicate both the dynamic elements supporting the current neoliberal consensus politics and the difficulty they pose to those wishing to challenge it. Since the work supports a distinctively political narrative of change that brought about such a consensus politics, the conclusion it will reach is that those difficulties are not insurmountable and that the latter can be changed by democratic means. Hence the appeal advanced in the Conclusion for a more normative approach to policy analysis that can combine political imagination and forward-looking thinking.

I.1. Setting the stage, why governance?

In the last twenty years, governance studies have developed into a very distinctive field of inquiry. In doing so, they have successfully managed to divert the attention of many social and political scientists from one set of topics that used to dominate their disciplines to another. The almost exclusive attention to questions concerning 'high' politics and the mechanisms of decision-making used in liberal democracies has thus given way to a growing interests into issues of 'low' politics: those pertaining to policy making and policy implementation.

The latter have slowly shed an aura of technicality that made them the exclusive object of study of very narrow subdisciplinary fields. Growing public awareness of the relevance that policy making and policy implementation have for high politics has also been accompanied by practical attempts to make those fields of activity more participatory. Several analysts are now supporting the opening up of administrative ambits hitherto left untouched by the various waves of democratisation which occurred in the post-war period. They also view these fields at the forefront of a new process of democratisation that is revitalising western liberal democracies (Vibert 2007; Warren 2009). The present work endeavours to investigate the full implications that 'governance', as opposed to 'government', is having or could have for democratic theory in general. Since the advocacy of governance-driven forms of democratisation challenges the realist arguments used in the past to oppose participatory models of democracy, the aim of this work is to evaluate the soundness of the claims made in support. Has governance theory the power to rescue participatory visions of democracy? Would this mean moving beyond the model of representative democracy established since the French Revolution? Or simply to complement it by introducing non-electoral forms of participation?

The reason for approaching governance from this abstract theoretical perspective rests on personal dissatisfactions which need to be spelt out right at the outset. My first dissatisfaction is with the ethical (and metaethical) perspectives that have come to dominate political philosophy since Rawls allegedly resuscitated it in the 1970s. To me, the proliferation of ethical analyses has had the regrettable result of hollowing out normative reflection on political content: they are often too abstract, far removed from the concerns of political life and tend to be either politically inconclusive or structurally unable to give any practical indication (Weinberg 2013). The practicality for implementation of ethical conclusions is only one aspect of the problem faced by political philosophy, though. Ethical approaches seem to share a commitment to pre-empt politics, to deny the value of politics as a normative and practical activity. Substantive principles of justice are thus always established at a very abstract theoretical level and assume the form of external side-constraints on political activities – they represent in effect a moral straightjacket with which to restrain the political (Nozick 1974). Leaving on one side the fact that the principles discovered by moral reasoning are always essentially contested (hence the Sisyphus-like attempt to shift the discussion on even more abstract meta elements upon which to build a hypothetical consensus), such an approach overestimates the motivational force theoretical arguments of this sort could have for individual compliance. Moreover, it denies that the political realm has any real autonomy. At best, politics is thought to be able to yield mere *modus vivendi* based on arbitrary, and therefore unstable, compromises: a matter of expedience rather than principle (Rawls 1993). This anti-political stance leads political philosophers to search for universal and timeless principles of justice which the political can never satisfy. At the same time, this search for absolute principles of justice promotes critiques challenging either their desirability or feasibility for which no universally valid answer is forthcoming. Philosophical reflection and political practice are, therefore, caught in vicious circles which help undermine each other in turn. The rights-based notion of citizenship developed in the post-war period is a clear case in point discussed in the first part of the book. Used to displace competing active models of citizenship, rights-based notions could not subsequently be defended properly against the accusation of promoting an entitlements culture supporting parasitic social attitudes. Hence the success of neoliberal attempts to turn questions of social justice into matters for philanthropy and charity.

My other dissatisfaction is with the anti-normative spirit that characterises political science. To borrow the words of two geographers grappling with mainstream research in their own disciplinary field, it is possible to claim that political science's

> treatment of politics is characterized by *theoreticism*. By this we mean a tendency to deduce desirable political outcomes from deeper interests, established outside political processes, into which the academic researcher has a privileged insight. This preoccupation is often combined with voluntaristic injunctions to the community of researchers, governments, or social movements to work to help bring these outcomes about. In short, the very terms in which [social and political scientists] have engaged in discussion of politics, justice, citizens, elections, have nourished an avoidance of reflection on the normative presuppositions of political institutions and on the basic criteria of political judgment underpinning democratic processes – criteria concerning what is right, what is just, what is good, and concerning *how* best to bring good, just, rightful outcomes about (Barnett and Low 2004: 3).

This is especially true in governance studies. Political and institutional change is here explained as the result of adaptive reactions to the pressure exercised by impersonal social and economic forces. Politics tends, therefore, to be treated as an epiphenomenon – a suprastructural element dependent on more basic elements, one lacking any power to influence change. The passage from 'government' to 'governance' is presented as both epochal and inevitable; it is assumed to reflect either technological, social, economic or even cultural innovations which have emerged outside of the political realm; it is considered either as the outcome of an ideological *coup d'état* carried out by neoliberal attempts to undermine the state, or as the unintended consequences produced by those attempts. As a set of political and institutional arrangements, 'governance' is then attributed positive qualities which make it a superior functional solution to 'government'. In the third part, I endeavour to show that these Panglossian functional accounts are highly problematic, if not downright bogus. Many of the supposed positive qualities attributed to networks, public private partnerships and governance regimes are not warranted at all, and those which are potentially so need to be cultivated politically to succeed. Even when desirable, the attempt to move beyond liberal democratic institutions could end up undermining democratic values altogether and bring about a worrisome post-democratic void (Mair 2013).

I.2. Stating the aim, what kind of governance?

Neoliberal reforms and globalisation have deeply transformed the institutions of the welfare state built in the post Second World War period (*les trente glorieuses*) and set the ground for the development of a new body politic and style of government. The passage from 'government' to 'governance' is said to entail three major innovations. First, the inception of governance marks a shift away from traditional hierarchical forms of organisation and the adoption of network forms of organisation. Second, the passage occasions a revision of the relationship between state and civil society in a more participatory direction. Third, governance is finally seen as responsible for having shifted the emphasis from statute law to more flexible forms of soft law and stressed the superiority of targets and positive incentives as a means for policy implementation. These innovations are assumed to have produced a more effective and efficient form of polity: one less dependent on command-and-control logics and hubristic developmental visions, and therefore less susceptible to government failure. New modes of governance are also held responsible for enabling the nation-state to restructure itself to meet the challenges posed by globalisation. According to various narratives proposed in governance studies, the post-war welfare state is in the process of being superseded by a model of polity where authority is progressively devolved to task-specific institutions with unlimited jurisdictions and intersecting memberships operating at sub- and sovra-national levels. For this new type of polity, the goal of government is not that of homogenising the political and social space enclosed by clear-cut and permanent national boundaries, but that of enabling individuals and local communities to operate autonomously in an increasingly open world, thus promoting sustainable forms of development. Given these core principles, the literature on governance has developed in many directions that this work wishes to track down in a sort of genealogical fashion, sharpening their analytical content in the process.

For empirically-minded analysts, the term governance identifies the institutions, techniques and practices of governing arisen in the last three decades (*les trente furieuses*) under the joint pressure of globalisation and neoliberal restructuring of welfare institutions. Network and multilevel governance represent for them novel systems of coordination established by those operating within the constellations of political agencies which emerged from the breakdown of the welfare state and the hollowing out of central government. As a result, a reconstructive approach is proposed the aim of which is to rationalise the innovations emerged so far. More theoretically oriented analysts have built on the findings of the empirical micro-studies carried out by the reconstructive approach to identify the general and more abstract features of this new system of governing. Viewed from this theoretical perspective, the term 'governance' is employed in a very specific sense to identify a conception of the state that opposes both hierarchical modes of government and interventionist policies enforced through the threat of public sanctions. The picture that emerges from this body of work is that globalisation and governance are engendering a self-regulating and polycentric social order capable of assuring coordination without the need of a Hobbesian sword (Sørensen and Triantafillou 2009). Hence, the state-centric accounts of political and institutional change used by political scientists in the past are rejected in favour of more socio-centric approaches. In developing a genealogical reconstruction of governance theory, the main aim of this work is to provide better analytical tools for conceptualising and understanding recent change. To this end, by juxtaposing socio- and state-centric conceptions, an assessment of governance claims and narratives is proposed, one that wishes to make sharper distinctions between factual, heuristic and prescriptive levels of analysis. Investigating the relevance that political and institutional change has for traditional themes in political theory related to state authority, democratic legitimacy and political accountability, the work assesses the heuristic and prescriptive value of the interpretations proposed by governance studies. As part of this endeavour, it aims at preparing the ground for a normative approach to policy analysis that could offer some indications on how to tackle the accountability gaps and democratic deficits affecting this emerging self-regulating and polycentric social order.

Although the work will pay special attention to the empirical micro-studies found in literature, its main focus is the analysis and evaluation of the interpretations proposed by mid-level rationalisations of change. The first objective of the second part of the book is thus to distinguish between rationalisations of change influenced by rational choice theory and others built on more socialised conceptions of agency. Although these two epistemic worldviews yield a rich variety of economics-centred and society-centred accounts of change, I maintain that they end up converging in identifying and justifying two distinct novel forms of political agency: the 'Regulatory State' and the 'Networked Polity'. I shall insist on the fact that these labels identify not only distinctive Weberian ideal types that are believed to have replaced (or are in the process of replacing) the welfare state and its style of government, but also normative ideals whose function is to influence the direction of change. I therefore treat them as 'performative' notions which are simultaneously used to describe and prescribe. It is because of this performative quality that the narratives supporting distinct models of agency tend to stress continuities and/or discontinuities with the policy tools and political values pursued by neoliberal visions of government and democracy. Theorists of the Regulatory State view it as an entity that could progress and entrench the neoliberal reforms of big government carried out in the 1980s by (i) furthering the delegation of decision-making functions to competing administrative agencies independent of the electoral process and (ii) giving people the opportunity of 'exit' – elements conducive to some form of 'shareholder democracy' that let them 'vote with their feet'. By contrast, theorists of the Networked Polity view it as the outcome of decentralised attempts to overcome the institutional fragmentation brought about by neoliberal reforms of central government: a bottom-up form of 'stakeholder democracy' attributing to all affected interests power of 'voice' in both policy making and policy implementation. Given the performative quality of these ideal types, the book develops an assessment that considers both their heuristic power as explanatory frameworks and their normative force as justificatory frameworks. The main claim advanced in this work is that, while the Regulatory State is a better heuristic category for understanding current change than its counterpart, the Networked Polity represents a less controversial ideal to engender for both empirical and theoretical reasons.

In approaching these interpretations from what I call a genealogical perspective, the second part of the book also distinguishes between institutional and processual accounts of change internal to these research programmes. The Regulatory State and the Networked Polity are not the outcomes of unitary and coherent undertakings, but of variegated narratives of change sharing some form of (Wittgensteinian) family resemblance. Both receive inputs and stimulus from a number of competing schools of thought and theories that I wish to bring to the fore. Within each epistemic outlook, homeostatic notions of equilibrium and mechanistic metaphors vie with functional analyses and organic metaphors, thus yielding often surprising and puzzling results. Among the perspectives influenced by economic theory, the development of dynamic accounts of change have unwittingly undermined the instrumentality that characterises rational choice approaches and thus reduced their critical and normative appeal; for rules and institutions end up reshaping individual preferences, desires and beliefs. A curiously reversed problem affects the studies influenced by sociological theory. The dynamic accounts of change proposed by those who subscribe to autopoietic notions, or Foucault's governmentality, have ended up producing what looks like sociological versions of the theories of spontaneous order found in neoclassic economics and raise, consequentially, similar theoretical and normative doubts. This variety notwithstanding, the first generation of governance studies has viewed the innovations brought about by recent change fairly sympathetically and stressed its more positive achievements. An emerging second generation of governance studies is, however, putting many of these supposed achievements under increasingly critical scrutiny. Expanding on these critical inquiries, the work points out that any ideal typical form of organisation is in itself susceptible to failure. It also warns about the growing accountability gaps and democratic deficits caused by the development of governance regimes at local, national and transnational levels. Using a state-centred perspective that explains change as the outcome of the political activism of various state actors (rather than their reactive adaptation to impersonal social and economic forces), the book also casts doubts on the viability of the justificatory frameworks proposed by governance theorists and investigates ways in which a more normative approach to policy analysis can help improve them.[1]

I. 3. Explaining the structure, types of governance and narratives of change

The book is divided into three main parts composed of three chapters each. The main aims of these parts are respectively: (i) to give an outline of the context in which change has taken place; (ii) to spell out the nature of the policy innovations brought about by this change; (iii) to analyse the side-effects produced by the dynamic of change. By and large, these parts are self-standing and develop according to their own inner logic. This choice has been made so that distinct types of readership can focus directly on those parts which suit them best without losing sight of its overall theses.

- The first part is principally directed to those whose main interest is to understand the evolution of the current neoliberal consensus politics. It attempts to contextualise current debate on change and the evolution of new modes of governance by discussing three main topics. First, it proposes an analysis of the predominant features which used to characterise the consensus politics established during *les trente glorieuses* and were at the root of the welfare state – the ideal-model of government new modes of governance are said to be replacing. Second, the weaknesses imputed to this consensus politics and to the ideal type of government that emerged in its wake (suggested mostly by the different strands of the neoliberal movement that became a dominant political force in the 1980s) are presented and assessed. Finally, it stresses the differences between the welfare state, as an ideal type of government, and those attributed to the models of polity engendered by governance. In reconstructing the general political context, standard accounts proposed by neoliberals and their critics are reassessed in ways which are meant to reinforce the arguments developed in the following two parts of the book: (a) that new modes of governance are not really tackling the cultural contradictions affecting the welfare state and (b) that they are affected by similar shortcomings to those which undermined neocorporate attempts to reform the welfare state endogenously.

- The second part opens with a presentation of the main conceptual elements composing the hard-core of governance theory as the sum of two distinct research programmes engaged in conceptualising and explaining recent political and institutional change. The first is derived from the new political economy (which emerged in the post-war period) and views the reforms undertaken in the last three decades as the catalyst for the rise of a neoliberal Regulatory State opposed to redistribution and majority rule. By contrast, the second is derived from sociological perspectives antithetical to the first which view governance as supporting the emergence of a Networked Polity set to overcome the limitations of market-based political visions. Here a genealogy of the distinct epistemic traditions that have influenced governance studies is carried out to stress both their diverse internal nature and their systematic blending of factual, heuristic and prescriptive claims. Given the detailed critical analysis proposed here of the schools of thought, authors and issues which have shaped the field and oriented research in it, this part is directed to those who have a special interests in the nitty-gritty of governance studies.

The two main claims advanced are: (c) that both research programmes are a blend of institutional and processual approaches to change pulling in different directions and (d) that there is an evident internal trade-off between their *heuristic* power and justificatory force.

- The third part discusses some critical questions raised by governance as both an ideal type of polity and style of government, and as a plausible reconstruction of the political and institutional innovations emerged so far. The three chapters in this part question: (i) the various accounts employed to explain the erosion of the nation state and the hollowing out of central government, (ii) the democratic anchorage of governance supplied by the two perspectives considered in part two (i.e. political economy's Regulatory State and political sociology's Networked Polity), (iii) the feasibility of the mechanisms of horizontal and managerial accountability underpinning the various governance regimes operating at sub-, national and transnational levels. The aim of the chapters composing this part is to show that the accountability gap and democratic deficit currently affecting liberal democracies is the outcome of the politics of centralisation of decision-making and decentralisation of administrative functions pursued by central governments during *les trente furieuses*. In short, change has not affected the nation state as such but only its democratic structures and in ways that justify the concerns expressed about the inception of a post-democratic age (Crouch 2004). This part is mostly directed at those wishing to challenge the current neoliberal consensus politics, for it highlights the dynamic elements that make this type of social order able to escape its own contradictions and periodically regenerate itself. The main claims advanced here are: (e) that the neoliberal consensus politics is supported by partnerships embracing state and market actors interested in reinforcing their positional power, rather than creating a market society, and (f) that each crisis bought about by the contradictions affecting this social order represent an opportunity to renegotiate the terms of those partnerships and regenerate them.

To a smaller extent I have attempted to structure each single chapter in a similar fashion and give the reader a flavour of the overall theses in them as well. In doing so, my main concern has always been to avoid unnecessary repetitions. The repetitions I found unavoidable are now mostly contained in Chapters Three, Four and Seven. These chapters either summarise or introduce the various parts they are in, so they inevitably end up overlapping with bits of the preceding or subsequent chapters where those same arguments are reconsidered more extensively. Read one after the other, Chapters Three, Four and Seven could, however, give a busy reader a shortcut to the full content of the book, sparing him/her the more demanding genealogical reconstructions and detailed critical analyses contained in the remaining chapters. The Introduction and Conclusion have not been thought as summaries and will not be able to do so to the same extent: they supply a more limited and fragmented picture of the book. Similarly, it needs to be acknowledged that the first part does not contain a detailed defence of the narrative of *les trente glorieuses* proposed therein. This is done intentionally to give context to the main topic – the development of new modes of governance and their role in determining the passage from 'government' to 'governance'. Any attempt to supply a full and detailed defence of it would have shifted the focus of the whole work onto another topic (i.e. government). Moreover, it would also have exposed the whole theoretical enterprise to a potential infinite regression dilemma. As I shall point out in the Conclusion, a somewhat similar problem was faced in relation to the post-2008 financial crisis. The narrative of *les trente furieuses* stops at the inception of the above mentioned crisis and does not deal with the subsequent fall out (and literature produced as a result in the meantime). At the time of writing, the resolution of this crisis is not at all evident and so it is not possible to assess the full implication it can have for governance studies in general, and for the reading supported here in particular. Since the book proposes a political interpretation of neoliberal consensus politics which likens new modes of governance to neocorporate attempts at crisis management in the 1970s, and imputes to them similar weaknesses, the theses of the book are open to refutation in the light of future developments.

Given my interest in normative analysis, my original intention was to investigate the contribution governance studies could bring to the critical assessment of the philosophical foundations of neoliberal thought, an investigation carried out as a PhD student (Palumbo 2000). Delving into this literature brought me to the conclusion that the differences between neoliberal theory and governance theory were not at all clear-cut. Hence the attempt to develop a narrative of political and institutional change on which to ground the normative approach to policy analysis I am keen to develop – what elsewhere I labelled 'principled' governance (Palumbo 2011). Runciman (1963: 165) wisely warns that 'even the most ingenious answers will prove inadequate when it is the wrong question which is being asked'. This work represents an attempt to set the question right, if we want to move beyond the current neoliberal consensus politics and tackle the problems brought about by the 2008 financial crisis. As I shall explain in the Conclusion, the answers supplied here are limited but far from being irrelevant, for they try to establish the possibilities (still) open to us. The first and most important element I will stress is that there is always a viable political alternative to extant institutional arrangements. Since, according to the narrative I propose here, the changes undertaken in the last three decades have been initiated by state actors and follow a specific political logic, the Thatcherite battle cry of TINA (there is no alternative, Berlinski 2008) needs to be unmasked for what it is – political cant. The second, and no less important, element I will stress is that both the restoration of the old welfare state and a return to Keynesian demand management policies are no longer possible. Those arrangements depended on the support of a social and political coalition that is long gone and will be very difficult to recompose in radically different historical conditions. Even more compelling is, to my opinion, the fact that the dissolution of that social and political coalition was due to the inner cultural contradiction affecting welfarist solutions – the exaltation of the value of individual and social autonomy that was then denied in practice by the acceptance of elitist perspectives and technocratic solutions. Last but not least, I will point out that the idea of giving back to the state its lost powers, popular in many academic quarters, is not only mistaken but also perverse. The current neoliberal consensus politics reflects a political logic, or so I will argue, that has allowed central governments to centralise decision-making powers while shedding political responsibilities. Relying on those same institutions to turn things around will only end up reinforcing that very logic of action. The austerity policies imposed since 2008 are a clear indication that this way of reasoning is self-defeating.

I.4. Clarifying the methodology, models, maps and metaphors

As a work in political theory, one particularly critical of the narratives of governance advanced by the first generation, I have adopted methodological tenets that do not conform to those used by empirically oriented social and political scientists. In the first place, this work deals with interpretations and does not add anything new to the body of empirical evidence collected so far. Broadly speaking, the arguments I present in support of given interpretations or against others are based on a case study: the reforms carried out in Britain from 1979 to 2008 by the conservative governments of Thatcher and Major, and the New Labour governments of Blair and Brown. But even this case study is based on a personal evaluation of contending interpretations of those reforms. I do not think it is possible to bypass interpretations and look directly at the facts. In a Nietzchean fashion, I believe that there are no political facts, but only political interpretations of given events. Upon this belief depend three main features of the present work: the attention given to epistemic questions, the role that personal intuitions and perceptions play in it and the style of exposition adopted. I take governance studies to be a blend of theories engaged in explaining recent political and institutional change. In classifying and analysing these theories, the criteria used are related to the epistemic, methodological and normative tenets subscribed by their authors, either explicitly or implicitly. Thus, in the second part I identify two main research programmes derived from distinct epistemic traditions (political economy on the one side and political sociology on the other), inspired by antithetical research methods (rational choice theory on the one hand and a variety of sociological alternatives on the other) and led to endorse specific principled forms of action (mechanisms of 'exit' in one case and channels of 'voice' in the other). Combining these elements in a coherent fashion, I arrive then at the identification of two ideal typical interpretations of political and institutional change in need of assessment: the Regulatory State on one side, and the Networked Polity on the other side.

I am fully aware that these are abstract theoretical constructions. But I also believe that they have significant heuristic power and am keen to investigate their relative ability to explain recent changes. These ideal types are supposed to simplify the issues I want to analyse without making them simplistic, and it is this criterion that I follow in proposing some ideal typical representation and in opposing others, in mapping the terrain I am investigating and in using metaphors to illustrate my remarks.

Concerning the relative plausibility of contrasting ideal types, I adopt a set of criteria at odds with the hard-nose empiricism dominating many cognate disciplines in the social and political sciences. Since I believe that any appeal to facts alone is not possible, I subscribe to a constructivist position very sceptical of logical empiricist notions of verification or Popperian ideas of falsification. In my case, this means that any reference to facts needs to be integrated with appeals to personal intuition and experience. The hypotheses I use throughout this work rest on a blend of these three elements. Furthermore, I contend that the ideal types populating governance theory have an ineliminable performative quality to them – that they are used to describe and prescribe at the same time, as already mentioned. Thus, the blend of facts, intuition and experience used to measure the plausibility of distinct ideal types has to be used to assess not only their heuristic power, but also their justificatory force. It is at this level that the anti-normative stance underpinning governance studies becomes problematic and the need for a normative approach to policy analysis is really felt. In attempting to assess the normative values of the Regulatory State and the Networked Polity, I am concerned with both their desirability and feasibility, and in doing this a number of theoretical and empirical arguments (dependent on deduction, observation and intuition) are once again deployed. Since I believe that the Regulatory State is a better heuristic device than the Networked Polity, and since I observe a growing dissatisfaction with current neoliberal policies, I arrive at the conclusion that the Regulatory State's feasibility is empirically questionable, and from this observation I try to investigate the features which make this justificatory framework also theoretically undesirable. Likewise, I notice that the Networked Polity is a normative ideal, rather than a tendency implicit in the current dynamic of change. Then I focus on the features that could make this ideal appealing and investigate the possibility to engender it – a positive undertaking that, alas, cannot be fully accomplished in this work for the reasons stated above.

Obviously, this way of proceeding can be challenged for not being scientific enough, and nowhere in the book do I engage in discussions directed at defending its scientific credentials. I am simply stating what methods I employ to make the reader aware of them from the outset; it is up to that reader to decide whether to continue reading it and what degree of plausibility the various statements contained in this work have. To borrow the words of Dean (2010: 12): 'if we are to understand our present, we need to do so not by mere replication of other's ideas, or the application of other's theories or methods to an empirical domain, but by way of the production of concepts'.

A second feature that makes this book unlike other works in governance studies is related to the way it deals with the related literature in the field. None of the following chapters have been thought as a survey of studies produced on the topics touched by them; especially if this is supposed to mean a review of the most 'recent' contributions from some sort of 'impartial' perspective. Although

I have taken into consideration a variety of perspectives and struggled to keep up-to-date with recent developments, the aim of this work is not to supply a more or less accurate picture of the state of the art.[2] Rather, my intention is to make a personal contribution to this research field. The bodies of literature discussed by the subsequent chapters are used as stepping stones to move my line of investigation along, crossing established disciplinary boundaries any time this is required by the interconnected nature of the political and institutional change analysed. To make this enterprise manageable, I have imposed two sets of limits on my inquiry. First, there are temporary limits: the ultimate goal is the analysis of change undertaken during *les trente furieuses*, as I call them; that is, the three decades that go from the election of Margaret Thatcher as Prime Minister of Britain in 1979 to the 2008 financial crisis. To put those changes in perspective and make my critical argument intelligible, I try to contextualise those events by proposing a theoretical link with the three decades that preceded it, the so-called *trente glorieuses*. If, as it is commonly stated, *les trente furieuses* are supposed to have made possible the momentous passage to 'governance', it is obvious to also supply an account of what it has allegedly replaced, 'government', even if only in outline. This account of government is meant to give the reader an idea of both continuities and discontinuities with the immediate past, and a better understanding of the ability of new modes of governance to solve the problems which affected their counterparts.

The second types of self-imposed limits are structural: the change under study pertains to the innovation of administrative practices related to policy making and policy implementation in Organisation of Economic Co-operation and Development (OECD) countries. Although my conclusions could have larger implications and even be applied to other forms of social change, my concern here is not to test their degree of application. In doing so, I point out that many of the shortcomings attributed to current neoliberal consensus politics in reality preceded it, that neoliberal reforms far from solving the government failures produced by the interventionist welfare state have actually reinforced them, and that the new modes of governance analysed here show a remarkable similarity with past attempts at crisis management, casting a shadow on their effectiveness. Again, it is up to the reader to decide what degree of originality my contribution has or whether it would have been better to do another survey of recent literature instead.

The last point I want to touch on concerns the nature of the inquiries I carry out and the style employed to expose them. For want of a better word, I refer to my inquiries as 'genealogical' analyses: narratives which try 'to explain a cultural phenomenon by describing a way in which it came about, or could have come about, or might be imagined to have come about' (Williams 2002: 20). Since the notion of genealogy is currently used to identify mostly a methodological approach developed by Foucault, I feel in need to clarify that I do not intend to work within that tradition of thought or to conform to the idea of genealogy established by it.[3] I discuss different genealogical perspectives in Chapter Six, Section 6.5 – to which I refer the reader, where I distinguish between Humean and Nietzschean endeavours. Both engaged in tracing the origins of social practices in a striking antithetical spirit: Hume sought to advance a normative justification of social conventions which look arbitrary from a philosophical viewpoint; Nietzsche wished to unmask moral attitudes and beliefs by showing that they were based on layers of resentment. Although Foucaldians are usually assumed to work in a Nietzschean critical spirit (Foucault 1998), in that section I point out that some authors arrive at a notion of governmentality lacking Foucault's critical edge; to the point that their conclusions sound eerily Humean. My approach follows a somewhat reverse route: I start from a Humean interest in tracing down the origins of notions, habits and practices to then deploy a critical Nietzschean scrutiny of innovations thought to be both epochal and positive and justified as such. In assessing those innovations in a Nietzschean critical spirit, my aim is not to dismiss them but to retain a sceptical perspective that can help us distinguish between 'different shades of grey' (an expression especially apt in a book dealing with reforms of public administration based on the British experience).[4]

As said earlier, while appreciating the contribution governance studies could bring to democratic theory – in particular to the re-evaluation of the participatory models dismissed by realists since Schumpeter's acclaimed rejection of the classic conception – I am also deeply suspicious of functional explanations, especially when the latter tend to collapse together heuristic, descriptive and normative levels of analysis. I also find particularly unwelcome the current tendency to mythologise the post-war settlement and the workings of its main institutional achievement – the welfare state. Such an attitude, although comprehensible at a popular level, leaves the collapse of that past experience unexplained and could have deleterious effects at a normative level, as I shall explain in the Conclusion. Given all these methodological clarifications, it should be clear to the reader why no attempt to hide the author's opinion behind some controversial scientific notions of impartiality or an impersonal linguistic style is made in this work. For good or ill, all the opinions expressed here are those of the author, and for them I bear full personal responsibility.

I.5. Plan of the Book

Chapter One pursues two main objectives. First, it gives an account of the various elements that eventually came to compose the model of 'government' that has allegedly been replaced by new modes of 'governance'. This account intends to explain the economic, political and social values which underpinned that particular model of government as a technology of power and set of public rules, institutions and processes. The second objective is related to understanding the crisis which engulfed that model of government and kick-started the process of change leading to the development of new modes of governance. The narrative proposed here rejects standard economic explanations concerned with the theoretical and practical limitations of Keynesianism in favour of a more political reading of the events. The breakdown of the consensus politics supporting the welfare state is imputed to the growing contradiction between the values of autonomy preached by the welfare state and the technocratic practices that it endorsed in reality. This contradiction is at the root of the discontent that led to the implosion of the social and political coalition supporting the post-war settlement and is used to explain both the ability of neoliberal forces to replace welfarist values with a restricted and even more elitist worldview and the political resilience of the neoliberal consensus politics established in the aftermath.

Chapter Two discusses two distinct but interrelated topics. The first topic concerns the theory underpinning the neoliberal counter-revolution. After explaining the post-war development of an integrated economic approach to politics and its methodological tenets, the work considers the academic eminence and political influence acquired by the New Political Economy since the 1970s. The second topic is related to the various waves of reforms implemented during *les trente furieuses* by governments who subscribed to neoliberal world views. Using the UK as the main point of reference, the chapter advances an account of the setting-up of the original template as part of the New Public Management programme for the civil service, and the subsequent application of this same template across various other public sector fields and in different countries. The main thesis supported in this chapter is that, far from attempting to implement the libertarian prescriptions derived from the New Political Economy, central governments have exploited the latter as a set of rhetorical policy instruments to impose a restructuring of the welfare state that maximises their decision- and policy-making powers *vis-à-vis* competing institutional and societal actors. It is the success of this strategy of administrative decongestion-cum-political centralisation that explains the resilience and diffusion of neoliberal consensus politics across policy areas and within OECD countries.

Chapter Three presents and discusses the political and institutional changes responsible for the alleged passage from 'government' to 'governance'. It starts by dividing the period that goes from 1948 to the financial crisis of 2008 into two cycles of thirty years each. The first (*les trente glorieuses*) coincides with the building of the model of 'government' that the reforms carried out in the second period (*les trente furieuses*) have attempted to dismantle, producing a shift towards 'governance' in the process. Then it clarifies the different conceptions of policy making, administration, citizenship and the state-civil society relationship which characterise 'government' and 'governance' as ideal types. In discussing the analytical features which are taken to mark out these ideal types as regulatory systems, modes of organisation and productive structures, the chapter contributes to governance theory by suggesting new and more refined conceptual distinctions. While appreciating the heuristic role ideal types can play for understanding current changes, the chapter warns about the risk implicit in using extremely simplified models which could end up reifying some aspects of the phenomena they are meant to explain. The chapter also casts some doubts on the alleged superiority of 'governance' *vis-à-vis* its counterparts by highlighting that coordination failures can affect network modes of organisation as well. These critical remarks are in line with the development of a second generation of research in governance studies less mesmerised by the seemingly limitless powers of networks and are meant to encourage a more normative approach to policy analysis.

The aim of Chapter Four is to summarise and reassess the innovations brought about by governance theory. It is argued that the notion of governance is a conceptual device that could help rationalise and articulate the changes undertaken by liberal democracies since the late 1970s. After presenting the novel policy instruments brought about by those changes, a better analytical distinction between 'network governance' and 'multilevel governance' is proposed and defended. Recalling the debates on the hollowing out of the state and on policy implementation, the chapter discusses some of the narratives advanced to explain the passage from 'government' to 'governance'. It suggests the need to distinguish between at least two separate research programmes making up governance studies, which are influenced by alternative epistemic traditions – political economy and political sociology. Rationalisations of change influenced by political economy support the idea that the outcome of recent political change is a market-oriented Regulatory State, while those influenced by political sociology see governance as supporting the rising of a Networked Polity. Since these research programmes blend together descriptive and prescriptive elements, the chapter advances a twin type of evaluation that tries to assess both their relative heuristic power and their ability to justify the normative ideals they seek to engender. The main claim advanced in the chapter is that, while the Regulatory State is a better heuristic category for understanding recent political change than that of the Networked Polity, the reverse happens when these two entities are considered as normative ideals to engender.

Chapter Five discusses the Regulatory State as a rationalisation of recent political and institutional change. Proposed originally by perspectives derived from the New Political Economy, the Regulatory State was later adopted by social scientists concerned about the negative side-effects of neoliberal reforms undertaken since the 1980s. Throughout this shift, the label has, however, remained an epistemic black box, the inner working of which is seldom analysed properly. The chapter endeavours to look inside this black box stressing the double role played by the state as regulator (when playing by the rule) and meta-regulator (when playing the game of the rules). In disagreement with the theories of state retreat, the Regulatory State is here presented as engaged in an attempt to reaffirm the control of central government upon parts of the public sector that post-war developments had unwittingly emancipated or left outside its remit. In the process, central government has shed past social and political responsibilities which made it responsive to Parliament and public opinion. The chapter further discusses the normative claims underpinning the Regulatory State. The latter endorse economic solutions committed to establishing mechanisms of 'exit' which would allow people to 'vote with their feet'. The theoretical and practical weaknesses of the justificatory framework employed for this are thus highlighted. First, it is pointed out that output-oriented modes of legitimacy overlook questions of social justice that impact negatively on the feasibility of the Regulatory State. Second, it is claimed that the multiple attempts to 'play by the rule' and play 'the game of rules' have simultaneously undermined the independency of regulatory agencies and failed to cut red tape. The upshot is the promotion of regulatory hypertrophy that is draining the already feeble legitimacy of existing liberal democracies and turning the Regulatory State into a political black hole.

Chapter Six discusses the sociological traditions and schools of thought that have contributed to the development of the Networked Polity as a conceptual alternative to the Regulatory State. It starts by proposing an analytical distinction between neo-institutional and processual approaches to political and institutional change on the one hand, and between instrumental and non-instrumental conceptions of rules on the other. By criss-crossing these two variables, the chapter arrives at a conceptual map useful (i) for locating the various contributions to rationalisations of change advanced by accounts of governance subscribing sociological tenets, and (ii) for classifying these accounts under distinct analytical categories. The chapter then identifies and analyses the main approaches to governance studies found in each of these four sectors of the conceptual map. Two main claims will be supported here. Against neo-institutional accounts, it is argued that, far from being the inevitable outcome of current trends, the Networked Polity is in reality a normative ideal and needs, therefore, to be justified accordingly. In relation to autopoietic and processual accounts, it is pointed out that the picture of the Networked Polity that emerges from these rationalisations is uncannily similar to that arrived at by the economic theories of spontaneous order influencing neoliberal thinking and is, consequently, affected by similar epistemic and normative weaknesses.

Chapter Seven discusses the alleged crisis of the nation state underpinning both globalisation and governance theory. Globalisation and governance are often presented as phenomena related to the breakdown of national frontiers, the growing ineffectiveness of public intervention and the policy relevance acquired by the private sector and non-governmental organisations. Accordingly, state institutions are said to be unravelling, soon to be superseded by new collective entities which operate along functional rather than territorial lines, are not committed to impose absolute forms of sovereignty but only systems of networked and multilevel governance, and which support plural and overlapping conceptions of citizenship. To this account is juxtaposed an alternative reading of change that views globalisation and governance as the outcomes of state action pursuing a genuinely political logic. From this perspective, the political and administrative reforms of the last three decades have had the overriding goal of strengthening the governability of existing liberal democracies by reinforcing the power of central government *vis-à-vis* Parliament, local government and civil society. The outcome has been the hollowing out of representative institutions rather than the state form. This alternative account of political and institutional change is developed by challenging three main theoretical antinomies influencing debates in these fields: the idea that there is an inevitable trade-off between the state and the market; the identification of the state with public hierarchies that are being inexorably supplanted by network forms of organisation; the allegedly terminal implications that internationalisation is having on the Westphalian system of power relations.

Chapter Eight contrasts the two distinct visions of democratic politics at the heart of governance theory. The first, connected to the notion of the Regulatory State, advocates anti-majoritarian solutions whose goal is to depoliticise public policy, while the second, derived from the concept of the Networked Polity, supports ultra-democratic reforms promoting the deliberative involvement of mini-publics in policy making. The chapter pursues three main aims. First, it proposes a reading of the weaknesses attributed to a model of democracy that characterises the post-war welfare state, Schumpeter's competitive leadership. Second, it clarifies the nature of the innovations advocated by those attempting to build a Regulatory State, and by those struggling to engender a Networked Polity. Lastly, a critical evaluation of these solutions and their democratic visions is carried out. It is argued that while anti-majoritarian solutions rest ultimately on disputed notions of social efficiency and contradictory appeals to pluralism, deliberative solutions are either likely to undermine political equality, or incapable of supporting the claims associated with the ideal of a Networked Polity.

Chapter Nine discusses the problems raised by the developments of new modes of governance in relation to the mechanisms of political accountability established by the post-war settlement. It starts by noting that, notwithstanding the relevance attributed to it by Schumpeter's competitive leadership model, the evolution of welfare states, with their large, centralised governments and administrations, conspired to progressively undermine the ability of their citizens to keep representatives accountable and political regimes responsive. The chapter then stresses that, far from reversing this trend, the structural reforms carried out since the late 1980s have ended up reinforcing this tendency, thus yielding worrisome accountability gaps. The alleged erosion of accountability brought about by neoliberal reforms of big government, globalisation and governance is mainly explained as the outcome of systematic attempts to substitute horizontal mechanisms of auditing for political and vertical forms. Although the introduction of new mechanisms of accountability is not considered, in principle, objectionable, but viewed as a means that could help compensate for the distortions yielded by big government, the attempt to employ them to free central government from parliamentary control is claimed to be at the root of the systemic legitimation problems liberal democracy is currently facing.

The Conclusion summarises the main issues raised in the book. Its aim is twofold. First, it endeavours to show that some of the difficulties encountered by liberal democracies worldwide are structurally related to governmental attempts to centralise political control by decentralising managerial functions and shedding the social responsibilities acquired in the post-war. Far from realising a consumer-friendly Madisonian democracy, market-based solutions are sought and implemented to bring under the control of central government a variety of local and peripheral branches of the state apparatus which welfarist policies had unwittingly emancipated by delegating to them policy-making and implementation powers. I contend that by making central governments less responsive to the citizenry and less accountable to Parliament, these attempts are undermining the representative model of democracy engendered by the post-war settlement and ushering in a troublesome post-democratic age. Second, the chapter wishes to clarify some of the normative shortcoming affecting the rationalisations of political institutional changes supplied by governance studies so far. To the extent that the new modes of governance analysed by the theorists of the Regulatory State supply a more convincing analytical framework of the change undertaken during *les trente furieuses*, the normative justifications for this state of affairs are daily shown to be wanting. The Regulatory State has failed to reinforce the output-oriented legitimacy of liberal democracies and is affected by accountability gaps and democratic deficits increasing the risk of a system-wide legitimation crisis like the one experienced earlier by the welfare state. By contrast, the accounts of change proposed by the theorists of the Networked Polity need to acknowledge their basic normative dimension and develop proper justificatory frameworks of the features they wish to engender. To this end, their supporters have still to indicate how is it possible to turn what is clearly a self-serving neoliberal policy template into an instrument for realising a deliberative policy environment and a system of self-service policy.

End Notes

1. My critical remarks should not in any way obscure the fact that the first generation has helped develop inter- and trans-disciplinary perspectives to political and institutional change which make my endeavour possible. I am not at all confident that such a broader approach will survive it, and can indeed see indications that the second generation is re-establishing old disciplinary boundaries, fragmenting knowledge in this field of inquiry as well.

2. To keep the book within a manageable size, no attempt has also been made to include references which were not strictly essential. Many noteworthy contributions to governance theory have therefore been left out.

3. Even if I am myself very keen on opposing the three Platonic modalities of history Foucault (1998: 385) imputes to Nietzsche: 'the first is parodic, directed against reality, and opposes the theme of history as reminiscence or recognition; the second is dissociative, directed against identity, and opposes history given as continuity or representative of a tradition; the third is sacrificial, directed against truth, and opposes history as knowledge [*connaissance*]. They imply a use of history that severs its connection to memory, its metaphysical and anthropological model, and constructs a countermemory – a transformation of history into a totally different form of time.' I would also like to point out that my approach is Foucauldian in the spirit attributed to it by Dean (2010: 61): 'genealogy strives to make intelligible forms of liberalism in relation to the practices of government to

which they are linked. To analyse liberalism in relation to these practices of government, rather than as a period, philosophy or form of state, is to seek to understand its plurality, capacity for reinvention and sheer longevity. In brief: genealogy is the patient labour of historico-political analysis and a contestation of existing narratives. It is animated by a particular ethos of permanent and pragmatic activism without apocalyptic or messianic ends.' This clarification is triggered by critical remarks on an earlier draft of this work expressed by Peter Triantafillou, who I wish to thank for the opportunity.

4. According to Hennessy (1990), this was the reply given by a retiring British senior civil servant to those asking him what so many years passed in Whitehall had really taught him about power.

PART I

CONTEXT

Chapter One

Les Trente Glorieuses: The Post–War Settlement and the Birth of the Welfare State

1.1. Introduction

The chapter aims at supplying an analytical sketch of the model of government brought about by the post-war settlement, and which is supposedly currently in the process of being supplanted by an alternative model of governance. This analytical sketch starts with a brief description of the political and social context in which it evolved and then examines the factors which helped it to consolidate and spread across OECD countries. Two main assumptions underlie this reconstruction: the idea that its evolution was achieved bit by bit, rather than as a result of political planning, and that it was driven by practical concerns, rather than an overarching ideological vision. This evolution spanned the first five decades of the twentieth century and developed in response to the cataclysmic events which accompanied those turbulent times. The activities which characterised the various phases of development were not only of a very practical nature, but also inspired by contrasting readings of the problems at hand coming from distinct conservative, liberal and socialist political traditions. Thus the welfare state, as the political entity that came to embody this model of government, must be seen as the result of two intertwining dialectics: one concerning the ideological and scientific debates on the side-effects brought about by modernity and the best way to address them, and another concerning the political forces engaged in devising ways to intervene in restricted policy areas. In contrast to the historical and sociological accounts interested in stressing the peculiarities of distinct socio-cultural contexts and of the solutions employed therein, my reconstruction highlights the common and overlapping elements between the national experiences which found themselves at the forefront of this historical development in OECD countries. This explains my interest in employing a Weberian methodology based on ideal typical representations of the phenomena under investigation. Unlike Weber, I see these ideal types as having an irreducible 'performative' nature: they are at the same time heuristic and prescriptive instruments whose goal is not only to explain political and institutional change, but also to uncover the ideological perspectives trying to influence the direction and pace of change. I will therefore pay special attention to and try to indicate the ideological influences and political alliances engaged in the attempt to shape the welfare state, and single out the policy tools through which those attempts were carried out.

As a political and administrative patchwork, the welfare state was riddled with tensions and contradictions. Since the beginning, literature on the subject has been replete with technical analyses of the shortcomings of the administrative tools employed and of the technocratic fixes adopted. The following chapters will deal with (some of) those analyses more or less extensively – a great deal of attention is paid in particular to those put forward by the New Political Economy at the root of the 1980s neoliberal counter-revolution (*see* Chapter Two). My interest here is to support instead a more political reading of the events that contributed to the crisis experienced by the welfare state (and the model of government it embodied) in the 1970s. According to this reading, the root cause of what was revealed to be a terminal crisis was the growing evidence of a contradiction at the core of the welfare state. Whereas, at a rhetorical level, the latter advocated a democratic vision that attributed to the citizen an expanding set of social and economic rights, in reality it pursued a minimalist politics of the ballot-box that deprived the citizen of any meaningful role in public policy, preferring to delegate policy-making power to technocratic polyarchies which were either unrepresentative of, or scarcely responsive to, the *demos*. Eventually, this contradiction determined the implosion of the social and political coalition supporting the post-war settlement and produced a political and institutional void successfully exploited by neoliberal forces seeking to impose their worldview and programme of government. I also maintain that this reading of events was pretty evident to many analysts and practitioners facing the popular discontent towards welfare policies and institutions, and inspired the endogenous attempts to reform the welfare state along neocorporate lines.

As a work in political theory, the reading I am proposing here has two main goals. First, it intends to support the account of the neoliberal counter-revolution outlined in the next chapter by stressing that the latter's success is far from being the result of an ideological *coup d'état* (its ability to brainwash all political forces supporting the current neoliberal consensus politics); it rests instead on an ability to fill the gap opened by the dissolution of the post-war welfare coalition and on the institutional equilibrium established thereafter – an equilibrium point which is capable of exercising significant power of attraction among ruling elites. Second, the reading of the inner weakness of the welfare state proposed here is meant to shed doubts on both the resplendent picture of *les trente glorieuses* proposed in the wake of the 2008 financial crisis and related attempts to re-affirm the validity of Keynesian macroeconomic policies. As I shall explain in the Conclusion, both persist in supporting technocratic visions of public policy which have proved to be highly defective and cannot be brought back to life in radically different historical conditions.

1.2. From the 'social service state' to the 'welfare state': the piecemeal evolution of a governing pattern

Far from being a political solution born fully-formed from a social democratic mind (Berman 2006), the sets of political and institutional changes responsible for the rising of the welfare state were the result of countless practical attempts to solve the policy problems produced by complex, diffuse and difficult social transformations. The first and most debated of these transformations is related to modernisation – a phenomenon that encompasses both the socio-economic changes brought about by the industrial revolution and the politico-administrative reforms which followed the French Revolution. While industrialisation and urbanisation on an unprecedented scale upset the practices which used to regulate and stabilise social intercourse, the formation of the nation state and its gradual democratisation redesigned the pre-existing political landscape, enlarging the scale, scope and reach of the body politic in the process (*see* Chapter Seven). The transition from this pre-existing political landscape to modernity and the side-effects brought about by the new social, economic and political orders caused a series of interconnected crises which engulfed many countries across several continents and culminated in the catastrophic world conflicts which took place in the first half of the twentieth century.

In order to understand the nature, shape and relevance of the political and institutional arrangements established by the post-World War II (WWII) settlement, it is necessary to follow the course of those events in a very selective way. Given the scope of this work in general, and this chapter in particular, I will refer to a restricted number of historical landmarks only and focus on the common tendencies between the (mostly Western) countries which were at the centre of the events mentioned (and of the post-war settlement that eventually produced *les trente glorieuses*). As such, the expression 'welfare state' will be used throughout to identify the ideal-type form of political agency adopted in this geographical context at the time, regardless of national variations and their degree of consolidation. In discussing this ideal type, I am concerned with analysing three of its constitutive elements: the constitutional architecture of the body politic (polity), the set of relations established within the public realm and between the latter and the social and economic realms (politics), and the administrative structures and instruments employed to regulate social intercourse (policy).

As for any other social phenomenon, the birth date of the welfare state is somewhat conventional and depends heavily on the disciplinary and ideological perspective of the analyst. Although it is generally assumed to be the outcome of the political settlement reached at the end of WWII, the various elements composing the welfare state have their own pre-existing social and political history.[1] It is a history that dates back to the last decades of the nineteenth century, reaching the conjuncture between two distinct sets of events: the culmination of the process of national formation in Western Europe with the political unification of Italy and (above all) Germany, and the unfolding of the first serious economic depression experienced by industrial countries in the 1880s. These two events helped establish a political pattern that will repeat itself during the next fifty years: a pattern according to which the state comes to gradually acquire new and more pervasive social and economic functions for social betterment – in breach of the *lasseiz-faire* public philosophy that had enjoyed intellectual (if not political) hegemony up to that point. This meant acquiring new political powers but also assuming new social responsibilities. The first led the state and its administrative arms to intervene in spheres of activity up until then considered private and thus beyond the remit of public authorities. The second committed the state to solve social problems affecting significant constituencies which, in the past, had to fend for themselves, and to compensate for misfortunes for which neither individuals nor groups could be held fully responsible.[2]

Changes in attitude about the role of the state *vis-à-vis* civil society are at the root of the development of what Briggs (1961: 15) calls the 'social service state', 'a state in which communal resources are employed to abate poverty and to assist those in distress'. The main policy instruments employed by political authorities to accomplish these newly-acquired functions were: (i) social insurance schemes protecting people from injuries, disabilities and lack of income due to protracted periods of involuntary unemployment; (ii) state pensions for elderly people no longer able to support themselves through paid work; (iii) factory legislation aimed at reducing the sources of social risks responsible for people's poverty and misfortune. The political pillars upon which the 'social service state' rested were, in turn, as follows: (a) the idea that state intervention in those areas had to be indirect, complementary and minimalist; (b) the promotion of prudential virtues by imposing on individual workers their contribution to national insurance schemes (complemented by public grants to reach required thresholds for the deserving poor); and (c) an instrumental approach to the 'social question' aimed at reducing class-based conflicts and the threats to social order posed by revolutionary movements.

In the course of the twentieth century, the recurrence of social crises of this sort but on an even larger scale and in a more vicious form, the development of mass democratic movements pushing for universal franchise and the administrative capacities acquired by the states involved in total wars, combined to eventually transform the 'social service state' into a 'welfare state' (*see* Figure 1.1):

> a state in which organized power is deliberately used (through politics and administration) in an effort to modify the play of market forces in at least three directions – first, by guaranteeing individuals and families a minimum income irrespective of the market value of their work or their property; second, by narrowing the extent of insecurity by enabling individuals and families to meet certain 'social contingencies' (for example, sickness, old age and unemployment) which lead otherwise to individual and family crises; and third, by ensuring that all citizens without distinction of status or class are offered the best standards available in relation to a certain agreed range of social services (*ibid.*: 14).

As Briggs explains, the crucial difference between the two forms of public intervention is that the welfare state

> brings in the idea of the 'optimum' rather than the older idea of the 'minimum'. It is concerned not merely with abatement of class differences or the needs of scheduled groups but with equality of treatment and the aspirations of citizens as voters with equal shares of electoral power' (*ibid.*: 15).

Figure 1.1: Evolution of welfare services

	How to	*Who for*	*What for*
Paupers	Charity and assistance	Needs and means	Charity
Poor	Regulation and insurance	Means-tested and universal coverage	Moral redress
Citizens	Public welfare	Universal coverage	Social solidarity

This is a progressive social vision that builds upon notions of citizenship brought about by the political activism of labour forces and the engagement of entire national populations (and overseas colonies) in the war efforts – two factors which the European ruling elites could not fail to consider in the aftermath of the war, given their responsibilities in determining that tragic course of events and their incompetence in dealing with the inevitable failure of their decision-making. These notions of citizenship would find their most influential rationalisations in the works of Marshall (1950) and Rawls (1971). I argue, however, that the notions of citizenship advocated by them were part of a larger milieu and that the subsequent prestige and appeal acquired by these liberal rationalisations were due to political developments which saw the gradual marginalisation of alternative democratic visions. I contend that it was the political hegemony acquired by liberal thought that explains the shape of the welfare state and the weaknesses it will show in the course of time.

The existence and nature of this milieu has been obscured by two contrasting readings of the welfare state which emerged subsequently: the neoliberal reading advanced in the 1980s, derived mainly from New Political Economy (NPE) (*see* Chapter Two), and the social democratic reading developed since the 1990s in reaction to the first reading. Against the first, I argue that the welfare state did not emerge as a result of a socialist form of planning, nor did it ever attempt to impose such a thing. The alleged parallels and similarities between the two logics exposed by neoliberal schools of thought are part and parcel of an ideological interpretation unsupported by both historical analysis and empirical evidence. But this can also be said about those who have sought to give to the welfare state a social democratic pedigree, presenting it as an endeavour to pave the road to socialism (Berman 2006; Streeck 2014). The political history of welfare policies and institutions is full of twists and turns, each of which is determined by the political response that variegated and changing coalitions of forces managed to produce in given historical contexts. Although socialist movements and ideals were a crucial component of those coalitions, their influence was often indirect. In relation to its predecessor, the 'social service state', Briggs shows for instance that the social reform movement that brought it about included religious conservative forces, radical utilitarians and new liberals. The then-emerging socialist movement represented a background factor against which progressive changes were justified: the menace of a revolutionary upheaval that needed to be neutralised in a humane and non-military manner.

The same account is proposed by Marshall (1961: 296), who clarifies that at the time 'the threat was not grave enough to make socialism in all its forms an untouchable idea. It was a label that was attached to, and often accepted by, most groups of ardent reformers, like Tory Socialists, Christian Socialists, Radical Socialists and even on occasion Liberal Socialists'. Once one attempts to analyse the content of this early socialism, the outcome is a blend of moral, political and organisational values which are characteristic of a utopian social tradition that Marxist thinkers and activists were busy fighting – and even among those committed to a scientific form of socialism the notion of planning and state intervention will emerge only after the 1917 Russian Revolution and the European experience of total war (Toye 2003). The characteristics of the social reform movement just outlined explain why, up to the mid-1930s, state intervention was advocated only in an indirect, complementary and minimalist way.

Harris (1992: 123–4) also shows that up to the mid-1930s the reformist coalition was dominated by idealist philosophical and social concerns:[3]

> the cultural hegemony of idealism was established at many different levels. It was apparent in popular as well as in academic studies, and it was found not merely in abstract treatises on political thought, but in statistic and descriptive studies of concrete social problems, whose subject-matter and methodology appeared on their face to be quite the reverse of idealist.

Politically, 'the vast majority of British idealists were unremittingly enthusiasts for "active citizenship" and popular democracy' (*ibid.*: 126).

Moreover, 'idealism united people who differed widely on political tactics; it generated a vocabulary of social reform that transcended political parties; and it helps to explain the enthusiasm for, or at least tolerance of, the growth of centralized social services within a political culture that had traditionally been hostile to any accretion of state power' (*ibid.*: 138). State intervention was viewed as an instrument for setting the pre-conditions for developing a form of participatory democracy based on the active involvement of its citizens in the management of public affairs. The state was not supposed to supplant the self-help societies and charitable organisations composing the social economy. Rather, it was seen as playing a complementary and supporting role the aim of which was to promote moral harmony through the political inclusion of the working classes. In fact, the main concern of these idealist reformers was no longer the 'pauper' but the 'poor'. For them, the objective of welfare services was not that of relieving people from hardship but that of 'inculcating citizenship as the ultimate goal of social welfare' (*ibid.*: 133). As a result, social policies and work were understood as part of a general programme of social education beneficial to all those involved.

> Thus it was not the material fact of a social-welfare benefit that was important, but its inner meaning and context. A benefit was allowable (even a state benefit) if it took place within an ethical context (that is, a reciprocal personal relationship between giver and receiver) and if its end was rational (that is, the

promotion of independent citizenship in the recipient). But it was not allowable, either from the state or from private charity, if it involved a mere mechanical and anonymous transfer of resources from one individual to another, with no element of moral purpose or ethical exchange (*ibid.*: 132).

Accordingly, the social reform movement was committed to establish local and municipal services run by dedicated but unprofessional personnel on a voluntary basis whose goal was 'not to keep the poor in their place, but to force the poor into active and prudent participatory citizenship' (*ibid.*).

A pragmatic and politically heterodox spirit also characterises the subsequent phase of development that, in Harris's (1992: 116) words, 'after the Second World War created in Britain one of the most uniform, centralised, bureaucratic and "public" welfare systems in Europe, and indeed in the modern world'. For instance, in rejecting the 'modern counterpart of the "Whig" historiography' which was (and still is) claiming that 'welfare states were the fruit of social democracy', Briggs (1961: 11) maintains that 'many of the "reforms" were designed as remedies for specific problems: they were certainly not thought of as contributions to a "trend" or a "movement". The sources of inspiration were multiple – socialism was only one of several strands – and this very multiplicity added to later complications and confusions'.

What, then, were the circumstances which explain the bureaucratic development of the welfare state? The most obvious were those bought about by the war experience – what Briggs calls the association between warfare and welfare. First of all, there was a generalised popular expectation that the crucial contribution of the working classes to the war effort needed to be recognised by dismantling the legal and structural factors hindering the democratisation of the state. Hence the social pressure for the extension of the franchise to all able bodies (regardless of their sex, status, education, religion and political belief) was accompanied by requests for a significant reduction of the material inequalities which made the concession of formal political rights void. This was a popular expectation fostered by the propaganda machines set up during both wars to strengthen national resolve and avoid the social and political turmoil generated at the end of the previous conflict by disappointing it – something that in Britain in particular explains the unexpected commercial success of the Beveridge Report as a publishing enterprise (Brown 1995).

A second but no less important factor was the administrative and financial capacity acquired by national governments and their bureaucratic apparatus; that is, the ability to organise and plan all productive activities according to rigorous managerial criteria based on command-and-control techniques. The general inference drawn from this was that such capacity could well be applied in peacetime to win the war on want. An inference justified to all concerned by pointing out the staggering amounts of money spent for the war cause in sheer contradiction with the public finance probity professed by the ruling classes in relation to the social question. To quote Briggs (1961: 226) once again, the argument was not simply that administrative problems would be simplified if structures were 'comprehensive' or 'universal' but that through 'universal schemes' 'concrete expression' would be given to the 'solidarity and unity of the nation', which in war has been its bulwark against aggression and in peace will be its guarantee of success in the fight against individual want and mischance.

To fully appreciate the shift towards the centralised and bureaucratic system of welfare, we need to consider the transformations that took place since the mid-1930s as well. For Harris (1992: 136),

> a creeping disenchantment with idealist forms of discourse as a theoretical framework for social policy can be detected in many quarters from the early 1930s [...] The revolt against idealism that had been lurking in philosophic circles for the previous twenty years burst into a torrent in the mid-1930s with the onset of linguistic positivism; and the speculative discussion of underlying principles that had been such a marked feature of social-policy debate over the previous forty years vanished virtually overnight from the organs of academic philosophy. Moreover the crash of idealism was more than just an episode in academic fashion. It took with it much of the intellectual capital of those who had built up the British social services and were in the process of constructing the British welfare state.

This anti-idealism brought back into fashion positivistic visions supporting organisational, managerial and professional values opposed to those that had dominated the previous movement for social reform. The emphasis on democracy and citizenship continued but, in the new cultural and political climate, the public debate came to be dominated by social forces which were, for diverse reasons, highly suspicious of, if not hostile towards, the *demos* as a legitimate and competent decision-maker, and democratic politics as an educational practice resting on learning-by-doing pragmatic tenets.

Among these social forces, there are three which stand out for their relevance: religious groups promoting a new form of Christian democracy, the reformist components of the socialist movement which in the interwar period had had some governmental role, and the remains of the liberal ruling classes which managed to regenerate themselves by joining the anti-fascist resistance. Each of them had good reasons for fearing forms of democratisation along the participatory lines indicated by their idealist predecessors (Müller 2011: ch. 4). As a traditional defender of the propertied classes, the liberal establishment was obviously concerned about the tyranny of the majority. Christian democrats subscribed to conservative and paternalistic values which were antithetical to the emancipatory spirit driving idealist reformism. Finally, socialist and labour parties (which had publicly betrayed the international cause and sided first with the nationalistic forces responsible for the 'imperialist' WWI and then with liberal forces engaged in repressing the revolutionary uprisings which followed it) were fast evolving into bureaucratic and professional political organisations more concerned with controlling their membership than empowering it. To round things up, since the 1939 collapse of the Spanish Republic, revolutionary socialism had come to be dominated by Leninist ideas and Stalinist tactics which destroyed any internal form of democracy and exacerbated factional divisions, making any endogenous revolutionary threat highly unlikely.

1.3. 'Let them eat cake': Overlapping elements of welfarist solutions

Converging together in broad coalition governments of national unity called on to carry out first the reconstruction process and later the Cold War, the forces promoting the post-war settlement ended up adopting values, policies and hierarchical modes of organisation justifying a very limited and superficial process of democratisation. In the first place, democratisation was restricted to state institutions only (Grugel 2002), leaving unanswered calls for: (i) economic and industrial forms of democracy advocated by trade unions and labour councils but vehemently opposed by liberals; (ii) democratic reforms of social institutions (like family and church) which entrenched non-legal forms of discrimination denounced by social reformists but strenuously opposed by traditional social and religious authorities; and (iii) turning cultural institutions and the newly emerging mass medias into tools of social emancipation (rather than control) as advocated by independent thinkers and producers against the wishes of oligopolistic corporate agents interested in exploiting them. Even within the public domain, the process of democratisation either failed to touch entire sectors which had strategic relevance (e.g. security, defence, diplomacy, public finances and administration), or had a very superficial impact (e.g. courts, tribunals and the administration of justice in general).

Unsurprisingly, the opening of liberal constitutional proceedings throughout OECD countries ultimately favoured agreements on procedural forms of democracy whose main objective was, mostly, to reduce popular participation to periodical electoral moments and to slow down the political process by imposing a separation of powers establishing veto points through which to check the *demos*. To this end, (i) decision-making was made the exclusive domain of professional political elites upon whom the electorate had few controlling powers once elected; (ii) policy making assumed the form of a technocratic activity gradually delegated to independent professional bodies whose task was to survey public opinion and aggregate individual preferences impartially; (iii) policy implementations remained the exclusive preserve of monopolitistic and vertically integrated bureaucracies whose democratic legitimacy and accountability was ever more remote. In the process, the notion of citizenship itself underwent a subtle but radical change, and from a set of duties people owed to each other and their communities, it was turned into sets of legal-claim rights against an impersonal state.

Intellectually, the procedural conception of democracy that came to inspire the political forces involved in the post-war settlement was the one suggested at the time by Schumpeter (1943) – the Competitive Leadership Model (CLM). This conception was the offspring of the anti-idealistic spirit described by Harris. It was predicated on a positivist worldview rejecting the abstract moral commitments shared by the various components of the *fin de siècle* reformist movement. The picture of the classical model of democracy supplied by Schumpeter against which to juxtapose his vision, notably failed to distinguish between a Rousseauian political tradition critical of the possibility of delegating the general will and a Benthamite utilitarian tradition that not only supported the delegation of power but also suggested an aggregative reading of the general will equivalent to the one proposed by the Austrian economist.[4]

The positivist spirit of CLM is also evident in Schumpeter's opposition towards value-laden analyses and the consequent adoption of an elitist realism derived from Weber. Accordingly, the classical model was rejected in favour of a conception that viewed democracy simply as a 'method' for selecting the ruling elite; that is, a procedure needed to choose those who were then called to make public decisions. The people as a sovereign entity was thus relegated to the background, called on to express its will directly only at scheduled electoral intervals. Schumpeter was so radically opposed to any foray of the people into politics that he decried any attempt to influence the deliberation of representatives in between elections – to the point that even the possibility for public-minded citizens to write letters to their local MPs was supposed to be forbidden. Since decision-making was presented as a highly technical activity defying the competence of ordinary citizens, it had to be reserved for the selected few who had the intellectual capacities and time to acquire political expertise dispassionately.

The trust Schumpeter puts in the judgment of professional legislators is justified by further limitations imposed on democratic politics on technical grounds. Parliamentary activities were in fact supposed to take place within a constitutional setting that established a clear-cut separation of power between elective and non elective bodies and made policy making and implementation the exclusive domain of institutions (executive offices, public bureaucracies and courts of justice) insulated from the electoral process and run according to non-political managerial criteria. The only real concession Schumpeter seemed willing to make to democratic thought concerned the justification of majority rule against the liberal preference for unanimity – a feature that, as I shall explain in Chapter Two, separate him from later neoliberal thinkers. However, even this justification is mostly a question of expediency, rather than due to a principled acceptance of democratic values: it was grounded on the practical difficulties entailed by unanimity, as in principle unanimity remained the only legitimate rule.[5]

The limitations of Schumpeter's realism are clearly evident in his description of the institutional aspects required by CLM. What he advocates is an idealised version of the British political system, a competitive bi-partisan parliamentary democracy headed by a strong cabinet and flanked by a politically impartial and organisationally autonomous civil service. This is, in fact, a prescriptive ideal type that is neither arrived at by logical inference of the institutional features required by his procedural definition of democracy as a method for choosing public decision-makers, nor based on an accurate historical assessment of the actual working of the British body politic and its ability to foster individual compliance. As a result, Schumpeter states that any such competitive bi-partisan parliamentary democracy would work in the end if, and only if, several prerequisites are already in place – prerequisites which CLM is not able to generate endogenously and can even undermine (Mackie 2009). Connecting these prerequisites together gives us an idealised picture of the English gentleman, a picture no less artificial and controversial but highly complementary to the one supplied previously.[6]

These same theoretical aspirations and limitations re-surface in a second conception of democracy that, born as a critique of realist elitism, in actual fact managed to reinforce the intellectual hegemony of CLM – the pluralist theory of democracy developed in the USA in the wake of the behavioural revolution in American political science (Farr 1995). Notwithstanding the distinct disciplinary, methodological and political orientations of the two, the features which characterise behaviourism as an intellectual movement are refinements of those indicated by Schumpeter. First and most evident is the rejection of previous approaches to politics and policy analysis for being overly ideological and lacking scientific validity. This expresses itself in the adoption of a hard-nose ism that despises and discourages normative analysis. Paralleling the logical empirist crusade against metaphysics, the latter is dismissed for failing to follow a very debatable 'is-ought' distinction that even the various behavioural approaches are evidently unable to uphold, as it will turn out. Starting from variegated theoretical angles, various authors thus converge on supporting the specious theses about the irrationality of mass psychology and the acquisitiveness of human nature at the centre of Schumpeter's theory.

These elements are then used to stress: (i) their role in undermining the stability of interwar democratic experiences, (ii) the need to pay attention to the condition of social stability in order to avoid a repeat of that failure in similarly polarising global conditions, (iii) the indispensable role leadership plays in bringing about both social change and order, and (iv) the functional role of apathy for the working of the political system. As critics were keen to point out, these theses were not based on empirical data, nor did the empirical evidence collected confirm their validity in line with the rigorous epistemic tenets advocated (Walker 1966). If anything, they reflected the anxieties behind the post-war settlement – mirrored by Parsonian sociology and welfare economics during the 1950s, the two disciplinary fields from which empirical political science derived its tenets. Thus, the observation that: 'the "sociological" approach of Berelson and the "economic" model favored by Downs, did, despite obvious methodological differences, lead to remarkably similar or at least congruent conclusions' (Ball 1995: 59).

A second feature showing the continuity between Schumpeter and American pluralism is to be found in the ideal types used by them. In both Downs' attempt to develop an economic theory of democracy along Schumpeter's lines and in Dahl's attempt to go beyond Schumpeter's elitism to arrive at an empirical political theory, the similarities abound. Like Schumpeter's CLM, these ideal types have an unmistakable deductive structure and performative nature. In other words, they are far from being the outcome of empirically-based and testable generalisations, and their ultimate goal is to support and celebrate American liberal democracy regardless of its shortcomings. As Ball (1995: 63) explains,

> the idea that there exist certain specifiable 'functional requisites' for a viable democracy was proposed by Lipset (1959, 1960) and other 'empirical theorists' of democracy and was picked up by Almond and Verba (1963), among other comparativists. When one examines these 'functional requisites' – low level of class conflict, the existence and legitimacy of competing parties, widespread consensus regarding the 'rules of the game', and so on – one discovers that they are met most fully in the United States. In the Almond-Verba version, a viable 'civic culture' are one in which these requisites are met. And not surprising, the ideal-type of the civic culture is most fully exemplified in the political culture of the United States.

In Dahl's work in particular, the notion of 'polyarchy' keeps oscillating between a Weberian ideal-type, an historical type and a prescriptive type: it is clearly a normative ideal type in the 1956 *Preface* (where it is juxtaposed to Madisonian and populist democracy), it becomes a historical type in the 1961 *Who Governs?* (derived from the restricted empirical study of New Haven politics conducted by the author), and wishes to be a Weberian ideal type in the 1970 book *Polyarchy, Participation and Democracy*.

Finally, the revision of CLM proposed by American pluralists during the behavioural revolution seems to have had the restricted objective of showing that an idealised picture of the US political system and of the American middle classes (*homo civicus*) could well fit the prerequisites uncovered by Schumpeter in order to have a stable democratic order. Even if the simplifications needed to do this required them to put to one side the previous 100 years of American social and political history and overlook the social and political cleavages criss-crossing the USA at the time. Fulfilling the role of methodological 'scavenger' attributed to it, empirical political science was indeed too preoccupied with preserving the post-war settlement to be able to appreciate the heuristic role popular movements could have in promoting political and institutional changes, and to catch up with contemporary developments in the study of those movements carried out by other social scientists.[7]

Also telling are the divergences with Schumpeter – who Dahl tends to associate with the Madisonian theorists. The first crucial difference concerns the relevance attributed to formal constitutional constraints as opposed to social constraints. The point is clearly stated by Dahl (1956: 83): 'we admire the efficacy of constitutional separation of powers in curbing majorities and minorities, but we often ignore the importance of restraints imposed by social separation of power. Yet if the theory of polyarchy is roughly sound, it follows that in the absence of social prerequisites, no constitutional arrangement can produce a non-tyrannical republic'. This point was already made and discussed at length in Chapter Eleven of Dahl and Lindblom (1953) – a book whose influence on policy analysis should not be underestimated. There, it emerges that the appeal to social pluralism is directed towards an interpretation of leadership as natural aristocracy characterising the tradition of thought that links Weber and Schumpeter via Michels. All of them fail to clarify the social basis of leadership and leave the latter either unexplained or the outcome of natural forces beyond human control.

According to Dahl and Lindblom, social pluralism is an indispensible prerequisite for fostering not only leadership but also the right kind of leadership required by polyarchy. As they explain,

> first, social pluralism means the existence of social organizations, organizational loyalties, and organizational leaders [...] Second, social pluralism facilitates competition by insuring the existence of rival leaders with differing loyalties and support. [...] Third, social pluralism facilitates the rising of political leaders whose main skill is negotiating settlements among conflicting social organizations. [...] Fourth, social pluralism increases the probability that one is simultaneously a member of more than one social organisation; hence action by a leader against what seems to be an enemy organisation may in fact strike against his own alliance. [...] Fifth, social pluralism [...] increases the probability that alternative sources of information not under direct government control will be technically available to citizens (Dahl and Lindblom 1953: 304–305).

This leads us to the second aspect of their revision, the relevance attributed to government responsiveness as a counterbalance to tyranny. Even if indirectly, democratic choice needs to be somehow connected to policy, otherwise, they claim, electoral competition would resolve in sectarian infighting, favouring the 'iron law' of oligarchy. This risk needs to be reduced by making leaders responsive to the preferences of the electorate, namely establishing a counteracting 'law' of reciprocity. And this is a point they elaborate with explicit reference to the Austrian economist: 'Schumpeter argued that political competition guaranteed only a choice among leaders, not among policies. Thus in his view the significance of political competition for translating citizen preferences into public policy was negligible. This assumption is false unless one can show that choice among leaders is completely divorced from preferences as to policy. Schumpeter did not show this, nor in our view could he' (*ibid.*: 283, n. 15).

The last crucial and more technical aspect of the revision proposed by Dahl and Lindblom worth considering here pertains to the set of policy instruments available to polyarchy. Although Schumpeter leaves the question unspecified stating only that public administration must be insulated from politics and run according to rational managerial criteria, his preference for the market mechanism could be used to support Madisonian objections against the welfare state. In rejecting objections of this sort, that the authors claim 'to be derived almost entirely from a priori reasoning', they develop an incrementalist approach to 'policy making that combines markets and hierarchies as mechanisms of control. If competition and negotiation are seen as social processes of control necessary for the acquisition and retention of decision-making power, hierarchy and command are needed for controlling policy making and implementation. 'Plan or no plan is no choice at all; the pertinent questions turn on particular techniques', they contend, 'who shall plan, for what purposes, in what conditions, and by what devices? Free market or regulation? Again, this issue is badly posed. Both institutions are indispensable' (*ibid.*: 5). Hence, they (i) identify four main socio-political processes of control: the price mechanism, hierarchy, polyarchy and bargaining; (ii) indicate the control function each of them satisfies: the price system as a mechanism for control *of* and *by* leaders, hierarchy as a mechanism for control *by* leaders, polyarchy as a mechanism for control *of* leaders, and bargaining for control *among* leaders; (iii) show how those controlling mechanisms can be combined together for economising the resources needed for choice and allocation. At each step, they take the time to point out that 'techniques and not "isms" are the kernel of rational social action in the Western world' (*ibid.*: 16).

Reservations about substantive conceptions of democracy and the cult of technocratic leadership in policy making and implementation are at the core of the managerial revolution cutting across the private and public domains at the time (Chandler 1977). This revolution was earlier noticed and analysed by Burnham (1941). Here I will consider one aspect overlooked by Burnham – the rising of a managerial class of gurus engaged in rationalising and spreading what Wolin (1960: 355) labels 'the new gospel of "enlightened management"'. To do so I restrict my attention to the field of public management for the obvious relations it has with the bureaucratisation of welfare institutions and the proceduralisation of social policy. The most remarkable piece of performative managerial analysis produced by the behavioural revolution is, undoubtedly, Simon's (1947) *Administrative Behaviour* – a work that established the theoretical basis of public management while reading as a step-by-step instruction manual. It originated as a critique of traditional administrative maxims, what the author calls 'proverbs of administration' (Simon 1946), and then went on to spell out both the various phases making up the decision-making process and the organisational arrangements required to support them (Simon 1944).

In Simon's (1947: 8) words, 'the administrative process are decisional processes: they consist in segregating certain elements in the decisions of members of the organisation, and establishing regular organisation procedures to select and determine these elements and to communicate them to the member concerned'. Decision making and organisation structure are described as following parallel procedural logics: there is a 'hierarchy of decisions' on the one side, and a hierarchy of roles and functions on the other side. Although Simon mentions the possibility of horizontal forms of specialisation, his main task is not just restricted to analysing vertical forms of specialisation but also spells out the reasons justifying them.

> First, if there is any horizontal specialisation, vertical specialisation is absolutely essential to achieve coordination among the operative employees. Second, just as horizontal specialisation permits greater skill and expertise to be developed by the operative group in the performance of their task, so

vertical specialisation permits greater expertise in the making of decisions. Third, vertical specialisation permits the operative personnel to be held accountable for their decisions: to the board of directors in the case of a business organisation; to the legislative body in the case of a public agency (*ibid.*: 9).

The crucial elements driving the whole administrative process are individual 'discretion' and personal 'responsibility'. The vertical proceduralisation proposed by Simon aims at reducing the organisation's dependency on individual discretion by mapping and ordering in a stepwise fashion all the various processes of production and in establishing a hierarchical order of roles and functions that could make it easy for managers to attribute personal responsibilities and monitor how they are gradually discharged.

The spirit leading this managerial enterprise is as far as possible from the concerns of socialists with human emancipation as it is from the educational aspirations of democrats. Its aim is to reaffirm order by juxtaposing it (in a stark way reminiscent of Thatcher's later battle cry of TINA) to chaos, and connecting control with the virtues of specialisation and accountability. On this point, Torgerson (1995: 240–241) rightly contrasts Simon's enterprise with Dewey's, from whom the procedural approach is derived in order to support a Schumpeterian conception of democracy: 'while he draws explicitly on [Dewey's book] *How We Think*, Simon does not mention the crucial role that Dewey affords to judgment. Dewey is invoked rather as the inventor of a stepwise model of problem solving'; Dewey uses judgment to advocate 'an active and educated public in a form of participatory democracy. In contrast, Simon restricts his concern to the responsiveness of administration in the context of a representative democracy'.

Indeed, Schumpeter's procedural redefinition of democracy as a method for selecting the ruling elite could work properly only if the chain of accountability connecting decision-making and law enforcement maintains its integrity, allowing the electoral mechanism to retain its power of deterrence as noted above by Dahl and Lindblom (*see also* Chapter Nine). Hence, Simon's preoccupation to establish procedural checks on (individual and technical) judgment, and empower a managerial class dedicated to that task. Finally it needs to be noted that the search for this sort of accountability has its root in the changes accompanying the development of the modern joint-stock company which brought to the fore the problems caused by the separation of control and ownership studied by Berle and Means (1932) – organisational forms which had in the meantime become a dominant feature of industrial societies (Palumbo 2009). In theory, the solution suggested by Simon not only applies to both private and public forms of production, but it represents an attempt to import into public administration the techniques developed within the private sector to manage public companies. It is thus an earlier instance to reshape the public sector in the image of the private sector, rather than an advocacy of socialist planning. As such, it is a crucial contribution to making Schumpeter's CLM a workable institutional solution.

1.3.1 Citizenship as a set of legal-rights claims

The procedural redefinition of democracy as a method for social choice and the subsequent revision of CLM to make it a workable institutional solution were complemented by a reinterpretation of citizenship. The outline of what Kymlicka and Norman (1994) call the post-war orthodoxy is given by Marshall in his 1949 Alfred Marshall Memorial lectures published (together with other essays on the subject) the following year (Marshall 1950). In those lectures, Marshall proposes an evolutionary and expansive account of citizenship as rights. Looking back at British social history, he claims that

> civil rights came first, and were established in something like their modern form before the first Reform Act was passed in 1832. Political rights came next, and their extension was one of the main features of the nineteenth century, although the principle of universal political citizenship was not recognised until 1918. Social rights, on the other hand, sank to vanishing point in the eighteenth and early nineteenth centuries. Their revival began with the development of public elementary education, but it was not until the twentieth century that they attained to equal partnership with the other two elements in citizenship (Marshall 1950: 27–8).

Such a rights-based reading of British social history matches the performative ambitions of Schumpeter and his behaviourist followers. While it is proposed as a neutral sociological reconstruction, in reality it is a very sketchy picture used to advance a justification of a specific understanding of citizenship – one that is advocating a 'marked shift of emphasis from duties to rights' (*ibid.*: 9).

In carrying out his reconstruction, Marshall either fails to mention alternative readings of citizenships (Harris 2010), or fails to engage with them properly. He notes (1950: 24) that the notion of social and economic rights he is keen to defend derives from legislation passed to deal with paupers and children; that is, subjects excluded from active citizenship. Marshall then explains that it was because of this connection that women's organisations fighting for political inclusion were particularly hostile towards any attempt to extend to them the protection offered by that body of legislation. For the suffragettes, the protection afforded by those rights meant in effect accepting a subordinate juridical role; something that was in strident contrast with their claim to be recognised as fully contributing members of society to whom was due both equal respect and political responsibilities.[8] While extolling the virtues of a legal rights-based conception of citizenship (its certainty, universality and fairness), he remains impervious to the shortcomings this shift could have at a political and motivational level.

In a similar fashion, Marshall (1950: 44) considers and dismisses the notion of active citizenship advocated by syndicalist movements. He takes issue with the way in which trade unionism used civil rights collectively for renegotiating aspects of the social contract and then spent the political consent acquired for strengthening its collective bargaining power. For him, not only rights and bargaining are inconsistent with each other, but he once again stresses the appealing universalistic feature of basic rights and the benefits they could assure to the working classes *vis-à-vis* collective bargaining. For him, legalism makes industrial democracy and the active notions of citizenship supporting it no longer indispensible, and rehabilitates the state, its administrative apparatus and system of courts and tribunals as the champions in the quest for social justice.

Such an approach completely overlooks the educational benefits attributed to more active forms of social, economic and political engagement and disregards both the motivational shortcomings it could produce and the dangers it could pose to emancipatory ideals. Social reformist movements were in fact well aware of the limits of paternalism and state institutions, and their inherent social biases. Thus, they viewed democratisation as the only means to achieve this while reducing the appeal revolutionary ideologies still exercised on some sectors of the working classes. In his dispute with trade unionism, Marshall's appeal to a rights-based model of citizenship is also deeply inconsistent, for it is predicated on a grand bargaining strategy that trades material advantages for socio-political gains.

This grand bargaining strategy is indeed the hallmark of the British welfare state and is supported by a large intellectual constituency that, in the aftermath of WWII, includes even the main exponents of the mutualist tradition of thought. As Harris (2010: 18) eloquently puts it,

> within this contest the message of Citizenship and Social Class may be set alongside the Beveridge Report and J. M. Keynes's General Theory in offering what apparently appeared to be a radical redistributive, constitutionalist – but also 'materialist' alternative to the attraction of Marxism. [...] market inequalities [...] can to some extent be mitigated by political intervention; but enforced equalisation of rewards beyond a certain point is self-defeating because it undermines productive processes. [...] a new form of social equality [...] based on equal access to full citizenship in the form of material social security [...] would substantially counteract and mitigated continuing inequalities inherent in the sphere of economic production. But there was no reason at all why these two quite different forms of resources-allocation should not co-exist together, the one generating the resources required to maintain and finance the other.

Within this intellectual milieu the success of Marshall's essay is pretty understandable. The economy of this work does not allow me to carry out a proper textual analysis, but it is my belief that the massive influence Marshall had in the USA can be traced in Rawls' (1971) attempt to develop a more comprehensive theory of social justice.[9] Although the American philosopher was reluctant to use the notion of rights as a fundamental moral category (and resisted attempts in this direction carried out by Dworkin (1975)), at the root of Rawls' enterprise there is: (i) a grand bargaining between Kantian notions of equality and utilitarian concerns with efficiency, (ii) an expansive notion of citizenship that allows only those inequalities which favour the worst-off members of society, (iii) an anti-political bias that leads him to trust abstract formal reasoning and constitutional courts above democratic politics – blamed for always reflecting asymmetries in bargaining power, and (iv) Marshall's 'implicit view that the new "classless" to be enjoyed by the mass of the people was to be a "middle-class classlessness" (involving universal access to education and high culture) rather than a working-class one (based on different kinds of occupation' (Harris 2010: 20).

Ironically, Rawls' philosophical restatement and refinement of Marshall's citizenship as social rights saw the light when the post-war consensus was already in tatters. Thus, its academic, intellectual and commercial success notwithstanding, it was not strong enough to stop the disintegration of the social and political coalition supporting the welfare state, or even dent the academic and political prestige acquired by neoliberal schools of thought, as we shall see in Chapter Two. In the next section, I try to show that this crisis was already brewing in the early 1960s and that the reason for this was that, in practice, the grand bargaining was failing to deliver – a failure some prominent supporters of welfare state were well aware of and tried to highlight by using the empirical evidence available to them.

1.4. The welfare state at work: aspirations, tensions and limitations

The previous section has given an outline of the intellectual climate wherein the welfare state took shape. It was a climate dominated by perspectives extremely concerned with the viability of mass democracy and highly committed to setting external side-constraints on the process of democratisation. As mentioned at the end of the previous section, the political forces leading the main popular parties of the time were, for their own reasons, as concerned with keeping their membership under control and avoiding dangerous *fughe in avanti*[10]. The post-war settlement converged thus on an embedded form of liberalism encasing democracy in a constitutional and organisational straightjacket. This embedded liberal vision was rhetorically presented to the public at large as the most realistic model of democracy possible. One that, based on professional leadership and objective knowledge, could combine market dynamic and social solidarity, and thus promote a progressive form of citizenship giving people expanding sets of social and economic rights. The *demos* was, therefore, gently asked to sit down, relax and enjoy the journey.

The point I want to raise here is that the actual working of the welfare state fell short of satisfying the expectations it had itself created, and that the growing awareness of the gap between the practices it condoned and the values it professed caused the spiralling crisis of the post-war settlement (and of the welfare state with it). Awareness of this contradiction was already evident in the early 1960s, and was painstakingly analysed by many social scientists who had actively supported that settlement. Towards the end of the decade, their disenchantment with various aspects of the welfare state, and the growing social discontent within the constituencies supporting it, politically pushed for reforms along neocorporate lines. As I will explain (*see also* Chapter Two), unfortunately these reforms were both too timid and too late; that is, they arrived when the social and political coalition supporting the post-war settlement had imploded, leaving the welfare state in a political and cultural void that neoliberal forces managed to exploit to their own ends.

In Britain, the country that pioneered the welfare state, a very cautious (but still encouraging) earlier assessment of post-war achievements was proposed by R. H. Tawney, a staunch defender who had converted to the welfarist cause in the 1930s. In the epilogue to the 4th revised edition of his *Equality*, he summarises the effects of income distribution during the 1939–1950 period thus:

> those whose command of wealth and economic power formerly gave them most now have somewhat less. Those whose poverty or weakness formerly allowed them least now have somewhat more. [...] The recipients of the larger incomes, the classes whose *métier* is enterprise, many professional men, and persons, whether well-to-do or poor, dependent on incomes derived from the ownership of property, are less free than in the past. The wage-earners and recipients of small salaries are freer (Tawney 1952: 266–67).

Ten years later, this cautious assessment was replaced by a more disenchanted and detailed critical analysis carried out by Richard Titmuss, the successor of T. H. Marshall at the London School of Economics. In a lecture given at the University of California, Titmuss (1963: 8) writes:

> since 1948 it appears that persons on National Assistance have received a smaller share in rising national prosperity and that the gulf between their standard of living and the national average has widened substantially. [...] the facts show that these schemes are not making the lower-income groups appreciably better off in relative terms. [...] Developments and changes in the social services during the last twenty years have not abolished poverty in Britain. [...] Full employment and a remarkable rise in the paid employment of married women, from about five hundred thousand in 1939 to over four million in 1960, have been the two main causes of higher living standards.

It was on the basis of this assessment that Titmuss even objected to using the expression 'welfare state' to identify what he thought was 'a confused and contradictory pattern of state provision in the fields of medical care, social security, and education (*ibid.*: 11). In dispute with his own publisher, he thus requested that the title of his collection of essays on the subject should at least carry that contentious expression in inverted commas – *Essays on 'The Welfare State'*.

The matrix reported below (*see* Figure 1.2) attempts to reproduce the confused and contradictory pattern of state intervention mentioned by Titmuss. At the heart of the ongoing assessment carried out by him and his various collaborators was the need to distinguish between the goals to which the welfare state was said to be committed and the policy instruments employed to achieve them (among which the funding streams used to pay for them were also included). According to

Figure 1.2: Matrix of welfare goals and policy tools

		Policy instruments		
		Social insurance schemes	*Public goods/ services*	*Economic/fiscal policies*
G	*Equality of conditions*	State integration	Needs-based & free at entry point	Compensatory
o				
a	*Equality of opportunities*	Compulsory universal cover	Universal but rewarding talent	Setting incentives
l				
s	*Equality of results*	Top up redistribution	Means-tested	Taxation rules

Titmuss, the major impact on the rising living standards of the working classes was mainly due to the set of conditions that brought about a period of full employment, promoting the entrance of married women into the labour market thus doubling the income of many working class families and the value of the 'fringe benefits' paid labour guaranteed as a result.

Among the conditions responsible for this state of affairs were, in order of relevance, (i) the objective needs of post-war reconstruction, (ii) a shortage of manpower that enabled trade unions to negotiate better salary packages and (iii) the Keynesian economic policies pursued by the government. In his account, integratory, compensatory and redistributive welfare policies had had negligible effects on the general poverty level and on the share of public wealth that went to the working classes. This, in turn, meant that if and when the reconstruction phase came to an end, that standard of living could not be sustained any longer and poverty would return again despite massive amounts of resources and energies the working classes had invested in building the infrastructure of the welfare state.

In fact, when this investment is factored into a cost-benefit analysis, the achievements of the welfare state start to look very doubtful. For Saville (1957–8: 21–22),

> the social services have developed in such a way that the financial burden upon the rich has been very largely cushioned. Even more striking however [...] is the growth of direct and indirect taxation upon working class incomes to the point where much of the spenditure upon social services is no more than a transfer of income by taxation within the working class. [...] to a very considerable extent the working class pay for their own social security benefits by compulsory contribution and a high level of indirect taxation.

In other words, the type of redistribution generated by the welfare state was mostly horizontal, rather than vertical from the rich to the poor. And this horizontal redistribution had been achieved by means of a grand social bargain that required (i) the nationalisation of a whole social economy and (ii) the transfer of decision and managerial powers from a) interlocking networks of friendly, self-help and mutual societies controlled locally, to b) a faceless national bureaucracy dominated by middle-class values, and c) only vaguely accountable to a professional political class even more (sociologically) unrepresentative of the working classes.[11] Particularly scathing are Saville's remarks on public education policies, those responsible for assuring some equality of opportunity:

> for the majority of our people the education ladder is still a greasy pole; all that has happened in the last few decades is that the intellectual elite of working class children have been provided with the necessary equipment to climb it. [...] Those who climb to University have to be very strong minded to resist the absorption of bourgeois values and ideas; for there is no better way of trimming working class ideas than by three years at our English Universities (*ibid.*: 18).

The jewel in the crown of the British welfare state was undoubtedly the National Health Service (NHS). Free universal services at the point of entry paid from general taxation combined to make it an institution run on socialist principles of social justice: from each according to his ability, to each according to his need. Alas, during the 1950s those principles were eroded by the removal of some medical services (dental and ophthalmic care) from the list of free services and the introduction of a flat-rate system of individual charges (Titmuss 1976: 138). Even more problematic, however, were the political and organisational foundations upon which the NHS had been established, and the way these influenced its daily managerial practices – problems on which Titmuss was the first to shed light and which deserve more of our attention to understand future developments.

Also delivered originally in the USA, Titmuss's lectures on the NHS followed a two-pronged task. The first was to debunk the claims put forward during the propaganda campaign mounted by the American Medical Association (with the complicity of its British counterpart) to oppose post-war calls for the establishment of a system of state-funded and -run medical care in the States. That propaganda rested on three main sets of objections (used successively to also disrupt Clinton's reforms in the 1990s and the current Medicaid legislation pushed through by the Obama administration) concerned with: (i) the financial affordability of public medical care schemes, (ii) the quality of care guaranteed by them *vis-à-vis* competitive private schemes and (iii) the restriction of liberty likely caused by the 'socialisation' of medicine. Using the British NHS as a case study, Titmuss demonstrates, in an empirical meticulous way, that all those claims were unfounded; that 'what evidence there is could in theory point the other way' (*ibid.*: 176).

Far more interesting, at least for us, is the second part of Titmuss's enterprise, his analysis of the weaknesses shown by the British experience and the implications those weaknesses could have for the future of the NHS. In doing this, he masterly combines a sociological analysis of professional developments in the field of medical science and practice with a study of the political implications of the bureaucratisation and juridification of the relations between suppliers and buyers (a category that includes patients and taxpayers alike).

Titmuss pointed out that the NHS was established at a time when scientific progress was transforming traditional medical knowledge radically. Changes in that field also meant the emergence of new professional figures – who were trying to replace traditional systems of authority favouring general practitioners (GPs), and the development of larger social expectations – which contributed to undermining the role and status of GPs. Based on the British experience, Titmuss explained first that those changes were unrelated to the establishment of the NHS, and then that the latter had played a major role in helping navigate the transition very sensibly indeed. In an understated English fashion, he writes that 'the National health service in Britain could not ensure that doctors, now invested with these greater powers and potentialities, would choose overnight to be "better" doctors; all it could do was to provide that particular framework of social resources within which potentially "better" medicine might be more easily chosen and practised' (*ibid.*: 171). He also pointed out that, alas, 'there is the danger of medicine becoming a technology [...] of a new authoritarianism in medicine which, in its turn, might lead to a growth of professional syndicalism. There is the problem of medical power in society; a problem which concerns much more of our national life than simply the organisation of medical care' (*ibid.*: 202).

Starting from a micro-sociological level, Titmuss explained the bureaucratisation of public medicine and the juridification of relations among all those involved in it as part of a more general process dependent on the growth of social expectations and responsibilities acquired by patients and their families, and on the corresponding impact this phenomenon was having on practitioners and public managers. According to him,

> the need for accuracy, orderliness and a strict observance of rules increases in proportion as clinical and surgical techniques become more complex, more scientific, more a matter of the co-ordinated and carefully timed activity of a medical and nursing team. [...] Thus, the system or rules and regulations which governs the performance of duties and the hierarchical relationships between different medical and nursing groups tends to become more complex and rigid (*ibid.*: 201).

At a more macro-sociological level, Titmuss noted (i) a growing dependence of doctors and patients on medical and pharmaceutical technologies, (ii) a concomitant shift in medical care from a policy of mass preventive education to one based on individualised emergency intervention, and (iii) the gradual dominance of professional and technical expertise above more social and political concerns. 'Socialised' public medicine risked, in his opinion, becoming indifferent to the social aspects of illness and care, and being run according to self-serving professional and technocratic logics. This last point was already more than a remote future eventuality. Titmuss used it in fact to account for the centralised organisational structure chosen for the NHS in 1946. At that time, many members of the profession [...] decided [...] that full-time or part-time service with a centrally controlled organisation was preferable to service with the municipal health authorities. Thus, in the political bargain struck between the profession and the Government of the day, the profession made it abundantly clear that it would enter the Service only on condition that all the hospitals, representing four-fifths of the hospital beds in the country, were taken out of the hands of municipal government. The profession's opposition to municipal ownership or control of hospitals is as strong today as it was in 1946, and partly explains way the organisation and structure of the Health Service takes the particular form it does (*ibid.*: 142–3).[12]

My claim is that not only similar dynamics were at work in other social and economic realms which gradually came under the direct and indirect control of the British welfare state, but also that a similar evolution occurred in the other OECD countries engaged in establishing their own version of the welfare state.

Could the negative consequences brought about by the bureaucratisation of public services and the juridification of relationships between citizens, users and administrators be redressed or at least contained? In my opinion they could not because the adoption of CLM, in its original Schumpeterian version or in the polyarchical form suggested by American pluralists, managed to turn democracy into a spectator sport relying on the apathy of large sectors of the citizenry; especially those lacking the required political competence and expertise. Thus, the attempt to build an embedded liberal democracy was in reality based on the atomisation of the working classes and the minimalist politics of the ballot box. This meant that the bargaining power of organised interests operating in various fields could not be counterbalanced by those representing larger and more diffused interests. A structural problem that became especially evident once the democratic game assumed a thoroughly national character, successfully excluding local and other intermediary layers of government from decision and policy making.[13]

In effect, while CLM relegated popular participation to electoral practices requiring a minimalist politics of the ballot box, the welfare state had deprived citizens and local communities of any responsibility in the delivery of public goods and services. As such, real existing liberal democracies turned out to be unmistakably governments *for* the people rather than governments *of* the people, and general elections ended up being only a remote link in a long chain of delegation enforcing accountability throughout the body politic. The actual working of these liberal democratic systems of government was, in addition, irredeemably biased towards the satisfaction of the preferences of a hypothetical median voter and predicated on the role of social buffer attributed to the middle classes against attempts at revolutionary transformations. Within this protective constitutional set up, the function of welfare policies was not only that of trying to minimise vertical modes of redistribution from the rich to the poor, but also that of co-opting the more successful members of the working classes within the cultural value system of the middle classes.[14]

The relentless search for stability thus meant actively depleting the political capital of the working classes while retaining a social and economic order based essentially on the bargaining abilities of the various components of the populace – a process to which the Marshallian notion of citizenship as legal-rights claim was giving a crucial contribution. Far from being restricted to the establishment of the welfare state, bargaining was a diffuse practice encouraged by polyarchies engaged in cultivating their segmented consensus at various levels of the body politic through forms of policy exchange – to whom empirical political science attributed colourful labels (horse trading, log rolling, pork barrel, etc.) in its quest to describe and classify them.

In this negotiating policy environment, (i) everything could be put up for sale – social and economic rights included, (ii) benefits and gains tended to reflect existing social, economic and cultural inequalities – hollowing out the constitutional provisions attributing a formal political equality to everybody, (iii) distinct organisational realms were encouraged to develop their own utility function and the institutional strategies to maximise it. Since the outset, centrifugal dynamics were, as a result, fragmenting the welfare state into a plurality of fiefdoms intent on exploiting their gatekeeping position in the administrative hierarchy by extracting some form of rent. In short, embedded liberalism employed welfare policies not only as a bulwark to resist social calls for democratisation, but also to actively hollow out the political ability of the working classes to mobilise and use their bargaining power collectively. Hence, after acquiring their juridical status, citizens were forced to continuously negotiate the rights claim formally attributed to them with a growing number of intermediary bodies insulated from the electoral process (lobbies, professions, administrators) and with the legal apparatus of the state supervising them.

Given the costs of collective action and the unresponsiveness of bureaucratic welfare institutions to electoral politics, popular dissatisfaction was channelled either through social movements exercising pressure from without or by means of class action (where allowed) using legal and lobbying instruments. In both instances, the credibility of formal democratic institutions was undermined and the democratic game gradually took the form of a competitive contest between minoritarian but well-organised interest groups unconcerned with the public good. It is therefore not surprising if the emergence of social rights movements in the USA and of extra-parliamentary activities in Europe in the second half of the 1960s were initially accounted for in terms of a general legitimation crisis affecting liberal democratic institutions. Coming from the left-wing side of the political spectrum, this diagnosis rightly imputed the legitimacy deficit affecting the post-war settlement to the stunted process of democratisation that had raised hopes for social change but failed to fulfil those promises repeatedly. This diagnosis also explains why the erosion of legitimacy affected the social constituencies which were supposed to benefit most from the welfare state, well before the alleged revolt of middle-class taxpayers and even where that revolt failed to materialise. As a staunch supporter of post-war social democracy eloquently notes: 'the beneficiaries of that order – whether Swedish shopkeepers, Scottish shipworkers, inner-city African-Americans or bored French suburbanites – were increasingly resentful of their dependence upon administrators, local councillors and bureaucratic regulations' (Judt 2010: 83–84).

From my perspective, the best testimony in support of this reading of events can be found in Dahl and Lindblom's 1976 Preface to a reprint of their 1953 volume *Politics, Economics and Welfare*. Right at the start, the authors point out the political limitations of liberal constitutionalism and in particular of the one at the root of the post-war embedded version: 'a constitutional structure adapted to a reconciliation of diverse interests may lack mechanisms for articulating common purposes, for mobilizing overwhelming majorities, and for asserting the collectivity's right to act no less than the subcollectivity's right to veto' (Dahl and Lindblom 1992: xxvi). Against the procedural visions of democracy preoccupied with assuring formal rights only, they now maintain that,

> we cannot move a great deal closer to political equality without moving closer to equality in access to political resources. We cannot move to greater equality in access to political resources without greater equality in the distribution of, among other things, wealth and income. And if certain options like voting, free speech and due process have to be established as 'rights' to make democracy work, so also does a fairer share of income and wealth have to become a 'right' (*ibid.*: xxxvi).

Finally, they cast doubts on the type of technocratic incrementalism advocated earlier, even if they claim not to have shared the boundless trust put in it by other empirical political scientists: 'we did not share that euphoria and do not now believe that more thoughtful, better informed, or more scientific problem solving is enough. The emphasis given to it in the last decade or two has diverted attention from more fundamental requirements. The decisionmaking and policymaking institutions themselves are seriously defective and need to be restructured' (*ibid.*: xlv–xlvi).

Restructuring them entails abandoning the reservation expressed in the past towards the more participatory forms of democratic engagement advocated by a new generation of students and scholars that during the late 1960s tried to connect with the working classes and revive both the values and alliances of a pre-welfarist age.[15] For Dahl in particular this meant retrieving the conceptual tools and practices of trade-unionism in order to democratise polyarchy. For, he comes to acknowledge that the political viability of polyarchy at the national level depended, to a large extent, on the democratic nature of related social and economic settings. Any polyarchical order based on social and economic arrangements with a similar polyarchical structure would generate the type of power elite described by Wright Mills (1956); that is, replicate the conditions which had made the welfare state and liberal democratic institutions worldwide unresponsive to their electorates.

In my opinion, the perverse side-effects produced by welfare institutions within an overarching polyarchical political order could also be used to explain the neocorporate turn and its limited answer to the widespread quest for democratisation of the early 1970s – even if there is no possibility to discuss this phenomenon properly here. Developed following the piecemeal logic of the welfare state, neocorporate solutions represented practical attempts to tackle the inflationary spirals and social conflicts that emerged in the second half of the 1960s. Employed originally by Scandinavian and other Northern European social democracies, they were soon copied elsewhere as a more effective and democratic political template. Rationalisations of these institutional innovations started to appear in the mid-1970s – coincidentally with the effect produced by the first oil crisis – and, in a manner uncannily resembling the new modes of governance object of our inquiry, they were immediately heralded as a turning point for the welfare state and for empirical political science as well.

Underpinning the neocorporate template were two main ideas: one extolling the virtues of social cooperation against competition, and the other highlighting the beneficial effects of participatory forms of democracy against the procedural forms subscribed to by elitist and pluralist thinkers. Since inflation and social conflict were viewed as the outcome of the adversarial logic promoted by the competition between political parties and in industrial relations, emphasis was now put on negotiating practices leading to mutual beneficial accommodations. Since centrally-imposed measures often failed to acquire social recognition and were actively opposed by large sectors of civil society, the role of governmental forces was now described as that of a neutral umpire called to bring together the various contending parties at the same negotiating table. Finally, since the aim of neocorporate arrangements was to reach a viable, practical accommodation, they operated mostly at the policy level and did not touch on constitutional issues concerned with decision-making and the formal architecture of the state. In practice, this meant opening the policy process to organised interests in various policy areas, letting them contribute to the establishment of regulatory frameworks more conducive to some sort of social harmony. The other main state actors were then called to ratify (legislators) and enforce (public officials) those frameworks. Within this political arrangement, organised interests were given informal policy-making power on the understanding that they then assumed responsibility for aggregating the preferences of their members and assuring individual compliance with the regulation they themselves had contributed to determine.

Seen from a broader theoretical perspective, neocorporate arrangements support an aggregative model of democracy that is particularly concerned with the legitimacy of policy outcomes, and willing to overcome traditional liberal suspicions towards the intermediary bodies operating in between the state and the citizen – suspicions which during the process of state formation had brought about rigid limitations to the right of association (Schmitter 1983). As shown in Figure 1.3, these features make neocorporate democracy slightly different from both (a) the procedural conceptions underpinning the post-war settlement, but also (b) the participatory ones which were finding support among the new left and even (c) the forms of guild democracy advocated by the old left in the interwar period. All of these were in fact concerned with more extensive forms of participation whose aim was to strengthen what, according to Scharpf (2000), can be called

Figure 1.3: Ideological map of aggregative democratic forms

		Legitimacy	
		Input-oriented	*Output-oriented*
I	*Diffuse*	Participatory democracy	Foot-voting democracy
n			
t			
e	*Organised*	Guild democracy	Neocorporate democracy
r			
e			
s	*Public*	CLM/polyarchical democracy	Guardian democracy
t			
s			

input-oriented modes of legitimacy. By opening up the policy-making process to organised interests only, neocorporate democracy was also at odds with two other visions of democracy: (d) the Platonic forms of democracy favoured by the monocratic elitism of the *caudillos* (Latin-American dictators) and single-party type considered by MacPherson (1966), and (e) the foot-voting forms advocated by neoliberals (*see* Chapters Two and Eight).

The distinctive location occupied within this broader ideological map of democratic forms also gives us an insight into the theoretical weaknesses of neocorporate modes of democracy. As Schmitter (1983: 916) explains,

> neocorporatism is manifestly contrary to the citizenship principle. It introduces elements of 'weighted' calculation and consensual bargaining with privileged minorities which clearly violated the sacred norms of 'one man, one vote' and 'the most vote win'. [Moreover, he maintains that] so far, neocorporatism has privileged interests organised along functional lines of production within a capitalist economy – classes, sectors and professions. Its relative success has depended on restricting the number and identity of participants and passing on the costs to those not directly represented in its deliberation: consumers, taxpayers, youths, feminists, irregular workers, foreigners, cultural minorities, nature lovers, pedestrians, prohibitionists, etc. (*ibid.*: 917).

In other words, it was an attempt to boost the vitality of the welfare state by grafting embedded liberalism, as political polyarchy, onto other social and economic polyarchies – an enterprise upon which Dahl had already expressed serious reservations.

My take on the theoretical and practical limits of neocorporate solutions is twofold. Although I think (with Dahl) that in the long run they would have eventually failed, their actual demise was not caused by those shortcomings. As I shall argue in Chapter Two, §2.3, with the electoral victories of Margaret Thatcher in Britain in 1979 and Ronald Reagan in the USA the following year – that is, two countries where neocorporatism failed to make a dent – a diverse set of neoliberal solutions was devised and gradually implemented. These solutions rested on a different reading of the crisis and proposed a revision of the model of citizenship. I maintain that it was the specific type of success achieved by this neoliberal set of solutions in freeing central authorities from the social responsibilities imposed on them by the post-war consensus that explains both the retreat of neocorporatism and the retrenchment of welfare institutions. However, I also believe that the new modes of governance investigated in the rest of the book follow closely on the footprints left by neocorporate experiments (*see* Chapter Three). Thus, understanding their normative defects is still useful in order to highlight the likely danger faced by new modes of governance. This is a claim that I shall try to substantiate only in the concluding chapter, once the features which characterise new modes of governance and their inner articulation have been spelled out and analysed.

1.5. Conclusions

At no time have *les trente glorieuses* looked so resplendent than since the 2008 financial crisis. The expression itself clearly reflects a backward-looking perspective that projects onto the past a light much brighter than that experienced by contemporaries. In fact, it was used for the first time in 1979 by the French economist Fourastié as title of a study of the social and economic transformations which occurred in France up to the mid-1970s. The second part of that book's title was, *ou la révolution invisible de 1946 à 1975* – a subtitle well chosen because, as it seems, those revolutionary events received a much more sombre coverage in many chronicles of the time. My aim in this chapter has been to go back to those chronicles and carry out a genealogical analysis of the theory and practice of welfare institutions as they developed following the post-war settlement. The picture I derive from this attempt seems apparently odd: (i) rather than paving the way towards a bright socialist future, the welfare state was the outcome of very conservative and suspicious attitudes towards mass democracy; (ii) these attitudes where shared to a large degree not only by the liberal establishment that tried to recycle itself after the traumatic events of the first half of the twentieth century (for which it was directly responsible), but also by the leaders of the Christian and socialist parties – the former concerned about preserving traditional social, gender and religious values, and the latter preoccupied about their ability to retain its hegemonic power within the working classes; (iii) welfare institutions therefore developed within a liberal constitutional framework full of built-in social and political biases whose main aims were to slow down the pace of change and set strict side-constraints on the process of democratisation; (iv) this defensive strategy meant blunting the political abilities of the working classes to mobilise and use their bargaining power collectively, and transferring decision and policy-making power to state actors (sociologically) unrepresentative of the working classes and only remotely accountable to the electorate.

I would like to point out that this picture is not derived from an idiosyncratic genealogy selecting the most radical and anti-systemic theoretical perspectives available. On the contrary, it has been built by using perspectives broadly sympathetic to the welfare state, but also genuinely concerned about its future prospects. In some cases, the disappointment with the evolution of the welfare state led some political scientists to discard behavioural tenets which could not help explain the widespread legitimacy deficit of welfare programmes even among the social constituencies which were supposed to benefit most from them. Among the mounting tensions between welfare institutions and the political forces supporting the post-war settlement, attempts were carried out to reform the welfare state along neocorporate lines. Based on an understanding of the crisis as the result of a stunted process of democratisation, the policy-making process was gradually opened up to the 'peak' organisations representing the productive forces of civil society. However, the move failed to solve the legitimacy deficit and soon deteriorated into 'iron triangles' engaged in endless renegotiations of aspects of a social contract that could not be properly enforced because of the generalised opposition of large sectors of civil society, including some of those represented at the negotiating table. The opening of the policy process to neocorporate agents was far too timid and arrived too late. On the one hand, it excluded more diffuse interests lacking organisational resources and abilities, thus failing to arrive at a better understanding of the public good. On the other hand, it relied too much on social organisations which, by then, enjoyed only a low degree of representativeness and precarious legitimacy, and for whom inclusion within 'iron triangles' meant the acquisition of a gatekeeping position they could use to strengthen their power of representation.

As I shall explain in the next chapter, neocorporate solutions ended up magnifying existing structural weaknesses producing a growing gap between the formal and material aspects of the post-war constitutional settlement. While the overall responsiveness of the welfare state depended on formal mechanisms of accountability ultimately dependent on electoral dynamics, the delegation of decision- and policy-making power to bodies insulated from electoral politics made those mechanisms very remote and highly defective. Not only were popular majorities unable to affect change, but even their elected representatives found the formal decision-making powers of legislative institutions ineffective. In practice, the bureaucratisation and juridification of policy decisions made the levers of power too rubbery to make themselves felt simultaneously across the body politic, but kept paying lip service to accountability rules which attributed full political responsibility for government failure to elective institutions. With the introduction of neocorporate solutions the problem worsened, for national executives, who were initially the main beneficiaries of the delegation process, now had to share their policy-making power not only with civil servants, but also with other societal agents while retaining full responsibility towards parliament for policy failure. It was this complex interplay between expanding delegated powers and persistent political responsibilities that neoliberal governments in the Anglosphere tried to address; and it is the policy template they helped establish that eventually swept across OECD countries, bringing to an end the attempt to reform the welfare state along neocorporate lines.

End Notes

1. Histories of the welfare state abound. This reconstruction relies heavily on the following works: Briggs (1961), Brown (1995), Flora and Heidenheimer (1981), Harris (1992), Marshall (1961), Saville (1958), Titmuss (1963) and Trattner (1994). The literature used is admittedly biased towards the British experience. In my view, this bias is however justified by the influence this historical experience had on the development of welfare policies and institutions in other countries and for understanding the pitfalls which will lead in time to Thatcher's successful neoliberal counter-revolution.

2. In Bismarck's celebrated words, 'the right that men have to be taken care of when, from no fault of their own, they become unfit for work' (quoted in Marshall 1961: 296).

3. Harris' study is restricted to Britain. For an outstanding analysis tracing the influence idealism had in the other parts of continental Europe and in the USA, not only as a cultural phenomenon but also as a reformist movement engaged in reshaping the education system of those countries, see Collins (1998: ch. 12).

4. A point that future critics never failed to notice: 'Schumpeter, an economist by profession, displayed an ignorance of the history of political ideas that would disgrace an undergraduate' (Birch 1993: 52). An extended critique of the classical model of democracy was carried out by Duncan and Lukes (1963).

5. 'Democratic government will work to full advantage only if all the interests that matter are practically unanimous not only in their allegiance to the country but also in their allegiance to the structural principles of the existing society' (Schumpeter 1943: 296). This instrumental defence needs to be compared with the principled justification supplied by Kelsen (1945), for whom majority rule is the only decision-making mechanism able to minimise public dissatisfaction. I owe this suggestion to Alfio Matropaolo, who has drawn my attention to Kelsen.

6. My hunch is that this picture of the gentlemen was derived from Alfred Marshall, but proving it is frankly beyond the remit of this work.

7. On the cultural context of the time in the USA, it is particularly interesting to reconsider Hofstadter's theses on populism and progressivism along the lines proposed by Brinkley (1985). This essay is a perfect companion to the one by Harris discussed above. For a more extended historical study of the US (semi) welfare state, see Trattner (1994).

8. The doubts of the turn-of-the-century suffragettes were restated after WWII by Arendt (1958a) in relation to the category of human rights, prompting Jean Cohen (1996: 169) to write that, 'Arendt sees human rights discourse [...] as the ineffectual chatter of moralists not much different from the language indulged in by societies for the prevention of cruelty to animals'.

9. Michele Mangini (personal communication) draws my attention on the fact that Rawls does not discuss citizenship explicitly and the subject is not even listed in the index of *A Theory of Justice*. If we understand citizenship to be concerned with the problem of inclusion/exclusion, connecting Rawls' 1971 work to it is obviously misleading. On the other hand, if we understand citizenship to be concerned with the entitlements which ought to be recognised to any member of a cooperative enterprise, then Rawls is engaged with this task regardless of whether he uses the expression or not. Note that even T. H. Marshall is not concerned with the question of inclusion, but only with the matter of entitlements.

10. This phrase is difficult to translate but is used commonly in left-wing circles to mean 'vanguard actions not yet understood by the masses'.

11. Rather than an unintended consequence, Brown (1995: 33) claims that this was an explicit aspect of the grand bargain: 'Beveridge made the point that this aspect of his Plan also meant that it could be implemented without any political or social tension. He stressed the popularity of contributory principles and the extent to which his proposals involved horizontal transfers of income – from the young to the old, the healthy to the sick, and the employed to the unemployed – rather than a vertical social redistribution across class line'.

12. What for Titmuss was a worrisome political imposition, for Marshall (1961: 298) represented a scientific achievement: 'the Health Service has nothing to do with class relations, poverty, subsistence or the defects of the capitalist system. It typifies humanity fighting against natural ills, as medicine has always done, it suppresses the economic market and replaces it by a calculus of needs, and those who give are distinguished from those who receive, not by superior wisdom, better morals or greater wealth, but by professional skill and knowledge'.

13. Offe (1987) comes closer to proposing such an explanation. Unfortunately, his neomarxist revision remains loaded with 'superstructural' elements (Harland 1987) pushing him to reject cultural and political accounts of this dynamic in favour of 'structural causes' which in the end originate 'from anonymous economic imperatives' (Offe 1987: 530). My explanation wishes instead to avoid relying on superstructural elements of any sort.

14. As Gould (1982) notes, 'the members of the salaried middle class seem to be the main beneficiaries of the welfare state. In pension, health, housing, and education it seemed that the better off you are the more you gained from the system. In terms of service, tax allowances and occupational welfare, the managers, administrators, professional, scientists, technological working for large organisations benefited considerably more than routine white collar workers'. In quoting this same passage, Offe however draws a different conclusion. According to him, 'such special advantages and upward redistributive effects have failed to buy the political support of those who

not only benefit from services and income-graduated transfers, but also from the secure and continuously expanding employment the welfare state had to offer' (Offe 1987: 532). Obviously, once the leaders of the working classes are co-opted and socialised into the value-system of the middle classes, their identification with the lower classes and sense of solidarity with the worst-off members of society was doomed to decline. But this was already foreseeable in the early 1960s without introducing controversial superstructural elements in the framework of analysis.

15. Signposts of this participatory model of democracy are the 1962 Port Huron Statement by the Students for a Democratic Society (http://coursesa.matrix. msu.edu/~hst306/documents/huron.html) and Pateman (1970). The social history behind those works is told by Blühdorn (2009) and Müller (2011: ch. 5).

Chapter Two

Les Trente Furieuses: The Neoliberal Counter-Revolution and the Politics of Depoliticisation

2.1. Introduction

It is generally acknowledged that the post-war welfarist settlement disintegrated in the 1980s and was superseded by the neoliberal consensus politics that is still dominating public life. Since the financial crisis of 2008, the ideological basis of this consensus politics has been scrutinised in growing detail – especially as the expected demise of neoliberalism has, so far, failed to materialise (Crouch 2011). Underpinning the great majority of works on the subject, there is the idea that neoliberalism somehow managed to carry out an ideological *coup d'état*, imposing the tenets of its political philosophy on opinion and policy makers across OECD countries, if not beyond (Mirowski 2013). Building on an earlier account of the neoliberal counter-revolution proposed by Foucault (2008), legions of authors who analyse it from variegated disciplinary and ideological standpoints follow an uncannily similar plot. They start by locating its origins in obscure liberal circles hostile to the then unfolding welfare revolution; then they go on to explain the influence neoliberal thought exercised on people like Margaret Thatcher and Ronald Reagan; and finally they arrive at the conclusion that neoliberal thinking has entrenched itself into the mindset of Western political elites, so much so that it blinds them to the existence of possible alternative ways of governing. Thus, the 2008 financial crisis is explained as a failure of neoliberal thinking while the unwillingness of those governments engulfed by it to adopt Keynesian macroeconomic measures is described as purely ideological in nature. Without even attempting to engage with this growing body of literature, the present chapter suggests a different account of the hegemonic force exercised by neoliberalism at government level. This account tries to keep separate the reasons behind the public prominence acquired by neoliberal thinking since the 1970s and the reasons behind the success of neoliberal policies and market instruments at an institutional level. The main reason for doing this is to move beyond the search for simplistic causal explanations, and look instead at the way in which policy ideas and practices keep interacting in a dialectical manner. The thesis I support in this chapter is that neoliberal ideas and policies have found support among institutional and political actors only when, and to the extent that, they helped them to either reinforce their power, or to undermine the power of competing institutional and societal actors. In other words, market solutions must be perceived as part of the policy weaponry used in the ongoing power games unfolding within the public realm. Their role is thus not that of undermining the role of the state *per se*, but of reaffirming central government control of state institutions to whom welfare policies had delegated significant policy-making power. Such an attempt also entails shedding social responsibilities acquired in the post-war period to free central government from the formal systems of accountability imposed on it by constitutional rules and conventions.

In this chapter, the next section proposes a reconstruction of the various schools of thought making up the neoliberal archipelago. Special attention is paid to the New Political Economy (NPE), from which the main policy suggestions responsible for *les trente furieuses* were originally derived. The aim of the section is to show the influence of NPE in changing the narrative of the crisis, shifting public attention from preoccupations with a stunted process of democratisation to concerns about democratic hubris and political overstretching so as to justify depoliticising various policy areas and attributing increased responsibilities to the individual and social actors dependent on welfare handouts. No sustained attempt to refute the arguments grounding these policy suggestions will be carried out here, for I deny that their political relevance is in any way related to the cogency of the arguments employed. Instead, I will point out some perplexing aspects of the neoliberal theoretical framework. The first concerns the fact that the narrative of the crisis of the welfare state re-directs the economic logic of market failures (used by progressives to criticise the imperialist aspirations of NPE and justify public intervention) to warn about the inevitability of government failure. Second, I argue that the resulting principled opposition to state intervention is not just debatable, but that it is framed in an ethical language sounding like the moralising idealism of pre-welfarist social reformist movements to justify a conservative equivalence between charity, social solidarity and justice.

Section 3 suggests seeing the continuing interest of central governments in market-based policy solutions as part of a self-serving strategy aimed at reaffirming their political control while promoting administrative decongestion and shedding social responsibilities. The section's focus is on the way in which the various building blocks of the neoliberal policy template were first put together in Britain under the leadership of Margaret Thatcher. The claim I support here is that it was the gradual (and fortuitous) success of Thatcher in defeating the trade unions, bringing local councils under the firm control of central government and restraining the British civil service that explains the adoption of that policy template by her successors and even abroad. Thus, far from being based simply on ideological conviction, neoliberal consensus politics rests mainly on the power balance made possible by the application of market-based policy instruments across the public sector. The last section of this chapter considers the process of policy transfer that has allowed this template to spread across policy areas, levels of government and countries. If, at the domestic level, such a process of policy transfer has been mostly reactive in nature, at the global level it has greatly benefited from the proselytising activism of the Bretton Woods Holy Trinity - the International Monetary Fund (IMF), the World Bank (WB) and the World Trade Organisation (WTO, formerly the GATT) and regional transnational authorities like the European Union (EU). Using the EU negative market integration programme, the section outlines the continental-wide dynamics which make the neoliberal consensus politics resilient despite the costs it imposes on gradually larger sectors of civil society.

2.2. Politics without romance: a basic genealogy of neoliberal thought

As argued elsewhere (Palumbo 2001), the attempt to develop an economic theory of politics follows the axiomatisation of neoclassic equilibrium analysis, the development of welfare economics and the widespread acceptance of Keynesian macroeconomics. Equilibrium analysis and its axiomatisation in the 1940s made it clear that markets were prone to failure and required government intervention to stabilise them. As Inman (1987: 650) puts it, 'there is a common problem which underlies all market failures, and that [...] common problem is uniquely handled by an institution which can enforce cooperative – that is, collective behavior in a world where non-cooperative behavior is the preferred individual strategy. Government is one such institution'.[1] Such an analysis parallels and complements Keynesian macroeconomics and the idea that state intervention is a necessary condition for achieving Pareto-optimality; that is, efficient allocations of social resources. For, left to their own devices market dynamics could easily lead to a multiplicity of suboptimal equilibrium states or magnify the impact of economic cycles creating 'boom-and-burst' sequences. In this conceptual scheme, the goal of public intervention is twofold. First, it aims at moving market equilibria towards the Pareto-frontier (and in the most heroic versions to expand the Pareto-frontier itself), thus solving problems of sub-optimality. Second, state intervention is crucial for reducing systemic risks which could lead to the implosion of the market itself or create troublesome cyclical instabilities. The justification of the economic role of the state as both market regulator and hierarchical form of production alternative and/or complementary to the market has been questioned ever since it was first stated. Theoretically, three main areas have been the objects of critical attention by post-war political economists which have a direct interest for this work: (i) the ability of democratic institutions to generate efficient social choices, (ii) the neutrality of public institutions in devising and setting public policy and (iii) the effectiveness of Keynesian political economy. By and large, what Inman (1987, also Mueller 1990) calls the New Political Economy (NPE) is the sum of the several bodies of literature dealing with those areas of inquiry.

The first critique is part of that body of economic literature known as 'democratic social choice'. It originates with the attempt to solve the problem of preference aggregation affecting the social welfare functions of Bergson and Samuelson. The criticism of democratic social choice is twofold. First, there is the claim that democratic choice faces problems of preference aggregation which lead to the well-known (im)possibility theorem elaborated by Arrow (1951). According to this theorem, far from arriving at an effective way of constructing social welfare functions, collective choice mechanisms impose an inescapable dilemma between dictatorial decisions or inefficient allocations of social resources. A second strand of democratic social choice argues that the effectiveness of collective action has an inverse relation with the size of the group: the bigger the group the more likely is the emergence of free-riding and therefore the difficulty in producing public goods and services (Olson 1965). Consequently, it is claimed that government action is either redundant when dealing with small groups, or unable to overcome free-riding problems when dealing with large groups. Following the works of Downs (1957) and Buchanan and Tullock (1962), the development of 'public choice' as an analysis of political processes and democratic institutions started. The hallmark of this approach is that the main public actors from whom the maximisation of social efficiency is demanded – legislature, government, public administration – are not the neutral and selfless agents depicted in political science.[2] Rather, they resemble the more traditional *homo oeconomicus* with his crude, self-seeking motivations and maximising drives. Public choice has been taken as complementing social choice theory because it demonstrates that even if aggregative procedures were available, the political process would be distorted so as to maximise the wealth and power of unaccountable politicians and parasitic bureaucratic élites (Niskanen 1994; Tullock 1976). Finally, economists from the Chicago and Austrian schools maintain that Keynesian political economy is unsuited to deal with the complexities of the information flows produced by centralist economic planning. Thus, they claim that while attempts to control the economy by means of monetary policies have resulted in the actual worsening of social efficiency – i.e. promoting inflationary cycles and stagflation (Friedman 1962), the increasing role of government as regulator and producer of public goods and services is gradually eroding both the entrepreneurial spirit of market societies and the rule of law, thus effectively paving 'the road to serfdom' (Hayek 1944; 1960).

Following Dowding (1995), it is possible to distinguish two aspects of NPE as an economic approach to politics: its behavioural and methodological foundations on one side, and its equilibrium analysis on the other. In line with neoclassic microeconomics, NPE regards each institution operating in the public sphere as a strategic player with a well-defined utility function and a simple goal: the maximisation of its expected utility. Finding inspiration in Hayek (1955), Niskanen (1994: 5) describes this approach as,

the 'compositive' method of economics, which develops hypotheses about social behavior from models of purposive behavior by individuals, [which] contrasts with the 'collectivist' method of sociology, [and] which develops hypotheses about social behavior from models of role behavior by aggregative ideal types. The [...] bureaucrat is the central figure [...] he is a 'chooser' and a 'maximizer' [...] not just a 'role player' [...] The larger environment influences the behavior of the individual by constraining his set of possible actions, by changing the relations between actions and outcomes, and, to some extent, by influencing his personal preferences.

In turn, the schemes of incentives and sanctions that characterise the institutional framework wherein interaction takes place are explained as the result of strategic equilibria arrived at by the players. Were this not the case, the political agents would find themselves either in a condition of permanent disequilibrium (resembling a Hobbesian trap), or would require the existence of a powerful sovereign capable of enforcing his/her own favoured scheme of incentives.

Although the several authors and schools contributing to NPE share this broad epistemic framework, equilibrium analysis is carried out by focusing on the strategic behaviour of diverse institutional agents: electorate, interest groups, politicians, government and public administration. Accordingly, there arise a number of separate equilibrium analyses each of which singles out a bargaining game. Those on which NPE has focused are the following:

- the *democracy game* between citizens and politicians for the production of public goods and redistribution of social resources – a theme explored by Riker (1982) and the Rochester school
- the *government game* between legislative and government officials for the definition of the objectives singled out in the previous game – a field developed by Buchanan (1972) and the Virginian school
- the *bureaucracy game* between politicians and bureaucrats for the implementation of political decisions and the delivery of cost-effective services – a subject brought to public attention pre-eminently by Niskanen (1994)
- the *implementation game* between the officials from whom is demanded the execution of policies and the subjects to whom those policies apply – a topic whose theoretical relevance was first highlighted by Peacock (1978, 1992).

Three problems arise from the economic approach to politics proposed by NPE which are worth restating here. The first concerns the fact that the various bargaining games underpinning equilibrium analysis are taken *as if* they unfold in an institutional vacuum. As a result, this approach blurs the distinction between the non-cooperative interaction taking place in state-of-nature-like contexts and the stability of alternative institutional solutions. Moreover, it does not attribute any relevance to the side constraints established by distinct constitutional settings, or to the fact that the relationship between players is often one of authority. These assumptions obviously cast doubts on the realism of NPE as a positive theory of politics, and sound so value-laden to require an explicit justification for them. Very seldom this normative justification is however supplied; but even in those rare instances when it is, it remains grounded on debatable notions of feasibility derived from a 'negative epistemology' (Hayek 1982, II: 98; Mackie 1982: 153) that is supposedly able to (i) point out possibilities and limits of human action in establishing and carrying out purposeful collective plans and (ii) show what the side-constraints on any workable moral system are – thus supplying objective reasons for 'striking off' all theories and principles of action which are far-beyond the limits initially discovered. The second problem relates to the fact that each of the games listed describe an interaction between collective agencies to whom is attributed a coherent utility function and an unambiguous motivational structure.

This 'black-boxing' of complex institutions like state, government and bureaucracy assumes away the strategic relations existing within each institution and is, therefore, inconsistent with the tenets of the 'compositive' method advocated.

Whenever an effort is made to tackle this methodological inconsistency, the results of the bargaining games analysed turn out to be as indeterminate as the studies carried out by the political and social scientists which NPE theorists want to replace. In fact, the clear-cut results of the equilibrium analyses proposed for each game are very often due to the biased way in which strategic power and/or information is distributed among the interacting agents. Typically, the bargaining games scrutinised by NPE analysts take the form of asymmetric interactions between a weak and fragmented institutional agent ('open box') and a monolithic opponent ('black box'). This means assuming that while one agent has greater difficulty in imposing its authority across the hierarchical line, the other has no difficulty whatsoever in doing so. Opening the second black box would raise the complexity of the game far beyond the analytical power of the compositive method even when the underlying connection between the various games is overlooked, and blunt the political relevance of the whole economic approach to politics. As a result, NPE is systematically and rightly criticised for yielding very rudimentary and questionable analyses of the overall working of those institutions composing the body politic in liberal democratic settings (Green and Shapiro 1994).

The attempts to reject these criticisms and justify the adoption of such a crude behavioural model of man and simplistic equilibrium analysis explain the emphasis NPE theorists put on the alleged equivalence between the market and the public arena, and the significance of government failures *vis-à-vis* the theory of market failures. Introducing a collection of works in public choice, Buchanan advances a strong criticism of the theory of market failures and related justification of government action. For him, 'criticism becomes justified only when the "failures" of market process identified in this way are presumed to be correctable by political or governmental regulation and control. This last step represents an arbitrary and nonscientific closure of the behavioral system, and as such, cannot be legitimate' (Buchanan 1972: 12). Buchanan's reaction to market failures is cloaked as an epistemic and methodological problem. If the maximising behaviour of the economic agents is supposed to produce suboptimal equilibria, on what grounds can it be claimed that the strategic behaviour of political agents represents a solution? Do we have to assume that economic and political agents operate according to diverse behavioural models? In effect, welfare economics suggests a clear-cut division of labour which attributes to economics the study of the transactions carried out within the market, while attributing to politics the study of the background institutions which define the boundaries of the market. In addition, this approach somehow accepts a behavioural model which portrays the individual agent as a *role-player*; that is, an agent capable of identifying with the values and aims of the social roles which he/she occupies accepted by many sociologists (Hollis 1977).

Buchanan opposes this division of labour. First, he claims that it leaves the economist without an understanding of whether the political game can really close the gaps left open by the market process. Second, he maintains that this division of labour relies on the implicit and highly questionable assumption that the same people behave differently when operating within or without the market. As he puts it,

> the post-Pigovian should not be allowed to generate excitement and ultimately to modify social policy by his alleged discoveries of 'market failures' without, and at the same time, acknowledging the comparable 'failures' of his proposed political-governmental correctives. The discovery of market failures is normally based on the usage of a narrowly constrained utility function which describes individual market behavior in terms of narrow self-interest. If, in fact, individuals behave in such a manner in the market place, the inference should be that they will also act similarly in other and nonmarket behavioral settings. The burden of proof must rest on the discoverer of market failure as he demonstrates that the behavioral shift into a nonmarket setting involves a dramatic widening of personal horizons. [...] Both the post-Pigovian welfare economists and the public choice economists should be required to work within broadly consistent analytical models. Both groups work essentially with an economic model; neither group should be allowed to slip into its own version of some Kantian-like hypothesis when and if this suits ideological prejudices (Buchanan 1972: 22 and 23).

Buchanan seems here to call for a unified method among the various economic schools and elects neoclassic microeconomics as the most suitable candidate.[3] His suggestion is backed by Tullock (1972), who in his contribution to that same volume, and as a conclusion to it, wishes to have it extended across the social sciences, thus advocating 'economic imperialism'. Without trying to advance any refutation of these epistemic arguments, I would like to note two things about Buchanan's reply. First, it relies on a misleading interpretation of the problems surrounding classical political economy and the attempt of welfare economics to avoid these problems by operating the division of labour mentioned above. Historically, the challenge posed to political economy by critics has been to show that within a pure competitive market framework the self-seeking actions of a number of unrelated agents result in an equilibrium that satisfies the criteria of Pareto-optimality. General equilibrium theory demonstrated that the alleged coincidence of private vices and public virtues obtains only within very narrow logical boundaries, if at all. Thus, the theory of market failures follows from the claim that optimal allocations of social resources can be achieved as *by-product* of individual self-seeking behaviour and describes the 'logical domain' wherein this claim could turn out to be true: a pure competitive market economy. Buchanan's (1972: 12) protestation that market failures arise as a result of the 'assumption that the persons behave as automatons' is misdirected, for that is the epistemic platform chosen by the political economist.

Moreover, Buchanan's complaint sounds frankly hypocritical, for he clearly believes that that behavioural model captures the essence of human nature and uses it to ground his constitutional political economy. Second, by calling for a unique method across the social sciences and proposing neoclassic microeconomics as the method to be adopted, Buchanan (and Tullock) is actually stating that (i) the model of action underpinning rational choice theory is to be employed to arrive at a general theory of social action, (ii) the pluralism which characterises the social sciences can only be a transitory feature and (iii) the epistemic validity of alternative perspectives and paradigms used in social sciences is questionable. Now, whatever the faults of welfare economics, it is Buchanan (and Tullock) who is (are) putting forward strong normative claims concerning both the 'right' model of man and the 'proper' way of undertaking social inquiry. As such, it is him (or they) who has (have) to produce proof confirming that the social sciences can be brought under a unified epistemology and that the neoclassic standpoint represents the 'right' epistemic basis for doing this.

Far from supplying a proper justification for those claims, further developments of NPE have not only made the neoclassic paradigm irrefutable, but also reinforced the chutzpah of economic approaches to politics. Following Arrow's (im)possibility theorem, the findings of the social choice theory have gradually been used to reject democratic politics in any form or shape even if no empirical evidence of decision cycles has ever been able to survive critical scrutiny (Mackie 2003). Moreover, building on Down's voting paradox, the notion of rational ignorance has been widely employed to undermine every democratic mechanism of supervision even if all available empirical evidence fails to support the existence of any such paradox (Green and Shapiro 1994: ch. 4). Last but not least, the theory of regulatory capture has somehow become an article of neoliberal faith used to promote highly biased and self-serving forms of deregulation in spite of its 'short and inglorious history' (Posner 2014). Taken together, these developments and their epistemic audacity contributed however to shift the narrative of the crisis experienced by the welfare state in the 1970s from one that connected it to its unfulfilled democratic promises (the legitimation crisis thesis) to one emphasising instead the pitfalls of democratic hubris (the political overloading thesis). I suggest that a crucial contribution to this achievement was also given by other strands of the neoliberal archipelago which are worth considering. For, they complement the allegedly value-free inquiries of NPE with a more moral diagnosis of the human condition under the welfare state and prescriptions indicating the managerial therapies which could revive the entrepreneurial spirit in advanced market societies, boost the economic efficiency of welfare institutions and engender the political accountability of public officers. It is these strands to which I briefly turn now.

2.2.1. The neoliberal morality tale: entitlement culture, welfare dependency and charity

Whereas NPE and the economic approaches to politics emerged from it have attempted to undermine the welfarist model of representative democracy (Schumpeter's CLM and its pluralist revision) established by the post-war settlement, the theories I consider in this section have as their main target the notion of social citizenship outlined by T. H. Marshall (*see* Chaper 1). Refined and made more philosophically sophisticated by Rawls (1971), the re-proposition of this progressive notion of citizenship launched a massive debate on social justice spanning two full decades, leading eventually to the recasting of the theory in 1993 (Maffettone 2010). The anti-welfarist worldview analysed here is the outcome of a counter-reaction to Rawls's progressive vision of social justice, in that it developed from the all-out attack against that very idea spearheaded by theorists like Flew (1981) and Hayek (1982, II).[4] The germination of this worldview took place in a fertile ground located between the academic world, the corporate world and the political world that has been dominated by neoliberal epistemic communities, policy networks and think tanks ever since. A suitable point of entry into this worldview is, in my opinion, Anderson's (1978) work: firstly because the author himself is a splendid representative example of this new breed of neoliberal policy analysts, secondly because that work supplies a clear early statement of the neoliberal notion of citizenship and lastly because the latter is conveniently summarised by the author in seven main theses which are reproduced below in their entirety.[5]

First Thesis: The 'war on poverty' that began in 1964 has been won. The growth of jobs and income in the private economy, combined with and explosive increase in government spending for welfare and income transfer programs, has virtually eliminated poverty in the United States. Any Americans who truly cannot care for themselves are now eligible for generous government aid in the form of cash, medical benefits, food stamps housing and other services (p. 15).

Second Thesis: the virtual elimination of poverty has had costly social side effects. The proliferation of welfare programs has created very effective marginal tax rates for the poor. There is, in effect, a 'poverty wall' that destroys the financial incentive to work for millions of Americans. Free from basic wants, but heavily dependent on the State, with little hope of breaking free, they are a new caste, the 'Dependent Americans' (p. 43).

Third Thesis: the overwhelming majority of Americans favour government welfare programs for those who cannot care for themselves, while at the same time favouring large cuts in welfare spending because of their strong belief that many welfare recipients are cheating. A guaranteed income is flatly opposed by a two-to-one margin. Although welfare is generally seen to be a serious problem, it holds very low priority with the public relative to other problems facing the country (p. 59).

Fourth Thesis: the clamor for radical welfare reform comes essentially from a small group of committed ideologues who want to institute a guaranteed income under the guise of welfare reform (p. 67).

Fifth Thesis: the institution of a guaranteed income will cause a substantial reduction – perhaps as much as 50 per cent – in the work effort of low-income workers. As long feared by the public, and recently confirmed by independent research studies, such a massive withdrawal from work would have the most profound and far-reaching social and economic consequences for our society (p. 87).

Sixth Thesis: radical welfare reforms or any variety of a guaranteed income is politically impossible. No radical welfare reform plan can be devised that will simultaneously yield minimum levels of welfare benefits, financial incentives to work, and an overall cost to the taxpayers that are politically acceptable (p. 133).

Seventh Thesis: practical welfare reform demands that we build on what we have. It requires that we reaffirm our commitment to the philosophical approach of giving aid only to those who cannot help themselves, while abandoning any thoughts on radical welfare reform plans that will guarantee incomes. The American people want welfare reform that ensures adequate help to those who need it, eliminates fraud, minimises cost to the taxpayers, and requires people to support themselves if they can do so (p. 153).

Several things need to be noted about the way in which Anderson frames the question of welfare assistance as a policy matter, for these aspects will be refined, qualified and expanded upon by various other authors later on outside of the policy context wherein they originated (the USA), and will inspire the concerted attempt to turn the 'welfare state' into a 'workfare state' carried out within several OECD countries since the 1980s (Handler 2003; Jayasuriya 2003). First of all, the issue of welfare is said to pertain to the poor and disadvantaged members of society rather than the citizen. According to this very American narrative, Roosevelt's New Deal effectively solved the problem of poverty by establishing public programmes for employment and assistance which established a minimum safety net. It was with the launch of the war on poverty during Johnson's Great Society that things started to get out of hand. The ambitious objective to eradicate poverty by imposing abstract principles of social justice à la Rawls not only proved to be hubristic, but ended up creating social disincentives on a large scale, in effect producing both welfare dependency and poverty traps. Second and consequently, the question is said to be not about welfare assistance to the needy but rather the attempt to transform it from a minimalist and temporary expression of social solidarity into an unconditional individual entitlement. For, this attempt has produced negative side-effects – above all moral in nature – which have (i) disconnected public help from social obligations, (ii) made it no longer possible to distinguish between deserving and undeserving poor and (iii) destroyed the working ethos of the lower classes in the process. Third, the economic and social problems experienced since the late

1960s are said to be a direct consequence of the breakdown of traditional forms of social authority on one hand, and the spreading of a culture of permissiveness on the other.

These two phenomena created a process of individual and social de-responsabilisation that has undermined basic institutions like the family (due to child illegitimacy), the neighbourhood (due to criminality) and the workplace (due to negative status rewards). As a result, they have also generated increasing unrealistic expectations about public intervention and the role of the state that cannot be met because the political system is overloaded and lacks moral authority. In order to redress the moral shortcomings of the post-war social conception of citizenship, the solution envisioned is the redefinition of the scale and scope of welfare programmes: the need to re-focus exclusively on the needy and supply only minimal forms of safety nets. In turn, this rescaling requires the reversal of social disincentives that could re-establish a connection between public assistance and social obligations, that is, use the discipline of the market to responsibilise the individual.

Before explaining how the envisioned solution could be turned into more operative policy suggestions, I think it important to briefly consider the resemblance between this moral reframing of the welfare question and the evolution of welfare thinking proposed in the previous chapter. What we have here it something sounding like the duties-based language used before the inception of the welfare state. Unlike the one employed by progressive reform movements, this language of social duties lacks any idealistic and emancipatory spirit. This can be seen clearly when the content of the obligations called to complement entitlements is scrutinised. A list of those obligations is supplied by Mead (1986: 242):

> work in available jobs for head of families, unless aged or disabled, and for other adult members of families that are needy[;] contributing all that one can to the support of one's family (but public assistance seems acceptable if parents work and cannot earn enough for support.)[;] fluency and literacy in English, whatever one's native tongue[;] learning enough in school to be employable[;] law-abidingness, meaning both obedience to law and a more generalised respect for the right of others.

In other words, these social obligations amount to a set of individual responsibilities for making oneself saleable on the labour market, regardless of the conditions of employment on offer. No attempt to define work *à la* Arendt (1958b) is made; for Mead and like-minded critics of the entitlement culture, it is common sense that work means only paid labour. Thus, if for the social reformists of the progressive era education was meant to promote abilities which could make the individual an active citizen, for Mead and later neoliberal followers it is only a form of training, an investment made in the expectation of a proper financial return.

This leads to a second aspect of the question, how is this list of alleged commonsensical social obligations arrived at? Mead supplies two contrasting answers, neither of which entails a public democratic engagement of all affected interests. Right at the start of the book, he is eager

> to emphasize that what standards to require is not for any one person to decide, and there is no right answer to it. It is a political question, indeed the supreme question in social policy. [...] For that reason social policy should be made in a political way by politicians, not, as it is often in Washington, in an expert and technical way, clothed in the language of economics, that admits only liberal goals or suppresses value questions entirely (*ibid.*: 11).

'The political' appealed to by Mead is the high politics of professional legislators, rather than the one suggested by the above-mentioned Arendt and thus does not entail the direct involvement of the citizenry. In the closing chapter, just before the bullet-pointed list of obligations is given, Mead specifies that 'we can infer some of those expectations from the social capacities in which government has taken an interest, often short of enforcement, as well as from the welfare debates and opinion studies seen earlier' (*ibid.*: 242). In short, it is arrived at by the author himself indirectly, by establishing what the public opinion on the matter is in the same technocratic way as the bureaucrats he criticises decide what policies maximise the public interest.

This is tantamount to saying that the dominant value system of the time must be accepted even if it reflects disproportionately the anxieties of the well-off members of society about the preservation of their own entitlements and the fears of the middle classes about a possible breakdown of law and order. That this sort of public opinion could reflect a dominant but highly contested value system is far from being perceived as problematic. Indeed, it even finds an endorsement in another influential exponent of this duties-based vision of citizenship. Assessing the impact of his work on welfare dependence (Murray 1984) two years after its publication Murray (1986: 28) writes:

> I am suggesting that we define the dependent variables of social policy, the measures for assessing whether poor people are progressing or losing ground, in terms of our own values, in terms of what we would want if we were poor.

The expression 'our values' is clearly used to refer to middle-class values, or perhaps those subscribed to by the likely readership of the *Cato Journal* where Murray's article was published; that is, a readership sharing a social background very unrepresentative of American society even now, after three full decades spent inculcating a neoliberal entrepreneurial culture.

Studies on the defects of the welfare state carried out by these authors are another example of *chutzpah* – one able to rival the economic approaches to politics discussed above. In attempting to explain the persistence of poverty and the lock-in effects produced by welfare programmes, these studies conveniently appropriate tools and concepts developed at the turn of the century by social reformists to mount a defence of conservative values. As such, they lack not only the idealistic spirit of their predecessors, but also the sociological, historical and political depth of the critical analyses proposed by the likes of Titmuss (*see* Chapter One, §1.4). To start with, the rescue of the notion of anomie (via Polanyi in Anderson's case) as an explanatory category is not done in order to understand the limitations of old forms of solidarity and the reasons why these need to be reconstructed on new political foundations, as in the Durkheimian tradition. Rather, it is simply done to reject neo-Marxist explanations based on the competing notion of exploitation (MacPherson 1973). As already hinted, for Anderson, Mead and Murray the so-called 'social question' belongs to the past and was fully solved by Roosevelt's New Deal. The persistence of a worrisome underclass is blamed instead on Johnson's Great Society programme; that is, the attempt to move from Briggs' social service state to the welfare state by attributing universal and unconditional welfare rights to all, deserving and undeserving poor.

This defence of conservative values is accompanied by the evocation of a mythological pre-welfare age when charity alone, and a bunch of voluntary organisations, were successfully providing social betterment (Beito 2000; Whelan 1996). Evoked to oppose the centralised and bureaucratic evolution of welfare services, the neoliberal social histories of past philanthropic movements are always deeply apolitical (Green 1993, 1999): they overlook the challenges faced and posed by these movements, and completely disregard the nature of the reasons and the identity of the actors behind the post-war grand bargain that led to the dismantling of the social economy they were part of. Hence the inevitable disciplinarian spirit of the policy suggestions advanced; for, to paraphrase Harris's words (*see* Chapter One, §1.2), their real aim is, as always, to keep the poor in their place rather than to force them into active and prudent participatory citizenship.

2.3. Making the British State lean and mean: building the neoliberal policy template

As noted in Chapter One, the attempt to reform the welfare state along neocorporate lines did not produce the expected results, but contributed to a further erosion of top-down governability by forcing governments to share policy-making power with other societal agents. In Britain, in particular, where there was no consolidated neocorporate tradition to speak of, attempts in this direction never managed to take off properly due to the objections of the Confederation of British Industry (CBI), and they eventually floundered because of trade union militancy. The latter obstructed the incomes policy negotiated by the British government with the Trade Union Congress (TUC) in 1975, and a year later forced the then-Prime Minister Callaghan to ask the IMF for a rescue package to save sterling, i.e. the pound (Kavanagh and Morris 1989: ch. 4).[6] This set the stage for the advent of Thatcher and the search for an alternative neoliberal solution to what became increasingly perceived as a crisis of governability due to overloading (King 1975). A first step in this direction was carried at Party level, where Thatcher's leadership marked the shift from 'one nation' conservatism, a political tradition that from Disraeli to Heath made a remarkable contribution to the construction of the British welfare state, to a neoliberal Toryism committed to dismantle it.[7]

In upturning this political tradition before being actually elected Prime Minister, Thatcher established a pattern that will be followed by her copycats ever since, regardless of their political convictions. As Prime Minister, Thatcher went on to impose a majoritarian reading of the democratic game that, up to that time, was alien to any Western political tradition, resembling more the style of dictators like Pinochet than that of democratically-elected leaders (Hall 1988). Democracy, in the Schumpeterian sense of the term, was used as in the satirical (and misogynist) depictions of her handbag circulating at the time – as a weapon with which to hit those daring to oppose her policies, or simply perceived as not 'one of us' (Young 1989). Among the various internal enemies against whom she directed the full force of her 'elective dictatorship', three stand out for their political and constitutional relevance: the trade unions, local government and the civil service. Thatcher's neoliberal programme of government developed, or so I argue, as a concerted attempt to neutralise the political role of these institutions by reshaping their *raison d'être* and denying them any constitutional right to define the public interest. In other words, she pursued a more radical form of depoliticisation than the one sought by means of negotiated incomes policies. This radical form of depoliticisation used market-based solutions for undermining the internal cohesion and political influence of competing social and institutional actors, while imposing upon them centralised, although indirect, forms of supervision. This strategy would gradually be imposed by a resolute application of the logic of TINA – the denial that, politically speaking, there is always a feasible alternative to the one proposed from the top (Evans 2004).

Two things need to be clarified at this stage. First, many of the building blocks making up Thatcher's programme of government were neither a British invention nor specifically neoliberal in origin. Some of the policies adopted were first tried in countries like Australia and New Zealand by Labour governments (Self 1993). The idea of 'hiving off' departmental functions to autonomous administrative agencies (at the core of the 'Next Steps' reform programme for the civil service) was first outlined in the 1968 Fulton Report commissioned by PM Harold Wilson and found its source of inspiration in innovations introduced into Swedish public administration by social democratic governments during the 1960s.[8] Second, the reason why was it possible to put those building blocks together in Britain rather than in Australia, New Zealand or even the USA, is related to the peculiarities of the British Constitution (Turpin and Tomkins 2007). Here, the absence of a written document and of a formal, functional separation of powers and mechanisms of checks-and-balances puts central government (which exercises various royal prerogatives as well) in a privileged position *vis-à-vis* both Parliament and the judicial system, making the British political system look uncannily like that of the Vatican, and the Prime Minister a power figure similar to the Pope. Lacking constitutional protection (and, in the case of the British civil service, even an act of parliament defining its role and organisational structure), the political autonomy of trade unions, local government and the civil service was gradually eroded by successive waves of reform. I have attempted to analyse the way in which the various building blocks were put together by Thatcher and her successors elsewhere (Palumbo 2004). In the rest of this section I will explain how those building blocks, singly and in combination, would serve the plan to depoliticise policy issues, help central government to shed social responsibilities and neutralise the mechanisms of accountability set out at the constitutional level, while expanding and entrenching governmental control throughout the British body politic.

What do we mean by depoliticisation? Colin Hay (2007: 80) has indicated three types of strategies used to depoliticise policy issues, which entail demoting them (i) from the governmental to the public domain, (ii) from the public to the private sphere and (iii) from the private sphere to the reign of necessity. For him, the reason why political actors engage in it is simple:

> depoliticisation [...] serves to insulate politicians and their choices immunizing them from responsibility, accountability and critique. It is a disavowal of democratic obligations of a government to its citizens in a democratic polity. It is a convenient mechanisms for disarming opposition, swiping under the carpet potentially contentious issues. And it is a technique that is likely to prove both especially useful and particularly insidious where the chosen reform trajectory is certain to prove to be unpopular (*ibid.*: 92).[9]

This definition rests on a rather simple understanding of the political. In reality, the politics of depoliticisation pursued by Thatcher and her successors employed subtle blends of policy measures which politicised and depoliticised various aspects of social life simultaneously. If the welfare state was predicated on a political philosophy that attempted to solve the social question by assuming responsibilities once thought to be private and requiring no political redress, the neoliberal programme of government pursued by Thatcher aimed at reversing that trend by returning a great deal of those responsibilities back into the private realm, making some aspects of the personal political in the process. In turn, this would (a) free central government from the supervision of other political actors constitutionally entitled to make it accountable (electorate and parliament), (b) tighten its power of control on local and peripheral branches of the administration by imposing new managerial mechanisms of accountability, and (c) force welfare claimants to assume obligations which made them even more dependent on government intervention while reinforcing their subordination to the labour market as well. Figure 2.1 below summarises the ways in which regulation, privatisation and marketisation were used to accomplish those goals in relation to actors who had thus far benefited from the policy-making delegation processes set in motion by the post-war settlement in its welfarist and neocorporative incarnations.

Figure 2.1: Depoliticisation induced by redesigning public powers and personal responsibilities

	De- and re-regulation	Privatisation	Marketisation
Trade unions	Flexiwork and internal democracy	Collective bargain and litigation	Trade-off between workers' and customers' rights
Local government	Capping rates and guardian democracy	CCT: transfer of managerial and supervising powers sideways	Reducing decision and policy-making powers while keeping responsibility for delivery of services
Civil service	Procedural vs substantive accountability	Strategic rescaling of services and manpower yielding an informal spoils system	Centralising policy-making power while passing responsibilities on to middle and lower managerial tiers

As we shall see in more detail later on (Chapter Five), the so-called policy of deregulation turned out to be a complex mixture of de- and re-regulation: ambits which were previously the object of self-regulation became formally regulated and, vice versa, others that were regulated in a traditional formal way were given the power to regulate themselves (Moran 2003). Industrial relations is the most emblematic case in point. Since the 1980s, British governments of different hues have systematically intervened in this ambit to de-regulate the labour market making it more flexible and entrepreneurial. To do so, they have imposed a formal regulation on the activities of trade unions, the aim of which was plainly to undermine their internal cohesion and bargaining power (Farnham 1990). The Conservative governments of Thatcher and Major were libertarian towards producers' industrial, professional and financial organisations, but unashamedly *dirigiste* towards trade union organisations. The only common aspect I can detect among of the panoply of acts, orders in council and other soft-law tools employed in this context seems to be the legal protection given to free-riders in general: businesses were granted the faculty to escape social responsibility for the consequences of their profit-driven maximising behaviour, and social organisations like the trade unions were forced to accept individual practices which weakened their ability to mount defensive counteractions. Justifications for this sort of free-rider-friendly legislation were always a matter of expediency and rested on an egregious use of double standards. No comparable type of legislation to the one used to protect trade union members and non-unionised workers was ever contemplated in order to protect the individual rights of citizenry from other forms of corporate power. For instance, in relation to political parties protecting the democratic rights of party members and voters; in relation to joint stock companies protecting the rights of minority shareholders and other stakeholders; or in relation to the privatised utilities protecting the rights of consumers and taxpayers – except when this could also be turned to strategic advantage by creating adversarial relationships between customers and workers legitimising intervention directed at guaranteeing the right of managers to manage, as with Major's Citizen's Charter (*see* Chapter Nine, §9.5.1).

In carrying this policy of biased regulation forward, *ad hoc* choices of legislative instruments, maximising the political position of the executive *vis-à-vis* Parliament, were repeatedly made. Statute laws were used if, and only if, this move minimised parliamentary opposition or the supervising role attributed to subcommittees. Soft-law was always the preferred solution whenever it improved the government's discretion and power of supervision. In other words, here we encounter a domestic version of the negative market integration policy that the EU and other transnational authorities employ to assure criteria of good governance worldwide – a form of colonialism based on what Wolf (1999a) calls the new *raison d'état* (*see* Chapter Seven, §7.5).

To many analysts, these contradictory practises and attitudes epitomised the power of conviction – the ideological force exercised by neoliberalism on the Conservative Party leadership, conviction reinforced by the fact that those double standards actually favoured the party itself financially and politically. Consequently, a policy reversal, if and when the Labour Party won back the people's mandate, was widely expected and often predicted. That these predictions failed to materialise, and the anti-union legislation was never repealed, should be ground, in my opinion, for revising the politics of conviction thesis. In the end, New Labour were shown to be more than happy to retain and even expand this body of legislation, in spite of the fact that it ran against its own self-interest, straining the relations with trade unions and draining party membership as a result (Daniels and McIlroy 2009). The set-up established by the Tories evidently suited the New Labour government so well that those costs were worth paying.[10]

Two other elements support my reading. First, what drove the conservative anti-union campaign was not the need to protect the individual from corporate power, as officially stated, but the challenge that type of corporate power brought to central government's attempt to claim an exclusive right to define the public interest. As entities representing both the working classes and autonomous local communities, trade unions claimed to have an independent right to define the public interest and posed, therefore, a political challenge that needed to be neutralised. Since other corporate actors could not claim such a right, or were not interested in doing so, their exercise of private power over the individual was politically irrelevant and did not need to be dealt with. That the unions had a legitimate claim to express the public interest is confirmed by the fact that the anti-union legislation *per se* did not produce the dramatic decline in membership expected, and that to dent their bargaining power the government had first to undermine the autonomy of the local communities and professional categories which they were expression of (Gospel and Wood 2003) a factor that can be easily evinced when the decline of trade union membership is compared with the collapse in membership suffered by traditional political parties over the same time period (Mair 2013). The second element is related to the fact that identical justifications used to undermine the bargaining power of trade unions were also used to carry out structural reforms of local government and the Civil Service – two institutions which historically contended central government's right to define the public interest – which changed the political and constitutional role of those institutions radically. In short, the policy of regulation pursued by British governments since Thatcher have had the aim of reducing the overall size of those ambits of the public sector which escaped their control, either directly or indirectly. A further and complementary aim was that of reneging the role of 'good employer' attributed to the public sector in the post-war. Together with the extended privatisation policies and the introduction of proxy markets, neoliberal style regulation aimed at disciplining various institutional and social domains by making the British State lean and mean (Reitan 2003).

If the post-war settlement stopped the development of local government by attributing to it residual policy-making powers and a predominantly managerial role in the delivery of public goods and services (Byrne 2000: 21ff), Thatcher's neoliberal consensus politics would try to turn that slow decline into an unconditional democratic surrender by reducing its autonomy in these two areas as well. Opposition by local and metropolitan councils to Thatcher's plans revealed in effect the relevance policy implementation and services delivery had *vis-à-vis* decision-making and high politics in general (*see* Chapter Four, §4.3). Fortuitous general election victories and the ability of the British executive to control parliamentary activities was put to good use by Thatcher and her successors by imposing a Platonic form of guardian democracy on local government. Privatisation, the capping of local rates and the introduction of Compulsory Competitive Tendering (CCT) would gradually hollow-out any political autonomy local government had managed to retain during *les trente glorieuses*. As enabling authorities, local councils were left with growing social responsibilities for the delivery of goods and services they could no longer manage directly (Horton 1990). In conjunction with the capping of local rates, they were made fully dependent on block grants distributed by central government in an *ad hoc* fashion and subject to a myriad of conditionality clauses supervised by newly established auditing systems and inspectorates (Power 1997a). Local councils were thus turned into mere executioners of orders issued from above and easy scapegoats for policy failure.

Resistance against this creeping centralisation was squashed by Thatcher earlier on by using the regulatory approach used against trade unions. As for the anti-unions legislation, central government's attempt to short-circuit local democracy produced social tensions which eventually caused the departure of Thatcher herself (victim of a *coup d'état* carried out by internal factions of the Conservative Party after the Poll Tax revolt) and the electoral annihilation of the Tories in local elections. Alas, even in this case, the expectations created by New Labour in the public opinion were only partially satisfied by a very cautious devolution programme that was more worried by the potential challenge devolved authorities could pose to central government than in reviving local democracy. As Byrne (2000: 598–9) noted at the time devolution was introduced,

> in general, local autonomy is going to have to be earned. And many (notwithstanding devolution) are concerned about what they see as centralist or autocratic tendencies, or continuities, in the new government – as evidenced, in the case of local government, by such actions as the imposition of national standards and targets, the extension of performance indicators and league tables, use of improvement or developing teams ('hit squads') inspections 'overload' […], the imposition of Health Improvement and Education Action Zones, compulsory health and social services partnerships, abolishing GM schools […], reinforcing of the national curriculum […], imposing performance-related pay for teachers, reinforcing LMS by squeezing the cap on funds retained by LEAs, replacing local authority Social Services inspection with regional commissions, continued privatisation, excessive guidance and regulation […], the failure to reduce quangos or to democratize them, greater use of specific grants and the retention of capping powers.[11]

In this context, the notion of 'enabling authority' (Gilbert and Gilbert 1989; Gyford 1991) has a special interest for us. Introduced in Britain with the Conservative CCT programme, this was later adopted by New Labour as an overarching category for understanding the goal of its flagship policy for the 'Best Value' delivery of local services – nothing more than a simple re-labelling of the old CCT. According to the documents issued to sell that new reform initiative to the British public, to turn local and district councils into enabling authorities meant to separate executive and non-executive functions, exercise the latter in a forward-looking strategic manner and pass along the former to private suppliers or appropriately established executive agencies competing with each other. In other words, becoming an enabling authority meant to turn local government into a strategic political actor (role occupied by municipalities before the inception of the welfare state) rather than an administrator overburdened with the direct production of goods and services (the functions attributed to it as result of the centralising plans of the welfare state). Freeing local government from routine, administrative tasks and daily managerial activities would, in this vision, empower citizens and consumers alike, by giving them the opportunity for meaningful choice, and revitalise local democracy. Lurking behind this New Labour rhetoric, there was in effect an attempt to exploit the lingering appeal of idealist/progressive era social reformist ideas to carry the politics of centralisation forward – an operation akin to the duties-based vision of citizenship that neoconservatives like Anderson, Mead and Murray were trying to set out on the other side of the pond, as seen earlier (Chapter Two, §2.2.1). Once again, emphasis was put on strategic thinking and political steering to ensure that local government did not regain the political role it once enjoyed (or rather wanted to have) and to take away the managerial and supervisory powers it had acquired in the meantime – powers which, at the implementation level, kept frustrating central government's quest to impose its own uncontested right to express the public interest. The list of restrictions and conditions which accompanied New Labour's modernisation programme supplied by Byrne above is, to my eye, hard empirical evidence confirming the soundness of this hypothesis.

2.3.1. Turning the civil service into a Rolls Royce fit for racing

Similar conclusions can be reached when the reforms of the civil service, undertaken since the late 1980s, are also considered from this theoretical perspective. In relation to the civil service, central government was particularly skilful in combining the various tactics used in relation to both trade unions and local government, accomplishing a constitutional counter-revolution that was crucial for the diffusion and consolidation of the neoliberal consensus politics within and without (Foster 2005). To appreciate the depoliticising logic behind the multiple and contradictory attempts to reform the British Civil Service, I will first try to clarify the complex strategic relations connecting the various parts of the whole administration, then highlight the sets of issues raised by those strategic relations for central government, and finally explain in what way the reforms carried out during *les trente furieuses* contributed to redress the balance of power between the executive and its administrative apparatus.

In Britain, a popular representation of the relations between ministers and civil servants was the one depicted in the satirical sitcom *Yes, Minister* (and its follow up *Yes, Prime Minister*), where the clever and devious permanent secretary, Sir Humphrey Appleby, always managed to impose a euphemistically called 'departmental point of view' on the well-intentioned but hapless politician, the Rt Hon. Jim Hacker MP, put in charge by the fortuitous events of the electoral process. Following a revised version of the plot used in Wodehouse's Jeeves and Wooster stories, the sitcom showed that it was the top level of bureaucracy (the so-called 'mandarins') who were actually in charge of public policy, and that they could use an inexhaustible variety of tactics to bring ministers along with them regardless of the policy commitments made by their Party during the electoral campaign. As for the economic theory of politics introduced in Britain by NPE (Buchanan *et al.* 1978), representative democracy was thus presented as a façade behind which power was exercised by unelected actors following their own corporate interests. In this case, the power of the mandarins rested on their staying in office, something due, in turn, to seniority rules which gave them informational advantage and policy expertise above a fluctuating political personnel lacking the necessary competence. By contrast with NPE models, from the sitcom it was possible to evince that the interest of mandarins overlapped (to a very large extent this was also true in real life) with that of Britain as a whole; for the mandarins saw themselves as engaged in keeping the British ship afloat and sailing across the ages, rather than simply intent on trying to avoid rocking the boat in between general elections. However, since the power enjoyed by civil servants could not be legitimised by democratic procedures and rested on a rather conservative definition of the public interest, it was periodically questioned by politicians and public opinion alike. At the end of the 1960s, the mandarins came under attack by Wilson's Labour governments, which questioned their actual expertise, while at the end of the 1970s it was Thatcher's turn, who, in addition to that, questioned both their loyalty and right to define the public interest against the wishes of the elected government of the day. Three consecutive electoral mandates gave Thatcher the chance to establish a new balance of powers through a blend of soft managerial and hard structural reforms – so-called New Public Management (NPM) – which reduced the permanency of senior civil servants and increased the staying power of central governments. In the process, the Civil Service became much more responsive to the wishes of the government of the day, even if that also meant freeing the latter from the scanty parliamentary supervision and minimalist forms of electoral accountability required by Schumpeter's CLM.

The way in which soft managerial changes and hard structural reforms managed to achieve this is perhaps the more interesting side of the whole story. First, the managerial innovations introduced with Rayner's scrutinies tried to undermine the internal cohesion of the administrative structure by mobilising the expertise of middle-rank operatives against the authority of the generalists who sat at the top. Second, privatisation and the Next Step reform programme were used to fragment the system in ways that undermined the mandarins' power of control and supervision over significant ambits of activity. Lastly, the introduction of proxy markets and market testing exercises gave the government the opportunity to periodically renew the administrative machinery by changing the rules of the game every time civil servants learnt how to play it. What has been the result of this array of institutional changes? The first element that strikes analysts is that NPM set in motion a permanent revolution. The system is in effect designed to never settle down into a stable system of administration, but require civil servants to update standards and benchmarks in a way that keeps it moving from one transition phase to another. The various heads of the Civil Service responsible for implementing changes in the last three decades have gradually enjoyed a much shorter tenure of office than their predecessors, and leave office reminding their successors that as much needs still to be accomplished (Press Association 2014). That NPM has not improved the overall responsiveness of the administrative apparatus towards Parliament, the electorate or its customers is clear in that managerial autonomy has undermined the ability of the first to supervise the constellation of administrative agencies created so far but left intact the power of interference ministers still have on managerial activities (Polidano 1999). Since the chief executives of those agencies are now appointed by using market criteria decided directly by the government itself (or by independent bodies controlled at arm's length by it), these agencies are indeed an integral part of a 'quango state' engendered to realise an American-style spoils system in a political context lacking the formal constitutional guarantees available there. Hence the recurrent preoccupation about the politicisation of the civil service (Peters and Pierre 2004) and the declining of its public ethos (O'Toole 2006).

The same can be said about customer satisfaction, or their ability to make meaningful choices (Clarke *et al.* 2007). For feasibility reasons, mechanisms of exit have never been considered seriously, notwithstanding the advocacy of neoliberal think-tanks for fiscal forms of federalism and models of foot-voting democracy (*see* Chapter Eight). Channels of voice, on the other hand, have never been part of the political agenda of the main political parties, despite the continuous reference made to stakeholder models of democracy and the values of great society in their electoral manifestos. According to central government, horizontal and managerial mechanisms of accountability are the only acceptable means to run proxy markets, perhaps because, as also part of the 'quango state', audit offices and inspectorates can be more easily controlled.[12] As Mehde (2006: 71) perceptively notes: '*governance* in this sense might be interpreted as just another technique for politicians and bureaucrats to divert responsibility for insufficient public services. *Governance* provides an inclusive model that brings in more actors that traditional administrative science and in this way also distributes responsibility for potential shortcomings'.

2.4. Modern-anglicisation by TINA: exporting the neoliberal policy template abroad

A growing body of literature on policy transfer is attempting to explicate the way in which policy instruments are borrowed and implemented across countries (Cashore 2002; Elkins and Simmons 2005; Henisz *et al.* 2005; Sandberg 2013). Building upon it, in this closing section my aim is to distinguish between various dynamics explaining the spreading of the policy template put together in Britain during *les trente furieuses*. In doing this, I also endeavour to clarify why it has been adopted in, and adapted to, distinct political and administrative settings by ruling parties belonging to contrasting political traditions. I claim that the neoliberal consensus politics seeks to modernise liberal democratic states by applying what is the basic template established in Britain. To this end, the same anti-political logic of TINA, effectively deployed there, has been repeatedly used regardless of the actual previous achievements of that template. In the process, this template has been 'personalised' and 'refined' to suit the specific needs of the social and political actors leading the charge. New modes of governance must, therefore, be seen as policy tools contributing to the attempt to reinforce this drive towards the political centralisation of state functions by decentralising administrative tasks and shedding social responsibilities taken up during *les trente glorieuses*.

In the changing political landscape, a crucial role has been played by epistemic communities and collective actors engaged in preparing the ground where the template was going to be transplanted; namely, the transnational authorities, regulatory agencies and policy networks supplying additional power, knowledge and legitimacy to the domestic authorities interested in setting the process of 'modern-anglicisation' in motion for self-serving reasons. According to the theoretical perspective inspiring this work, the spreading of neoliberal consensus politics is never the outcome of a reactive adaptation to the pressures exercised by systemic and impersonal global forces. Rather, it requires the proactive mobilisation of domestic forces capable of exploiting the opportunities available to them by establishing partnerships with other collective and institutional actors operating at national and transnational levels willing to do so. By using the European integration process, I outline this complex process of consensus building and the challenges it poses to any Polanyian counter-movement wishing to influence the pace and direction of change from the bottom up (Munck 2007).

Inspired mainly by comparative political science, the literature on policy transfer tends to focus on horizontal processes of expansion; that is, the ability of market-based instruments to spread across boundaries – state boundaries in particular. My aim here is to point out that this process also entails two further elements: (i) the cross-fertilisation between interconnected policy areas, and (ii) the ability of these policy instruments to penetrate vertically through the fabric of the body politic. Since the latter is the most neglected strand of the two, an outline of this vertical process of absorption is, in my opinion, the best starting point.

In describing the policy of depoliticisation employed in Britain, the previous section also pointed out that it was accompanied by fierce resistance throughout, and that its success (and subsequent global power of inspiration) rests on the peculiarities of the British political system on one side, and on the fortuitous opportunity of the Conservative Party to win four consecutive electoral mandates on the other.[13] The defeat of the miners in 1984, of metropolitan and local councils at the end of that decade, and the failure of the mandarins to resist the fragmentation and marketisation of the civil service in the 1990s determined, in effect, a shift from an all-out resistance to governmental plans to an attitude of passive acquiescence. This shift was strengthened by the generational changes which intervened as a result: old supporters of the post-war settlement occupying apical institutional positions either retired or moved on, while those who could not afford to do so gradually tried to switch side and use their political and administrative expertise to improve their lot. Given the fact that now market-based reforms made it possible to really appropriate part of the bureau's budget, and that the new ruling class was extremely relaxed about becoming rich quick when given the opportunity, this type of conversion could be easily apprehended without recourse to more demanding hypothesis – i.e. what Mirowski (2013, Mirowski and Plehwe 2009) calls the Neoliberal Thought Collective (NTC). Slightly different instead was the position of those occupying institutional positions operating under constitutional rules which prohibited individual strategies of this sort, such as local government and other central and peripheral parts of public administration. In fact, these actors have actively contributed to turning the neoliberal policy template into a Foucauldian form of governmentality (*see* Conclusion), even when this meant alienating the sympathies of the constituencies upon which their authority and legitimacy rested to benefit those sitting at the top – not to mention the commercialisation of the non-profit organisations and voluntary associations which had become an integral part of policy networks and public-private partnerships.

From my perspective, the explanation rests, in part, on the opportunity left open to these actors to replicate, in their sphere of influence, the strategy employed by central governments: to pass administrative functions along to middle-rank managers and street-level bureaucrats, thus shifting onto them any responsibility for policy failure. In other words, delegated authorities have been able to shed managerial tasks sideways and downwards onto other public and private agents (or appositely established combinations of the two) and use market solutions to deflect their newly acquired responsibilities. This explains why: (i) local councils have become regularly willing to wear the hat of enabling authorities and externalise administrative activities whenever that frees them from centrally imposed managerial duties; (ii) ministerial departments have done likewise in relation to all activities which can be contracted out to autonomous administrative agencies; and (iii) the main private businesses involved in service delivery have systematically attempted to do the same with their sub-contractors. As a result of these regressive dynamics, the policy of depoliticisation outlined above has ended up producing ripple effects which swiftly encompass distinct but interconnected policy areas and levels of government, causing the rise of a post-democratic landscape where pre-modern uses of private power coexist with post-modern forms of stakeholder involvement in policy making and service delivery (Crouch 2011; Newman and Clarke 2009).

A complementary explanation concerns the reason why so many individual and collective actors are apparently willing to play this game and assume administrative and managerial functions which make them fully responsible for the delivery of public goods and services even when they have scant managerial autonomy. Obviously, in some cases these actors have either no other option at all, or a very restricted set of alternatives available to them. Street-level bureaucrats and the employees of externalised lines of production fall into these categories. For them, refusing to play along means resigning from their jobs and seeking employment elsewhere in a labour market where working conditions are steadily becoming similar across the board. Finally, there are countless societal actors who are willing join the fray in the expectation that they can somehow win. To appreciate the logic underpinning what looks like a not fully rational belief, the actions of corporate and individual agents holding such beliefs need to be understood in relation to other structural features characterising contemporary neoliberal societies.

As I shall point out in the conclusion, the neoliberal consensus politics has established sheltered islands where a chosen few are able to rest and enjoy their privileged positions. Since the 2008 financial crisis, it has been repeatedly noted that the system brought about by three decades of relentless change is composed of two main tiers: a very large tier run accordingly to market principles and another, located at the very top of the social pyramid, run accordingly to socialist principles assuring that 'no banker is left behind' (to quote the title of a 2011 Ry Cooder's song). Among the plethora of public services which are now run according to for-profit criteria, corporate agents tend to assume control in either of two cases: when the policy framework established by central authorities has clearly separated 'responsibility' from 'liability', or when they are legally allowed to develop secondary markets which let them separate the two. In the first case, the assumption of broader social responsibilities for service delivery does not entail any financial liability, and it is the tax-payer who always has to bear the financial burden of corporate failure or the actions of predatory private businesses. In the second case, secondary markets allow the companies who acquired the service contracts to pass any liability on to other private investors and subcontractors interested in entering that sector. Evidently, private companies find it fairly easy to assume social responsibilities they know they cannot discard insofar as that does not increase their financial risks as well. Hence the readiness of governments to re-design policies which have been unable to attract prospective suppliers by shielding them from financial liabilities or establishing very appealing exit clauses – as the histories behind the privatisation of public transport and national utilities, private financial initiative schemes and student loans, CCT and various other forms of outsourcing solutions experimented so far amply illustrate (Jones 2014; Meek 2014). By assuring safe strategies of exit, these friendly contractual arrangements make it clear to all and sundry that the only route for accessing the neoliberally engineered socialist archipelago goes upwards. This explains the scramble at the bottom to try to master the only game in town in the hope of moving up from one level to the next. Working jointly, these motivational factors make sure that a highly dysfunctional and exploitative neoliberal consensus politics can reproduce itself while continuing to expand both horizontally and vertically.

The expansionary dynamics that have allowed this consensus politics to spread across OECD countries and beyond is by now well documented (Soederberg *et al.* 2005). It has mostly depended on the political activism of the international institutions created at the end of WWII by the then winning side at Bretton Woods: the IMF, the WB and the WTO. Established to manage the transition phase from a war economy to a welfare growth economy in ways which had to avoid the financial and social turbulences experienced in the wake of WWI, the real objective of those institutions turned out to be that of re-establishing the pre-existing economic set of fixed exchanges and capitalist relations worldwide under the leadership of the USA (Helleiner 1994; Wade 2003). With the implosion of the post-war settlement in the 1970s, the role of these institutions shifted dramatically from one that committed them to ensure the stability of embedded forms of liberalism based on the concerted macro-management of domestic economies along Keynesian lines, to that of pursuing a global negative integration of markets within a system of free and flexible financial exchange rates (Hart and Prakash 1997; Helleiner 1994; Ruggie 1993, 1998). In carrying out this task, they would eventually be joined by several other international regulatory agencies and transnational authorities which emerged overtime, the leading light of which are those of the EU.

As I shall explain in Chapter Seven, the logic underpinning these global processes of diffusion tends to replicate, *mutatis mutandis*, the one already described. Once again, the pro-active changes set in motion by domestic forces hoping to benefit from the restructuring of state institutions along neoliberal lines trample any alleged reactive adaptation to impersonal global forces. The neoliberal policy template has in fact been adopted in, and adapted to, not only those political contexts which, like Britain, did not have a neocorporate tradition and experienced similar problems of governability. It has also found a very fertile ground in the North European and Scandinavian countries where neocorporate arrangements have had a long and illustrious history. As Christiansen *et al.* (2007: 41) explain, though traditionally a reluctant reformer, over the last five years Norway has become more eager to implement NPM reforms. The regulatory arrangements involve both more horizontal and more vertical specialisation, but what has occurred is not simply an automatic adjustment to international administrative doctrines.

Evidently, there too the radical form of depoliticisation offered by Thatcher's programme of government has exercised a significant power of attraction, pushing domestic forces of various hue to impose it on their recalcitrant populations by using the unyielding logic of TINA.

The policy of negative market integration used in the EU to bring these political arrangements about has in effect risen to the status of what Wolf (1999a and b) calls a 'new *raison d'état*': the strategic exploitation of self-binding international agreements to reinforce the positional power of some governmental actors against other competing institutions of the state and domestic social forces – especially those connected to past neocorporate arrangements. In the author's own words: 'challenged by the emancipation of their societal and sub-state environments, governments develop a "new *raison d'état*" […], a common interest in instrumentalising intergovernmental governance structures for the maintenance of their internal autonomy' (Wolf 1999a: 233). The outcome of the competitive dynamics between state and non-state actors, and public and societal agencies is, for Wolf, the establishment of biased forms of multi-level governance (*see* Figure 2.2). That is, institutional arrangements which are justified for fostering transnational cooperation and the functional coordination between multiple levels of government, but which in reality maximise the power of some state actors in competition with other domestic authorities to define the public interest.

Applying this analytical framework to European integration makes it possible to understand several paradoxes noted so far in the field of European studies (*see* Chapter Seven, §7.5): why do negative market integration policies tend to affect distinct policy issues and policy areas differently? How does this differentiated impact widen the gap between the material and formal aspects of the constitution? Why are attempts to redress the lack of responsiveness of state and transnational institutions by making them ultimately more accountable end up promoting an even larger democratic deficit and more virulent populist reactions? As we shall see in Chapter Seven, this analytical framework is not only heuristically better than the rationalisations of political and institutional change put forward by both the theorists of the Regulatory State and those of the Networked Polity. More than that, it supplies better analytical categories for understanding the nature of the neoliberal consensus politics and the driving forces behind it. Furthermore, this framework clarifies why this system of domination is able to reproduce itself notwithstanding the various, supposedly terminal, crisis affecting it. Since 2008, the financial meltdown, provoked by the American subprime crisis, and the Eurozone crisis, emerged in the wake of policies imposed to bail out financial institutions engulfed by the subprime crisis, have failed to affect the neoliberal orientation of European

Figure 2.2: Policy transfer leading to a biased multi-level governance

		Strategic environment	
		External interaction	*Internal interaction*
G	*Self-seeking*	Anarchic setting	Biased multi-level governance
o			
a			
l	*Public value*	Cooperative	Functional coordination across
s		intergovernmentalism	levels of government

ruling parties. On the contrary, crisis and emergencies are easily exploited by the same subjects who caused them in the first place for justifying a new round of negative market integration. Even more striking is the ability of national governments to play the same game on different tables each time and support austerity measures more unpopular than the incomes policies of the 1970s without major political consequences.

Seen from Wolf's new *raison d'état* perspective, the EU negative market integration supports a centralisation of power that, by hollowing-out representative institutions from the minimalist democratic content imposed by Schumpeter's CLM in the past, allows the establishment of various forms of domination proceeding as interlinked concentric circles. The outer circle is produced globally by the 'Washington Consensus', a system of domination that, by means of good governance programmes promoted by the Bretton Woods 'Holy Trinity', is perpetuating the worldwide hegemony of the USA and its allies. A second inner circle is made up of the transnational authorities established to regulate social life in more restricted regions of the world. Like the EU, these regional transnational authorities, far from challenging the hegemonic power of the only remaining superpower, are committed to engender a similar system of domination at the continental level – one that in Europe favours Germany and other Northern European countries at the expense of Southern Mediterranean countries. But even within member states it is possible to uncover a third inner circle which allows hegemonic coalitions to shift the burdens of austerity measures taken to solve the Eurozone crisis and imposed by the so-called 'troika' (the tripartite committee made up of the European Commission, the European Central Bank and the International Monetary Fund) on those living outside of the sheltered socialist archipelago and on the political forces linked to them by the mechanisms of accountability established by the post-war settlement and still in place. Within this third circle, Schumpeter's CLM keeps working in ways which paradoxically undermine the authority of elective institutions (legislative bodies mostly), while reinforcing the informal powers of the institutions insulated from electoral dynamics and able to connect themselves with the outer circles (mostly executive bodies). The stalemate created by electoral politics at the parliamentary level is then easily exploited by those called to 'rule the void', to use Mair's (2006, 2013) apt expression – political actors who thrive in any sort of emergency situation, for the latter are seen as opportunities to reposition themselves by trampling on constitutional rules and conventions.

Within these interlinked concentric circles, hegemonic positions are systemically challenged by competing coalitions of political and societal actors. What is not challenged, however, is the system of domination that allows any winning coalition to enjoy the position of power guaranteed by the newly established post-democratic set up. The new liberal consensus politics in the end rewards even those belonging to the losing coalitions who managed to reach one of the sheltered tropical islands making up what an aerial view would depict as a socialist archipelago at the top. So, nobody among the elites has an incentive to rock the neoliberal system of governmentality; their dominant strategy is to act pro-actively and creatively in order to improve their own chances of success. Thus, a dysfunctional, but also highly dynamic, neoliberal consensus politics keeps expanding regardless of the challenges faced periodically.

2.5. Conclusions

If, in the 1950s, there were the likes of Titmuss who travelled to the USA to explain to the American people the achievements and limitations of the British welfare state, in the 1970s the flow reversed and there was now a motley coterie of new political economists and neo-conservative thinkers who travelled to Britain to explain to the British people what was wrong with their welfare programmes and what policy solutions could fix them. In reversing the flow, a leading role was played by the neoliberal think-tanks operating there (Cockett 1995). The involvement of the latter is often taken as decisive evidence supporting two claims which I have been keen to avoid in this chapter. The first concerns the relevance of Mirowski's NTC in influencing the policies responsible for undermining the welfare state and establishing a neoliberal consensus politics. Although I appreciate the role ideas play in politics, I am also very suspicious of any attempt to consider politics as an epiphenomenon dependent on more basic non-political factors, whether cultural, social or economic. Thus, in this chapter, I have tried to show that in the case at hand – the establishment of a neoliberal consensus politics – we confront a complex interaction between ideas and practices defying any simple causal explanation; that the adoption of neoliberal ideas and policies by various British governments since Thatcher's election in 1979 (or for that matter Reagan's in 1980) was due neither to the cogency of neoliberal arguments, nor to the ability of neoliberal think-tanks to gradually convert friends and foes alike to their cause. On the contrary, I advanced an alternative explanation that views the spreading and deepening of neoliberal consensus politics as based on two joint political factors: the inability of neocorporatism to solve the problems faced by welfare states on one side, and the success of neoliberal solutions to address those problems in a convenient way on the other.

In adopting market-based solutions, Thatcher, Reagan and their successors did not attempt to 'roll back the frontiers of the state' and engender a Madisonian model of democracy even more minimalistic than Schumpeter's CLM. Rather, I suggested that their aim was to 'roll forward the reach of the executive' by re-establishing centralised forms of control upon local and peripheral levels of government to which significant policy-making powers were delegated. Market-based solutions also allowed central governments to gradually shed social responsibilities acquired in the post-war era by handing them down to lower levels of government, civil society organisations co-opted into the delivery of goods and services, and 'prosumers' – the end-users requiring those very goods and services (*see* Chapter Three, §3.2, note 5). The second claim from which I tried to depart concerns the relevance of the USA in establishing this neoliberal model of government. Although I appreciate the relevance of NPE and American neoliberal schools of thought in shifting the narrative of the 1970s crisis from one focused on the democratic deficit of liberal democracies to another preoccupied with their top-down governability and, later on, in helping export that model of government worldwide, the various building blocks composing the neoliberal policy template were first put together and tested in Great Britain. This explains the overall relevance attributed to British politics and welfare reforms in this book.

In reviewing Friedman's (1962) book *Capitalism and Freedom*, MacPherson (1973: 149) maintains that 'the placing of economic coercive power and political coercive power in the hands of different sets of people, as in the fully competitive capitalist economy, does not lead to the first checking the second but to the second reinforcing the first. It is only with the welfare-state variety of capitalism, which Friedman would like to have dismantled, that there is a certain amount of checking of economic power by political power'. *Pace* MacPherson, the thesis supported in this chapter claims that by retaining a centralised and partially democratised political system (and an even more centralised and undemocratic economic system), the post-war settlement left open the possibility that political and economic powers could operate as members of a competitive partnership, helping each other in moments of need while exploiting each other's weaknesses to periodically renegotiate the terms of their partnership. The check political power, in the guise of the welfare state, exercised on economic power was thus both partial and self-serving. To the point that the contradiction between the values preached and the practises condoned became gradually more evident, fuelling discontent and social unrest. Given the fact that constitutional rules and conventions kept attributing political responsibility to electoral bodies which were unable to impose accountability along the chain of delegation, discontent and social unrest ended up producing the political turmoil experienced in OECD countries since the end of the 1960s.

I argued that to understand the development of a neoliberal consensus politics we need to pay attention to the way in which the policy template established by Thatcher and tested in Britain managed to solve those contradictions without undermining the liberal system of domination. Thanks to the implosion of the post-war social and political coalition supporting the welfarist settlement, Thatcher showed that a radical policy of depoliticisation could be more effective than the income policies introduced by neocorporate solutions. This lesson was learned by her British successors first, and then by countless others worldwide, setting in motion a remarkable dynamic of policy transfer that has gradually extended and entrenched the neoliberal consensus politics regardless of the cost to traditional representative institutions and to gradually larger social constituencies.

End Notes

1. Market failures can be listed under five headings: (i) public goods, (ii) externalities, (iii) economies of scale, (iv) incomplete information, (v) transaction costs. Since the common feature underlying these types of failure is the non-cooperative nature of individual interaction, the role of government is that of transforming social and economic interaction in cooperative enterprises.

2. In NPE literature, political science and sociology are used as labels which identify approaches and methodologies the behavioural assumptions of which are inconsistent with the one used in rational choice theory. Often NPE theorists use to refer to Kantian and Weberian models of man loosely to identify an agency which is 'selfless', 'plastic', or 'role-taking. It needs to be noted that very seldom are these references substantiated by proper scholarship. Thus, some authors attribute to Kant and Weber what others deny, while others attribute to Kant and Weber theoretical positions they actually criticised. To cite just two examples, Buchanan (1972) sees Kant as supporting an epistemology incompatible with rational choice, while Sugden (1991) claims that the Bayesian approach is essentially Kantian. Alternatively, Niskanen (1994) attributes to Weber a holistic methodology, whereas Boettke (1998) maintains that Weber is methodologically akin to the Austrian economists. For critical analyses of the debate concerning *homo economicus* vs. *homo sociologicus* see Hargreaves-Heap (1989), Hollis (1977) and Weale (1992).

3. Buchanan speaks always *as if* the argument is directed towards fellow economists, calling on them to retain methodological consistency by conforming to the standard *homo oeconomicus* model. Welfare economics is thus accused of having betrayed its neoclassic roots. Such an attitude cannot disguise the fact that Buchanan's conception of agency is eminently normative, though its normative content has shifted from the need to have a unique behavioural model for the positive analysis of social institutions (1972) to the need to have a single model of man for constitutional choice and comparative institutional analysis (Brennan and Buchanan 1985).

4. Although Nozick (1974) is also usually included in this group, the Lockean theory used to oppose egalitarian claims crucially rests on the legitimate acquisition of extant property rights. Whenever extant entitlements violate just principles of acquisition (never specified by Nozick), then compensation is required. The scale and means required for compensation of historical

violations are so complex and staggering to contemplate that Nozick himself suggests that a patterned criterion of social justice *à la* Rawls would in the end represent the best practical solution. So, theoretically at least, Nozick's theory is more compatible with Marxist approaches to social justice than with neoliberal critiques.

5. In reality the book contains eight theses. The last thesis, however, is more an assessment of President Carter's Welfare Reform Plan in the light of the previous seven theses that the author uses as a QED.

6. 'In many respects income policy is a history of the attempt to depoliticise one aspect of the union question and to curb market forces in wage bargaining. Expert or impartial commissions and norms were designed to give voice to the consumer or the national interest, as determined by government. Although the policies produced temporary slow-downs in inflation, the out-turn of hourly wages invariably exceeded the target set, and by the second and third year the policy collapsed. The lack of central authority within the TUC, or within many unions, made it difficult to operate a long-term policy. Unions were just too unsuited to being responsible and authoritative partners for government. The positive features of corporatism found in some other countries, notably Sweden, were absent in Britain' (Kavanagh and Morris 1989: 66).

7. It needs to be noted that Heath won the 1974 general elections on a radical neoliberal programme. In actual fact, his administration very soon reverted to the type of incomes policies established by his predecessor. This u-turn could possibly explain the subsequent hostility of the Thatcherite camp towards Heath and the trade unions.

8. It is indeed possible to prove that the whole ideal of internal markets underpinning the New Public Management is derived from market socialist thinking rather than Mirowski's NTC. Within this tradition of thought (Buchanan 1985; Le Grand and Estrin 1989), the one who really attempted to 'think the unthinkable' (to use Cockett's words) was the little known Hungarian economist Tibor Liska (2007). This explains the interest in proxy markets of Le Grand (2007) and other New Labour policy advisers since the 1990s.

9. Recently, he seems to have revised his opinion. Commenting on a monographic issue of *Policy & Politics* (42, 2, April 2014) on 'Depoliticisation, governance and the state', Hay (2014: 301) writes 'the point is that we do not need to appeal to the instrumental motives of political elites in order to explain the pervasive depoliticisation we have witnessed. Altogether more credible, I think, is that political elites engage in depoliticisation not because they think it is in their own self-interest so to do, but because they have been convinced (and have convinced themselves) that it is in our interests for them to do so. They are almost certainly wrong in this conviction; and we need now to convince them that this is indeed the case. Calling their motives into question is unlikely to prove an

effective means to that end'. Although I agree with his reservations about the simplistic way in which self-seeking behavioural models are used in politics, I am also concerned about the way the politics of conviction is used. The latter explains even less and comes perilously closer to a conspiratorial view of political history than the former.

10. For Crouch (2004), this dynamics is at the root of the transformation undertaken by political parties all over Europe, detaching their leaderships from the base and turning them into post-democratic entities. Support for Crouch's thesis is given by Mair (2013).

11. The referendum for independence held in Scotland in September 2014 is a clear indication of the failure of the British political system to take seriously the centrifugal forces produced by the colonising aspirations of Downing Street upon the communities living in the British Isles.

12. The most compelling evidence is presented fortnightly in the satirical magazine *Private Eye*, whose back pages are the last refuge of investigative journalism in Britain.

13. As Dunn (2000: 147) aptly observes, 'in its way just as remarkable as the Conservative Party's achievement in winning these four consecutive elections was the Labour Party's achievement in losing all of them. [...] it is easier to attribute the dismaying Labour share of the vote to the Party's own power of repulsion than to the Conservative Party's power of attraction'. The consideration expressed by Dunn need to be integrated with the analysis of the implosion of the post-war settlement carried out in the previous chapter. It also needs to be kept in mind that in Schumpeter's CLM the electoral system can be used in two distinct but complementary ways: either to punish the ruling elite that failed to govern properly, or to reward the ruling elite thought to be better than its counterparts. For a more extended discussion on this point see Heath *et al.* (2001: ch. 3).

Chapter Three

From 'Government' to 'Governance': Change, Rationalisation, Ideal Types

3.1. Introduction

The shift from welfarist to neoliberal consensus politics discussed in the previous chapters was meant to supply a sketch of the broader political context wherein more restricted sets of political and institutional changes are supposed to be taking place. These subsets are, in turn, responsible for the alleged passage from 'government' to 'governance'; a passage often presented as having momentous and wide-ranging implications for: the political arrangements brought about by modernity (the nation state), the relations political actors entertain within and without the political realm (democratic politics) and the ways in which society is regulated and administered (government). Since the interest of this work resides in governance theory, and not in a general intellectual history of the post-war period, it is with the passage from 'government' to 'governance' and its implications that I shall be concerned henceforth. This means that the focus of the whole discussion will be restricted to the changes set in motion since the end of the 1970s, and is mainly concerned with the way these changes are said to be reshaping the model of polity, form of politics and instruments of policy inherited from before. In short, I shall be concerned with the phenomena which can help us understand the features characterising the current neoliberal consensus politics, the dilemmas raised by this consensus politics at present and the means we have at our disposal for addressing those dilemmas.

According to governance theory, the joint pressure exercised by neoliberal reforms of big government and the globalisation of socio-economic relations has set in motion processes of change which are radically transforming the architecture of the modern polity, its inner workings and its ability to intervene and address the problems generated by an increasingly complex society (Bevir 2013). The alleged passage from 'government' to 'governance' entails three main shifts: (i) from an hierarchical state structure to more flexible forms of organisation; (ii) from a technocratic approach to policy making to a more open and deliberative policy environment; (iii) from an administrative process relying on command-and-control strategies to more horizontal and consensual managerial practices based on networking. This passage is also said to be turning upside down the logic used to connect the various institutional and processual aspects of the political process. While real existing liberal democracies in their welfarist phase used to attribute a logical and normative priority to constitutional issues (pertaining to the architecture of the polity), then consider the political questions surrounding the legitimacy of decision making and finally look at the technical aspects of policy making and implementation, governance reverses the theoretical focus moving from policy to politics and then to the polity. Hence the current concern with implementation issues and the way in which involvement in policy making could contribute to the effectiveness and legitimacy of the body politic from the bottom up.

The aim of this chapter is to present, analyse and discuss how governance theory accounts for this momentous passage from 'government' to 'governance'. To start with, in presenting the ideal typical features assumed to characterise government and governance (*see* §3.2), I propose a chronological re-articulation of *les trente glorieuses* and *les trente furieuses* that divides these periods into two main sub-phases, corresponding roughly to the ascendant and descendent slopes of the post-war settlement parabola and of the subsequent neoliberal consensus politics parabola. I contend that the 2008 financial crisis represents the end-point of a general crisis of the neoliberal consensus politics: an end-point that closely resembles the one that marked the end of the post-war settlement. I also contend that the more progressive forms of governance must be seen as a set of attempts to overcome this crisis by adopting policy solutions reminiscent of the neocorporate solutions sought during the 1970s. Once the main features of an ideal type of governance are identified, in Section 3.3 my task will be to explore them in detail and propose some conceptual distinctions which are, I believe, needed to help clarify the power and limitations of this ideal type as a rationalisation of current political and institutional change. This will lead me to consider the various epistemic and normative perspectives contributing to governance studies as a new field of research. The chapter will close with a short discussion on the epistemic and methodological tenets underpinning governance studies. Thus, in Section 3.4, I distinguish between the approaches, research programmes and generations making up this field of study and contributing to its development. The intent of this discussion is to make as clear as possible the nature of my approach, its restricted focus and real intention. As already mentioned (*see* Introduction), this genealogy is carried out from a state-centric perspective and will, accordingly, consider only those notions of governance that have a direct relevance for the public realm and the nation state. Forms of governance unrelated to the public realm (corporate governance) are not considered in this work, while others which touch on the nation state only from without (global and good governance) will be briefly discussed in Chapter Seven.

3.2. Government vs. governance: forms, values, actors and cycles

As I see it, governance theory puts forwards a rather simplified account of the passage from 'government' to 'governance'. Thus, in this section my aim is to propose a more nuanced account that employs a thicker and multifarious set of ideal types, and rearticulates the chronology of the alleged passage by distinguishing between two main parabola-like cycles: one parabola concerns the form of government established by the post-war settlement, while the other is related to the new modes of governance introduced since the 1980s supporting the current neoliberal consensus politics. In identifying the salient features which characterise government and governance as theoretical constructs, I follow three distinct steps. First, I identify the values, procedures and actors these ideal types privilege at the decision-making level, the policy-making level and the policy implementation level. Then, I discuss the state-civil society relationship trying to identify each time the actors these ideal types take to be the embodiment of civil society itself. Finally, I present and analyse the ideals of citizenship connected with government and governance respectively. Since my re-construction considers the ascendant and descendent phases of each parabola in turn, the ideal types of government and governance considered here will be further subdivided into two main variants: welfarist and post-welfarist conceptions of government on one side, and neoliberal and post-neoliberal conceptions of governance on the other.

Chapter One made it clear that the outcome of the post-war settlement, the welfare state, adopted a system of government whose salient features are those summarised below in Figure 3.1. The matrix distinguishes between three levels into which the political process can be analytically disaggregated: the level at which legitimate public decisions are made, the level whereby these decisions are turned into public policies, and the level where those policies are implemented. For each of these levels, the matrix identifies the values which were supposed to orientate action, the procedures established to carry state action forward and the actors to whom the relevant functions of government were attributed. As the only feasible form of democratic politics for large nation states, the widespread acceptance of CLM (in its Schumpeterian version or in the revised pluralist version supplied by the American behaviourist school) established the cultural hegemony of liberal elitist values. As a result, decision making became the exclusive domain of elective representative bodies filled with professional politicians upon whom the people, as the ultimate sovereign agent, had very limited powers of control. Representatives' commitment to the public good, rather than private or sectoral interests, was enforced indirectly through three main constitutional devices adopted by all Western countries during the post-war reconstruction: (a) periodic general elections giving those dissatisfied with the government of the day the opportunity to 'kick the rascals out', and thus deter representatives from courting special interests only; (b) procedures establishing a separation of power and mechanisms of checks-and-balances between elective and non-elective bodies whose function was to reduce the risk of the tyranny of the majority; (c) vertical and legal mechanisms of accountability used to transmit democratic legitimacy and enforce individual guarantees across the various levels of government.

Since this liberal vision of democracy rejected any idea of the general will sought by the Rousseauian political tradition, the public good was to be arrived at by an impartial aggregation of individual preferences.[1] The latter were also defined indirectly by using either public opinion surveys carried out by a specialised polling industry, or analytical tools establishing a logical utilitarian

Figure 3.1: Model of government I: welfarist

	Values	*Procedures*	*Actors*
Decision-making	Liberal/elitist	Aggregative	Political representatives
Policy-making	Hierarchical	Planning	Ministers
Implementation	Legalistic	Command & control	Bureaucrats

equivalence between the consumer operating in the market of private goods and the citizen called to choose in the political market. In both settings, competitive dynamics were supposed to bring about overall beneficial results as a by-product of individual rational choices.

Given the complexity of decision making under these constitutional rules, policy making assumed the form of a very technical task that was gradually delegated to the executive branches of government and their planning offices. A similar process of delegation took place, albeit in a slightly restricted form, in relation to policy implementation as well. The beneficiaries of the delegation process were an expanding number of civil servants and public managers working within the administrative departments called to supply the public goods and services required by the citizenry. In both cases, the process of technical delegation of public authority initiated a subtle but increasingly evident shift in the balance of power between the various political and administrative actors interacting within the public realm – a process that would eventually create a growing gap between the formal and material aspects of the constitution. On the one hand, the executive branches of government came to acquire an informal political pre-eminence over the legislative branches – one that tended to turn the latter into glorified rubber-stamp bodies for decisions taken in reality elsewhere. This was a phenomenon that came to characterise not only presidential systems, where the separation of power established some form of co-decision, but also those political systems where formal sovereign authority remained entirely with parliament – an institutional evolution reinforced by the relevance acquired by mass parties during the establishment of what Schattschneider (1942) called 'party government'. On the other hand, the growth of government functions and administrative personnel meant that ministerial powers were also gradually limited by the development of organisational logics and departmental points of view produced by appointment rules and socialisation processes building a permanent state apparatus with a distinct identity and public ethos (du Gay 2000). Regardless of the constitutional architecture of the body politic and political orientation of the governmental forces in charge, ministers soon became aware that access to the levers of power was often not enough to make changes happen. In spite of these difficulties and of their common knowledge among those involved in the policy process, the legal and vertical mechanisms of accountability kept attributing political responsibilities in line with formal constitutional rules increasingly at odds with political reality.

The three decades of seemingly continuous socio-economic growth that followed the post-war settlement played down, at least initially, the political relevance of these constitutional side-effects. Reinforced by the parallel success Keynesian macroeconomic measures were apparently having in controlling economic cycles by aggregate demand management, the policy process became dominated by a technocratic logic requiring only the minimalist politics of the ballot-box. According to this technocratic vision of democratic politics, public apathy, far from being a worrisome political malaise, was now seen as an indication of high degrees of public satisfaction with both the constitutional arrangements of real existing liberal democracies and their practical achievements. Such a Planglossian attitude was eventually challenged by the social unrest experienced by OECD countries at the end of the 1960s. Contrary to the neoliberal account of the crisis that prevailed in the 1980s, it is possible to argue that that social unrest was due to the growing dissatisfaction of some constituencies towards the welfare state – constituencies often indicated as the main beneficiaries of its social and industrial policies: the urban working classes enjoying full and secure employment and the expanding middle classes enjoying high degrees of upward social mobility (*see* Chapter One). Moreover, it is possible to claim that the misgivings of those two constituencies towards the welfare state were far from being unreasonable. Two distinct narratives of the crisis were proposed at this juncture: a left-wing narrative accusing the welfare state of having betrayed its most progressive promises to help build a 'defensive' type of democracy subservient to capitalism; a right-wing narrative that accused the welfare state of having raised public expectations so much that they could no longer be satisfied without undermining fundamental individual liberties and the ability of the economic system to deliver growth (Goetz 2008; Müller 2011). The first saw the emerging social unrest as the result of a systemic legitimation crisis due to a stunted process of democratisation (Habermas 1976), whereas the latter viewed those same phenomena as the result of systemic overload due to democratic hubris (Crozier, Huntington and Watanuki 1975).

Under the mounting pressure of student movements and grassroots workers' organisations, it was the left-wing narrative of the crisis that initially prevailed in the public debate. Earlier attempts to reform the welfare state were thus carried out with the aim of opening up the political process by including the social agents representing the organised interests of labour and producer associations. This neocorporate move supported a post-welfarist model of government whose main features are summarised in Figure 3.2. The main novelty introduced by neocorporate solutions was a more consociative approach to decision making that attributed to democratically-elected legislative bodies the task of formalising the policy agreements negotiated by representatives of labour, producers and governmental forces. Policy making became thus the domain of so-called 'iron triangles', where the government played the role of the impartial umpire between contenting social forces called to strike a bargain having the status of a general social contract. Although slightly watered down, governing retained,

Figure 3.2: Model of government II: post-welfarist (or neocorporate)

	Values	*Procedures*	*Actors*
Decision-making	Liberal/consociative	Aggregative	Social representatives
Policy-making	Hierarchical	Bargaining	Iron triangles
Implementation	Legalistic	Command & control	Bureaucrats

by and large, a technocratic aspect, even if it was now inclusive of a restricted set of unelected social representatives. Policy implementation fully retained its legalistic aspect and remained the exclusive domain of public officers and civil servants employing command-and-control managerial techniques. The new political arrangements failed to address the gap between the formal and material aspects of the constitution. The latter was even worse than before, in fact, because national core executives now had to share part of their policy-making prerogatives with other societal actors but retained full formal responsibility for government failures – even when these were due to the inability/unwillingness of those societal actors to comply with the compacts to which they had willingly subscribed.[2] What brought to an end the neocorporate experiment were not these shortcomings though. The end of the post-war settlement was the result of the inflationary drives caused by the oil crises; which were due, in turn, to the boycott of the Arab oil-producing countries in response to the military support given by the West to Israel during the 1973 Yom Kippur War. In other words, it was more the result of foreign policy failure than the alleged weaknesses of Keynesian macroeconomics.[3] Whatever the cause, the failure of neocorporate solutions to stabilise prices, industrial relations and political systems shifted the terms of the public debate reinforcing the intellectual prestige of the neoliberal narrative of the crisis. With the election of Margaret Thatcher in 1979 in the UK and Ronald Reagan one year later in the USA, the parabola of the welfare state comes to an end and a new political cycle starts to unfold slowly.

The key features which will eventually come to characterise neoliberal governance are listed in Figure 3.3. All three levels into which the political process was disaggregated would be affected in the course of time. At the decision-making level, libertarian values celebrating free enterprise and minimalist visions of the state came to replace progressive and consociative democratic conceptions. Although the forces supporting those values presented themselves as anti-establishment, in reality they were the expression of restricted sets of organised interests which perceived the political process in more elitist terms than their welfarist counterparts. Once they found themselves able to influence government policy, their main goal was to dismantle all political obstructions previously set in the way of the free market, and to accomplish this goal they advocated the adoption of policy solutions directed at actively transforming the political preferences of large constituencies thought to be in the thrall of the welfare coalition from the top-down. The panoply of

Figure 3.3: Model of governance I: neoliberal

	Values	Procedures	Actors
Decision-making	Libertarian	Transformative	Market
Policy-making	Horizontal	Competitive	PPPs*
Implementation	Entrepreneurial	Contracts	Agencies

* Public-Private Partnerships

market tools and strategies adopted across the public domain did not aim at letting individuals follow their alleged natural instincts to produce and barter. Rather, market mechanisms were gradually introduced to force people to take responsibility for their own lives by acquiring the behavioural traits attributed to the fictitious rational agents populating neoclassic economics. To this end, policy making was delegated to networks and partnerships encompassing all entrepreneurial forces untainted with previous neocorporate arrangements. This meant barring labour organisations and collective bargaining from public policy. A similar policy of exclusion was gradually enforced towards the public bureaucratic actors to whom welfare policies had unwittingly granted informal powers without formal responsibilities. Thus, the ambits of the public sector which could not be privatised, were made to feel the discipline of the market indirectly, through the imposition of new public management programmes and proxy markets. In time, large administrative departments would be fragmented into constellations of administrative agencies in competition with each other and linked to the strategic managerial centre located within the old ministries by contractual relations having a private legal status. Competition rather than co-determination became the battle cry of the neoliberal model of governance, and the neoliberal insistence on government failure was used strategically to undermine the hegemony public bureaucracies exercised upon the implementation process (*see* Chapter Four, §4.2.2).

The neoliberal model of government has been the object of widespread social opposition. In the mid-1990s, a succession of social movements were mobilised to combat Thatcher's dictum that 'there is no alternative' (TINA). An endless stream of works celebrating these opposition movements and the demise of neoliberalism have seen the light since then – a stream that has become a flood since the 2008 financial crisis and the austerity policies imposed subsequently (Castells 2012; Chomsky 1999; Frank 2000; Gray 1998; Harvey 2001; Saad-Filho and Johnston 2005; Schäfer and Streeck 2013; Stuckler and Basu 2013). Evidently, given the much restricted social basis upon which the neoliberal consensus politics rests, and the increasingly high costs imposed by market solutions and austerity measures on gradually larger social constituencies, the eventuality of a systemic crisis on a scale similar to that experienced by the welfare state cannot be discounted lightly. Post-neoliberal models of governance should be viewed, from this perspective, as endogenous attempts to reduce the risk of a systemic crisis by introducing crucial reforms of the neoliberal model of governance. As for the neocorporate solutions discussed above, the various attempts to go beyond neoliberal governance seek to open up the political process in order to broaden the social basis upon which the current neoliberal consensus politics rests. Figure 3.4 summarises the main aspects of what is still a post-neoliberal model of governance in the making.

Concerning decision-making, the post-neoliberal model of governance subscribes to post-democratic values. The repeated use of the prefix 'post' twice is meant to convey the degree of uncertainty about the direction in which this model is evolving. The vision of democracy such a model is trying to replace is, instead, well known to us from Chapter One: Schumpeter's CLM and the revised form proposed by the American behavioural school. Neoliberal reforms of big government did not try to change the formal aspects of liberal democracy. However, they were carried in a way that increased the gap between the formal and material aspects of the constitution further. Contrasting narratives of the current crisis converge on the assumption that this gap is a source of systemic risk and suggest, therefore, reforms which can close it by adopting revised models of representative democracy.[4] As Bang (2003b: 260) explains,

> representative institutions are not at all designed to deal with a social world in which the capacity to 'make' is considered as intrinsic to democracy as are values and norms. They are constructed to appeal to rational actors and to masses, not to 'ordinary' reflexive individuals. Their modus vivendi is predominantly for the people – elitist, bureaucratic, emancipatory, procedural and calculative – not by and with the people as reflexive individual would demand to be it today.

The two main contending alternatives considered in this work are what, in Chapter Eight, I label 'anti-democratic' and 'ultra-democratic' visions. The first wishes to introduce a form of 'shareholder democracy' that would make people 'vote with their feet' by letting them move across the various jurisdictions of a multilevel Regulatory State. By contrast, the second advocates a 'stakeholder democracy' that would let all affected interests take part in the political process at any level, including the implementation stage thought to be crucial for achieving a multilevel Networked Polity from the bottom up.

Figure 3.4: Model of governance II: post-neoliberal

	Values	*Procedure*	*Actors*
Decision-making	Post-democratic	Deliberative	Societal
Policy-making	Subsidiarity	Cooperative	Networks
Implementation	Participative	Multilevel	Prosumers

Both alternatives seek functional solutions able to improve the effectiveness and legitimacy of the body politic. Ultimately they end up supporting democratic experiments introducing innovations at the policy level which could have positive systemic effects on the effectiveness and legitimacy of public action. Hence the emphasis attributed to the principle of subsidiarity and the value of the people's direct participation in producing the goods and services wanted as prosumers.[5] Engendering these values entails, finally, engaging various societal actors by using deliberative procedures able to refine individual preferences, and adopting network modes of organisation which could counterbalance the unjustified faith put in state action by welfarist conceptions of government and the mystical belief in the beneficial effects of markets by neoliberal modes of governance. In the next section I shall explore the content of the post-neoliberal model of governance and highlight the internal differences between various readings of the features included in it by alternative schools of thought. Here I want to bring my presentation of the passage from 'government' to 'governance' to a close by considering the state-civil society relationship these abstract ideal types envisage, as well as the notion of citizenship they tend to advocate.

Among the supposedly epochal changes brought about by the passage from 'government' to 'governance' special emphasis has been put on the revision of the state-civil society relationship (Pierre and Peters 2000: 199).[6] In spite of the ubiquitous role the expression 'civil society' has in political science (Cohen and Arato 1994), its real meaning is rather ambiguous. Harris (2006: 131) distinguishes between four main understandings of civil society vying against each other:

> one central tradition of writing about civil society has portrayed it as virtually coterminous with government, law-enforcement, and the cluster of institutions that comprise 'the state' (Model 1). A very different tradition has identified civil society with private property rights, commercial capitalism, and the various legal, institutional, and cultural support-systems that these entail (Model 2). Yet another line of thought has seen civil society as quintessentially composed of voluntaristic, non-profit-making, civic and mutual-help movements, coexisting with but nevertheless quite distinct in ethos and function from the spheres of both states and markets (Model 3). And in very recent discourse 'civil society' has come to be increasingly identified with the enunciation of universal standards of democracy, fair procedures, the rule of law, and respect for human rights [...] (Model 4).

Obviously, the implications civil society has for democratic politics varies accordingly with the definition chosen by the analyst. Figure 3.5 proposes a synoptic picture of the main types of state-civil society relationship to be found in literature. Rows indicate the societal actors assumed to embody civil society in distinct traditions of thought, whereas columns identify the nature of the link between those societal agents and state institutions sought by these traditions.[7]

Figure 3.5: Types of state-civil society relationships

Institutions	Relation with the state		
	Independence	*Autonomy*	*Connection*
Businesses	Libertarian	Third sector	Corporative
Associations	Voluntarist	Mutualist	Leninist
Groups	Movementism	Pluralist	Polyarchical

The welfarist model of government brought about by the post-war settlement retains a very modernist dislike for civil society, especially when the latter is used to identify intermediary bodies which can challenge the absolutist aspirations of the nation state. For it, modernisation means, above all, either dismantling pre-modern corporate bodies or refashioning them as subordinate organs of the state. The welfare state pursued this modernist task by starting processes of vertical integration which brought under the supervision of the state those institutions of the social economy set up since the turn of the twentieth century by various mutual societies and professional associations (Palumbo and Scott 2005). It is with the introduction of neocorporate solutions towards the end of *les trente glorieuses* that the attitude towards civil society changed and the state started to actively co-opt the representatives of major social forces. And even in this case, only a few societal actors representing labour and producer organisations were included. Moreover, the opening up of the state towards civil society was based on a not too subtle *quid pro quo*: a top-down social pacification that could reduce inflationary pressures and the risk of a systemic legitimacy crisis. Accordingly, civil society organisations were treated in a Leninist fashion as mere 'transmission belts' whose function was to bring instrumental support to their political sponsors – players engaged in endless tactical moves often without a clear strategy in mind. The advent of neoliberal governments in the Anglo-sphere brought with them a strong aversion towards neocorporate solutions (and in particular towards trade-unions and red tape). Using the notion of civil society to refer to the business community and its social referents, neoliberal governments supported, at least rhetorically, a libertarian understanding of the relation that committed them to reduce any interference of the state in the private sector. Hence the slogans about the rolling-back of the state, the entitlement culture and redistributive policies. Opposing the terms of a metaphor that has been repeated endlessly since Osborne and Gaebler (1992) first proposed it, neoliberals refused to attribute to the state either the role of 'rowing' or even that of 'steering'. What they advocated instead was a vision of the state as 'enabler' (Gilbert and Gilbert 1989); that is, one willing to reverse the neocorporate logic and make state institutions the transmission belts for the multifarious businesses operating in the private sector – a reverse of logic that, it can be argued, is at the root of the growth of corporate welfare discussed later on (*see* Chapter Two, §2.3 and Chapter Nine, §9.2). I argue that it is this idea of the state as 'enabler' that keeps resurfacing in governance theory, notwithstanding the many references to the distinction between rowing and steering to be found in literature together with the claim that governance means steering (Mayntz 2003).

Government, governance and their internal variants identify with and support distinct conceptions of citizenship. The matrix reported in Figure 3.6. distinguishes between four main ideal types derived from intersecting rights-based and participatory conceptions with expansive and protective political aspirations.[8] Following Marshall's (1950) work, it becomes natural to identify the welfarist model of government with a social democratic conception of citizenship; that is, one that attributes to the citizen expanding sets of social and economic rights. As argued in Chapter One, this conception was never realised in practice and was at the root of the popular dissatisfaction with the welfare state that eventually caused the implosion of the social and political coalition supporting the post-war settlement.[9] It was also the one blamed by neoliberal ideologues for creating an unsustainable and parasitic entitlement culture (*see* Chapter Two, §2.2.1). Neoliberal attempts to bring the discipline of the market into the public sector and develop an alternative enterprise culture meant adopting a liberal conception of citizenship concerned with assuring only minimalist safety nets which would not interfere with the competitive dynamics responsible for social and economic innovation. At a theoretical level, the works which mark the cultural shift between these two understandings are Rawls's (1971) treatise on justice and his (1993) revision. In *A Theory of Justice*, Rawls advances a conception of citizenship that justify a redistribution of social resources aiming at compensating, as far as possible, every natural and social inequality for which the individual could not be held morally responsible. In *Political Liberalism*, Rawls recognises that the second principle of justice cannot be the base for an 'overlapping consensus' and proposes instead the principled adoption of a safety-net system more or less equivalent to the one proposed by Hayek (1982) for merely instrumental reasons – to preserve the liberal order from the catastrophic consequences great inequalities and mass unemployment could cause.

The unintended but amply predicted consequence of neoliberal attempts to engender this liberal model of citizenship by moving away from the welfare state towards a workfare state – an attempt backed by those political and intellectual forces subscribing to the 'third way' (Blair 1998; Giddens 1998, 2000), has been to provoke waves of populist movements which have kept the OECD boat

Figure 3.6: Models of citizenship

	Rights	*Participation*
Expansive	Social democratic	Republican
Protective	Liberal democratic	National populist

rocking since the late 1990s. Fuelled by the resentment of the white working classes towards the traditional political parties which used to cater to them, this populism has given a new lifeline to right-wing ideologies and political forces which the post-war settlement managed to marginalise and exclude from parliamentary politics (Albertazzi and McDonnell 2007; Berezin 2009). The common features of these populist movements are: (i) calls for a more direct form of political participation whose aim is to protect local communities from the ethno-cultural creolisation imposed by globalisation, and (ii) the rejection of neoliberal reforms responsible for exposing local communities and the white working classes to (what are perceived as) unfair forms of competition (Palumbo 2009, 2011). These populist movements subscribe to traditional values and push for protective social policies. They also view political participation in a Weberian fashion, as mass mobilisation in support of charismatic leaders committed to 'kick the rascals out' (Cuperus 2004). Post-neoliberal governance theorists speak instead a republican language of citizenship. Here rights-based moral justifications are abandoned in favour of more political justifications for participatory policy instruments. Participation, however, takes a dialogical aspect wishing to rely on the force of forceless reason and use involvement in the policy process as an educational tool (Fung 2006; Nabatchi 2010; Warren 2009).[10] Since the participation advocated applies at the implementation stage as well, its educational effects are meant to proceed from the bottom up and move from policy to politics to the polity. This seemingly republican conception of citizenship is committed to responsibilise the citizen as prosumer by invoking the deep-down democratisation of the public realm.[11]

3.3. Aspects of governance as a polycentric model of social order

Governance theory draws attention to new conceptual categories which are meant to complement traditional pair-wise juxtapositions: state vs. market, public vs. private and hierarchy vs. anarchy. As a result, the outline of more complex bi-dimensional analytical spaces populated by novel ideal types is laid down. The conceptual categories marking one of the extremities of these triangular spaces are the notions of 'network' and 'soft law', which are given a different meaning to that attributed to them by previous theoretical approaches which also used them to oppose state-centric theories of social change – in particular those with a neoliberal pedigree (Stringham 2005). Networks, the resulting polycentric order they generate and the soft law tools they use in the process, identify logical spaces other than the state, formal rules, procedural policy instruments, hierarchical forms of organisation as well as command-and-control managerial techniques. In addition, governance perspectives influenced by economic sociology insist on showing that networks and networking follow a logic of social action alternative to market modes of organisation, competitive forms of interaction and sets of monetary incentives (Thompson 2003). The epistemic aim of those who employ these conceptual categories is to show that the paradoxes generated by the interaction of self-seeking individual agents employed in neoclassic economics can be avoided, and in particular that complex forms of social coordination can be established and maintained without the exogenous intervention of the state (Ostrom *et al.* 1992; Scharpf 1994). To quote Rhodes (2006: 440), 'coordination is the holy grail of modern government, ever sought, but always just beyond reach, and *networks* bring central coordination no nearer. However, they do provide their own messy, informal, decentralized version'. To explicate the ways in which these anti-statist regulatory tools and flexible mechanisms of enforcement can contribute to the resolution of collective action problems, a triple definition of governance as a regulatory system, organisational type and form of production is proposed here.

As a regulatory system, governance theory concerns itself with the changes affecting the following elements: (i) the political and administrative institutions to whom the power to define and supervise rules is attributed; (ii) the procedures according to which these institutions are supposed to operate; (iii) the criteria used for evaluating the content of the rules themselves and their practical achievements. At the institutional level, governance theory seeks to rationalise the extensive forms of delegation meant to transfer decision- and policy-making power to authorities operating above, below and alongside the nation state (Ansell 2000; King 2007). Since globalisation is supposed to be fast eroding the ability of the central state institutions to deal with externalities and to govern global commons through intergovernmental agreements, a systemic need to create and empower new transnational public authorities is said to follow. Moreover, since technological innovation is giving individuals and organisations the opportunity to interact across national borders (thus setting gradually stricter limits to the state's ability to enforce its policies from the top-down), subnational authorities are also viewed as indispensable intermediaries for social regulation. Finally, governance theorists explain that the blurring of lines between public and private domains and the redefinition of the relationship between the state and civil society induced by neoliberal reforms of big government calls for a revision of the logic of command-and-control upon which public authorities used to rely. Thus, Walker and de Burca (2006: 525) point out that

> new governance in that sense is defined as something that is not only *different from* but actually *in contrast with* law (e.g. because of its different sources, or symbolic associations, or cluster of institutional features and associated values or functions – being 'softer', *less* hierarchical, *more* revisable, *more* flexible, *more* experimental, *more* inclusive of non-traditional institutional actors, *less* reliant on courts and formal legislation, etc.), and so, it follows, different from and in contrast with hitherto prevalent forms of government and governance which rely to a greater extent on law.

For Hooghe and Marks (2003), this entails creating new functional regulatory agencies to supplement traditional territorial authorities, switching from a model of authority with general scope and permanent jurisdiction to one based on specialised and transitory forms of intervention, and adopting an overlapping system of authorities using heterogeneous modes of organisation. In other words, they suggest seeing current political and institutional change as causing the emergence of a multilevel system of governance where rules are produced by a variety of public and semi-public authorities operating at distinct jurisdictional levels, following partially diverse policy objectives and changing over time in number, status and organisational structure (*see* Chapter Four, §4.3 and Chapter Seven, §7.4). In this context, political and administrative actors operate within a regulatory patchwork giving them significant discretionary powers and are supervised by myriads of audit agencies having a similarly large degree of discretion. The political process comes to rely, therefore, on a panoply of regulatory instruments distinct from statute laws (Lobel 2004; Mörth 2004; Scott 2003; Trubek and Trubek 2006; Walker and de Burca 2006). Nowadays, elected representative institutions issue only very broad guidelines which then need to be fleshed out by soft law tools whose validity and effectiveness can no longer be derived from parliament and are thus semi-legal in nature. Given this semi-legal status, soft law tools escape traditional control-systems based on judicial review and courts of justice; their supervision is thus demanded of systems of audit and peer-review operating in a quasi-juridical manner.

The pluralisation of normative sources, legal instruments and juridical systems is explained by retrieving and building upon the socio-legal critiques of legal positivism advanced to rationalise the shortcomings of past welfare institutions and policies (Nonet and Selznick 1978). In doing so, governance theorists suggest seeing soft law tools as a distinct set of regulatory instruments to add to traditional distinctions and juxtapositions between social norms and formal rules, thus proposing a representation of the socio-legal space like the one given in Figure 3.7. The regulatory maze outlined by this representation is then argued to be such that it goes beyond the abilities of state actors to enforce it by command-and-control techniques. Its harmonisation increasingly requires the adoption of self-reflexive legal attitudes and flexible juridical practices (*see* Chapter Six, §6.4). As stated in the abstract of Teubner's (1983: 239) most influential article: 'instead of taking over regulatory responsibility for the outcome of social processes, reflexive law restricts itself to the installation, correction, and redefinition of democratic self-regulatory mechanisms'.

Treib *et al.* (2007: 5–7) distinguish five thematic areas where the adoption of new modes of governance has introduced crucial socio-legal changes.

1. *Legal bindingness versus soft law.* Negotiated and agreed upon soft law tools are not backed up by the authority of the state and therefore lack external enforcement mechanisms. Policy guidelines, memoranda of understanding, standards and benchmarks issued by regulatory authorities located at various levels of the policy process thus come to acquire the character of non-binding recommendations.

Figure 3.7: Soft law and the new socio-legal space

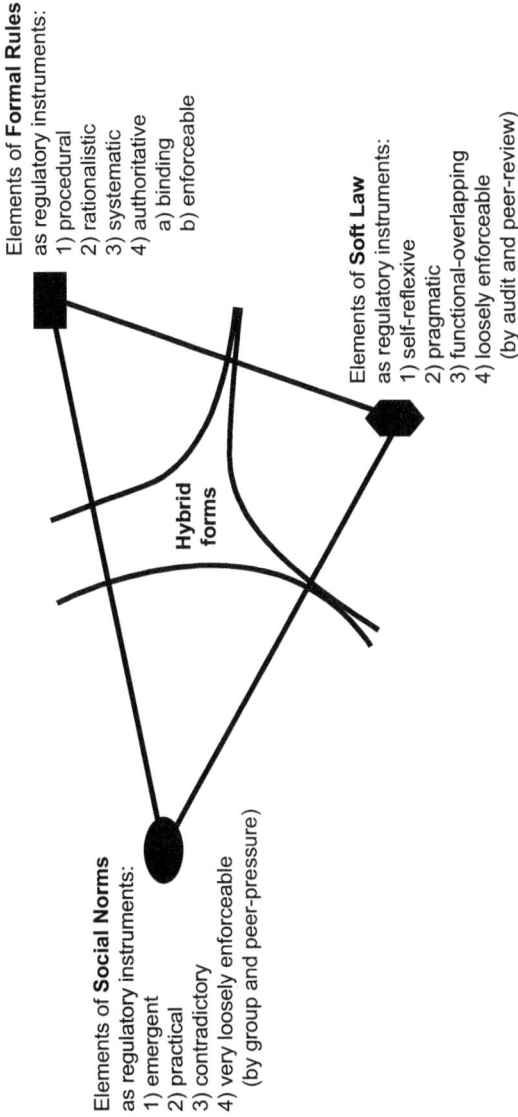

Elements of **Formal Rules**
as regulatory instruments:
1) procedural
2) rationalistic
3) systematic
4) authoritative
   a) binding
   b) enforceable

Elements of **Soft Law**
as regulatory instruments:
1) self-reflexive
2) pragmatic
3) functional-overlapping
4) loosely enforceable
   (by audit and peer-review)

Elements of **Social Norms**
as regulatory instruments:
1) emergent
2) practical
3) contradictory
4) very loosely enforceable
   (by group and peer-pressure)

Hybrid forms

2. *Rigid versus flexible approach to implementation.* Similar flexibility characterises the implementation process: 'they [soft law tools] may leave norm addressees and implementing actors more leeway in adapting them to local circumstances or individual interests (e.g. by providing a range of alternative options to choose from, by offering possibilities to derogate from individual provisions or to exempt certain groups of persons or branches of the economy from being covered by the rules)' (*ibid.*: 6).

3. *Presence versus absence of sanctions.* Since the policy process now relies on non-binding recommendations, sanctions are often not contemplated any longer by a variety of soft law tools. But even when formal sanctions are established, soft law tools leave to the regulatory agencies in charge ample discretion about the opportunity to issue them or not.

4. *Material versus procedural regulation.* Soft law tools tend to adopt a substantive approach to regulation. They not only contemplate the possibility of using procedural shortcuts which could strengthen the effectiveness and efficiency of the policy process, but also require the continuous upwards revision of the standards set to assess individual and organisational performance.

5. *Fixed versus malleable norms.* Adopting a material perspective on regulation means that any overall legal framework has to rest on evolving sets of rules. The latter need to be adapted to distinct contexts and evaluated according to standards capable of measuring their actual performance. As such, soft law tools tend to be 'comparatively more open-textured, revisable and integrated with other norms and policies' (*ibid.*: 7).

According to governance theory, openness, flexibility and reflexivity in the socio-legal domain combine with a deliberative democratic vision that shapes the content of rules in a more egalitarian way (Mörth 2004). In Low's (2005: 47) words, 'the social relations of the network combine a sense of equality among the participants with a sense of mutual obligation that is not, however, normally legally binding. Actors in a network do not command and obey. Nor do they buy and sell. But they do exchange, and what they exchange is information, political support, and trust'. This claim is upheld, among others, by Bevir (2006) and Peters (2002), who maintain that regulation arrived at through deliberative engagement is a precondition for fulfilling a democratic notion of social autonomy.

As an organisational model, governance theory is committed to develop a neo-institutionalist perspective that can complement, if not supersede, the economic analyses of social institutions proposed by NPE (Rowe 1989; Schotter 1981). Governance approaches interested in complementing the latter build upon Williamson's (2000) New Institutional Economics. By and large, their main goal is to revise the protective belt surrounding the individualist research programme adopted by NPE to improve the empirical content and/ or predictive power of rational choice explanations. Besides Williamson and his followers, this enterprise has involved distinguished social theorists like Coleman (1994), Gambetta (1988) and Hechter (Hechter and Kanazawa 1997,

Kiser and Hechter 1998). Governance approaches willing to replace rational choice explanations are mainly derived from economic sociology.[12] For them, Williamson's continuum between hierarchy and market is simplistic and fails to consider the distinctive role played by network modes of organisation in resolving coordination problems and structuring social interaction (Podolny and Page 1998; Powell 1990; Thompson 2003). Consequently, they maintain that networks are not hybrids combining markets and hierarchies, but distinctive forms of social organisation operating according to a logic antithetical to that used within hierarchies and markets alike (*see* Chapter Four, §4.3).[13] In both cases, the organisational continuum between markets and hierarchies proposed by Williamson is replaced by a bi-dimensional triangular space replicating the picture of the socio-legal space reported above (*see* Figure 3.8).

As reported above in quoting from Low's, networks are organisational forms where social interaction is not based neither on relations of authority nor on the maximisation of expected utilities. A network can thus be defined as an (i) informal, (ii) high density and (iii) permanent system of exchange between (iv) socially embedded agents (Powell 1990). Within a network, roles and functions have a voluntaristic basis reflecting individual inclinations; they are, consequently, more flexible than those attributed within hierarchies but less fluid than the contractual relations established by markets. As a mechanism of social coordination, interaction within a network is neither dependent on codified legal procedures nor on the signals sent by the price-system. Rather, coordination is achieved through dialogical social practices where individual and groups have been given the opportunity to (a) express their opinions, (b) revise their preferences and (c) select the course of action to follow democratically (Sabel 2004). Networks are also distinct from hierarchies and markets in relation to the types of incentives they use to solicit individual and organisational compliance. While hierarchies rely on full-time and long-term employment contracts rewarding seniority and impartial service, within a network incentives are always informal and reward local attachments and personal loyalties. Also, market transactions depend on monetary incentives, whereas network forms of organisation support systems of exchange based on the gift economy (Mauss 1954) or the economy of excess (Bataille 1985, 1997). As a result, markets tend to produce strategic equilibria based on short-term criteria of mutual advantage. By contrast, networks are heavily dependent on trust, common identities and feelings of solidarity. To quote Thompson (2003: 107),

> we might say that a network logic operates on the 'edge' of the reciprocated gift and the nonreciprocated gift. Any deferred return embodied in the gift of an economy of utilities obligates one individual to another and therefore creates a social debt between them, while a non-reciprocated gift of the economy of excess secures its social bond in an unrecognized and unrealized form by the slight of hand of the counterfeit and disguised engagement with the place of the 'beyond'.

Figure 3.8: Networks and the new organisational space

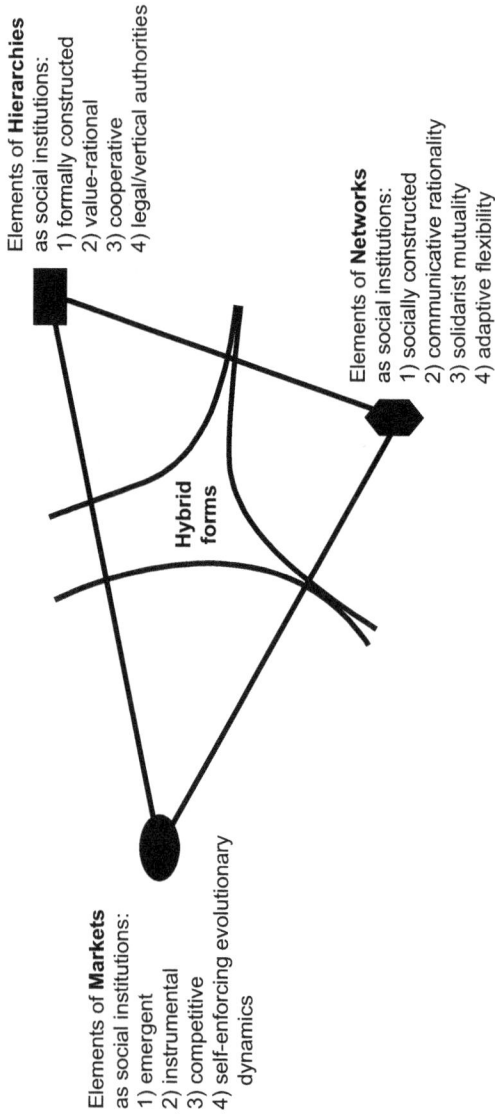

Elements of **Hierarchies**
as social institutions:
1) formally constructed
2) value-rational
3) cooperative
4) legal/vertical authorities

Elements of **Networks**
as social institutions:
1) socially constructed
2) communicative rationality
3) solidarist mutuality
4) adaptive flexibility

Hybrid forms

Elements of **Markets**
as social institutions:
1) emergent
2) instrumental
3) competitive
4) self-enforcing evolutionary dynamics

Governance theory views networks as privileged types of organisation through which civil society can be involved in the policy process and the production of public goods and services. From an abstract perspective, this entails turning (i) hierarchies into more horizontal and decentred forms of organisation connecting the terminal nodes of civil society and those of public authorities operating at local, national and transnational levels (Ansell 2000); (ii) the individual agents located within these nodes from gatekeepers, committed to control all traffic going in and out, to gateways, committed to establishing new and more effective channels of communication which would enhance the exchange of information, knowledge and resources (Kajer 2004); (iii) decision making, policy making and policy implementation from highly centralised technical activities into deliberative practices involving changing mixes of experts, stakeholders and prosumers (Yee 2004); (iv) permanent and exclusive territorial jurisdictions into variable sets of specific, non-exclusive and overlapping functional jurisdictions which will cease to exist once their task is accomplished (Hooghe and Marks 2003). According to governance theorists, the joint effect of these reforms will cause the formation of heterarchies which could stimulate the autopoietic ability of civil society and engender a democratic and polycentric political order (Bang 2003a; Jessop 2003; Kooiman 2000; Teubner 1983).[14]

Governance theory builds upon and applies to the body politic the hypotheses developed by economic sociology in relation to the so-called post-Taylorist turn in industrial organisation (DiMaggio 2003). As for the 1980s managerial reforms of the economic firm, neoliberal reforms of big government have disaggregated the centralised institutions of the state in constellations of regulatory authorities, administrative agencies and auditing bodies connected by multiple horizontal linkages. This disaggregation implies the revision of the main governing functions the post-war settlement attributed to the welfare state. First of all, public intervention is no longer seen as directed at the uniform social and economic development of the nation state. Rather, the state is now operating as an enabling agent whose role is to support the endogenous and sustainable development of local communities, economic businesses and civil society organisations. This means dismissing the notion of the state as (i) a direct producer of public goods and services, (ii) an employer of last resort and (iii) an agent engaged in compensating regional and social disparities by the authoritative redistribution of social resources (Majone 1994). Uniform development is replaced by a flexible form of public intervention directed at supporting local characteristics and individual vocation, and thus helps people, groups and communities to compete successfully on the global stage. In turn, it entails (a) devolving the production of public goods and services to administrative agencies and PPPs in competition for public funding; (b) establishing flexible forms of labour regulation and workfare programmes which could boost national rates of employment; (c) guaranteeing safety nets and minimal wage rules which could protect the worst-off members of society without undermining market incentives (Brenner 2004). As a result, the

Keynesian macroeconomic management of the aggregate demand is abandoned in favour of a supply-side approach whose goal is to help the creation of new societal nodes and the stimulation of an enterprise culture. Moreover, general and long-term development plans are replaced by project-based programmes which could help integrate individuals and communities into larger and more resourceful networks. Furthermore, crucial decisions about state support and the allocation of public resources are devolved to regulatory authorities located at the local level and, therefore, better able to assess the viability of the projects to be publicly funded (Low 2005).

The interpersonal and interorganisational networks induced through calibrated public intervention are supposed to work along the lines followed by the constellations of productive forms brought about by the post-Taylorist managerial revolution. As Sabel (1995: 3) eloquently explains,

> the large, centrally directed bureaucracy that defined efficiency in corporations and public administration is giving way to more decentralized and federated structures. The basic unit of these new structures is the team or work group charged with responsibility and given the means for achieving a goal as it determines, and this whether or not it has the formal autonomy of a legally independent entity. Coordination of these groups is by means of iterated goal setting: General projects such as, for example, the design of a new car, are initially determined by evaluation of best practice and prospects of competing developmental alternatives. These general goals are in turn successively decomposed, again by reference to leading example and comparison of possibilities, into tasks for teams or work groups. Then the goals are modified as groups gain experience in prosecuting the tasks as originally defined. Through these revisions, modifications in the parts lead to modifications in the conception of the whole, and vice versa. The same procedure of monitoring decentralized learning, moreover, allows each part to observe the performance of the other collaborators accurately enough to determine whether continued reliance on them, and dedication of resources to the joint projects, are warranted. Because of this connection between joint exploration of collaborative possibilities and mutual evaluation I call these systems learning by monitoring.

Within the body politic, the basic units are the PPPs charged with the realisation of specific project-based programmes. Their inner working is decided by deliberative procedures with two main functions: (1) enhancing the information flows between the various individuals, groups and organisations involved in the programme and (2) monitoring the various partners with whom it is worth to continue working in future projects. With time, the knowledge accumulated by the members of PPPs is to cause the crystallisation of 'deliberative polyarchies' interested in carrying out further projects and programmes. The learning abilities and selective strategies employed by these deliberative polyarchies ensure better adaptive powers to network modes of production than their traditional counterparts. In this account, systems of learning by monitoring allow networks to effectively address the bureaucratic sclerosis affecting hierarchies while keeping under control the free-riding problems undermining market solutions. In the process, a system of individual and social responsibilities controlling the rise of excessive expectations and the spiraling of governmental costs (as experienced by the welfare state) is established and enforced in a decentraliszed manner (Warren 2009).

3.4. Governance as an evolving research field

The research on new modes of governance produced since the early 1990s covers various aspects of the political process, the jurisdictional levels where this unfolds and the individual and organisational actors involved in it. This research also encompasses an ample number of disciplinary and methodological perspectives and, by now, distinct generations of analysts and practitioners. Figure 3.9 gives an overall analytical summary of the topics emerged in governance studies during this period. It distinguishes between three main types of research: empirical microstudies of restricted policy areas, mid-level rationalisations derived from these empirical microstudies and system-theoretic analyses discussing the overall social dynamic explaining (or else generated by) the introduction and diffusion of new modes of governance over time. These types are then criss-crossed with two main theoretical orientations characterising the various strands of research: a reconstructive approach dealing with the way in which many policies have been applied in specific policy areas, together with the outcomes they have generated in the process, and a comparative approach using ideal typical representations of governing styles, organisational forms and administrative practices through which the determinants of change are explained and justified. The aim of this section is not to present all these lines of inquiry but, more modestly, to outline the areas which will be taken into consideration in this work (emphasised in bold below). In general, only those areas of analysis which have a particular and direct relevance for political

Figure 3.9: Governance as a research field: approaches and types of research topics

	Empirical microstudies	*Mid-level analyses*	*System dynamics*
Reconstructive approach	Government failures New public management Policy networks	Hollowed-out state **Network governance** **Multilevel governance**	Collibration Governance networks Interactive governance
Comparative approach	Deregulation Audit/delegation Self-regulation	**Regulatory State** **Networked Polity** Global governance	Governamentality Metagovernance Autopoiesis

theory will be investigated throughout the volume, and within this restricted set only those that have special significance for the nation state, as the locus of legitimate political authority, will receive systematic attention.

By far, the greatest part of governance studies is made up of empirical studies pertaining to restricted policy areas. Two things need to be noted about this body of work. First, the term 'governance' is here employed as a synonym of government and the heuristic role of distinguishing between contrasting ways of governing is attributed to qualifiers like 'old' and 'new' (or, more seldom, 'Type I' and 'Type II'). Second, although it is possible to identify approaches which have mostly a reconstructive intent and those which have instead a comparative intent, the line of demarcation between the two is very thin and not followed in a systematic manner. These distinctions loom large in the body of literature located at the mid-level. Here a sustained analytical attempt to use 'government' and 'governance' as labels characterising diverse styles of governing, modes of organisation and political worldviews is carried out and defended – even if the various arguments employed to do so remain contentious and the term 'governance' periodically keeps being used as a synonym of government as well. At this mid-level of analysis, approaches which have reconstructive and comparative intent are not only easier to identify, but the line dividing them also tends to be followed more systematically by single authors or within disciplines. Although less prolific than its empirical counterpart, mid-level analyses of new modes of governance are growing at a perceptibly fast pace and are exercising an increasingly noticeable influence on empirically oriented research; for these analyses are committed to supply general analytical frameworks through which empirical evidence can be systematised and further research orientated. In pursuing these ambitious epistemic objectives, mid-level analyses confront themselves with more restricted but no less ambitious scientific perspectives engaged in system-theoretic studies of social change – perspectives which find their inspiration in the works of authors like Easton, Foucault and Luhmann or cybernetic modelling. Against the neo-institutional conceptions dominating mid-level rationalisations, system-theoretic approaches stress the role of processes above structures, evolutionary dynamics above static comparisons and functional analyses above causal explanations (*see* Chapter Six, §6.3). From this perspective, 'governance implies a variety of recursive practices oriented to both the creation of identity and the enhancement of the governing faculties of individual and groups to produce effective and relevant outcomes through the processes and projects in which they are interacting' (Bang 2003a: 20).

While I keep in great consideration empirical research and case studies, the focus of this work will be primarily on mid-level analyses of governance. From my perspective, it is at this level that the theoretical and normative presuppositions driving governance studies are made explicit and excuse the direct engagement of political theorists in this field of studies. The hollowing-out of the state and the emergence of network and multilevel forms of governance are said to mark a momentous passage from past conceptions of governing (modernist) to new ones (post-modern), which are, in turn, presented and justified as better functional solutions to the political and organisational problems which undermined the viability of welfare institutions and policies. As superior functional solutions to traditional policy problems, network and multilevel governance are also said to be setting in motion processes of change causing the emergence of new political actors, policy instruments and mechanisms of implementation. In short, their working and diffusion is linked to the establishment of new powerful historical subjects capable of replacing the nation state. These post-modern and post-statal political entities are said to favour novel conceptions of sovereignty, seek alternative criteria of legitimacy and supports new forms of embeddedness. It is therefore evident the relevance these transformations have for political theory and the interest governance theory raises (or ought to raise) for political theorists – an interest that the blend of restricted empirical studies, sweeping generalisations derived from them and a vocal dislike for normative analysis that characterises governance theory at present is far from satisfying.

Focusing on mid-level analyses, the contribution political theory, as I perceive it, could bring to governance theory is twofold. In dealing with the approaches which have a mostly reconstructive interest, this contribution is primarily concerned with sharpening the analytical categories and distinctions proposed so far. A case in point is the distinction between 'rowing' and 'steering' discussed earlier. Many governance theorists subscribe to the claim that the passage from 'government' to 'governance' entails dropping a conception of governing as 'rowing' (that is, a view of the state as both the engine and driving rod for social change) and adopting a less demanding conception of governing as 'steering' (that is, a view of the state as engaged in simply directing the social changes generated by a dynamic civil society). I have pointed out that the notion of 'steering' was already employed by the neocorporate variant of the welfare state. It cannot therefore be used to characterise the post-statal entities allegedly brought about by governance without also diminishing the supposedly epochal nature of the changes occurred in the meantime. Moreover, in the literature on governance an alternative notion is repeatedly used to indicate the development of a more subtle form of political intervention: 'enabling'. Hence, I suggest that, for analytical reasons, 'enabling' rather than 'steering' should be used to indicate the kind of interventions public authorities are now committed to undertake.

In the next chapter (*see* Chapter Four, §4.3), I shall also suggest a better way to distinguish between network and multilevel governance. The aim is to avoid the proliferation of labels indicating identical things and the conceptual confusion that usually arises from this. To these conceptual issues, we need to add several analytical confusions found among the approaches which have a more comparative interest. The first type concerns the set of ideal types used to compare between past and more recent styles of governing, modes of organisation, mechanisms of implementation, etc. As the reconstruction carried out above indicates, the political developments which occurred during *les trente glorieuses* yielded two variants: a welfarist model of government that, towards the end of the 1960s, become engulfed in various crises, and a neocorporate model of government summoned to overcome what was diagnosed as a legitimation crisis, but which was unable to reverse the decline of the welfare state. I also pointed out that currently we face a similar problem when trying to identify the ideal type that is supposed to have replaced (or is in the process of replacing) the welfare state. Consequently, I indicated that in relation to the political and institutional changes brought about by *les trente furieuses*, we also need to distinguish between neoliberal and post-neoliberal forms of governance, where the latter are attempts to solve the policy mess generated by the former – about whose eventual fate at present we can only speculate. Far from dismissing ideal type-based methodologies altogether, I try to address their shortcomings by refining the models used in governance literature, while pointing out, each time, the heuristic powers and limitations of those introduced. The refined models I propose are grounded on the assumption that while abstraction (and simplification) is a *sine qua non* condition for any kind of theorising, simplifications which reify aspects, features and characteristics of the phenomena under scrutiny need to be avoided (O'Neill 1989).

Tightly related to the issue surrounding the use of ideal types are questions concerning the narratives proposed by governance theorists. Are new modes of governance trying to consolidate the reforms of big government carried out during the 1980s? Or should they be viewed as decentralised political solutions to the coordination problems generated by the institutional fragmentation caused by those reforms? Is current political and institutional change causing the emergence of a Regulatory State committed to empower the individual by letting him vote with his feet? Or is it promoting the development of a Networked Polity committed to empower civil society by developing a new form of stakeholder democracy and deliberative policy environment from the bottom up? In trying to adjudicate between these contending narratives, I will carry out a genealogical analysis of governance theory that distinguishes between various approaches, methodologies and worldviews used to rationalise current political and institutional change. This genealogical analysis will eventually lead me to identify two main research programmes making up governance theory: one derived from political economy and the other influenced by political sociology; one based on the fictitious utility maximisers employed by NPE models and the other adopting instead a more embedded model of agency; one that sees implicit in current change the development of a Regulatory State that is freeing civil society from politics and another that predicts, by contrast, the rising of a Networked Polity willing to open the political process to all affected interests. The distinction between, and the inner articulation of, these two research programmes (carried out in Chapters Five and Six) allow me to assess them as both heuristic frameworks attempting to explain change and justificatory frameworks trying to influence its pace and direction. In doing so, no effort will be spared to avoid falling into some sort of analytical Manichaeism, namely the temptation to use pair-wise analytical distinctions to express value judgments surreptitiously, rather than to help better understand the nature of the phenomena under study. To this end, matrixes offering no less than four alternative analytical categories will be used throughout this work, and special attention will be taken to keep separate the evaluation of the explanatory aspects of a research programme from the assessment of its prescriptive suggestions.

A concluding remark on the waves of research which have contributed to the development of governance as an independent field of study is in order at this point. According to Sørensen and Torfing (2006), since its inception in the 1990s, the remarkable body of work on new modes of governance has been due to two generations of research. The two Danish authors use the term 'generation' to refer to cycles of research rather than the age of those engaged in it: 'The emergence of a new generation is neither a matter of new and younger researchers entering the field nor a matter of a clear break with the past; rather, it is a matter of a gradual renewal and enlargement of the research agenda' (*ibid.*: 14).[15] As I see it, the main difference between them is that the second generation is questioning several theoretical assumptions shared by the first. The assumptions undergoing critical scrutiny concern: (i) the role of the state in promoting and supporting the political and institutional changes responsible for the passage from 'government' to 'governance', (ii) the functional accounts used to explain the adoption of new modes of governance and their diffusion across policy areas and countries, and (iii) the sort of redefinition representative democracy and accountability are undergoing as a result of the transformations in progress. I shall briefly summarise the matter at stake in these three ambits and indicate the contribution this present work could bring to the further development of the critical turn in governance studies.

The first generation maintains an outspoken aversion towards state-based approaches to policy analysis. This anti-statist stance leads analysts and practitioners to concentrate their efforts on cases of 'governance without government' and neglect the evidence concerning the no less relevant forms of 'governance with government' and 'governance of government' – to use the tripartite definitions suggested by Sørensen (2004). Sometimes this neglect turns into an attempt to play down the role of state institutions in initiating and supporting the changes analysed in governance studies throughout. Building on the parallel literature on globalisation (*see* Chapter Seven), state activism and persistent regulatory intervention are explained away as adaptive reactions to the pressure exercised by impersonal social forces operating at a systemic level. This leads governance theorists to put an overwhelming emphasis on unintended consequences and heterarchic forms of social order. To quote Bell and Hindmoor (2009: 6),

> in this view [first generation's], hierarchy, power struggles and conflict seem to get marginalised or replaced by contracts, bargaining, negotiation, networking, mutual dependence, or reciprocity and trust relations. This is a horizontal view of politics in which the state is receding or playing a more marginal role in a system of "self-organising networks" built on bargaining and negotiation, rather than authority structures. [...] In other words, the

role of government is marginalised or rendered seemingly equivalent to that of private actors amidst processes of horizontal bargaining and negotiation.

Reacting against what Bell and Hindmoor call 'society-centred governance', many analysts are now refocusing on the role played by state actors to gauge their actual crucial relevance within governance regimes as meta-regulators, ultimate sources of legitimacy, arbours for institutional anchorage and shadow forces for soliciting individual and organisational compliance.[16] In adopting a state-centric perspective, I suggest considering new modes of governance as policy tools employed by powerful state agents (central governments above all) to pursue a strategy of political centralisation-cum-administrative decongestion that reinforces and extends state control on civil society. By letting national executives govern at a distance, new modes of governance in reality (i) free them from the burdens imposed by an expansive model of social citizenship, (ii) undermine the mechanisms of accountability established to make non-elective state institutions legitimate and responsive and (iii) shift onto civil society the costs associated with rules enforcement and policy implementation.

The celebratory attitude towards the alleged demise of the state is usually accompanied by a no less emphatic celebration of the virtues of network modes of organisations and networking logic. It is thanks to the latter that new modes of governance are reputed to be able to avoid the government failures which undermined the viability of welfare states and succeed in reconciling equality and efficiency, social entrepreneurship and solidarity, political inclusion and policy effectiveness. First generation research employs networks as a powerful epistemic category to refute not only the Hobbesian dictum 'promises without a sword are but words', but also to deny any role to political activity in stabilising emergent forms of social order. According to the worldview and methodological tenets subscribed to by the various governance theorists, networks are then used either to corroborate the Hayekian notion of the market as a self-sustaining 'catallactic' order able to turn foes into friends (with the little help of a friendly and much reduced Regulatory State), or to justify the viability of a socially embedded Networked Polity equally distant from states and markets. These corroborations are grounded on an array of functional explanations meant to highlight the comparative advantages of either markets against states or networks against both markets and hierarchies. By introducing into this networked world the notion of governance failure, the second generation is developing an approach to policy analysis less mesmerised by the seemingly infinite possibilities offered by networks. Methodologically, this also implies debunking the functional analyses employed to show the theoretical validity of the notion of spontaneous order (in both its neoliberal and post-neoliberal versions). In turn, this entails questioning the soundness of the rationalisations of political and institutional change supplied by showing that the empirical evidence available can be used to support alternative, and no less plausible, accounts of change. The genealogical analyses of Regulatory State and Networked Polity carried in the second part are consequently meant to show: (iv) the similarities between the two version of the spontaneous order thesis upon which they are grounded, (v) the theoretical limitations affecting each of the analytical frameworks proposed in support of this thesis, (vi) the alternative ways in which empirical evidence can be read once a constructivist and state-centric perspective, suspicious of both causal and functional explanations, is adopted.

Notwithstanding the celebratory and Panglossian spirit pervading it, the various strands of governance theory retain a principled opposition towards any attempt to develop a normative approach to policy analysis. Echoing the heydays of the logical positivist crusade against metaphysics, this principled opposition leads governance analysts and practitioners to deny either that theoretical reflection could make any genuinely new contribution to knowledge and understanding, or even that there exists such a thing as governance theory – suggesting instead that we must view governance studies simply as a collection of loosely related empirical studies on specific policy areas. The multiple suggestions given to influence the direction and pace of change are thus presented as technical fixes, and usually resolve in the systematic advocacy of new technological tools to make democracy more participatory, policy making more inclusive and policy implementation less top-down. From the critical viewpoint of the second generation, such an anti-normative attitude, and associated cult of ICT, hinders the ability of those working in the field to uncover social deficiencies which keep affecting extant networks (virtual and real). As Peters (2011: 66) wisely notes: 'there is a tendency to think of formal and informal institutions for *governance* as somehow strictly alternatives, but these structures may assist one another in providing *governance*'. Awareness of the limitations networks show has led several authors to advocate forms of metagovernance which can combine diverse modes of organisation in ways that could help neutralise each other's weaknesses (Jessop 2003). In addition, the possibility of governance failures has brought back into play the role of public institutions and politics as indispensable factors for assuring stability to governance regimes. Despite these theoretical green shoots, even within this emerging second generation, normative policy analyses and approaches are still underdeveloped and viewed with suspicion. The present work wishes to contribute to the rediscovery of politics by helping develop a genuine normative policy analysis. To this end, it will investigate (vi) the features of the alternative democratic visions the diverse strands of governance theory subscribe to, (vii) the contribution given by these attempts to deepen democracy to the growth of worrisome democratic deficits and accountability gaps, and (viii) the normative tools political theory could bring into policy analysis in order to address the post-democratic drift noticed within OECD countries.

3.5. Conclusions

In this chapter I have proposed a revised account of the passage from 'government' to 'governance'. Compared to the accounts supplied by the first generation of research, the one proposed here identifies four governing styles replacing each other in the six decades that followed the post-war reconstruction. Two of these styles are connected to the model of government established by the political settlement reached after the WWII and trace the parabola-like trajectory of the welfare state. The other two are connected to the model of governance that came to replace the welfare state and trace the parabola-like trajectory of the current neoliberal consensus politics. I clarified that in each case the evolution from one governing style to another was the outcome of endogenous attempts to address the dilemmas raised by its predecessor. Thus, while neocorporate solutions were an attempt to overcome the legitimation crisis affecting the welfarist model of government espoused by the welfare state, post-neoliberal modes of governance should be seen as attempts to solve the legitimation crisis engulfing at present the neoliberal consensus politics. For each of the ideal types identified in this way, I have presented and analysed the values, procedures and actors they tend to privilege at the decision-making level, the policy-making level and the implementation level. Furthermore, I clarified the distinctive visions of democratic politics they endorse by spelling out the ideal of citizenship subscribed to, and the state-civil society relationship envisioned. In doing so, I pointed out the similarities between neocorporate and post-neoliberal solutions. Both of them are predicated on a reading of the crises affecting their predecessors having to do with issues of legitimacy and endeavour to address those issues by opening up the political process. I also noted that similar weaknesses affect these two attempts. As for past neocorporate solutions, new modes of governance are not able to live up to the democratic standards they claim to uphold. Moreover, by supporting democratic experiments wishing to replace traditional conceptions of representative democracy, I pointed out that they risk actively contributing to the inception of a worrisome post-democratic age.

Focusing on new modes of governance, I then analysed the novelties they have introduced as regulatory tools, modes of organisation and forms of productions. Building on past critiques of legal positivism, governance supports the adoption of soft law instruments and systems of audit against statute laws and formal means of enforcement. From this perspective, flexibility, responsiveness and adaptability have replaced the value of legality, certainty and impartiality that used to characterise public action. This means, in turn, abandoning old models of organisation based either on vertical hierarchical lines of command or on horizontal forms of market exchange to adopt network modes of organisation. According to governance theory, networks and networking are better able to cope with complexity and can therefore address the coordination problems at the root of both government and market failure. In short, they are considered as superior functional means for producing public goods and services through the involvement of stakeholders and prosumers. The reconstruction of the regulative, organisational and productive features attributed to governance was carried out by discussing various epistemic perspectives and methodological approaches contributing to this field of studies. In doing so, I distinguished between the research programmes and generations of research making up governance theory.

Moreover, in noticing the differences between them, I also tried to spell out the thematic areas upon which the rest of this work will focus and the contribution it wishes to bring in these areas and to the field of governance theory overall. As a work in political theory, the objective of this book is to help sharpen the conceptual distinctions used so far and to contribute to the critical turn kick-started by the second generation by developing a normative approach to policy analysis. The following chapters will try to accomplish this by discussing at length and in greater detail crucial aspects of governance theory and of the research programmes contributing to its development.

End Notes

1. General works in political science surveying the events analysed here are Allum (1995) and Birch (1993). A more recent intellectual history is to be found in Müller (2011).

2. Indeed these neocorporate actors had to deal with their own internal crises of legitimation producing centrifugal dynamics. If joining the so-called iron triangles gave them access to resources which could reinforce their political legitimacy as gatekeepers, this strategy also exposed them to the criticism of being colluded. Hence their inner difficulty in complying with the clauses of the social compacts they had signed themselves.

3. Up to the mid-1980s, public intellectuals like Marquand (1988) still used Austrian neocorporate arrangements and policies as an example to follow for Britain against the then unfolding neoliberal revolution launched by Thatcher.

4. It seems like the terms of mid-1970 debates between those who attributed the cause of the crisis to a growing deficit of legitimacy and those who blamed it on systemic overloading are re-proposing themselves in relation to the troubles OECD countries are experiencing since the 2008 financial crisis (to say the least). A reference to the similarities between these two structural crises was earlier proposed by Goetz (2008). Streeck's (2014) is a clear re-statement of this connection.

5. The term prosumer is borrowed from Ritzer and Jurgeson (2010), who use it to identify the new subjects promoted by the development of self-service forms of production by the new economy, from catering to Web 2.0 technologies. In governance studies the expression *everyday makers* (Bang and Sorensen 1999) is meant to identify the subset operating in the public domain. To my knowledge, the best description of this self-service politics is to be found in Offe (2009: 559):

    at the micro-level of everyday behavior, citizens become in a way the ultimate executive agents of public policies (or, as the case may be, the ultimate cause of policy failures). In this role, the citizen does not primarily respond to government's authoritative commands nor to material incentives, but to political *signals* in the form of recommendations, information that has implications for behavior, programs with the purpose of consciousness creation, role models, alerts, disapproval, shaming, encouragement, appeals for prudent and responsible behavior, hints, moral campaigns and other "soft" forms of political communication between policy makers and citizens. Such signals differ from formal legal norms in that they appeal to social and moral norms rather than threatening sanctions or promising gains. They address citizens in their capacity as, for example, users of highways, parents, consumers, clients of education and health care systems, residents of neighborhoods, cities and eco-systems. But more generally they address citizens as responsible authors of their own life plans and life styles who are capable of both developing a reflexive awareness of their conduct and of binding themselves to situationally relevant social norms.

6. 'A move towards governance is predicated on a decreased significance of the public-private distinction in a variety of ways, whether we consider of governance as networks [...] or as more or less improvised types of public-private cooperation. The overall emphasis is on closer, more continuous and more informal contacts between political institutions and their environment' (Pierre and Peters 2000: 199). Later on (*see* Chapter Eight), however, I will show that this assumption has negative implications for the alleged connection with deliberative models of democracy—a connection used to sustain and justify the legitimacy of the dialogical policy environment generated by new modes of governance.

7. Chambers and Kopstein (2006) suggest an alternative scheme that uses six types of relation: (1) *apart from* the state, (2) *against* the state, (3) *in support of* the state, (4) *in dialogue with* the state, (5) *in partnership with* the state and (6) *beyond* the state.

8. The labels used to identify them are admittedly more part of a European political vocabulary than of an American one. Here the distinction between 'social' and 'liberal' democratic conceptions would likely be replaced by a 'progressive' and 'moderate' political terminology.

9. In Dean's (2010: 68) words,

the 'welfare state' was more an ethos of government or its ethical ideal and much less (and to varying degrees in different national contexts) a set of accomplished reforms and completed institutions. Above all, the welfare state was to be the telos (i.e. the final end or goal) of particular problematizations, interventions institutions and practices concerning unemployment, old age, disability, sickness, public education and housing, health administration, and norms of family life and childrearing.

10. This educational function is put at the forefront by Bang (2003b: 253):

> political culture is not merely a matter of having the right attitudes to the democratic regime but of co-operating in partnerships and networks in a democratic political community where people accept and recognie each other as capable and knowledgeable human beings.

11. On the different aspects of contemporary republican thought and on the problematic relations it establishes with governance theory and deliberative democracy see Honohan (2002: ch. VII) and Honohan and Jennings (2006).

12. Here I am simplifying the epistemic landscape somewhat. Concerning economic sociology, Fourcade (2007) claims that within it readings of networks which are meant to be supplementary and alternative to economics vie with each other. Similar claims can be put forward in relation to the new institutional economics as well. Some authors, Williamson included, used this approach to reinforce the individualist paradigm, while other economists view it as an opportunity to move beyond it. For a thorough survey of this field of study, see Hodgson (1998, 2007).

13. In this new organisational space (*see* Figure 3.8), hybrid forms of organisation keep floating beyond the gravitational pull exercised by the ideal types located at the vertexes of the triangle. These ideal types represent points of attraction creating their own gravitational field. Likewise can be said about the ideal types generating the socio-legal space in Figure 3.7.

14. According to the definition found in Wikipedia, 'A heterarchy is a network of elements which share the same "horizontal" position level in a hierarchy. Each level in a hierarchical system is composed of a heterarchy which contains its constituent elements'.

15. On this point, Rhodes (2006: 441) begs to differ and proposes a remarkable biographical reading of events:

> it is not just the story of the rise of an idea. It is about a new generation of political scientists. 'Young – well youngish – Turks' carved out a reputation for themselves by challenging their elders and betters. Sound and fury are essential to such uprisings. [...] The rise of *governance* was our story of how British government had changed. It was not the story in the graduate and postgraduate texts on which we were raised. We abandoned the eternal verities of the British constitution. In sharp contrast to the fuddy-duddies, we could explain both continuity and change. Of course, we were wrong but we weren't about to admit it.

Anyway the spats were fun! [...] The story of *policy networks* is a story of a success. The 'Young Turks' won their elevation to the professorial peerage, ran out of steam, and moved on. A flood of doctorates and case studies followed. It is no longer an innovative idea but a commonplace notion in almost every nook and cranny of both political science texts and British government textbooks in particular. It is ripe for challenge.

16. A point also stressed by Pierre and Peters (2000: 198):

government and governance are not altogether each other's opposites: governance can never be successful or give an accurate interpretation of political preferences among the populace unless it involves to a significant extent representative structures and an institutional means of translating these preferences into political and administrative action. Only the state can play these roles, and only the state can give meaning, objectives and direction to governance.

And even more emphatically by Mayntz (2003: 31–32):

the state not only legitimises, but also often helped to establish various forms of self-government. Where state actors participate in policy networks, they are a very special and privileged kind of participants; they retain crucial means of intervention, and this holds even where decision making has been devolved to institutions of societal self-government. In particular, the state retains the right of legal ratification, the right to authoritative decision where social actors do not come to a conclusion (e.g. in negotiations about technical standards), and the right to intervene by legislative or executive action where a self-governing system [...] fail to meet regulatory expectations. Thus, hierarchical control and societal self-regulation are not mutually exclusive. They are different ordering principles which are often combined, and in their combination, self-regulation 'in the shadow of hierarchy', can be more effective than either of the 'pure' governance forms.

PART II

CONTENT

Chapter Four

Interpreting Political Change:
Governance as a Research Programme

4.1. Introduction

Governance, like 'trust' and 'social capital', is another of those pivotal concepts endowed with a virus-like ability to spread across research fields in a remarkably short time. Like them, it has proved able to inspire a number of novel researches supplanting more traditional themes and approaches which were dominant in political science. Thus, it can be viewed as a paradigm-generating concept. The aim of this chapter is to summarise and reassess the innovations brought about by governance theory since its inception roughly two decades ago. This inquiry is carried out from the perspective of (normative) political theory and is therefore interested in mid-level studies which highlight the theoretical implications the switch from 'government' to 'governance' has had for traditional questions related to authority, sovereignty, legitimacy and accountability. It is argued that the notion of governance is a conceptual device that helps rationalise and articulate the changes undergone by liberal democracies since the late 1970s. However, the claims that view governance as ushering in a new political entity and style of intervention capable of 'governing without government' are found to be particularly problematic. Even less convincing are the statements affirming the inherent superiority of this new entity and its style of government from that of its predecessor. The chapter is structured as follows. The next section is concerned with the theoretical shifts promoted by governance as both an ideal-type of polity and style of government, and as a plausible reconstruction of the policy innovations emerged so far: the shift in scientific focus from abstract interests in the macro-dynamics of the polity to more concrete micro-studies of policy instruments, and from the high politics questions surrounding decision making to the low politics issues pertaining to policy implementation. Section three discusses the two main conceptual elements composing governance as an alternative paradigm: network governance and multilevel governance. The final section proposes a distinction between two broad research programmes contributing to governance studies, which are, in turn, composed of a blend of distinct analytical and justificatory frameworks. The claim I support here is that any critical evaluation of governance theory needs to pay attention to these internal differences and suggest criteria for assessing both the heuristic and prescriptive content of the approaches composing this field of studies.

4.2. Interpreting governance: shifting levels of analysis

The literature on new modes of governance is part of broader scientific endeavours to rationalise political and institutional change and justify using the notion of governance as the proper conceptual tool for understanding it. As seen in the previous chapter (§3.4), it is possible to identify two main approaches to governance studies: a reconstructive and a comparative one. The reconstructive approach is composed of myriad empirical micro-studies of the changes occurred in fields related to decision making, policy making and policy implementation. The comparative approach is instead interested in theoretical inquiries where abstract analytical categories are elaborated and compared with each other. We can also distinguish between three levels of analysis characterising governance studies. By far the most prominent part of governance research is composed of empirical micro-studies of restricted policy areas. However, this literature has limited or ambiguous relevance to political theory. For the conclusions arrived at by those studies are rarely clear-cut and cannot be easily generalised. To this empirical literature must be added a smaller, but no less prolific, body of work that operates at a more abstract middle level and tries to develop hypotheses encompassing larger sets of phenomena and policy areas. The rationalisations proposed tend to attribute to 'governance' a distinct analytical content and employ it as a Weberian ideal-type to juxtapose to 'government'.[1] In short, they elaborate theoretical frameworks through which to understand and assess change. A final and even more abstract level is composed of systems-theoretical analyses that find inspiration in authors like Easton, Foucault and Luhmann as well as cybernetics and autopoiesis. Here, the neoinstitutional perspectives that dominate mid-level analyses are supplanted by more dynamic conceptions emphasising (i) process above structure, (ii) evolutionary analysis above static comparisons and (iii) functional relationships above causal ones. Since it is at the mid-level that governance theory advances the more intriguing claims for political theorists, it is to this level that I shall direct my attention in this chapter.

4.2.1. From polity to policy

The development of governance studies promoted a shift in theoretical focus from polity, as the agent and locus of legitimate authority, to policy. In other words, it has forced political scientists and theorists alike to pay attention to the inner working of the various black boxes composing the political system – public administration above all. This shift is due in equal parts to two factors: the theoretical weaknesses attributed to traditional forms of government intervention and the outcomes of the reforms called for to solve government failure since the late 1970s (Mayntz 1993). The political landscape emerging from three decades of neoliberal restructuring of the public sector is presented as a fragmented one and, consequently, riddled with large-scale coordination problems. Governance theory suggests ways in which the new entities populating this landscape can be governed by indicating policy instruments other than those suggested by liberal democratic theory (Lascoumes and Le Gales 2007). According to the latter, legitimate decision-making rests with elected bodies representing people's sovereign authority (*see* Chapter One). To them alone is granted legislative power and the right to define the public interest and the means to bring it about. Given the complexity of some policy areas, liberal democratic theory also acknowledged the need to delegate policy making and the selection of policy instruments to more technical and executive branches of government, which, in turn, relied on public bureaucracies staffed with career officers dedicated to the enforcement of statute laws. Clear lines of accountability were established to guarantee political principals some degree of control over the delegation chain and help preserve democratic legitimacy across organisational boundaries (*see* Chapter Nine). The linearity of the political process just outlined has always been a constitutional fiction, of course. In reality, policy making was often beyond the technical ability of elected legislatures and relied heavily on the expertise of unelected public officials upon which representatives had only remote and indirect forms of control. The complexity of the administrative machine also meant that even ministers could not have meaningful knowledge of the various activities carried out by their departments to exercise proper supervision and be reasonably held responsible for failure (*see* Chapter Two). In the 1970s, the growing chasm between the formal and the material aspects of the post-war constitutional settlement caused widespread popular discontent with the minimalist politics of the ballot box advocated by liberal democracy and growing concerns about the bureaucratic rule of unaccountable technocrats.

In their attempt to bring runaway bureaucracies under governmental control, while reducing the political relevance of the then dominant welfare coalition, neoliberal reforms of big government introduced measures aimed at making the state and the public sector more responsive (*see* Chapter Two). The outcome of the neoliberal demolition work has been twofold. Delegation of decision-making power to non-elective bodies has led to the flourishing of Public-Private Partnerships (PPPs) and policy networks which now take an active part in the policy making (Atkinson and Coleman 1992). Devolution of policy authority at sub- and transnational levels has multiplied the points of entry into the political process and increased both the opportunities and the number of societal agents involved, well above the levels reached by past neocorporate solutions (Kettl 2000). This more open policy environment is neatly captured by Howlett (2000) in the figure reported below (*see* Figure 4.1).[2]

The graph highlights changes in three main dimensions of the political process posed by the shift from 'government' to 'governance'. The first concerns the objectives of public policy. Traditional models of government conceived public policy as a means to supply high levels of goods and services. By contrast, governance is committed not only to a low-level provision of goods and services, but also to indirect forms of production involving the private sector – this is indeed the hallmark of Majone's (1997a, 1999) Regulatory State discussed later on. The second aspect concerns the policy instruments employed. Moving from high to low supply of goods and services also entails moving away from state

Figure 4.1: Howlett's (2000) reading of the shift from 'government' to 'governance'

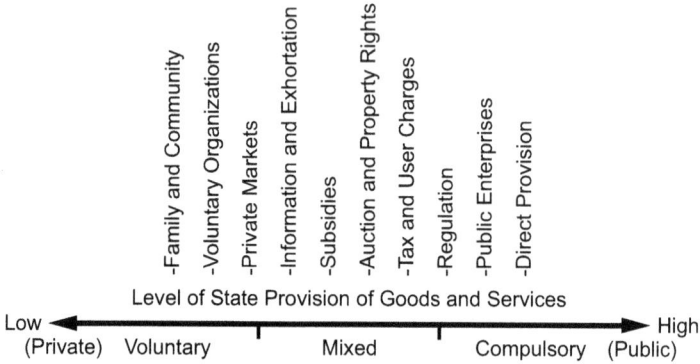

provision towards forms of family and community self-production (Eriksson 2012). Building on the critique of the dependency culture moved against welfare policies by neoliberals (*see* Chapter Two, §2.2.1), governance theory seems to advocate a model of citizenship that wishes to turn citizens, families and local communities into what Ritzer and Jurgenson (2010) aptly call 'prosumers' – consumers called to contribute to the production of the goods and services they want to consume. The third element highlighted by Howlett's graph concerns the normative force of public policy. While government operates through public policies having compulsory power, governance now adopts soft law instruments which solicit instead the voluntary compliance of the individuals, groups and communities affected.

In that same work, Howlett uses the same basic graph reported above to represent the spectrum of policy instruments available to the various agents who now operate within the public realm. The resulting Figure 4.2 highlights three dimensions of public policy, the first of which concerns the level of manipulation sought by the state. High levels of manipulation require the restructuring of institutions and organisations, whereas low levels of manipulation can be carried out through managerial means. According to this scheme, governance follows the neoliberal heavy restructuring of the public sector of the 1980s and early 1990s, and is characterised by a more managerial approach – one whose main goal is to re-establish permanent links between the array of administrative agencies, regulatory authorities, PPPs and policy networks composing the (by now hollowed out) nation state. 'Joined up government' and 'network management' are the expressions that crop up in policy literature to refer to this changed style of governing (Bevir 2010; Rhodes 2000a).

Moving towards this more managerial style of governing entails using more indirect and informal means of social persuasion and consensus building: from granting funds to using focus groups to the suppression of crucial information – what Dunsire (1996) refers to as 'collibration' (*see* Chapter Six, §6.3.3).

Figure 4.2: Howlett's spectrum of procedural policy instruments

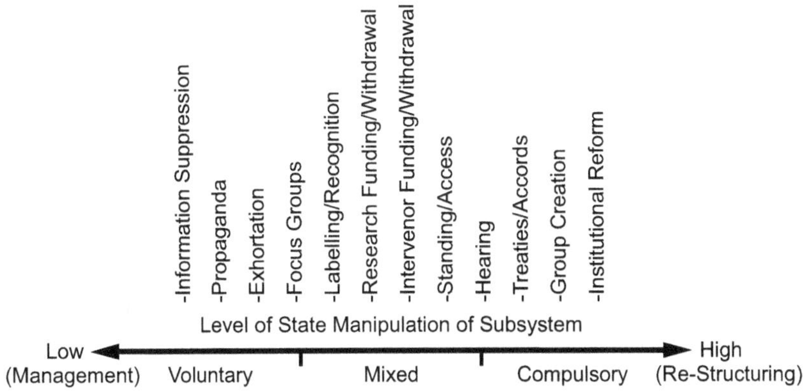

Level of State Manipulation of Subsystem

Low ← → High
(Management) Voluntary | Mixed | Compulsory (Re-Structuring)

Labels on spectrum (left to right): Information Suppression, Propaganda, Exhortation, Focus Groups, Labelling/Recognition, Research Funding/Withdrawal, Intervenor Funding/Withdrawal, Standing/Access, Hearing, Treaties/Accords, Group Creation, Institutional Reform

As seen above, this managerial style rests more on the voluntary compliance of the main societal agents than on the state's ability to impose those measures authoritatively. Tellingly, Howlett (2000: 422) thinks that this managerial turn in public policy is dictated not only by the preoccupation with efficiency gains, but above all with the need to 'construct or regain legitimacy'. From this perspective, governance can be seen as an attempt to halt, or even compensate for, the loss of legitimacy caused by neoliberal restructuring of welfare institutions. The widespread perception is that the changes imposed so far have failed to improve the quality of public goods and services, while the reduction in their quantity has had a negative impact on social inequalities and cohesion. Hence the growing attention of governance theory towards legitimacy issues and meta-theoretical questions (Bekkers *et al.* 2007).

4.2.2. From decision-making to implementation

A second momentous shift promoted by governance studies concerns the greater attentions paid to implementation issues *vis-à-vis* decision making and high politics questions in general. Indeed, policy implementation represents a field of inquiry where governance has focused on uncovering the root cause of government failure and to assess the impact of neoliberal reforms on the democratic legitimacy of the policy process within a hollowed-out nation state (Hill and Hupe 2002). According to governance theorists, government and governance subscribe to two distinct visions of the implementation process. The former supports 'top-down' mechanisms, whereas the latter advocates 'bottom-up' approaches. From a government perspective, implementation is 'an essentially top-down administrative and hierarchical follow on process. Policy, once formulated and legitimated at the "top", or centre, is handed in to the administrative system for execution, and successively refined and translated into operating instructions as it moves down the hierarchy to operatives at the "bottom" of the pyramid' (Barrett 2004: 252). The limits of this conception are several and have been repeated too many times to warrant more than a cursory reappraisal (Ham and Hill 1984: ch. 6).

A first problem concerns the effectiveness of the authority relation underpinning administrative hierarchies. Rational choice theorists maintain that the equilibrium solutions yielded by a hypothetic implementation game could turn out to be not only at odds with those intended by the 'top', but deeply suboptimal (Palumbo 2001). Although doubts have been cast on the epistemic assumptions of rational choice inspired accounts of the implementation game (Bowen 1982), the validity of authority as an effective motivational element seems to require a no less problematic over-socialised model of agency committed to a supererogatory ethos of public service – that is, a spirit of self-abnegation akin to the one depicted in Ishiguro's 1989 novel *The Remains of the Day*. Besides, nothing ensures that the practical judgements of those operating at the bottom of the hierarchy will automatically coincide with the political judgments of those at the top, even if the former are taken to be selfless (Lipsky 1980). Since the perception of middle- and street-level bureaucrats could systematically diverge from that of their political principals whenever problem-solving requires them to exercise their individual discretion, the implementation process is always a relevant source of government failure (Mayntz 1993).

It has indeed been pointed out that soliciting information from those operating at the bottom to improve both delivery and customer satisfaction requires not just sheer conformity with pre-established commands, but a more active engagement with the definition of policy objectives and the identification of the means most suitable to achieve them. This is tantamount to say that there is a likely trade-off between the pressure to 'conform' and the demand to 'perform'. Were this the case, the top-down vision of policy implementation as a politically neutral technical process would turn out to be too simplistic, if not contradictory. As Barrett (2004: 253) writes, 'the political processes by which policy is mediated, negotiated and modified during its formulation continue in the behaviour of those involved in its implementation acting to protect or pursue their own values and interests. Policy may thus be regarded as both a statement of intent by those seeking to change or control behavior, and a negotiated output emerging from the implementation process'. It is this more negotiated and participative type of implementation process that governance theory wishes to engender.

The development of bottom-up forms of policy implementation in the last three decades is directly related not just to the shortcomings of top-down alternatives, but significantly to the institutional changes occurred in the meantime. In this more fragmented policy environment, implementation necessarily requires the collaboration of a variety of administrative agencies and societal agents. Given the structural similarities between the type of interaction taking place at the top and the one developing at the bottom, it is not surprising then to also observe a growing similarity in the dynamics characterising policy making and policy implementation. Both aim at the resolution of complicated social dilemmas and require, therefore, negotiated consensual agreements that can yield horizontal forms of coordination and robust patterns of cooperation. As already mentioned, the switch towards more negotiated and consensual approaches to policy implementation has, in turn, meant the preferential selection of some policy tools above others. Far from relying on compulsory forms of compliance backed up by legal sanctions, effective policy implementation is now viewed as demanding innovation, collaboration and creativity (Kassim and Le Galès 2010).

Underpinning current research in policy implementation and drives towards bottom-up approaches are also ideological reasons that need to be highlighted. Neoliberal narratives explain the allegedly scarce attention traditional policy analysis paid to implementation dynamics as a paradigmatic example of the limitations affecting Keynsianism and, by extension, all worldviews that claim democratic politics and welfare policies indispensable for social change. In fact, O'Toole (2004: 313) notes that behind the Reagan Administration's enthusiastic support of implementation research there was an ideological rationale, 'more studies would reveal more failures and more reasons why programs cannot be expected to achieve, thus catalysing support for shrinking the agenda of government'. In other words, implementation issues are often part and parcel of neoliberal attempts to dismiss political and moral arguments for state intervention on feasibility grounds. Ideological undertones also characterise current debates between those who support bottom-up approaches against top-down alternatives. As O'Toole (2004: 314) explains,

> top-downers and bottom-uppers differ not just on some key puzzles of empirical theory [...], and not simply on matters of research methods [...], but also of normative orientation. Top-down analysts often express themselves clearly in support of a representative regime and the consistent execution of choices made by political leaders. [...] Bottom-up analysts, on the other hand, abjure the virtues of complex overhead representational schemes and endorse the emergence of meaningful policy effort in the discretionary choices of actors, including non governmental actors, far from the oversight of political principals.

As we will see below, the two further advocate distinct conceptions of legitimacy, with the bottom-uppers favouring often substantive criteria over the procedural forms employed by top-downers.

The divisions between the different strands that compose the bottom-up camp are, however, no less interesting or profound, raising awkward theoretical questions about the validity of the various accounts of change found in governance studies and their normative, as opposed to descriptive, nature. As I try to show in the next section, this body of work has emerged at the confluence of two main streams of policy research that find their source and inspiration in distinct theoretical worldviews. Thus, they tend to differ in regard to both the epistemic and normative values that drive these scientific enterprises. Understanding these values is, therefore, crucial to appreciate and assess the contribution of governance theory as both an analytical framework concerned with explaining political and institutional change and a justificatory framework interested in influencing its direction and pace.

4.3. Modeling governance: conceptual innovations and distinctions

Conceptually, governance theory has supplied two main typologies. The first derives mainly from organisational, managerial and administrative fields, and is based on network forms of organisation. Governance is here taken to identify a shifting political interest from institutional arrangements, based on hierarchical command-and-control strategies (government) and from neoliberal contractual solutions (market) to network forms of organisation (Börzel 2011). Hence, the label 'network governance'. The second conception finds currency in political science, European studies and international relations and focuses instead on the momentous transformations undergoing national sovereignty. Governance deals here with the re-articulation of national authority between the state and a growing number of territorial and functional jurisdictions located above, beneath and beside it (Hooghe and Marks 2003). Hence, the expression 'multilevel governance'. In this section, I explore the content of these two forms of governance by focusing on both the methodological tenets and normative implications these tenets are claimed to have.

4.3.1. Network governance

What is the importance of network theory for political science and governance theory in particular? In my view, it is twofold. The first is empirical and aims at supplying a more accurate account of political and institutional change which has occurred over the last three decades. The second is more normative in that it aims at supplying a theoretical platform for evaluating, and possibly influencing, the direction of change. Empirically, the evidence political scientists confront indicates that since the early 1980s multiple processes of change have transformed the institutions, tools and goals of governing. In the first place, the traditional divide between public and private has progressively lost its relevance and with it the hierarchies that used to monopolise the policy process. This is now carried out by constellations of networks composed of old-fashioned bureaux, newly-constituted regulatory agencies, corporations and non-governmental organisations (NGOs). As a result, the political process does not rely on command-and-control techniques backed up by the state's power of sanction, but on complex deliberative procedures, often informal and lacking strong enforcement power (Hajer and Wagenaar 2003). In this context, governing does not aim at regulating the economy from without, but focuses on network management – the non-invasive steering of societal agents through soft law and a revised system of incentives (Kooiman 2003).

Like the capitalist firm, the state seems to have undergone a process of dematerialisation-cum-delocation. Thus, governments now tend to operate as strategic managerial boards. As such, traditional methods and concerns which used to dominate political science find themselves obsolete or in need of radical revision. First, at national level the formal institutions of the state cease to be the locus of decision and action (Strange 1996). For, it is societal agents operating beyond parliament and central government that have become crucial for the policy process (Rhodes 1997). Equally, at the international level. Here both intergovernmentalism and regime theory are felt as outdated approaches for understanding world affairs and the dynamics of change unfolding therein (Rosenau 1992). National states and their diplomatic harms are no longer the main protagonists; they have been supplanted by the agents of an emerging global civil society (Slaughter 2003). Governance theory attempts to supply a rationalisation of these multiform processes of change extolling the virtues of network forms of organisation *vis-à-vis* markets and hierarchies (Thompson 2003). In doing so, it supplies competing accounts of change, each with its own reading of networks as both explanatory categories and normative solutions.

Since Coase's seminal work on the firm, political economists have suggested viewing all social institutions as lying along a continuum, whose ideal poles are hierarchies and markets (Williamson and Winter 1993). Following Granovetter (1985), economic and political sociologists have supplied a revised account of social institutions, which turn political economy's linear dichotomy into a bi-dimensional space with three poles of attraction (*see* Figure 3.8 in Chapter Three). Beside hierarchies and markets, sociologists identify a third distinct ideal-typical pole: network forms of organisation (Powell 1990). As already explained (*see* Chapter Three, §3.3) network form of organisation is a persistent, high density and informal system of exchange between embedded social agents. As an organisational form, networks are characterised by three main features. First, in a network, roles and functions are performed voluntarily, thus they are more flexible than those established by hierarchies, but less transient than market relations. Second, as tools of social coordination, networks do not depend on codified procedures or on market prices. Coordination is instead assured through dialogical social practices wherein people and groups have the opportunity to express their opinions, revise their preferences and beliefs, and reach collectively binding deliberations regarding the course of action to undertake. Finally, networks supply a system of individual incentives other than those employed by hierarchies and markets. Whereas bureaucracies base labour relationships on seniority and impartiality, networks tend to reward reputation and personal loyalty; whereas markets rest on crude monetary incentives, networks appeal to non monetary forms of exchange like those found in the gift economy. In short, 'networks are an alternative to, not a hybrid of, markets and hierarchies and they span the boundaries of the public, private and voluntary sectors' (Rhodes 1997: 52). Thus, they represent a genuine institutional ideal-type which the analytical framework supplied by political economists fail to capture. This makes political economy unsuitable as a general theory of social organisations and also casts doubts on its ability to account for the institutional innovations brought about by the post-Fordist restructuring of capitalist economies. Hence the current interests in a revised institutionalist approach based on a thicker model of agency.

Networks remain, however, part and parcel of wider attempts to expand the methodological individualism developed in political economy into non-market domain (Coleman 1994). In this context, they play the role of heuristic categories that help explain the emergence of spontaneous forms of social cooperation between self-concerned rational agents interacting in non-cooperative settings. Network effects and externalities are used to account for actual behavioural regularities and social institutions that would otherwise be left beyond the explicatory power of neo-classic economics. The aim of the various theorists engaged in this enterprise is obviously not that of overcoming the research programme of political economy. To use Lakatos's vocabulary, they rather wish to protect its 'hard core' from refutation by modifying some of the elements that constitute its 'protective belt', and reinforcing its descriptive power. The same can be argued about the notions of trust and social capital recently emerged in the social sciences. These too represent theoretical categories employed by political economists to support their attempts at economic imperialism (Rothschild 2008). Even more remarkable is the fact that these competing paradigms (political economy and economic sociology) are criss-crossed by similar internal tensions and fault lines separating those who stress the epistemic relevance of social institutions and those who focus instead on processes and social dynamics. Thus, as we shall see later on, in some cases analysts urge to distinguish between 'network governance' and 'governance networks' (*see* Chapter Six, §6.3.1), while in others it is suggested that 'regulatory capitalism' (Braithwaite 2008) represents a better heuristic category than the Regulatory State (*see* Chapter Five, §5.3).

The normative frameworks advanced by these contrasting perspectives have attempted to explicate the comparative advantages of network governance and help promote further and better institutional innovations. Normatively, the main claims put forward by governance theorists are two. The first concerns the superiority of soft law instruments *vis-à-vis* traditional statute law (Mörth 2004). Following Nonet and Selznick (1978), governance theory perceives statute law as an inflexible and ineffective tool of social regulation: it is too remote from the people and situations it aspires to regulate, and shows a remarkably cavalier attitude towards the complexities related to its enforcement. As an alternative, network governance uses regulatory tools that 'rely on broad framework agreements, flexible norms and revisable standards; and use benchmarks, indicators and peer review to ensure accountability' (Trubek and Trubek 2006: 541). The second concern of governance theory goes beyond legality and focuses instead on the question of legitimacy mentioned before. Modern liberal democracies justify coercive power, and the authority of those who are called to exercise it, by means of formal procedures regulating the decision and policy-making processes and the selection mechanisms for legislators and public officers. Since it is the fairness and impartiality of these procedures that define their legitimacy, democratic legitimation is claimed to be mainly procedural and of *ex ante* nature (Dahl 1979).

Governance theory has highlighted the shortcomings of both the exclusive reliance of the modern nation state on legality and the formalistic and procedural type of democratic legitimacy upon which liberal democracies rest. Procedural correctness never guarantees substantive justice and it can often prove to be a burden for the policy process. Thus, in network governance the emphasis shifts away from 'input-oriented' modes of legitimacy towards 'output-oriented' forms of legitimacy directly concerned with 'substantive criteria of *buon governo*' (Scharpf 1997: 153). As I shall discuss in the next section, such a shift also entails a revision of the criteria of accountability inherited from liberal democratic thought. Whereas liberal democratic models of government rest on vertical lines of accountability, network governance relies on more horizontal and managerial solutions – above all peer review-monitoring systems. In Sabel and Simon (2006: 402) words,

> peer review imposes on implementing 'agents' the obligation to justify the exercise of discretion they have been granted by framework-making 'principals' in the light of pooled comparable experience. In peer review, the actors at all levels learn from and correct each other, thus undermining the hierarchical distinction between principals and agents and creating a form of dynamic accountability – accountability that anticipates the transformation of rules in use. Dynamic accountability becomes the means of controlling discretion when that control cannot be hard wired into the rules of hierarchy.

4.3.2. Multilevel governance

To disentangle multilevel governance from network governance is not an easy task. The literature on these subjects derives from separate disciplinary fields, rather than clear-cut analytical distinctions. This has led to the charge that the two labels basically identify the same thing and are thus responsible for increasing conceptual complexity and causing confusion in the process (Peters and Pierre 2002). From my perspective, a case for keeping them analytically distinct and meaningful can be made if we connect multilevel governance to questions regarding sovereignty, rather than administrative and organisational issues.[3] According to this perspective, multilevel governance does not deal with the restructuring of governmental institutions *per se*, but with the consequence that this restructuring has had (or is having) for the traditional notion of sovereignty as the locus of legitimate political power. It is from this angle that the discussion will be carried out here. To do this, a few words are first required to explain what I mean by the traditional conception of sovereignty.

Since Hobbes, sovereignty has been tied to the authority of the modern state (Sassen 2006). Such a state-centric notion of sovereignty is at the core of the Westphalian system of international relations that has dominated world affairs for the last three centuries. Within the Westphalian system, the state is sovereign in two ways: first, it has the monopoly of legitimate force in a given territory; second, it enjoys the exclusive power of representing the subjects living within that territory. Analytically, the features that characterise the Westphalian notion of sovereignty are the following. First, 'territoriality' as the primary ordering principle: that is, the belief in the possibility of dividing the crust of the earth into discreet entities each of which represents a homogeneous and autonomous political space. Second, 'hierarchy' as the most effective organisational criterion: in short, the idea that government is to be structured as a system of nested authorities to avoid contradictory and conflicting claims which could affect both the certainty of law and the individual's ability to comply with it. Third, 'formalism' as the main mode of administration: namely, the tendency to manage the public affairs of territorial sublevels by means of permanent jurisdictions having universal competence and reach. Lastly, 'exclusivity' as an associational value: in essence, a generalised hostility towards overlapping systems of authority and multiple loyalties.

Domestic political principles of this type yield an international arena lacking sovereignty. In this context, the resolution of collective action problems connected to (a) externalities, (b) the management of global commons or (c) conflicting territorial claims is demanded of freely established contractual agreements negotiated between national governments. International law is thus viewed as the outcome of intergovernmental bargaining whose effectiveness rest entirely on the voluntary compliance of its subscribers. The shortcomings of intergovernmentalism periodically stimulates calls for a world government that could extend the template of the modern state to the international arena in some form of planetary vertical integration (Held 2010). In the course of the twentieth century, these aspirations eventually caused the consolidation of various international 'regimes' that went beyond intergovernmentalism (Hasenclever *et al.* 1997). By and large, however, they failed to undermine the state-centric notion of sovereignty upon which the Westphalian system of international relations was grounded (Waltz 1999).

Multilevel governance is used to describe the governing tools and concepts for a post-Westphalian political order; an order where state sovereignty has been undermined domestically and internationally but no comparable substitute to fill this gap has as yet appeared, or will ever appear. As Strange (1995: 56) puts it, 'state authority has leaked away, upwards, sideways, and downwards. In some matters, it seems even to have gone nowhere, just evaporated. The realm of anarchy in society and economy has become more extensive as that of all kinds of authority has diminished'. The analytical features that characterise the sovereignty of a multilevel body politic are in many ways the reverse of those used to describe its Westphalian counterpart. On the one hand, there is a significant rescaling of territorial space as an ordering principle (Sassen 2006). This rescaling is required by two sets of changes. First, decentralisation and devolution policies have eroded the internal unity and coherence of the nation state making it increasingly polycentric, while the rise of regional authorities and the consolidation of transnational regimes has blurred the boundaries between state and non-state actors. Second, crucial political functions (i.e. policy making, implementation and enforcement) have been progressively attributed (or contracted out) to a host of autonomous agencies (quangos) and NGOs, thus blurring the public/private divide. On the other hand, the adoption of more experimental and heterarchical administrative tools is necessitated by the restructuring of the policy process along functional, rather than territorial, lines (Hooghes and Marks 2001). The multilevel body politic is now composed of multiple and variable jurisdictions created to pursue specific administrative goals. Their remit and lifespan is related to the accomplishment of those goals, thus making the overall number of jurisdictions fluctuate accordingly. In this context, authorities overlap as a matter of course, while affiliation takes on pluralistic features and allows citizens and local communities to interact globally without the intermediation of central authorities – forming what Jessop (1997) calls 'intermestic' policy regimes.

The arena where multilevel governance has found its most fertile application is the European Union (EU). In its attempt to carry the process of integration forward without clashing with national governments, the EU has experimented with new forms of regulation aimed at freeing the policy process from its dependence on fiscal tools and command-and-control strategies. Moreover, the impossibility to impose new taxes, from which it derives its revenue, has pushed the EU to develop novel means of political intervention directed at eliminating the obstacles opposing European-wide market integration (Majone 1997a). The resulting 'negative integration' approach has relied on a European jurisprudence and system of courts which parallels that of the Member States, but lacks the enforcement powers of the latter. The implementation and enforcement of EU resolutions have thus been carried out by involving national and local authorities directly in the policy process. To do this effectively, the EU has favoured the employment of: 'common guidelines to be translated into national policy, combined with periodic monitoring, evaluation and peer review organised as mutual learning process and accompanied by indicators and benchmarks as means of comparing best practice' (Borrás and Jacobsson 2004: 188). Similarly, the EU has attempted to bypass national parliaments as sources of democratic legitimation by developing new forms of political engagement (Sabel and Zeitlin 2008). Each step of the policy process in various areas has seen the involvement of a myriad of committees composed of experts, national representatives, euro-bureaucrats and NGOs, setting in motion what is distinctively a European 'open method of coordination' (Christiansen and Larsson 2007). Criticism against the technocratic and somewhat secretive nature of the comitology system have, in turn, been met by 'open government' initiatives and extended form of consultations with civil society associations. The EU has not been just a large-scale laboratory for those interested in demonstrating the viability, or otherwise, of multilevel governance, but also a model for other less developed regional entities and for the future institutions of global governance alike (Slaughter 2003).

Even in relation to the notion of multilevel governance, attention needs to be paid to two main features that characterise this research field. The first concerns the fact that, like network governance, this is another heuristic category that blends explicatory and prescriptive elements; aspects that for analytical clarity is, once again, necessary to keep separate. As I shall argue next, the validity of this heuristic category for understanding the effects change is having on sovereignty does not depend on the validity of the justificatory strategies deployed. So, distinct criteria need to be devised for assessing explanatory and justificatory endeavours. A second, but no less relevant, feature to keep in mind is that the narratives of change proposed depend on the epistemic outlook of each approach and tend, therefore, to diverge significantly. As I endeavour to show next, in governance studies the theorists of the Regulatory State view negative integration dynamics as part of a larger tendency to restrict public intervention to hands-off forms of economic regulation and justify this systemic shift instrumentally. By contrast, theorists of the Networked Polity prefer to emphasise the transformation undergone by the old comitology system into a form of deliberative supranationalism and link the justification of the latter to the empowerment assured by emerging sets of interlinked dialogical policy environments.

4.4. The Regulatory State vs. the Networked Polity: confronting accounts of change

As already hinted, it is possible to identify two distinct research programmes contributing to governance studies. Broadly speaking, one is derived from what Inman (1987) calls the 'New' Political Economy (NPE), whereas the other builds upon sociological perspectives antithetical to this scientific paradigm (Hollis 1977). Notwithstanding the fact that both deal with the same empirical evidence, deep down their accounts of change tend to differ. The former suggest seeing recent political and institutional change as an attempt to consolidate the enterprise culture of the 1980s (Greene *et al.* 2008). By contrast, the latter present it as the outcome of decentralised attempts to solve the policy mess caused by neoliberal reforms of big government (Rhodes 2000b). Methodological divergences end up shaping their normative outlook as well. One claims that the outcome of three decades of restructuring of the public sector is a Regulatory State committed to a form of Madisonian democracy. The other suggest that the upshot is rather a Networked Polity engaged in large-scale democratic experiments – experiments that are undermining traditional liberal divisions between state and civil society, domestic and international domains, high and low politics (Ansell 2000). In clarifying the features that distinguish these two research programmes, I maintain that any assessment of the accounts of change proposed needs to consider both (i) their heuristic value as analytical frameworks and (ii) their normative adequacy as justificatory frameworks.

4.4.1. Regulatory State and Networked Polity as analytical frameworks

As analytical frameworks, the accounts inspired by NPE are grounded on a disembedded model of agency and equilibrium analyses emphasising the positive role of monetary incentives and competitive dynamics. Those derived from sociological paradigms assume a socially embedded model of agency and stress the positive role played by non-monetary incentives and relations of trust. This has noteworthy implications concerning the strategies invoked to assure horizontal coordination. One side views the market as the main institutional device capable of solving the dilemmas affecting the decentralised actions of strategic (collective and individual) actors and thus presses for the mandatory disclosure of information and the promotion of the individual's freedom to choose (Le Grand 1991a). By contrast, the other side retains network forms of organisation superior solutions to markets and support the dialogical engagement of those affected by the political process at both policy-making and policy implementation levels. In other words, the Regulatory State adopts refined versions of the classical *homo oeconomicus* endowed with a set of well-defined and self-originating preferences, whereas the model of agency underpinning the Networked Polity is embedded in a myriad of social relations that shape its desires and beliefs accordingly. The first also views social institutions and practices as strategic equilibria between maximising individual agents and tends to treat individual action as invariant across institutional domains. The second is committed to highlight the non-contractual elements upon which economic life rests. From this Durkheimian perspective, it is the very existence (or absence) of dense social networks surrounding the individual that explains: (a) its power to establish and maintain cooperative relations in highly uncertain social settings; (b) its relative success in actual existing markets *vis-à-vis* other competing individuals and groups; (c) its ability to coordinate without centrally imposed and sanctioned directives.

The narratives of change proposed are likewise at odds with each other. The aim of the Regulatory State is threefold: (1) to focus on regulatory activities, rather than Keynesian stabilisation policies; (2) to assume a strategic steering role within a dynamic market society, rather than that of main provider of goods and services and engine for economic growth; (3) to promote an entrepreneurial working ethos that would enable individuals and local communities to take responsibility for their own fate, rather than paternalistic attitudes reinforcing a perverse welfare dependency culture. In short, the Regulatory State represents an attempt to refine, consolidate and accomplish the restructuring of state institutions initiated by Thatcher and Reagan. Behind the Networked Polity there is, on the contrary, a narrative that stresses the discontinuities between neoliberal reforms of big government carried out since the late 1970s, and the subsequent evolution of the political process. At an institutional level, the growth and pre-eminence of network forms of organisation is accounted for as the result of several attempts to recompose the fragmented political landscape from the bottom up. The Networked Polity is thus presented as the embodiment of an alternative 'third way' to both state and market solutions – a pragmatic attempt to transcend the ideological divisions fueling the political imaginary of modernity. Far from being a short cut to the market or a form of compassionate neoliberalism, as imputed by critics, this pragmatic third way is proposed as an effective means for the renewal of social democracy in a post-modern global age (Giddens 1998). Although these narratives are predicated upon political ideals which make them rather value-laden (Schwarzmantel 2005), I think it interesting to confront these two accounts of change by assessing their heuristic power as analytical frameworks in the first place.

To start with, both frameworks have been the object of strong criticism concerning the very idea that the power of the state has been undermined so much that its ability to reclaim sovereignty internally and externally is now permanently affected (*see* Chapter Seven). Thus, in his review of Regulatory State literature, Moran (2003: 6) argues that,

> after the great crisis of the 1970s, the state in Britain did indeed scale down many of its central ambitions, but [...] it also acquired some startling new ones. [...] the turn to a regulatory mode also greatly widened the range of social and economic life that was subject to public power. The Regulatory State is a colonizing state with its own utopian projects quite as ambitious as those that characterized Scott's high modernism. And the image of a turn from command is [...] hard to reconcile with the growth of a vastly expanded apparatus of surveillance and control within the public sector [...] and with the transformation of self-regulation [...] where the direction of change has been towards more hierarchy, more formality, and more state control.

A similar assessment is put forward by Jayasuriya (2004: 490), 'dispersal of governance and the consequent segmentation of the state does not necessarily lead to the weakening of the executive. In fact, the "core executive" of the state takes on a pivotal role as the coordinator of metagovernance [...] the decentring of the "state" is paralleled by a concentration of executive power within the new Regulatory State'. And on this position also end in convergence Levi-Faur and Gilad (2004: 116), who notice both the strategic aims behind state regulation and its success in extending the control of central government over institutional ambits that post-war welfare developments unwittingly emancipated (i.e. local government, NHS, public education, etc.) or social contexts that somehow managed to escape welfare consolidation (i.e. professions, mutuals, charities, etc.): ' [...] the state did not lose control, but it rather centralized a control it never possessed. The increase in relational distance between regulators and regulatees was intentionally constructed as a tool of centralisation'.

These remarks on the heuristic shortcomings of the Regulatory State are often accompanied by invitations to move beyond the rational choice perspectives influencing regulation studies to adopt a more socio-centric perspective. In my opinion, this is welcome given the limitations shown by the economic readings of politics advanced by NPE to date (Green and Shapiro 1994), and the shortcomings of the neoliberal prescriptions derived from those readings (Self 1993). However, it is also somewhat problematic, for the sociological approaches supporting the idea of Networked Polity are, heuristically speaking, even less reliable. An emerging second generation of governance theorists, less mesmerised by the explicatory power of networks and networking activities, is casting serious doubts on the main claims put forward by the generation who started this field of inquiry: (i) the 'hollowed-out state' thesis, (ii) the shift from a re-structuring to a managerial approach, and (iii) the overall relevance attributed to the very idea of 'governing without government' (Bell and Hindmoor 2009; Davies 2011). *Pace* Rhodes (1997), the crucial question that these theorists are raising is not simply about which actors initiated and have supported the various waves of reform carried out during *les trente furieuses*. Rather, they question both the conceptual soundness and empirical validity of the notion of unintended consequences upon which the whole idea of Networked Polity is predicated. If the functional explanations employed to account for the rise of new forms of agency and policy instruments are highly controversial, then the attempts to connect the alleged passage from 'government' to 'governance' to the electoral fortunes of political parties with different complexions are even less convincing (Bevir 2010).

To begin with, those supporting the notion of Networked Polity tend to focus almost exclusively on alleged instances of 'governance *without* government', neglecting to consider the relative importance of alternative phenomena that can be identified as 'governance *of* government' and 'government *with* government' (Sørensen 2004). And in doing so, they also underplay the fact that 'governance *without* government' always unfolds 'in the shadow of hierarchy' (Scharpf 1997: ch. 9). As argued by Jessop (2003), networks and networking activities are as prone to failure as their market and bureaucratic counterparts to be the outcome of social selection mechanisms rewarding their relative advantage. Moreover, across OECD countries, neoliberal and 'third way' governments seem to share similar principles of action, systems of beliefs and attitudes to employ identical policy instruments to make what are described as 'global' and 'epochal' transformations dependent on the vagaries of electoral politics (Crouch 2011). As a working hypothesis about long-term political trends, the Networked Polity is, therefore, either unsupported by the available empirical evidence, or based on an improper generalisation of restricted empirical evidence (Hill and Lynn 2005). Thus, despite the limitations of the Regulatory State, heuristically the Networked Polity represents a much more problematic analytical framework in that it exacerbates some of the weaknesses affecting the former.

I contend that a more nuanced account of the alleged passage from 'government' to 'governance' is required, and that the analytical framework supplied by the more critical readings of the Regulatory State represents a good base for doing this (*see* Chapter Five). At an explanatory level, this revised account needs to pay more attention to two aspects: (i) the ways in which seemingly antithetical policy tools can be strategically used by diverse state actors pursuing their own political objectives, and (ii) how in their interaction with other societal agents those policy tools can reinforce the domination of those very state actors – rather than engender individual choice or empower civil society, as it is often claimed. To this end, I advance two assertions which will be fully substantiated in the following chapters. First, that the outcome of the various waves of reform undertaken in the last *trente furieuses* have in reality promoted a dual dynamic of political centralisation-cum-administrative decongestion that has reinforced the power of core executive institutions *vis-à-vis* their legislative counterparts. Second, I claim that the Regulatory State paradigm could account for this dual dynamic if its analytic focus switched towards the meta-game wherein the regulatory game unfolds, so as to consider the ability of state actors to play at both constitutional and post-constitutional levels, occupy several positions at once and switch roles at will.

It must, however, be noted that this revision would undermine the justificatory role attributed to the Regulatory State and cast doubts on its ability to promote its own alternative forms of legitimacy (Bader 2010). As Somers (2011: 30) explains,

> 'market-driven governance', [...] is not simply the use of market incentives; rather, it entails an institutional complex of political interventions and public policies which in no way are driven by actual free market practices. It is a hybrid mix of free market ideology, in tandem with government-driven market interventions and legal arrangements that redistribute wealth upwards. Market driven governance only exposes the poor and the middle class to real market discipline. Wealth and capital, by contrast, is fully supported by state and government regulations that make market outcomes predetermined in their favor. The genius and the alchemy of market-driven governance is that it puts a heavy political thumb on the societal scales, while behind the veil of free market ideology it appears that the rigged outcomes are actually the natural results of the free market at work.

I argue that such a dynamic will inevitably cause the rising of Polanyian counter-movements challenging this state of affairs and the consensus politics supporting it (*see* Conclusion). The various crises emerged since 2008 could be taken as an indication of the empirical weaknesses affecting the justificatory framework of the Regulatory State and of the need to develop a proper normative analysis of the policy instruments endorsed by governance theorists.

4.4.2. Regulatory State and Networked Polity as justificatory frameworks

That both the Regulatory State and the Networked Polity are not merely Weberian ideal-types, but also normative ideals akin to those employed by political theorists, is acknowledged by their advocates as well. On this point, Majone is explicit: 'the Regulatory State is (also) a *normative* idea, it could help assess, as well as intervene into, real existing political administrative systems' (La Spina and Majone 2000: 38, emphasis in original). Since the supporters of the Networked Polity subscribe to post-positivistic epistemologies, this acknowledgment is stated in a reverse form. For them, the Networked Polity must be understood, 'Not just as a normative statement of how we would like to see the relation between citizens and the state, but also, and more importantly, as an empirical observation of the direction things take in contemporary society' (Hajer and Wagenaar 2003: 24). According to their advocates, the Regulatory State and the Networked Polity pursue an identical goal – to boost the legitimacy of real existing liberal democracies, even if they impute the risk of a legitimation crisis to diverse sets of phenomena: the problems of ungovernability affecting welfare institutions in one case; the institutional fragmentation caused by reforms of big government in the other. The justificatory frameworks proposed by these two research programmes deal with three nested questions, with decreasing levels of abstraction, concerning (a) the type of legitimacy that needs to be boosted, (b) the kind of democratic vision more apt to do this in pluralist societies and (c) the mechanisms of accountability through which this goal can be achieved. I shall discuss each of them in turn.

Legitimacy. From the growing body of literature produced so far in governance studies, we can discern two main directions in the search for answers to the alleged legitimacy deficit of actually existing democratic regimes. The first adopts a rational choice account that attributes the difficulties of the post-war consensus to its reliance on procedural values. Accordingly, a three-pronged course of action is suggested: (i) developing a more effective problem-solving strategic attitude; (ii) adopting flexible policy instruments and forms of organisation; (iii) importing managerial techniques used in the private sector into the public sector. As already mentioned, the intention is to move from what Scharpf (2000) calls an 'input-oriented' mode of legitimacy to an alternative 'output-oriented' mode concerned with the effective delivery of public goods and services. Moravcsik (2002: 614, emphasis in original) explains the virtues of output-oriented notions of legitimacy thus: 'first is *the need for greater attention, efficiency and expertise in areas where most citizens remain "rationally ignorant" or non-participatory.* [...] Second is *the need impartially to dispense justice, equality and rights for individuals and minority groups.* [...] Third is *the need to provide majorities with unbiased representation*'.

The reverse solution is sought by those stressing the democratic potential of the Networked Polity as a dialogic policy environment. From this perspective, the switch from 'government' to 'governance' opens the political process in several ways. First, it overcomes rigid liberal distinctions between state and civil society, so as to give the latter access into institutional domains which were previously the exclusive field of technocratic bodies (i.e. policy making and implementation). Second, it introduces novel forms of representation that could complement the electoral ones traditionally employed by liberal democracies (i.e. descriptive forms of representation and stakeholdership). Finally, deliberative engagement in the policy process makes it possible to establish feedback mechanisms that can remove obstructions in the information flows between centre and periphery that are responsible for government failure (i.e. excessive expectations and institutional capture). As Warren (2009: 8) clarifies, 'the strategy amounts to a functional compensation for the low global legitimacy of electoral democracy by generating legitimacy 'locally' – issue by issue, policy by policy, and constituency by constituency'.[4]

Democracy. Evidently, these diverging understandings of legitimacy support distinct conceptions of democracy. Hirschman (1970) supplies the analytical vocabulary for shedding light on these different visions. Those supporting the consolidation of a Regulatory State share the objective of promoting mechanisms of *exit* that will give citizens the ability to 'vote with their feet'. This entails setting constitutional constraints on central government by territorial, functional and fiscal forms of decentralisation which would allow prosumers to move across jurisdictions and in so doing develop forms of interjurisdictional competition (Vanberg 2000). This solution would not only make democratic politics compatible with the market mechanism, but it would also avoid getting entangled in the collective action problems yielded by any instrumental evaluation of policy decisions at group level. As Somin (2011: 211) puts it,

> foot voters don't need comparably detailed knowledge. It is enough for them to know that conditions are better in one state than another, and then be able to act on this knowledge by moving. So long as public officials themselves know that their policies can affect social conditions in ways that attract foot voters, they will have an incentive to implement better policies in order to appeal to potential migrants. Not only does foot voting create a stronger incentive to acquire knowledge than ballot box voting, it also usually requires less knowledge to implement effectively.

The Networked Polity camp appeals instead to deliberative conceptions of democracy that seek to establish channels of *voice* able to give all affected interests the power to influence the policy process. Engendering this democratic model requires three main steps: (i) the adoption of a more self-reflexive policy approach, (ii) the construction of a more participatory political environment and (iii) the development of an active form of citizenship. Hence, the welcome with which diverse types of democratic experimentation are greeted, and the encouragement given to the deliberative activities of mini-publics at local, national, regional and international levels. Once again, Warren (2009: 8) spells out the rationale of these developments, 'elected governments have become increasingly aware that electoral legitimacy does not translate into policy-specific legitimacy. Thus, legislation has for some time directed agencies to establish processes for "public input" or required "community representation" during policy development. From this perspective, governance-driven democratization is supplementary to electoral democracy – shoring up its functional weaknesses'.

Accountability. The criticisms moved against proceduralism and hierarchy as organising principles have deep implications for the notions of accountability established in the post-war.[5] Building upon the iron logic of the agency theory supplied by NPE, supporters of the Regulatory State argue for a neat separation between strategic and administrative functions and for the development of managerial forms of accountability (*see* Chapter Nine). The latter combine two forms of control and supervision. The first, often labeled as 'performance accountability' (Bevir 2010: 33ff), is characterised by the definition of substantive standards of evaluations useful to indicate whether policy objectives were achieved effectively and efficiently. The second, identified as 'horizontal accountability' (O'Donnell 1998), refers to the supervision carried out by a growing number of regulatory agencies established by those who retain strategic policy power. Here, individual problem-solving abilities are allowed to bypass lines of authority and procedures that could obstruct or delay the accomplishment of given policy objectives. The main goal of managers is, in turn, no longer viewed as that of cultivating a mythical public service ethos (du Gay 2000), but of satisfying the wishes of their sponsors. External controls are, finally, carried out by authorities who are not hierarchically linked to the entities under scrutiny in semi-juridical ways and by using quasi-legal means (Power 1997b).

Rejecting the analyses based on agency theory, the theorists of the Networked Polity support the need to overcome the traditional distinction between 'enactment' and 'enforcement' (Sabel and Simon 2006). This leads them to support only the second of the two new forms of accountability sought by their counterpart, wishing to replace the first with what can be called 'downward accountability' (Scott 2000). The differences between 'downward' and 'performance-based' forms of accountability are subtle but considerable, for they reflect the diverse relevance attributed to competitive dynamics and dialogical cooperation by their respective advocates. If those in charge of delivery need to be made accountable to those whose interests are going to be affected, then engendering accountability means establishing channels of voice open to various stakeholders, in particular those at the bottom for whom public goods and services are crucial, rather than to political sponsors only. Subtly diverse also is the support given to the notion of horizontal accountability. In a Networked Polity, its function is that of embedding regulatory authorities in civil society by transforming them into a multiform population of mini-publics engaged in constantly revising and fleshing out serially and dialogically the constitutional framework of a pluralist society (Bevir 2006).

Which of these two justificatory frameworks is more appealing? Obviously, there is no easy answer to such a question. From my perspective, any assessment needs to consider the matter by using the three criteria of evaluation suggested by Hamlin and Pettit (1989): (a) desirability, (b) electability and (c) feasibility. My opinion is that on all three counts, the Networked Polity is a superior justificatory framework than the Regulatory State. This is due, to a large extent, to the weaknesses affecting the latter. In the first place, the supporters of the Regulatory State base their utilitarian calculations on allegedly value-free notions of social optimality that are utterly inconsistent with their principled defence of pluralism. Secondly, they maintain a remarkably cavalier attitude towards the question of social justice and a mystical faith in the catallactic power of the market mechanism. Finally, if the evaluation arrived at above concerning the higher plausibility of the Regulatory State as an analytical framework is at all sound, then we need to conclude that its feasibility is also deeply questionable.

The financial crisis that started in 2008 and is now engulfing various social and institutional domains across all advanced liberal democracies could indeed be used as empirical evidence of its actual shortcomings. The various attempts to engender features of the Regulatory State seem to have aggravated the accountability gap that affected past welfare institutions. Moreover, they have developed perverse competitive dynamics which have further undermined the political effectiveness of representative democracy, reinforcing the risk of a systemic legitimation crisis.

In reversing the assessment proposed above concerning the heuristic power of our research programmes, I wish however to stress that this evaluation does not amount to a full endorsement of the Networked Polity either. Rather, my claim is that, insofar as the latter's superiority is restricted to its more prescriptive elements, we need to revise the picture of the Networked Polity offered by its many advocates. First of all, it needs to be recognised that far from being 'an empirical observation of the direction things take in contemporary society', the Networked Polity is primarily 'a normative statement of how we would like to see the relation between citizens and the state' (Hajer and Wagenaar 2003: 24). Second, I maintain that a proper normative analysis of the various aspects of the Networked Polity needs to be developed so as to test its desirability, electability and feasibility.

4.5. Conclusions

The chapter has analysed both the content and the presuppositions of governance theory from the perspective of political theory. In acknowledging the usefulness of this term for rationalising the variegated sets of reforms carried out in the last *trente furieuses*, I have attempted to: (i) explicate the policy innovations brought about by (or often imputed to) the passage from 'government' to 'governance'; (ii) clarify the analytical differences between network governance and multi-level governance; (iii) distinguish between the various approaches that compose this heterogeneous field of studies. In tilling this field, my main concern has been twofold. First, I tried to spell out the implications that the shift to governance entail for traditional conceptions of legitimacy, democracy and accountability. Second, I endeavoured to define what sort of criteria we need to assess the validity of claims put forward by governance theorists. According to my analysis, it is possible to identify two main research programmes contributing to governance studies: one that is inspired by the NPE and the other that appeals to distinct sociological paradigms. I then suggested that, since these research programmes blend together descriptive and prescriptive elements, a twin type of evaluation is required to assess both their relative heuristic power and their relative ability to justify the normative ideals they seek to engender. Briefly, rationalisations of change influenced by NPE support the idea that the outcome of recent political change is a 'market-oriented' Regulatory State, while those influenced by sociology view governance as supporting the rise of a Networked Polity whose aim is to 'govern without government' dialogically. The main substantive claim advanced in the chapter is that, while the Regulatory State is a better 'heuristic category' for understanding recent political change than that of the Networked Polity, the reverse happens when these two entities are considered as normative ideals to engender.

End Notes

1. Thus for Rhodes (1997: 52–3, emphasis in original), 'it would seem that *governance* has too many meanings to be useful, but the concept can be rescued by stipulating one meaning and showing how it contributes to the analysis of change in British government. So, *governance refers to self-organizing, interorganizational networks*'. Similarly, Stoker (1998: 17, emphasis added) writes: 'Reviews of the literature generally conclude that the term – governance – is used in a variety of ways and has a variety of meanings [...] There is, however, a baseline agreement that governance refers to the development of governing styles in which boundaries between and within public and private sectors have become blurred. *The essence of governance is its focus on governing mechanisms which do not rest on recourse to the authority and sanctions of government*'.

2. Note that the published article reproduces only a simplified version of the figures used here. These figures were, however, contained in an earlier draft of that work I was able to access.

3. According to Piattoni (2009: 172, emphasis in original), 'MLG is at the same time a theory of political mobilization, of *policy*-making and of *polity* structuring, hence any theorization about MLG may be couched alternatively or simultaneously in politics, *policy* or *polity* terms.' So broad a definition makes it impossible to keep multilevel governance analytically distinct from network governance: the two are either equivalent to, or in competition with, each other; either way, the conceptual proliferation decried by Peters and Pierre (2002) is encouraged.

4. Bekkers *et al.* (2007: 43ff) propose a more complex tripartite distinction between 'input', 'throughput' and 'output' legitimacy. This distinction is reiterated and fleshed out by Schmidt (2013). To me, the analytical value of this distinction is still not clear. As I see it, throughput legitimacy is an articulation of input legitimacy rather than a distinct analytical category. If I am correct, there is the risk here of increasing the terminological complexity of this field of studies without improving its heuristic power.

5. To quote Pierre and Peters (2000: 67), 'democratic theory posits that power and accountability must rest with the same actors in order for some form of electoral control to be real and meaningful. Governance to some extent confuses that linkage by moving non-accountable actors into the political process.'

Chapter Five

Governing by the Market: The Political Economy of the Regulatory State

5.1. Introduction

What is the outcome of the variegated and relentless waves of reform carried out in the last *trente furieuses*? Following Majone (1994, 1997a, 1999; La Spina and Majone 2000), several analysts assume that the Regulatory State represents a heuristic category able to make sense of the changes which occurred in those three crucial decades.[1] In agreeing on the label, these analysts differ, however, on the content of the Regulatory State: its rationale, structure and goals. If Majone views it as the embodiment of a Madisonian form of government trying to consolidate the reforms of welfare institutions initiated by Thatcher and Reagan, authors like Levi-Faur (2013) dismiss its neoliberal pedigree and focus instead on the institutional and processual changes surrounding traditional forms of regulation and rule-making, thus denying that the emphasis on regulatory activities entails a corresponding reduction in redistributive practices. The aspiration here is that of employing the label to identify an ideal type of the global entities that have come to populate the political landscape at the dawn of the new millennium. On their part, King (2007) and Moran (2003) are less keen on the global heuristic aspirations of Levi-Faur and endeavour to highlight the limitations of this label as an explanatory framework. Thus, their critical accounts end up converging with those that deny the existence of a trade-off between the globalisation of regulatory regimes and the nation state as a sovereign entity (Jayasuriya 2005b), or else endorse the Networked Polity as a better rationalisation of current change (Bevir and Rhodes 2010).

The aim of this chapter is twofold. First, I shall clarify and sharpen some distinctions used in this literature. The clarification starts with the presentation of an analytical scheme discussing the relevance that norms and rule-making have acquired in the social sciences, as well as the change of perspective that occurred in the meantime. From epistemic concepts originally employed to refute the accounts of change proposed by political economists, norms and rule-making have been appropriated by a variety of economic perspectives engaged in the resolution of collective action problems and theoretical paradoxes affecting the latter when applied to non-market domains. Similarly, the notion of regulation has evolved from a progressive policy tool advocated by left-leaning thinkers and movements in the first half of the twentieth century to its antithesis – a theoretical alternative to state interventionism. Drawing on a traditional distinction between regulatory and constitutive rules, the chapter develops a more nuanced account of regulatory regimes than those suggested in literature.

The second objective of the chapter is to indicate a set of criteria for assessing the validity of the Regulatory State as a rationalisation of political and institutional change. Although heuristic and prescriptive element are inextricably interrelated, I maintain that, for analytical reasons, a proper assessment of this approach has to consider them separately, so as to arrive at distinct evaluation criteria. In developing this two-sided assessment, my conclusion is that the Regulatory State works much better as a heuristic device than it does as a justificatory tool. In other words, I claim that it can explain the rationale behind some of the processes of change carried out in the last *trente furieuses* better than competing sociological accounts supporting the notion of Networked Polity. At the same time, I argue that those same processes of change have eminently failed to supply to the Regulatory State with the widespread support and democratic legitimacy it requires. Thus, I conclude by casting serious doubts on both the feasibility of this new form of agency and the strategies of justification employed to support it.

5.2. Playing the game by the rules or the game of the rules? A conceptual scheme

The Regulatory State is a label used to indicate two things: (i) a set of activities connected to the regulation of social life in its manifold manifestations, and (ii) a set of institutions to whom the power to shape and supervise those activities is attributed. In practice, behavioural regularities are always the product of complex relations developed by these two sets of elements. Rules set constraints on individual action, but they also enable individuals to act meaningfully and constitute the agencies carrying out their enforcement. Hence, any understanding of the nature and relevance of regulatory regimes requires an explication of both: the ways in which regulation as an activity is conceived and the sort of institutional elements needed to assure its continuity over time. The matrix reported below (*see* Figure 5.1) endeavours to give a synoptic representation of this complex social phenomenon by criss-crossing two main variables. The first is derived from a classical distinction that, since Kant first (at least in modern times) stated it, has been periodically reiterated, though in subtle diverse form.[2] This is the distinction between (a) rules that have a predominantly regulative function and (b) rules that have a predominantly constitutive function. Such a distinction has been credited with the power of opening new vistas on the nature of rules as a theoretical construct and on the epistemic validity of the approaches employed to explain them. In this context, I re-propose the distinction to emphasise the double level at which the Regulatory State operates within and without its own jurisdictional boundaries. In doing so, my main objective is to make sense of the many contradictory claims made about the Regulatory State in a globalising political environment. The second variable concerns the means by which rules can be generated. In very abstract terms, they are the result of activities that can be either (c) cooperative or (d) competitive. Stressing one means of generation above the other entails not only choosing between epistemic paradigms operating in the social sciences, but also subscribing to normative outlooks concerned with the 'right' means by which regulation, as a social activity, must be carried out. My aim here is to show that, despite its progressive pedigree, in its most recent incarnation the Regulatory State is ineluctably connected with neoliberal attempts to impose market-driven forms of governance (Somers 2008), even if some of its advocates do not subscribe to a neoliberal worldview.

Traditionally, the notion of rule and rule-following behaviour has been at the centre of several epistemic approaches engaged in (i) showing the limitations of the explanations put forward by classic and neoclassic political economy and (ii) opposing the latter's attempts to impose some kind of methodological imperialism. For the schools of thought that share sociological tenets, rules are perceived as 'social facts' embodying the non-contractual elements upon which all contractual relations rests and are, thus, constitutive of social practices. To a large extent, the interest of the New Political Economy (NPE) in rules and rule-based behaviour is connected to the attempt to expand its inquiry beyond market behaviour, and the need to solve the countless problems and paradoxes this attempt yields – namely, the relation between action and structure, and the micro-macro transition. The popularity acquired by game theoretical representations of paradigmatic choice situations, and of the prisoner's dilemma in particular, are symptomatic of the recent shift in interest on rules which has occurred within the social sciences. Critics have always pointed out that in 'strategic' contexts of choice, where individual actions are interrelated, individualist methodologies lead either to indeterminacy or to a Hobbesian trap – results that undermine any rational reconstruction of actually existing social phenomena. Answering those critics, Petitt (1990) explains that the problems and paradoxes caused by the application of rational choice theory outside 'parametric' contexts can be easily avoided if individual behaviour is taken to follow rules, rather than straightforward utilitarian calculations. Hence, the attempts to develop rationalisations of rules consistent with the tenets of rational choice theory (Hechter and Opp 2001).

Rules also have a normative relevance that rivals the epistemic interests of those committed to value-neutral explanations. Political economy, in its various forms, has never been engaged in a merely explanatory enterprise, but has more or less explicitly tried to promote (and/or influence the direction of) change by indicating what rules can bring about optimal social outcomes. Brennan and Buchanan's (1985) *Constitutional Political Economy* represents the most sustained and sophisticated endeavour to establish this 'science of legislation' along the lines indicated by Adam Smith (Haakonssen 1981). The pillars underpinning such a science of legislation are three: (i) *homo oeconomicus* as a 'universal' model of agency, (ii) Pareto optimality as an 'objective' criterion for evaluating social outcomes, and (iii) equilibrium analysis as the 'correct' tool for investigating social phenomena. Blended together, these three elements supply a seamless theory of feasibility able to tell, according to its advocates, which values, principles or norms would create the conditions for their own self-enforcement and which would rather promote perverse side-effects, making their enforcement a very costly, and ultimately doomed, exogenous enterprise.

Figure 5.1: Regulation as a meta-game, social activity and research field

		Means of generation	
		Cooperative Activity	**Competitive Activity**
Level of application	**Rules of the Game**	• Post-constitutional models of *rule-following* in cooperative settings • Rules as the *outcome* of social practices (constructivism) • *Dialogical* dynamics directed at soliciting conformity	• Post-constitutional models of *rule-following* in competitive settings • Rules as the *by-product* of individual interaction (naturalism) • *Strategic equilibria* enforcing individual compliance
	Game of the Rules	• Constitutional models of *rule-making* in cooperative settings • Rules as the *outcome* of political deliberation • Establishment of channels of *voice* and mechanisms of *accountability*	• Constitutional models of *rule-making* in competitive settings • Rules as the *by-product* of social evolution • Establishment of the right *monetary incentives* and mechanisms of *exit*

Since feasibility studies supply a negative epistemology that points out the possibilities and limitations of human action in establishing and carrying out purposeful collective plans, the science of legislation developed has mainly had a critical import. Firstly, it has been deployed against all doctrines that conceive law as the formal deliberation of legitimate political bodies. Against those voluntaristic conceptions of law, it has been claimed that laws, norms and rules are to be understood as the precipitate of customs that have somehow passed the test of social evolution – the result of human action but not of human intentionality (Hayek 1987). Secondly, it has been used to undermine the division of labour between politics and economics suggested by welfare economics. By showing that political action is susceptible to produce worrying governmental failures, NPE has dismissed the theoretical relevance of market failures as a logical justification for state intervention (Buchanan 1972, Stigler 1971). NPE has thus stressed the virtues of deregulation and the ability of markets to police themselves effectively even when they are susceptible to failure, for government failure is presented as both more likely and burdensome than market failure (Winston 2006).[3]

5.2.1. The radical roots of the Regulatory State: a puzzling genealogy

Historically, the Regulatory State has been used to denote radical forms of state intervention, even when the nature, rationale and politics driving those interventions are antithetical. According to US legal literature from which the label is derived, the Regulatory State represents a configuration of political forces and institutional forms yielded by the reformist movements of the Progressive Era and the New Deal (Law and Kim 2010). Those reformist movements were part of a wider phenomenon affecting all industrialised countries at the time, often analysed under the heading 'the rise of protectionism'. They developed as a reaction to previous *laissez-faire* phases in which the state disengaged from direct, authoritative intervention in economic affairs, and were crystallised during the two main depressions that engulfed the then global economy. In his account of those events, Polanyi (1944) notes that political economy found protectionism very difficult to explain from its chosen methodological standpoint. Thus, it ended up attributing the development of state regulation to some implausible political conspiracy. To rebuff the charge, NPE engaged with the topic of regulation extensively, eventually promoting the birth of 'law and economics' as a distinct field of inquiry (Posner 1974).

Assessing the impact of this research field, Glaeser and Shleifer (2003: 417) point out that 'the economic analysis of regulation since the 1970s has been dominated by the "capture" or "interest group" theories, which see regulation as shaped primarily by producer or bureaucratic interests [...]. According to this view, producers either water down regulation to render it irrelevant, or else subvert it for their own benefit, such as by rising prices. Bureaucrats, in turn, use regulation to enhance their budget or bribes'. Rather than rebuffing Polanyi's critique, this conclusion seems no more than a restatement of the conspiracy theory arrived at by the generation of political economists targeted by the Hungarian author. Consequently, even two sympathetic reviewers like Glaeser and Shleifer (2003: 419) cannot avoid casting doubts on the soundness and empirical relevance of the overall approach: 'in the end, the evidence appears to point to significant social progress happening at least coincidentally with the Progressive Era reforms, as well as significant instances of regulatory capture by industry'. A more recent book length review of this approach is to be found in a volume edited by Carpenter and Moss (2014). The conclusion supported by this work basically repeats the critical remarks made by Glaeser and Shleifer, underscoring the fact that its ideology-driven overtones tend to distort its empirical findings and make it both heuristically and normatively unreliable:

> the essential idea that policymakers are for sale, and that regulatory policy is largely purchased by those most interested and able to buy it, remains central to the literature. And far too much of the relevant empirical work has sought to confirm this thesis (often rather casually), rather than test it or discover its limits. [...] As a result of these trends in the literature, we know much more about how regulation can fail due to capture than about the conditions under which regulation succeeds, or can be made to succeed, when capture is constrained (Carpenter and Moss 2014: 10).

Since the 1990s, while US legal analysis of the political re-organisation undertaken during the last three decades has described it as an attempt to replace the Regulatory State by an emerging 'presidential administration' (Kagan 2001), in Europe, thanks to Majone's efforts, those very changes áre described as having engendered a US-style Regulatory State. Moreover, while American legal and administrative theory is concerned with the rationalisation of changes occurred mostly, if not exclusively, at the federal level, in Europe the Regulatory State has been employed to rationalise multiple types of change which have occurred at distinct jurisdictional levels. The first and most evident phenomenon for which the label has been used is to account for the restructuring of national public administrations (Moran 2003). The second ambit where the label has proved even more successful is that of European studies; the EU is said to embody the Regulatory State to an extent not yet reached by its member states (McGowan and Wallace 1996). Since the EU is taken to be either a trend towards which other less evolved regional regulatory regimes are moving, or the main example for those regimes to follow, the Regulatory State is also employed to indicate a departure from the intergovernmentalist logic that shaped both international law and the institutions created for its enforcement (Jayasuriya 2001, 2005b).

Employing the same expression to rationalise phenomena occurring at different levels is justified by the alleged isomorphism of the dynamics of change unfolding at those levels. This isomorphism will be the object of the next section. As for the presidential administration, the images of the Regulatory State are often presented as positive developments – functional solutions to the problems that confronted their welfarist counterparts on both sides of the Atlantic. A conclusion reached in spite of the value-free empiricism that both US and European analysts purport to affirm and an indication of the, not always stated, justificatory role played by the rationalisations of political and institutional change supplied. There is some irony, if not a plain contradiction, in the fact that a concept used to indicate a positive development in the administrative architecture of world affairs, is in reality derived from a body of literature committed to show its shortcomings. In fact, several authors dispute both Majone's characterisation of the EU as a Regulatory State and his description of the latter as the embodiment of Madisonian government. Indeed, the growing literature on network governance suggests that the real novelty is the advent of a larger, more variegated and reflexive form of agency, presenting a picture of national and transnational regimes more akin to a Networked Polity than to a Regulatory State (Sabel and Zeitlin 2012). And even several of those who wish to retain the Regulatory State as an heuristic category are ready to point out the limitations of Majone's account and the epistemic and normative tenets supporting it.

My aim here is to propose an account of the Regulatory State at variance with both perspectives. First, I will propose a reading of the Regulatory State that stresses its debt to NPE's methodological and normative orientations. According to this reading, in the last three decades, the various waves of reforms that have transformed our political and institutional landscape have been driven by an unbreakable faith in market solutions and an overwhelming commitment to substitute channels of 'voice' with mechanisms of 'exit'. I will then show that the aim of these market-driven reforms was not to roll back the frontiers of the state, but to undermine the democratic nature of the institutions established in the previous era. Far from establishing a Madisonian system of government, they have reinforced the top-down governability of liberal democratic systems and the role central government plays in those systems. I contend that it is this attempt to hollow out representative institutions of any democratic content that explains the growing accountability gap and democratic deficit affecting real existing liberal democracies. And it is the inevitable Polanyian counter-reaction of those who try to resist this logic of depoliticisation that explains the inability of regulatory regimes at national and transnational levels to establish their own autonomous forms of legitimacy.

5.3. Features of the Regulatory State as an analytical model

Three main features contributed to the development of the Regulatory State as a model of government analytically distinct from its predecessor and/or alternative readings of political change: (i) the increasing importance of soft-law policy instruments (*vis-à-vis* state legislation and treatises) as flexible means of regulation; (ii) the diffusion of autonomous (or semi-autonomous) regulatory agencies as a result of pressures to delegate regulatory powers to non-majoritarian institutions; (iii) a growing reliance on horizontal mechanisms of accountability based on market evaluations of institutional and individual performance. In this section, I will clarify the content and inner articulation of these elements by comparing the different images of the Regulatory State emerging in literature. To this end, I shall sharpen internal distinctions and disagreements. In doing this, my aim is not, however, to show that the various representations of the Regulatory State are somehow contradictory and dismiss them on logical grounds. Rather, my aim is to recombine these accounts into a more articulated and dynamic picture of the Regulatory State – a task that will be carried out in the next section. An additional objective is to stress the conceptual links between the Regulatory State and NPE, even when some of its theorists cast doubts on the latter's underlying assumptions and normative aspirations. The influence of NPE is evident, as already stated, in the Regulatory State's explicit preference for market solutions and managerial policy tools designed to engender competition. At a conceptual level, the justification for mechanisms of 'exit' against channels of 'voice' remains deeply indebted to the alleged shortcomings of democratic theory and practice highlighted by NPE (Mitchell and Simmons 1994). I contend that accounts of the Regulatory State that embrace trust-based explanations of regulatory delegation and relational justifications of extended accountability are in themselves unable to break the epistemic links with NPE. However, I will point out that at a normative level these accounts are indeed at odds with neoliberal desiderata.

5.3.1. Formal and substantive elements of the Regulatory State

The focus on regulation, as a relevant research field for social and political analysts, follows the extensive projects of privatisation undertaken in OECD countries during the 1980s (Bishop *et al.* 1995). Justified as necessary solutions for cutting red tape and stimulating an entrepreneurial culture, these reforms in reality promoted complex dynamics of de-regulation and re-regulation in need of more sophisticated theoretical explanations. Even more puzzling than the growing level of regulation is the way in which regulation was carried out. To start with, regulation was pursued through a panoply of regulatory instruments located along a logical multidimensional continuum, the ideal poles of which were statute law at one end, and self-regulation at the other (Mörth 2004). When employed at all, formal legislative acts established only a general normative framework that left detailed regulation to other non-legislative instruments: contracts, franchising, audit and charterism (Loughlin and Scott 1997). Furthermore, and perhaps consequently, enforcement was delegated to autonomous agencies which followed procedures that were neither fully juridical nor merely political (Schneiberg and Bartley 2008). In short, regulation was transforming into a quasi-legislative phenomenon carried out through semi-juridical procedures by agencies with overlapping jurisdiction crossing the traditional internal-external and public-private divides.

For Majone (1994), the explanation of this state of affairs required a change of theoretical perspective: a shift in the level of analysis from the 'polity' to the 'policy' and the adoption of the methodological approach developed by NPE, and the Chicago school in particular. He explains that, 'regardless of what the law says, the process of regulation is not simply one where the regulators command and the regulated obey. A "market" is created in which bureaucrats and those subject to regulatory bargain over the precise obligations of the latter' (Majone 1994: 89). Majone's account of the rise of the Regulatory State rests on two theoretical claims that have subsequently been questioned and are, therefore, worth re-considering. First, Majone states that the heightened attention on regulatory activities is causally linked to a corresponding decline in the positive commitments of the welfare state. The Regulatory State progressively withdraws from the role of service provider and employer of last resort emphasised by Keynesian macroeconomics, renounces the redistributive functions attributed to it by the expansive conception of citizenship advocated by T. H. Marshall (1950), and elects as its core task the regulation of economic activities. Majone (1994: 80) hastens to explain that privatisation and deregulation means neither 'a return to *laissez-faire* or an end to all regulation', nor to 'a retreat of the state': 'what is observed in practice is a redrawing of the borders of the public sphere in a way that excludes certain fields better left to private activity, while at the same time strengthening and even expanding the state's regulatory capacity in other fields [...]'. Second, he also contends that the legitimacy of the Regulatory State can no longer depend on the fairness of its procedures, but on its ability to deliver the goods and services required by the citizenry. In so doing, he jettisons procedural justifications of state activities in favour of alternative strategies based on substantive conceptions of legitimacy.

Majone's attempt to strengthen the descriptive side of his account of the Regulatory State and play down its neoliberal connotations is far from convincing. In fact, his account seems to dovetail with Thatcher's political aspirations to 'roll back the frontiers of the state' and justifies viewing it as a neoliberal conception of the state derived from NPE tenets. This impression is reinforced when the set of constraints imposed on regulatory activities are considered in detail. First, Majone restricts the function of the Regulatory State to the resolution of a minimalist list of market failures. From this list are excluded: (i) Keynesian interventions directed at stabilising the economic cycle, (ii) social regulation designed to prevent exploitation or socially undesirable outcomes, and (iii) redistributive policies that aim at reducing domestic inequalities. This restricted function is further subjected to the proviso that the costs of government action should not offset those imposed by the market failure it aims to correct: 'an important recent development is the recognition that market failures provide only a *prima facie* case for intervention, since the costs of public intervention may exceed the benefits' (Majone 1994: 82). Second, the yardstick with which this cost-benefit analysis is to be carried out is the notion of Pareto-optimality exalted by political economists old and new, and that in Majone's framework assumes the form of an 'essentially uncontestable' concept. Lastly, the Regulatory State is depicted, by and large, as a politics free zone – a context where controversies and disagreements can always be objectively resolved by technocratic bodies insulated from the democratic process (*see* Chapter Eight).

Other eminent theorists of the Regulatory State have questioned Majone's account on more empirical grounds. The most contentious point is the trade-off that Majone introduces between regulation and redistribution. For Levi-Faur (2012: 15), 'the reason is simple: there is nothing in the rule orientation of the United States that prohibits redistribution and there is nothing in East Asian developmentalism that prohibits more rule-based governance'. According to him, nothing could prevent the Regulatory State from pursuing substantive goals that go beyond those listed by Majone and promote wider forms of social regulation – those strongly opposed by the economic theories of regulation mentioned in the previous section. A second sticking point is Majone's substantive approach to regulation. For Jayasuriya (2005a: 385), the hallmark of the Regulatory State is 'a flowering of assertive legalism and constitutionalism in economic and political decision making. [...] This legalism in turn reflects the importance of a form of "proceduralism" in economic policy making within the new Regulatory State'. The author then goes on to explain that, as a meta-regulator, the goal of the Regulatory State is to

> enhance or generate the self-regulation capacities of these sites of governance. [...] Proceduralism, then, transforms stateness or statehood in two respects: first, governance strategies are seen as establishing the self-regulating capacities of independent agencies; second, and perhaps more importantly, they establish something resembling 'meta-procedures' that govern the linkages between various sites of governance (Jayasuriya 2005a: 385).

So, the Regulatory State is procedural after all, and this proceduralism does not lead towards a minimalist liberal conception of the state either, but towards one supporting societal self-governance. This procedural notion of the state as 'enabler' (upon which strongly insist the theorists of the Networked Polity discussed in the next chapter) clashes with the rationalisations of political and institutional change developed in national contexts. For Moran (2003), the UK Regulatory State is the combined outcome of the failure of self-regulation that followed the neoliberal privatisations of the 1980s and central government's attempts to exploit this failure by expanding its remit to fields of activities and ambits of civil society that had until then escaped direct political control. A perspective upon which end up converging the several studies of transnational regulatory regimes proposed by Djelic and Sahlin-Andersson (2006).

5.3.2. Regulatory delegation, policy credibility and social trust

A second empirical feature underpinning the Regulatory State is the spreading of independent regulatory agencies worldwide. This is also an event that still requires a proper theoretical explanation. As Majone (1999: 3) puts it, 'one of the most striking features of this mode of governance is the extensive delegation of policy-making power to non-majoritarian institutions – institutions which fulfill public functions but are not directly accountable to the voters or to their elected representatives'. Even on this point, the literature supplies several overlapping rationalisations which are not always consistent with each other. Given its relevance, my starting point is once again Majone's, where the increase of regulatory delegation to independent agencies and a widespread systemic need to enhance the policy credibility of political actors operating at different levels are functionally connected (*see* Chapter Eight). Majone's account builds upon a blend of critiques derived from various NPE sub-fields. The crisis of the system of government established in the post-war period (and variously identified as Keynesian, positive, redistributive or even *dirigiste*) is here explained as the outcome of a twin process of rising individual expectations and institutional ungovernability. Majone also shares the normative solutions suggested by NPE and later experimented in several Anglo-Saxon countries: privatisation, deregulation and marketisation. The main disagreement between Majone and NPE seems to be related to the second dogma of the neoliberal consensus – deregulation. For, in Majone's account regulation remains the defining activity of the state and is presented in positive terms. In my opinion, this disagreement is pretty superficial and cannot be taken as an indication of an epistemic break with NPE's tenets, as I will illustrate.

As pointed out above, Majone's call for regulation is restricted to issues with broad economic relevance: public utilities, consumer protection, negative externalities. From the list of market failures requiring state intervention, he strikes out all elements that NPE retains theoretically suspect. And as seen before, even within these constraints, regulation is justified, if and only if, its expected costs are not higher than the negative effects of market failures. This means engaging in cost-benefit analyses based on the strict application of the notion of Pareto-optimality, as suggested by both the Chicago and Virginia schools. Even more indicative is Majone's rationale for the growth and diffusion of regulatory delegation to independent agencies at the global level. According to the latter, the case for independent administrative agencies to whom regulatory functions are to be delegated rests on the need to reinforce the policy credibility of legislative authorities – an explanation that clearly draws upon the reading of social choice theory advanced by the Rochester school. The lack of credibility depends on the populist tendency of majoritarian decision making to promote policy cycles, and the negative response of the economic agents whose investments are crucial for financing state activities in the long run (Riker 1982).

Majone's sharp distinction between regulation and redistribution aims at curtailing the powers of future democratic majorities and is intended to shield foreign investors and wealthy internal minorities from the reach of progressive forms of taxation. Delegation of regulatory powers to agencies insulated from electoral politics is crucial for the effectiveness of these protective measures because it ties state intervention to the satisfaction of Pareto criteria. At regional level, these mechanisms of delegation allow transnational regulatory regimes like the EU to engage in negative integration policies aimed at expanding market opportunities, while denying them the powers to impose corresponding duties on those benefiting from market expansion. Above all, they make it possible to envisage forms of democratic expression even more minimal and individualistic than the Schumpeterian politics of the ballot box advocated by previous generations of liberals. In a context populated by constellations of independent regulatory agencies, democratic legitimacy and political responsiveness could in fact be achieved by giving people the power to 'vote with their feet', as suggested by several eminent political economists since Tiebout (1956) started the post-war reflection on fiscal federalism.

Theorists of the Regulatory State less susceptible to the charm of political economy have supplied distinct rationalisations of regulatory delegation to independent agencies. Notably, Jordana and Levi-Faur (2004) maintain that the crucial element explaining this global phenomenon is not the type of policy credibility sought by Majone, but a broader need for social trust. According to them, 'trust-centred explanations are interesting enough. While in no way a substitute for political analysis, they might help us frame our analysis in broader terms, namely sociological, and thus somewhat challenge the dominance of the political-economy analysis in the study of regulation and the Regulatory State' (Jordana and Levi-Faur 2004: 15). For them, the theoretical advantages of a trust-centred perspective are several: (i) it makes better sense of phenomena like the audit explosion and regulation inside the state; (ii) it accounts for the retreat from traditional types of self-regulation and the decline of professional authority; (iii) it supplies a more convincing rationale for the expansion of social regulation; (iv) it highlights the shift in the balance of trust between different social groups without assuming the existence of monodirectional causal relations. I shall come back to these features in the next section. Here I would like to clarify two things about the trust-based alternative endorsed by Jordana and Levi-Faur.

The first is methodological and has to do with the relevance the notion of trust has acquired in social sciences and their wish to challenge the dominance of NPE in the field of regulation. Political economists, and other social theorists who share the same type of methodological individualism, have been at the forefront of the recent revival in trust-based perspectives (Coleman 1994; Gambetta 1988). In themselves, trust-based perspectives are neither incompatible with the sort of equilibrium analyses developed by NPE, nor do they depart very much from Majone's;[4] to the point that they could be easily integrated into the explanatory frameworks proposed by NPE. Trust and its twin notion, 'reputation', represent conceptual tools employed in economic theory to explain the possibility of cooperation in strategic contexts lacking external sources of law enforcement. On the other hand, various sociological perspectives of the type invoked by our authors have proposed rationalisations of political and institutional change that play down the theoretical relevance of delegation and regulatory agencies. For instance, Eriksen *et al.* (2003) contend that since Maastricht the real innovation brought about by EU integration is not the growth of regulatory agencies, but the transformation of the comitology system into what they call 'deliberative supranationalism'. Indeed, the growing and parallel literature on network governance suggests that it is the rising of a larger, more variegated and reflexive form of agency, the real novelty, presenting a picture of national and transnational regimes more akin to a Networked Polity than to a Regulatory State (Sabel and Zeitlin 2012).

Things turn out to be different from a normative perspective, a level of inquiry that the various theorists of the Regulatory State often shun for being scientifically suspect. Trust-based explanations are shared by a growing number of analysts who are dissatisfied with both the exclusive reliance on market solutions and the efficientist justifications put forward for them. While Majone's search for policy credibility is concerned with the support of restricted groups of economic and financial actors operating on global markets, trust-based accounts of the Regulatory State wish to appeal instead to broader social constituencies composed of individuals, groups and organisations still dependent on local markets and for whom the nation state continues to be a source of identification. The search for a larger social and political base upon which to ground the legitimacy of the Regulatory State leads these theorists to re-evaluate systems of 'voice' against means of 'exit', and to investigate the contribution deliberative forms of democracy and horizontal mechanisms of accountability could make in this direction. While fully appreciating the normative relevance of these aspirations, it needs to be pointed out that within the Regulatory State paradigm these lines of inquiry remain marginal and under-developed, especially so when they are compared to the growing relevance the theorists of the Networked Polity attribute to them (*see* Chapter Eight). This whole approach remains, alas, wedded to a strong empiricist outlook that not only underrates the role normative analysis can play in policy studies, but has developed in parallel with network governance studies with little cross-fertilisation.

5.3.3. *Enhancing democratic legitimacy by flattening accountability*

As a rationalisation of recent political and institutional change, theories of the Regulatory State have tried to shed light on two further elements: the notion of legitimacy most suitable for this emerging political entity and the mechanisms of accountability that can help ground it. As Majone (1997b: 13) succinctly puts it,

'Political principals can transfer power to their agents, within limits set by law, but they cannot transfer legitimacy in the same way. The new institutions have to achieve their own legitimacy'. Although Majone acknowledges that in any constitutional democracy the more appropriate criteria of legitimation are of a procedural kind, he maintains that, in relation to the Regulatory State, substantive conceptions could do a better job. For him,

> the existence of non-majoritarian institutions is due to the fact that all liberal democracies consider credibility, expertise, independent or fair judgment more important than direct responsibility towards the electorate. Hence, the relative ability to produce better results (accountability by results) in a given field, in relation to other institutional solutions, represents another valid method of legitimation (Majone 2003: 19).

After the positive role attributed to regulation, this is a second issue upon which Majone seems to depart from NPE, for the latter retains a strong proceduralist outlook. My opinion is, again, that this departure could be seriously overstated and that differences on this point need to be contextualised rather than emphasised. From the passage just quoted it is clear that regulatory delegation to independent agencies represents a functional solution to the problems created by majority rule. Majone (2003: 18) presents these problems in the terse language of NPE: 'at both national and international levels, non-majoritarian institutions are needed to precisely avoid some inevitable consequences of the democratic method, in technical terms, to reduce the transaction costs yielded by the application of the majoritarian principle'. In his scheme, the role played by non-majoritarian solutions is indeed equivalent to the one NPE attributes to procedural constraints – hinder the full force of majority rule; with the notable difference that the latter operate mainly at a constitutional level, whereas the former apply them at the post-constitutional level as well. It is for this reason that non-majoritarian and counter-majoritarian solutions are often treated alongside and defended on similar grounds (Moravcsik 2002).

In this context, the shift from 'procedural' to 'substantive' criteria or, to use Scharpf's (2009) systemic jargon, from 'input-oriented' to 'output-oriented' modes of legitimation has additional virtues that suit the current neoliberal consensus far better than the procedural constraints sought by public choice theorists. The procedural constraints invoked by the latter had the objective of slowing down the working of democratic systems dominated by political forces committed to egalitarian values. In a different context and political climate, these could turn out to be highly counter-productive. Since the 1980s, procedural criteria and acquired formal rights have been used by the remnants of the post-war welfare coalition to oppose the sweeping changes advocated by neoliberals (Somers 2008). Insisting on substantive criteria, or some form of unprincipled pragmatism ('what works in practice'), is thus a way of avoiding rigidities that could hinder the negative integration of distinctive geographical areas, domains of activity and communities of faith. The same can be said about two other pillars of liberal constitutionalism: separation of powers with a system of checks and balances, and traditional mechanisms of accountability. These changes are scrutinised in detail by Scott (2000) who also tries to go beyond the economic arguments used by Majone.

Traditional forms of accountability revolved around two main solutions: political avenues involving ministers and parliament as hierarchical principals, and legal avenues of judicial review involving the courts as external umpires. According to Scott, the Regulatory State is characterised instead by extended accountability structures arising from multiple strategic responses to the problems affecting its welfarist counterpart. 'In its narrowest form, an adequate accountability system would ensure that all public bodies act in way which corresponds with the core juridical value of legality, and thus correspond with the democratic will' (Scott 2000: 43). However, for Scott this model is not only too simplistic, but it is 'also very weak at holding public bodies to account for decisions which affect the collectivity, but have little bearing on the welfare of any individual' (*ibid.*). Hence, Majone's search for additional substantive criteria. Scott notes though that 'substantive tests of the effectiveness of accountability mechanisms create difficulties of measurement and do not indicate any appropriate way to recognize the conflict between desired values which is inevitable within particular domains' (*ibid.*). Drawing on the neoinstitutional notion of layering, Scott (2000: 49) then explains that 'market accountability forms have frequently been laid over hierarchical structures. The investigation of any particular policy domain reveals complex structure of extended accountability, best characterized a hybrid in character'.

Taking into consideration both (i) the changes introduced at the structural level (that is, the modifications of vertical mechanisms of accountability with the introduction of upward and downward responsibility towards non-constitutional principals – managers and customers, and the expansion of horizontal forms of accountability towards internal and external auditors) and (ii) the enlarged set of substantive and procedural values used to measure and assess the individual and collective performance of public bodies, Scott charts a more complex map of the accountability patterns established by the Regulatory State that is worth reporting (*see* Figure 5.2 below).

Particularly interesting is the dual kind of justification that Scott advances for such an extended pattern of accountability: a justification that attempts to go beyond Majone's 'thin' economicism and adopt the 'thick' relational perspective developed in network governance studies. This dual justification is

> premised on the existence of complex networks of accountability and functional equivalents within the British state structure. Close exploration of the structures of extended accountability in the United Kingdom reveals at least two different models which have developed which feature overlapping and fuzzy responsibility and accountability: interdependence and redundancy (Scott 2000: 50).

Figure 5.2: Examples of linkages between values and accountability institutions

For what? To whom?	Economic Values	Social/Procedural Values	Continuity/Security Values
'Upwards' accountability	Of departments to treasury for expenditure	Of administrative decision-makers to courts/tribunals	Of utility companies to regulators
'Horizontal' accountability	Of public bodies to external and internal audit for probity and VFM*	Review of decisions by grievance-handlers	Third-party accreditation of safety standards
'Downwards' accountability	Of utility companies to financial markets	Of public/privatised service providers to users	Consultation requirements re: universal service requirements

* value for money

Source: Scott 2000: 43

I will come back to the implications this shift in perspective has for the Regulatory State paradigm in the next section. I would like to close this section by noting that, like trust, network analysis can also be developed along economic lines and be fully integrated within an NPE outlook. Majone (1997b: 12) himself does this when discussing 'the network as a bearer of reputation'.[5] Indeed, in the next chapter I shall argue that a great deal of theoretical research on network governance often sounds eerily like a sociological version of the spontaneous order thesis supported by political economists and is, therefore, susceptible to similar criticisms at both the epistemic and normative levels. Those accounts also rest on very debatable notions of unintended consequences that systematically make political and institutional change dependent upon functional reactions to external impersonal forces even when many of those changes have clear political origins and rationale. Hence, the tendency I note to produce celebratory works that embrace complexity and variety uncritically, and which are sometimes impervious to the fact that those very features can be strategically exploited to boost the ability of some state agents to exercise power at a distance and unaccountably, rather than to empower previously excluded societal agents and stakeholders.

5.4. The Regulatory State as a research programme: Heuristic and normative questions

In the previous sections, I have discussed the shift in meaning for the Regulatory State label and presented the conceptual features at the centre of this paradigm. In doing so, I have emphasised the relationships current theories of the Regulatory State entertain with NPE as both (i) an approach to the study of political and institutional change and (ii) an ideological framework committed to influencing the pace and/or direction of change. In this section, I shall carry out an evaluation of the Regulatory State as a research programme committed to supply a rationalisation of the reforms initiatives undertaken in OECD countries during the last *trente furieuses*. The thesis I support is that, overall, the Regulatory State works much better as a heuristic framework than as a justificatory tool. In particular, I maintain that while the former could be fleshed out and re-articulated so as to fill obvious gaps and overcome apparent inconsistencies, the latter is wanting at both theoretical and empirical levels and would require revisions affecting the (normative) hard core of the research programme. Accordingly, this section is divided into two parts, one dealing with explanatory issues and the other with more prescriptive questions.

5.4.1. Opening the regulatory black box: The state as a meta-ruler, the market as a policy instrument

The doubts expressed about NPE notwithstanding, I believe that, as an analytical reconstruction of recent change, the Regulatory State is a superior alternative to rationalisations based on divergent sociological tenets supporting the notion of Networked Polity. This belief depends on a number of reasons related to the heuristic relevance the state still retains within this paradigm. To appreciate it, it is worth recalling the classification of governance forms indicated by Sørensen (2004): 'governance *by* government', 'governance *with* government' and 'governance *without* government'. From my viewpoint, governance literature celebrating the advent of a Networked Polity has focused on the study of one form, 'governance *without* government', almost exclusively and to the detriment of the other two. This gives the impression that non-hierarchical forms of governance have come to dominate both hierarchies and modes of co-governance. In turn, this has lent support to unwarranted claims about the erosion of the state and promoted celebratory studies of network as organisational forms and tools for democratic empowerment (*see* Chapters Seven and Eight). By contrast, literature on the Regulatory State supplies, in my opinion, a more balanced treatment of all three forms of governance indicated by Sørensen. It also acknowledges (although feebly and intermittently) that even forms of 'governance *without* government' unfold 'in the shadow of hierarchy', to use another successful phrase popularised by Scharpf (1997). Similar considerations can be expressed, and have indeed been expressed (Djelic and Sahlin-Andersson 2006; King 2007), in relation to the 'state', the political role of which is misleadingly underrated by those who wish to replace it with the term 'polity' to describe the more horizontal and multi-level nature of emerging governance regimes at both the national and the transnational level.

Prima facie, this claim could sound rather paradoxical, for I have previously attempted to show that the Regulatory State strongly resembles the minimal (if not ultra-minimal) state advocated by neoliberals. My concern here is, however, with the explanatory value of the general approach and not with its prescriptive side. From this (analytical) perspective, the picture I derive from the rationalisations of the Regulatory State put forward so far is one where the state (a) retains relevant regulatory powers, which it then (b) exercises either (i) directly (governance *of* government), (ii) jointly with other actors (governance *with* government) or (iii) indirectly, by delegating (some of) them to independent agencies (governance *without* government). What is clearly under-theorised in this literature is both the role of the state as a 'meta-ruler' as well as its ability to switch roles or to play multiple roles simultaneously – that is, the strategy-set employed by the state in the regulatory meta-game.

Drawing on the scheme proposed in Figure 5.1, it is possible to identify various aspects of regulation and the pivotal role the state still retains in each of them. First, the state has the power to shape the constitutional setting wherein regulatory agencies interact. It not only defines the terms of delegation, but it also establishes, as a meta-ruler, the co-operative or competitive environments in which the actors to whom regulatory power is delegated are then supposed to operate and interact. The meta-ruling powers of the state cast serious doubts on the real independence of regulatory agencies and/or autonomy of existing regulatory networks; a theme whose interest is slowly gaining ground (Gilardi and Maggetti 2011). Whereas regulatory agencies and networks are supposed to 'play by the rules' established at the constitutional level, the state is free to 'play the game of the rules', changing the latter periodically at will. Moreover, while the discretion of an agency and/or the room for manoeuvre of a network is kept in check by the co-operative or competitive settings in which they are called to interact, the state retains considerable leeway at national, transnational and international levels, even if this is far from being unlimited. Finally, the state remains the agencies' main financial sponsor, a political arbour for institutional anchorage and the ultimate source of democratic legitimacy.[6]

The main negative implications of this inability to take the power of the state, as a meta-ruler, seriously are two. The first is related to the seemly contradictory nature of the statements about the Regulatory State put forward in literature. Is there a trade-off between regulatory and redistributive activities? Does the rise of the Regulatory State entail abandoning Keynesian macro-economic policies, as claimed by Majone? Or are those claims only an expression of the (neoliberal) commitments of the Italian author, as suggested by Levi-Faur? And again, is the Regulatory State dependent on the outcome-oriented mode of legitimation suggested by Majone? Or does its legitimation rather rest upon the type of proceduralism evoked by Jayasuriya? Finally, is the latter right to attribute to the Regulatory State the role of enabler of self-regulation? Or should we view it as a solution to the structural failure of self-regulation, as claimed by Moran? My hunch is that these contradictory pictures of the Regulatory State are not an indication of deeper theoretical inconsistencies, but rather the outcome of the failure to give proper weight to the meta-ruling powers of the state, together with its ability to take on multiple roles simultaneously and switch among them at will. Once these elements are factored into our explanatory framework, we get a more complex and dynamic picture of the Regulatory State as a political actor able to play 'the game by the rules' and the 'game of the rules' simultaneously, to use a variety of policy instruments (contracts, franchising, audit and charterism), and to appeal to seemingly incompatible modes of legitimation (procedural and substantive).

A second and even more important question concerns the lack of a political rationale underpinning the various accounts of change proposed. Is the rise of the Regulatory State the outcome of impersonal forces that have undermined the viability of traditional forms of regulation and related policy instruments? Or can the changes witnessed at the national and the transnational level be more plausibly attributed to specific political actors driven by strategic considerations with political objectives in mind? To clarify, all the authors mentioned (Majone included) tend to distance themselves from naïve beliefs in the demise of the nation state and stress, more or less forcefully, the pivotal role state actors played in the waves of reform that have reshaped the public sector since the 1980s. However, it has been correctly pointed out that

> fields of transnational governance and transnational regulatory dynamics tend to wrap themselves in discursive references to efficiency and best practices – legitimized by science and measurement or market mechanisms and validated through rational benchmarks and scales. The discourse and self-presentation of actors involved in transnational governance processes is often neutralised – void of references to issues of power and interests' (Djelic and Sahlin-Andersson 2006: 198).

My aim is thus to flesh out those accounts by giving a closer scrutiny inside that epistemic black box called 'the state'. I contend that it is only by opening up this black box that we can understand the internal dynamics that have fuelled (a) the generation of new waves of reform within a given national context (engulfing distinct social and institutional domains in the process), and (b) the spread of these reforms (broadly based on a similar template) across OECD countries and beyond (*see* Chapter Two, §2.3 and §2.4).

A correlation that has been repeatedly noted in OECD countries is the hollowing-out of parliaments and a corresponding reinforcement of the powers of central governments. In parliamentary systems, this is described as a creeping process of presidentialisation (Poguntke and Webb 2005), while in presidential systems like the USA, it is depicted as a strengthening of the presidential administration (Shapiro and Wright 2011). Indeed, the various features that compose the Regulatory State indicate systematic and restless attempts to restrict the role and relevance of national parliaments and other elected subnational bodies. As mentioned, soft-law instruments have undermined the role and functions of statute law and of the political actors involved in it. But no less dramatic has been the curtailment of the supervisory power of these same institutions caused by the redefinition of the separation of power and systems of checks and balances imposed through market-driven forms of governance. To appreciate these internal changes, I propose in outline a re-construction of the way in which the regulatory meta-game has been played in the UK, focusing in particular on the changes promoted in the practice of accountability following the introduction of NPM and quasi-internal markets (Marquand 2004; Self 1993). Here, the lack of both a written constitution and a formal (as opposed to social) separation of powers with systems of checks and balances have turned British political institutions into what Vernon (2011) aptly calls the 'canary in the coal mine' – a lab for global experiments in institutional engineering.[7]

Diceyan constitutional theory suggests viewing the British political system as resting on two main forms of accountability: legal and political. Legal accountability is assured through the judicial review carried out by the courts and represents a form of accountability whose relevance has progressively increased since the UK joined the then EC in the 1970s. Still, it remains far less relevant than its American counterpart and open to criticism since the UK lacks the formal separation of powers and systems of checks and balances that make US courts independent from central government. The transmission of democratic legitimacy to the executive and administrative branches of government rests, consequently, on the ability of Parliament to take these branches to account for policy failures and abuses of power. The two main ways in which parliamentary supervision has been imposed over time considers the overall responsibility of government for policy decisions (collective accountability) and the responsibility of individual ministers for business carried out by the departments they are in charge of (ministerial accountability). Both forms are part of a vertical conception of accountability that attributes full democratic legitimacy and political sovereignty to Parliament (Woodhouse 1994).

Now, if the evolution of the Westminster system in the course of the twentieth century made Diceyan constitutional theory far too simplistic, the introduction of new managerial practises and internal markets have had the effect of enlarging pre-existing accountability gaps, hollowing out ministerial accountability altogether (*see* Chapter Nine). Delegation of regulatory powers to an increasingly complex network of agencies has shifted the institutional balance from vertical to horizontal types of supervision with a quasi-legal status and enforced in a semi-juridical manner. In addition, NPM has established a system of formal managerial autonomy that makes the indirect control Parliament exercised on civil servants a mere constitutional nicety. Through the introduction of competitive market tendering and the relentless drive to marketise community-based services, a similar process has taken place in relation to local authorities, whose regulatory and supervisory powers have gone the same way as their managerial ones. Given the fact that these changes have established very few and restricted 'exit' mechanisms directed at strengthening output-oriented modes of legitimation, managerial auditing takes on increasingly ritualised forms and is carried out by appointed personnel struggling to acquire its own legitimacy and highly susceptible to capture by organised interests (Power 2003).

In the process, central government has been freed from both the social responsibilities imposed on it by an expansive, rights-based conception of citizenship and the democratic supervision imposed by flexible constitutional conventions. These responsibilities have been either individualised, since they are now ascribed to middle- and street-level bureaucrats who have to meet countless standards, or depoliticised – namely, attributed to a variety of social and private actors involved in the delivery process but lacking any decision-making power.[8] In turn, constitutional conventions have been re-interpreted and utterly transformed under the unrelenting pressure to modernise the public sector (Marquand 2004). Hood (2010: 19), with his usual theoretical sophistication, suggests viewing these changes as the outcome of a blame-avoidance game:

> The blame-avoidance perspective may offer us one way of making sense of the much-remarked development of semi-autonomous public bodies, multilevel governance, and partnership arrangements in modern (and not so modern) government. It may also help to explain why elected politicians and senior bureaucrats often seem to spend a remarkable amount of their time on the fine print of organizational design while often professing that all they care about is 'results'.

Unfortunately, the author says very little about the way in which the rules of this blaming game relate to the accountability game outlined above: how they have combined and evolved, been enforced and revised, and who are the meta-rulers playing those games. The combined effect of this regulatory activism is nevertheless striking: the transformation of British democracy into a Prime Minister-led 'elective dictatorship': a type of American-style presidential administration lacking all the constitutional mechanisms and guarantees offered by the latter. This twin process of political centralisation-cum-administrative decongestion and its accompanying effects (depoliticisation of various policy areas, deresponsabilisation of crucial political actors, etc.) has not only benefited the dominant ruling parties and thus contributed to establishing a neoliberal consensus politics at the top. I contend that it has also suggested itself as an example to emulate in national and transnational contexts suffering similar problems of governability. Hence, the policy transfer that has allowed the British template to spread worldwide and, with it, the neoliberal consensus politics upon which it is based (*see* Chapter Two, §2.4).

5.4.2. Failing standards: The Regulatory State as a political black hole

Lurking behind the accounts of the Regulatory State discussed so far are functional explanations presenting it as the outcome of beneficial evolutionary processes. As seen, Majone explicitly states that the Regulatory State is a functional solution to the difficulties faced by previous forms of state intervention, above all those based on public ownership and command-and-control managerial philosophies. First, by focusing on regulation, political authorities avoid getting involved in conflicts generated by redistributive policies. Regulation is, in fact, presented as a positive-sum game, whereas redistribution is depicted as a zero-sum game. Avoiding social conflicts is, in turn, viewed as a crucial step for reducing the likelihood and magnitude of political cycles at the root of the structural lack of credibility that marred Keynesian stabilisation policies. Second, by delegating powers to independent regulatory agencies, political principals adopt self-restraints that boost the confidence of foreign investors and internal minorities. Political and bureaucratic discretion is, in fact, tied to objective criteria of social optimality that only allow changes which lead society towards the Pareto frontier and/or favour its outward expansion. The imposition of rational self-restraints is presented as something that will strengthen both the policy credibility and overall substantive legitimacy of the Regulatory State. The latter is then not just more stable than its Keynesian counterpart, it also represents a virtuous solution capable of seemingly unlimited powers of self-improvement. Since these functional explanations are either based on, rely upon, or replicate arguments used to prove the unintended beneficial consequences of Smith's invisible hand and, more recently, the efficient market hypothesis, the theoretical doubts expressed against those arguments can be reiterated against Majone's substantive justification of the Regulatory State.

Right at the start, we can observe that the comparative cost-benefit analysis proposed by Majone rests on contradictory claims. On the one hand, the Italian author acknowledges that, even if it is not a minimal state, the Regulatory State is a lighter version of its predecessor. The welfare state was committed to engendering a rights-based conception of citizenship requiring large-scale interventions aimed at reducing social and geographical inequalities. By contrast, the Regulatory State renounces any commitment towards this model of citizenship. Consequently, it is not at all clear whether the positive result of Majone's cost-benefit analysis depends on the efficiency gains ensured by delegation or is simply the result of a ruthless cost-cutting exercise. The Regulatory State might well require lower running costs and hence a lighter taxation burden, but this is perhaps because it no longer supplies relevant public goods and services which its welfarist counterpart felt compelled to do.

This revision of the *raison d'être* of the state raises a host of normative questions that make Majone's substantive justification extremely problematic. Who is going to supply those public goods and services, and at what cost? Or, if no-one is going to do it, what are the likely social costs of public inaction in the domains Majone wants to depoliticise? Redressing problems of political governability by shifting the costs onto society or onto the individual could cause even more subtle and vicious forms of ungovernability. Failed states, for instance, are an increasingly worrying phenomenon creating dangerous regional instabilities whose costs are rarely factored in the cost-benefit analyses carried out by political economists. This analytical myopia has, however, noteworthy implications for the feasibility of the institutions advocated. When affecting approaches that elect feasibility analysis as the main theoretical means for assessing alternative values, principles of action and rules, this myopia is an indication of contradictions located at the hard core of their research programme.

Normatively, the substantive justification of the Regulatory State proposed is even more wanting. Employing rhetorical devices borrowed from NPE, Majone claims that since redistributive policies are politically controversial, it would be better to abstain from pursuing them. However, Majone fails to supply any convincing answer to those who repeatedly point out that doing so would mean, *ipso facto*, adopting market criteria of distribution; that is, criteria whose legitimacy could be even more controversial, giving the impression that he implicitly accepts the morality of the *status quo* the Regulatory State is called upon to improve by impartial means.[9] On this point, it is worth noting that the logical distinction between 'acting' and 'blocking action', employed by Buchanan and Tullock (1962: 256) to refute criticisms of that kind against their constitutional model of public choice, is not available to Majone who advocates a negative market integration policy that commits the Regulatory State to action, regardless of the procedural objections from remnants of the post-war welfare coalition opposing market-driven forms of governance.

Furthermore, it is not even clear who and how, in Majone's substantive account, is supposed to carry out the impartial assessment upon which the legitimacy of the Regulatory State is said to rest. Given Majone's inclination towards NPE tenets, a likely extension of his reasoning would contemplate the creation of a constitutional setting wherein individuals are free to move across jurisdictions, thus giving citizens the power to 'vote with their feet' (Somin 2011). This model of democracy would avoid troublesome collective action problems and establish the type of fiscal federalism Majone is very keen on. Once again, it is far from clear that this model of democracy would pass the feasibility test indicated. Roughly, we could say that it would appeal to the social and economic constituencies crucial for the kind of policy credibility Majone has in mind – multinational corporations and the financial and political backers supporting the current neoliberal consensus politics. It is, however, doubtful whether those constituencies can assure the overall stability of national and transnational regulatory regimes. The economic crisis that started in 2008, and still with us at the time of writing, is, if anything, a reminder of the inner weaknesses and tensions that affect this consensus politics and its shaky democratic legitimacy.

These doubts rest on solid empirical grounds. Reviews of literature on the Regulatory State often find it difficult to classify and evaluate the relevance of an approach identified as 'regulation inside government' developed by Hood and colleagues (Hood *et al.* 1998, 1999, 2000).[10] Although restricted to the study of regulation in the UK, this is a very nuanced and sophisticated reading of change that also sheds light on the shortcomings of regulation as a post-command managerial tool (to which I cannot, alas, do full justice here). Of the two elements that are important for my work, the first has only indirect normative implications but fits in very well with the dynamic picture of the Regulatory State suggested above. To start with, Hood and his collaborators identify four ideal types used to check government activities: (i) traditional hierarchical forms of 'oversight', which have a decreasing overall weight; (ii) market and quasi-market forms of 'competition' that follow NPE's suggestions and are by now ubiquitous; (iii) horizontal forms of 'mutuality' upon which the theorists of Networked Polity have focused in their search for alternatives to both oversight and competition; (iv) 'contrived randomness', that is control exercised by the random application of processes, or the random revision of pay-offs – forms whose relevance and frequency the authors are keen to stress. Although these types are currently presented as alternative policy tools and connected to distinctive theoretical and normative outlooks, the authors show that in practice regulation within government is enforced through hybrids using different mixes of all four:

> we discovered not only that comptrol or oversight within government comprises a variety of forms, but also that oversight mixes with other inspector-free modes of control to produce a range of hybrids. Nor do the compound forms consist only of simple pair wise hybrids. Sometimes we find three or more of the types combined, […], which not only combines randomness with oversight […], but also elements of competition between state-run and contracted-out prisons (Hood *et al.* 1999: 17).

As regards network governance, regulation is enforced by hybrids containing a degree of oversight, and thus unfolds always 'in the shadow of hierarchy'.

This aspect comes to the fore when the inner life of the Regulatory State is scrutinised. According to our authors,

> the growth of the 'Regulatory State' […] in society at large is paralleled by an increase of regulation inside the state. […] with internal regulation in some way moving in the opposite direction from operational management, as increased managerial discretion is balanced by more intrusive regulation. [There are] some areas (notably local government in relation to central government) in which, far from a mirror-image process taking place, increased regulation was accompanied by decreases in managerial discretion – a 'double whammy' rather than mirror image pattern – even if mirror image processes could be observed inside local government itself (Hood *et al.* 1998: 65).

In other words, a good deal of regulation pertains to the inner working of the Regulatory State itself, rather than privatised utilities and other economic and social activities carried out by the private sector ('mirror image' metaphor). Within this subsector, regulation has affected operational agencies differently, where managerial discretion has been tightly constrained, and regulatory agencies, which have instead been bequeathed broad delegatory powers ('double whammy' metaphor). Hence the conclusion that 'Regulation inside government has grown topsy-like, with no overall rationalisation or consistent practice. [New] reviews ha[ve] added layers of new regulators to the existing ones without ever taking anything away, producing a crowded and largely uncoordinated regulatory system. And the regulation of government is itself regulated at best patchily, being little exposed to the kinds of disciplines it imposes on its regulatory clients' (*ibid.*).

This is indeed the picture of the Regulatory State as both ruler and meta-ruler that not only switches roles at will, but also uses standards tailored to the different roles it occupies. Once this account is coupled with the one related to the changes in the structure of accountability outlined above, what we get is a twin process of political centralisation-cum-administrative decongestion that makes Lord Hailsham's (1978, Chapter XX) notion of elective dictatorship a 'dread come true'; with the significant twist, chronicled by Mount (2012: 175), that in the process Parliament itself has been made redundant, while 'the office of the British PM now [holds] a concentration of formal power greater than that of almost any other country in the developed world'. Within the UK, various waves of reforms have freed the central government from a range of Marshallian social commitments and the weak democratic control Parliament used to exercise on its executive and administrative counterparts. At the same time, regulation within government has strengthened the grip of the cabinet on peripheral and local branches of the public sector and de-Sir-Humphreyfied the Civil Service, to the point that nowadays the latter is considered no longer part of the British Constitution. Since similar dynamics have filtered through the system and are now being imitated by authorities located at various levels, the overall picture is that noted by Moran (2003: 146): 'the expansion of the state's regulatory domain into new social spheres'. It is this twin process of administrative decongestion-cum-political centralisation that is being adopted in the rest of continental Europe through the aegis of the EU Regulatory State; and it is this model of regulation that inspires the drive towards 'modern-anglicisation' promoted by an overlapping set of global regulatory authorities (UN bodies, Bretton Woods institutions, rating agencies, arbitration agencies, NGOs, etc.) committed to good governance (Djelic and Sahlin-Andersson 2006).

The second, and normatively more important, feature highlighted by Hood and colleagues concerns the allegedly comparative lightness of the Regulatory State. During the last three decades, regulation inside the UK has shown a tendency to grow in a way worryingly similar to that observed during *les trente glorieuses*. Hood *et al.* (2000: 285) estimate that, at the end of the Conservative time in power, the overall costs for the British taxpayers were around two billion a year; an amount that includes, in roughly equal proportions, actual running costs and 'the compliance costs of such regulation – what it costs regulatees to meet the requirements of those who regulate them'. Moreover, they maintain that the changes introduced by the subsequent New Labour governments, far from reducing that burden, contributed to its growth, balancing, if not offsetting, the savings accrued by cuts in services and manpower across the public sector in that same period.

Even more striking are their remarks concerning the effects of these reforms on red tape: 'regulation of government seems to have become more formal, complex and specialized in many of its domains despite – or perhaps because of – the ostensible "New Public Management" drive to "let managers manage" in the public services' (Hood *et al.* 2000: 284). In short, regulation has failed to cut big government, red tape, or even to engender the supposed shift towards an entrepreneurial culture. For, the introduction of performance-related schemes has been accompanied by a parallel strengthening of procedural forms of control. The *Modernising Government* reform programme undertaken by New Labour did not even attempt to revise the double standards affecting operational and regulatory agencies, but simply endeavoured to fine tune its working with the introduction of 'enforced self-regulation', a policy innovation that 'has the rhetorical advantage that government appeared to be doing a great deal about public service failure without having too many authorities in the chamber of execution' (Hood *et al.* 2000: 294).

The features of regulation inside government outlined above explain why the Regulatory State currently finds itself facing a sort of legitimation crisis similar to that suffered by its Keynesian counterpart in the mid 1970s.

Regulation is developing into a parallel but unaccountable system of government. It is a system that multiplies official interventions because of the numbers involved. It lacks the independence of courts because of appointments by ministers; it bypasses the impartiality of the Civil Service and the accountability of ministers to Parliament. It threatens an over-burdensome bureaucracy, loss of direct government and a democratic deficit in the conduct of our affairs (Hodgson 2006: 252).

This crisis is not restricted to the UK government, but has spread to those political systems which have in the meantime adopted the British template, as well as to transnational authorities and regulatory regimes worldwide.

The EU is a startling case in point, and not only for its central role in Majone's account, but for helping spread the Regulatory State template directly and indirectly. If the 2005 constitutional debacle brought to light the existence of a widespread popular resentment towards the policies of negative market integration, since then the inability of the EU to deal with the financial crisis of 2008 is endangering the monetary union, and with it the very idea of a European commonwealth itself. Majone's confidence in the technocratic powers of the Regulatory State to promote its own policy credibility and political legitimacy by jettisoning redistribution and delegating regulatory powers to independent agencies is, therefore, unwarranted. And thus, we must remain deeply sceptical about the new phase of unification currently endorsed by the so-called Troika, a phase 'characterised by the same mix of centriped and centrifugal logic that has shaped its course since Maastricht: asymmetrical integration, combined with inegalitarian enlargment' (Watkins 2013).

But the theoretical accounts that attempt to distance the Regulatory State from Majone's account show similar weaknesses, as does Hood's reading of these recent developments. In his latest major work, Hood attributes the result of the 2005 French referendum to a tactical miscalculation. For him, the then French president Jacques Chirac 'failed to calculate that a referendum on a new European constitution in 2005 would act as a catalyst for everyone in France who was discontented with his rule rather than a grateful endorsement of a new grand vision of European unity' (Hood 2010: 12). And he then goes on to mislabel what are in reality mere 'tactics' as 'strategies' of blame avoidance. My hunch is that perhaps the EU publics who voted against the European constitutional project (as well as those currently opposing the austerity policies imposed by the Troika) understood the meta-ruling strategy of domestic and communitarian executives (now joined by the USA under IMF cover) better than Hood. What they then tried to do, and still keep doing, is to put a halt to the collusive meta-game wherein national and transnational authorities play the roles of 'good cop' and 'bad cop' in turn to enforce the shock therapies contained in various autocratic memoranda of understanding. If this hunch is at all correct, the EU could risk going down in history as the first real-life example of a failed Regulatory State.

5.5. Conclusions

Seen from a theoretical perspective, the Regulatory State represents a heuristic category that supplies a far-fetched interpretation of the variegated processes of change which occurred in OECD countries in the last *trente furieuses*. Epistemically, its interest lies in the fact that it supplies a rationalisation of political and institutional change influenced by NPE tenets. As such, it presents those changes as progressive attempts to expand and consolidate the neoliberal innovations introduced by Thatcher and Reagan. In so doing, this interpretation is at odds with sociological readings that suggest viewing those same events as ushering in a Networked Polity incompatible with the neoliberal aspirations of those two politicians. In proposing a genealogical reconstruction of the Regulatory State, the chapter has pursued two main objectives. On the one hand, it has stressed the connections with NPE, even if some of its most distinguished theorists do not subscribe to a neoliberal worldview and are critical of the type of methodological individualism employed by political economists. On the other hand, the chapter has attempted to flesh out this reading by looking inside the Regulatory State black box and suggesting a theoretical framework that could harmonise the seemingly contrasting pictures supplied to date. I argued that more attention must be paid to both: (i) the meta-game through which the state controls the constellation of independent regulatory agencies created in the last three decades and (ii) the political logic underpinning the strategy sets of the various state actors involved in this meta-game. I contend that, once this is done, several claims concerning the role of the state in a globalising political landscape needs to be revised and/or qualified. The state still retains massive leeway at national and transnational levels, but its internal balance of power has been dramatically modified in ways that have increased the role of central governments and executive authorities *vis-à-vis* parliaments and representative bodies. Hence, rather than hollowing out the state, those changes have had the combined effect of undermining the democratic nature of representative institutions and thus their responsiveness to public opinion.

The chapter discusses the prescriptive role the Regulatory State also plays in practice when used as a justificatory framework. The authors more directly influenced by NPE tend to stress the benefits brought about by (a) the introduction of mechanisms of 'exit' in the public sector, (b) alternative forms of democratic expression to the competitive leadership model (CLM) that used to dominate in the first half of the post-war period, and (c) the adoption of substantive criteria of evaluation against mere procedural forms of justification. Those who are more critical of neoliberal solutions and wish to play down the Regulatory State's association with market solutions tend to rely instead upon trust-based explanations and highlight the potential beneficial effects of extended patterns of accountability yielded by institutional layering. The chapter discusses both types of justification and casts doubts on the feasibility of the Regulatory State. Against neoliberal justifications, I pointed out that the substantive criteria of evaluation suggested are theoretically deficient and empirically unsubstantiated. The Regulatory State has not only failed to give people the power to 'vote with their feet', but has actually increased red tape and political control on sectors of civil society that were outside the remit of central government. I also noted that the twin dynamics of political centralisation-cum-administrative decongestion has freed the now dominant political actors from the responsibilities imposed by rights-based conceptions of citizenship and vertical mechanisms of accountability. The conclusion I draw from this is that, far from boosting the governability of OECD political systems, the Regulatory State has become a political black hole that is further undermining the already feeble legitimacy of real existing liberal democracies. Since 2008, the financial crisis and related austerity policies have exposed a number of fault lines that question the ability of the Regulatory State to preserve representative democracy from a systemic legitimation crisis. As a justificatory framework, the shortcomings of the Regulatory State cannot be underrated and need to be tackled properly. Unfortunately, the Regulatory State paradigm is wedded to a strong empiricist vision of policy analysis that plays down the relevance of normative inquiry and is, therefore, structurally unable to do so.

End Notes

1. The literature on the Regulatory State is very rich, although its growth is somehow declining. Besides Majone's seminal contributions, here the main focus will be on the work of Jayasuriya (2001, 2005a, 2005b), King (2007), Levi-Faur (2013, Jordana and Levi-Faur 2004) and Moran (2002, 2003). The Marxist theory of regulation developed during the 1980s, and thoroughly surveyed by Brenner and Glick (1991), remains outside the remit of this study.

2. Kant (1998 [1787], Part II, Div. II, Chapter II, Sect. VIII, p. 520 ff) uses the constitutive/regulative distinction as part of his illustration of the antinomies of pure reason. The distinction re-surfaces in Wittgenstein's (1958) theory of language games to express the difference between 'rules that define a game' and 'rules that tell you how to play such a game'. Rawls (1955) re-proposes the distinction to avoid several misconceptions about utilitarianism. Hart (1961: 79) employs it to show that law is the union of primary and secondary rules. More recently, the distinction has been re-deployed by Searle (1995: 28) to oppose relativistic and constructive readings of Wittgenstein's theory.

3. Note that the notion of government failure follows from the application of economic analysis to politics; application that is based on the controversial equivalence of political and economic markets. Thus, Stiglitz's (2008: 3, n. 5) ironical comments: 'many economists have donned the hat of a political scientist, arguing that political processes are inherently inefficient. But there is no general theorem asserting the inevitability of "government failures" outweighing market failures, and no persuasive "counterfactual" analysis that a world without regulation might look like as compared to the current regime'.

4. This is evident when all six elements that compose Majone's (1994: 84–5) functional explanation are considered: (1) 'agencies are justified by the need of expertise in highly complex or technical matters', (2) 'an agency structure

may favour public participation', (3) 'agencies separateness from government is useful [...] to free government administration from partisan politics', (4) 'agencies [...] provide greater continuity and stability than cabinets because they are one step removed from election returns', (5) an 'agency [...] provide[s] flexibility not only in policy formulation but also in the application of policy to particular circumstances', (6) 'agencies can protect citizens from bureaucratic arrogance and reticence [...]'.

5. 'But how is reputation established in the first place? By definition, a network is not hierarchically structured and so lacks formal mechanisms for monitoring the behaviour of its members and enforcing control. In time, however, the network develops informal standards and working practices that create shared expectations. Knowledge about agencies that do not fulfill the expectations of their partners spreads through the network by informal means. In this way, the network performs the crucial task of deciding which members are in good standing and communicating that information to other members. Only agencies with a reputation for independence, expertise and trustworthiness will be sought as partners. In short, the network becomes an intangible asset bearing a collective reputation and conferring that reputation upon the agencies in good standing. Independence, trust, reputation will be crucial to the viability of European regulatory networks, and thus to the practical implementation of the principle of subsidiarity in the areas of economic and social regulation' (Majone 1997b: 12).

6. The need for institutional anchorage is especially relevant to the growing number of private agencies involved in the regulatory process (Scott 2002). Without anchorage they would be floating in an institutional void and their power of influence would be similar to that of 'think-tanks'.

7. Vernon refers to current reforms in higher education worldwide. However, I contend that these reforms follow the template originally employed to reform the British Civil Service (*see* Chapter Two, §2.3) and later applied to all other institutional ambits composing the British public sector (Palumbo 2004). The distinction between formal and social conceptions of the separation of powers is derived from Ryan (1991).

8. The sustained attack on the entitlement culture also means that many public responsibilities have vanished altogether or been transmuted into individual duties. By and large, it is possible to claim that the depoliticisation of public domains and the deresponsabilisation of corporate actors has been accompanied by the politicisation of areas of private life with a related increase in individual responsibilities. Hacker (2006: 8) calls it 'The Personal Responsibility Crusade': 'a political drive to shift a growing amount of economic risk from government and the corporate sector onto ordinary Americans in the name of enhanced individual responsibility and control'.

9. Recent empirical research shows that neoliberal reforms have had a negative impact on horizontal and downward redistributive flows, that is policies

favouring different sections of the middle classes and the overall amount of resources allocated to poorer members of society. Increasing reliance on market criteria has, however, increased the upward redistributive flow, that is the concentration of social resources at the top. Cf. OECD (2011).

10. A case in point is Schneiberg and Bartley (2008), who even fail to mention it.

Chapter Six

Bringing Society Back In: The Political Sociology of the Networked Polity

6.1. Introduction

A number of analysts influenced by methodological tenets derived from various sociological perspectives have advanced rationalisations of political and institutional change at odds with those put forward by theorists of the Regulatory State. For them, the unintended outcome of thirty years of reform in the public sector is the rise of Networked Polity, a political and administrative entity based on network forms of organisations and the networking activism of the many and varied embedded societal actors who now find themselves involved in the policy process. Those who work within this sociological paradigm are keen to stress the novelties brought about by governance and use the latter term no longer as a synonym of government, but as a radically distinct way of conceiving both political activity and the administration of public affairs. The distance separating this account of change from the one advanced by Regulatory State theorists is so wide that these two bodies of work have developed without significant cross-fertilisation, and sometimes they have even downplayed each other's contribution to governance studies. Methodological differences concerning the agency responsible for change and the dynamics at the root of the alleged passage from 'government' to 'governance' often overlap with a host of competing normative claims concerning the desirability and feasibility of new modes of governance. Trying to distance themselves from neoliberal visions, the theorists of the Networked Polity link governance to the emergence of dialogical policy environments and bottom-up mechanisms of implementation the aim of which is to empower civil society. In so doing, they have lent growing empirical support to deliberative conceptions of democracy against both the procedural and aggregative models fashionable in the post-war period, and the foot-voting models advocated by Regulatory State theorists.

In subscribing to sociological notions of agency, network and trust, and in appealing to the political virtues of discussion and democratic deliberation, the theorists of the Networked Polity supply a spectrum of readings of recent political and institutional change that compete against each other, in that they (i) advance contrasting definitions of governance, (ii) put forward distinct analytical frameworks explaining its impact and diffusion, and (iii) support alternative justificatory frameworks elucidating its desirability and/or feasibility. To start with, definitions of governance as an institutional form of organisation compete here with others that conceive it as a more fluid and interactive social process. In addition, conceptions of governance having instrumental value are often juxtaposed to others that stress the reflexive nature of the policy innovations analysed. Thus, while the first perspective considers new modes of governance as tools for problem-solving and tries to assess its relative effectiveness and efficiency *vis-à-vis* more hierarchical forms of organisation and traditional policy instruments, the second perspective avoids getting engaged in comparative cost-benefit analyses of this sort altogether. Criss-crossing these two main variables we get a 2 x 2 matrix that divides the conceptual space into four subsectors, each of which encloses several ideal typical conceptions of governance and related visions of Networked Polity. The aim of this chapter is to clarify the analytical features that characterise these conceptions, as well as the value-systems with which they identify more or less explicitly. Once again, I wish to stress that the distinctions proposed here have a merely heuristic value whose goal is to point out the critical issues faced by these ideal types at both epistemic and normative levels. In so doing, the aim of the chapter is not to carry out a survey of literature on the topic, but to propose a genealogical analysis of Networked Polity that allow us to assess its theoretical standing as a rationalisation of political and institutional change.

6.2. From governance to metagovernance

Although I have previously mentioned approaches to governance which conceive it as a process, the bulk of my discussion has so far dealt with those which treat it as an organisational structure and link it to network forms of organisation. Far from reflecting a specific personal preference of mine, this unbalanced treatment reflects the pre-eminence acquired by neo-institutional perspectives in the field of governance studies, or at least among the first generation of analysts who turned governance issues into an autonomous field of inquiry.[1] A peculiar neo-institutional attitude characterises even those authors and schools of thought which employ systems-theoretic analyses and cybernetic models (as I shall try to show below) and who end up proposing a conception that can be labelled as 'interactive governance'. What characterises the various strands which compose this first generation of governance studies is its shallow critical attitude towards the emerging new modes of governance. Indeed, the general impression is that its main exponents are so mesmerised by the possibility of a 'governance without government' that they downplay not only its relative relevance *vis-à-vis* other types (i.e. governance of government and governance with government), but also the shortcomings affecting networks forms of organisation and deliberative policy instruments. A later second generation, worried about governance failure, has focused its attention on aspects and questions located at a meta-level of analysis, spurring several studies interested in analysing the '*governance* of *governance*' (Kooiman and Jentoft 2009: 819), or else the 'organisation of self-organisation' (Jessop 1998: 42), or even the 'regulation of self-regulation' (Sørensen and Torfing 2009: 246). In this section, my aim is to discuss the three conceptions of governance just mentioned (*see* Figure 6.1) and highlight the reasons behind the progressive shift towards questions of a meta-theoretical nature.

Figure 6.1: Instrumental approaches to governance as an institutional form

	Instrumental approach	*Reflexive approach*
Institution	Neo-institutionalism Interactive governance Metagovernance	
Process		

6.2.1. Neo-institutionalism and governance theory

The label 'institutionalism' is often used to identify the scientific approaches which stress the role social institutions play in directing and shaping the actions of those involved in social interaction. These approaches define themselves in opposition to the radical individualism of political economists, for whom social institutions are always the outcome of equilibria solutions reached by self-seeking individual actors. More specifically, 'neo-institutionalism' refers to a variegated movement that, starting from the late 1960s, reacted against the combined effort of NPE and behavioural political theorists to impose some sort of 'economic imperialism' across the social sciences (Tullock 1972).[2] Following Hall and Taylor (1996), it has become commonplace to distinguish between three types of institutionalism: historic, economic and sociological. This classification conflates chronological and epistemic features. It can be claimed that historical institutionalism also represents a blend of economic and sociological reactions against the then rising relevance of neoclassic economics. Furthermore, it can be pointed out that, among neo-institutionalisms, only the sociological component has sought to promote an epistemic break with neoclassic tenets. The versions developed in economics (in particular Williamson's NIE) all look like Lakatosian attempts to modify the protective belt of the individualist research programme so as to protect its hard core from refutation. As seen before (Chapter Five), rules conventions and institutions have been introduced into economic reasoning as a means to solve the paradoxes of collective action brought about by the attempt to employ rational choice theory beyond the parametric setting of a pure competitive market.

The neoinstitutional manifesto that has a special importance for us is the one proposed as far back as 1984 by March and Olsen. According to them, the scientific strands which fuelled the so-called behavioural revolution in political science (briefly discussed in Chapter Two) share a basic vision with five main features: it

is (a) *contextual*, inclined to see politics as an integral part of society, less inclined to differentiate the polity from the rest of society; (b) *reductionist*, inclined to see political phenomena as the aggregate consequences of individual behavior, less inclined to ascribe the outcomes of politics to organisational structures and rules of appropriate behavior; (c) *utilitarian*, inclined to see action as the product of calculated self-interest, less inclined to see political actors as responding to obligations and duties; (d) *functionalist*, inclined to see history as an efficient mechanism for reaching uniquely appropriate equilibria, less concerned with the possibilities for maladaptation and non-uniqueness in historical development; and (e) *instrumentalist*, inclined to define decision making and the allocation of resources as the central concerns of political life, less attentive to the ways in which political life is organized around the development of meaning through symbols, rituals, and ceremonies (March and Olsen 1984: 735).

Appealing to a 'classic' conception of politics (one we would now call 'republican'), March and Olsen present the then rising neo-institutional approaches as engaged in the attempt to

deemphasize the dependence of the polity on society in favor of an interdependence between relatively autonomous social and political institutions; they deemphasize the simple primacy of micro processes and efficient histories in favor of relatively complex processes and historical inefficiency; they deemphasize metaphors of choice and allocative outcomes in favor of other logics of action and the centrality of meaning and symbolic action (*ibid.*: 738).

These ideals overlap with those professed by many analysts supporting the notion of Networked Polity for reasons that are quite easy to understand. Given the latter's critical stance towards the various waves of reform carried out by neoliberal governments during *les trente furieuses*, and the general negative perception of their overall results, the elective affinity between neo-institutionalists and governance theorists has led to a 'holy union' begetting the vast body of literature on new modes of governance. Thus, a quarter of a century after March and Olsen's manifesto, Bevir (2009: 18–19) proposes an evaluation of this new endeavour by repeating their original endorsement almost verbatim:

sociological institutionalists focus on values, identities, and the ways in which they shape actors's perceptions of their interests. They argue that informal sets of ideas and values constitute policy paradigms that shape the ways in which organisations think about issues and conceive political pressures. Hence they adopt a more constructivist approach to governance […]. They concentrate on studies of the ways in which norms and values shape what are often competing policy agendas of welfare and administrative reform.

The idea underpinning the neoinstitutional approach is that a 'network' has to be represented as a persistent institutional form and not 'as a practice – an accomplishment on the part of strategic actors (or the organizations they nominally 'represent') – which takes place within a strategic (and strategically selective) context which is itself constantly evolving through the consequences (both intended and unintended) of strategic action' (Hay and Richards 2000: 14).

As Ansell (2006: 75) explains 'a network can be thought of as an institution to the extent that it represents a *stable* or *recurrent* pattern of behavioral interaction or exchange between individuals or organizations [...] the network approach views networks as critical mediating variables that affect the distribution of power, the construction of interests and identities, and the dynamics of interaction'. Thus, following on March and Olsen's footsteps, he indicates four meta-principles that characterise '*network institutionalism*': (i) 'a *relational* perspective on social, political, and economic action [for which] relationships [...] are not reducible to individual attributes – as the basic unit of explanation'; (ii) 'a presumption of *complexity* [for which] groups and organizations are not neatly bounded, certainly not unitary, and are often interpenetrating'; (iii) the idea that 'networks are both *resources* and *constraints* on behavior'; and that they (iv) 'mobilize information, social influence, resources, and social capital in highly *differentiated* ways. Not only is the social world complex, but also highly biased' (*ibid.*: 75–76, italics in original).

Also easy to spot are the main divergences between March and Olsen's theoretical expectations and many neo-institutional analyses of governance without government proposed by the first generation of theorists. The first and most striking divergence concerns the relation between the state and civil society. If for March and Olsen neo-institutionalism was going to 'deemphasize the dependence of the polity on society in favour of an interdependence between relatively autonomous social and political institutions', Ansell's *network institutionalism* advances a picture of the Networked Polity wherein the distinction between the political and the social simply disappear. Network and multilevel governance are presented as capable of reflecting and satisfying the needs and aspirations of societal agents without political intermediation, while the citizens are able to step into the role of political prosumers seamlessly. This neo-institutionalist reading also seems to play down the role of politics in fostering social order. The networking of individual and groups, unmediated by politics, is here used to support not only the plausibility of a social order without the exogenous intervention of the renowned Hobbesian sword, but also to affirm the superfluity and/or derivative nature of politics as such. A second but no less striking divergence concerns the assumption that neo-institutionalism is somehow incompatible with an instrumental perspective. As repeatedly mentioned, policy networks, partnerships, peer-review systems and bottom-up mechanisms of implementation are systematically presented as policy instruments superior to both those based on command-and-control, and the contractual solutions favoured by neoliberals.[3] More than that, in fact; the Networked Polity is deemed to be not only a more efficient and effective organisational set-up than states and markets, the dialogical and deliberative policy environments it promotes are also depicted as novel sources of democratisation which can reverse the legitimacy deficit experienced by actually existing liberal democracies (*see* Chapter Eight). In short, the neo-institutional approach to governance retains three of the main features March and Olsen decry about the post-war behavioural revolution: (a) contextualism, (d) functionalism and (e) instrumentalism.

6.2.2. Interactive governance

These features are also to be found in the second line of research included in this sector of our map: interactive governance. This line of research analyses governance through the lens of complexity theory and is strongly influenced by systems theory, of which it re-proposes both the scientific vocabulary and graphic representations (Duit and Galaz 2008; Klijn 2007, 2008). Although it is, by and large, dominated by analysts belonging to North European research centres (Dutch and Scandinavian mostly), its intellectual roots are to be found in Anglo-American sociological traditions; that is, the structural-functionalism of Parson and Easton and cybernetics, rather than in Luhmann's functional-structuralism or in the French post-structuralist school. The label interactive governance is derived from the work of Kooiman and associates, to which I will devote my attention here; it is, however, reclaimed and applies also very well to the work of authors like Bang, Sørensen and Torfing (Torfing *et al.* 2012).

As hinted above, the goal of interactive governance is to supply a more dynamic analysis of new modes of governance than that arrived at by neo-institutional approaches. This dynamic analysis remains, however, within the gravitational pull of the neo-institutional paradigm, and because of this it can be distinguished from the approaches that view governance as a process included in the sector located below (*see* Figure 6.2). As I understand it, interactive governance represents a perspective that wants to propose a middle course between the opposing methodological positions of Luhmann and Scharpf, whose scientific relevance has so far dominated research on *politische steuerung* in the German-speaking world. Thus, Kooiman and van Vliet (1999: 368) explain that

> no headway can be made in a social-political governance when the emphasis is either on the actor or on the structural level. Both have to be taken into consideration as they are to be considered as the two sides of one coin, as being inescapable analytical views on any social subject. Structure has great influence on action in the short run, and action has great influence on structure in the long run, to put it simply. This applies particularly to social-political governance.[4]

These are theoretical stances that keep evolving towards more abstract meta-analyses, thus approaching the thin line that separates institutional and processual visions of governance. More marked, however, are the differences that separate them from the reflexive conceptions located to the right side of the map (see Figures 6.3 and 6.4). Interactive governance retains a strong instrumental perspective: 'networks that do not contribute to the production of public purpose in this broad sense cannot be counted as governance networks' (Sørensen and Torfing 2006: 11).

In Kooiman's work, such an approach represents a development of the notion of socio-political governance suggested by the author at an earlier stage (Kooiman 1999, 2000, 2003). In this context, the qualifier 'interactive' is meant to translate the Dutch expression *Wisselwerking*, a word to which the author attaches special relevance, not only because there is the need to conceptualize the interactions between those governing in public and private roles, and the interaction between those governing and those governed, but also there is a need to conceptualize the interactions between structures and processes in societies and their sectors. *Wisselwerking* is the nice Dutch word that covers all those ways and modes of interactions: in *Wisselwerking* the way interacting entities influence each other in an active fashion is expressed (Kooiman and van Vliet 1999: 369).

Lets start then by identifying the features which characterise Kooiman's socio-political governance before moving to the subsequent refinements advanced by the author.

Kooiman's starting point is the identification of the independent variables responsible for the evolution of governance as a superior socio-political solution to states and markets alike: dynamics, diversity and complexity. Taken together, 'they continuously present these societies with problems, but also with opportunities' (Kooiman 1999: 75); they impose changes in relation to the policy instruments employable and indicate the way for finding out viable alternatives.

To be effective – that is to say, up to standards such as efficiency, legitimacy and fairness – social-political governing itself has to reflect the diverse, dynamic and complex character of the challenges it faces. Often problem definitions are too simple, policies too static and audiences too generalized: this might be one of the primary reasons why so much governing seems to be inefficient, governance unjust and governability weak (*ibid.*).

And again, 'to be able to govern, the governor needs ideas on where the system to be governed is, where it needs to be and how the actual situation may be turned into the desired situation' (*ibid.*: 76).

All viable solutions indicated must also work simultaneously at three distinct levels: at a *first-order* pragmatic level where the daily problems we confront each time are solved; at a *second-order* structural level where the conditions required to solve first-order problems are set; at a *third-order* meta-level which acts directly upon the second-order structural conditions 'because its central theme concerns the way "governing or governors are governed"' (*ibid.*: 79). Initially, Kooiman's task was restricted to analysing the first two levels (and the second in particular, for this coincides with socio-political governance). But lately he has been engaged with the study of the third level as well. Socio-political governance is concerned with the three main types of governance indicated by Sørensen (2004): governance *of* governments, governance *with* government and governance *without* governments. In his earlier studies, however, Kooiman focused only on the last two and on hybrid forms that combine them in various ways. As he writes, 'the most important governance task is to organize or institutionalize the mix of three modes of governance: self-governing, co-governing and interventionist governing.

[...] So my plea is definitely not for withdrawal or non-interventionism of public authorities in the governance of present-day societies; it advocates well-designed mixes of the three modes' (*ibid.*: 85). And this leads us towards meta-theoretical approaches to governance.

6.2.3. Metagovernance as a conceptual trinity

Kooiman is among those few governance theorists who recognise the relevance of normative questions for policy making and have shifted their attention to the more abstract meta-level where these can be discussed properly. For Kooiman and Jentoft (2009: 819), 'meta-governance, that is, the governance of governance, occurs in our opinion when governance system values, norms and principles are discussed, formulated and applied in governing processes'. Their discussion of these questions distinguishes two initial steps: one *ex ante*, wherein normative standards and benchmarks used to orientate future activities are established, and one *ex post*, wherein the congruence of policy decisions with the previously defined normative standards is evaluated. A further preoccupation of the authors concerns the possible distinction between values, norms and principles, as well as the analysis of the way in which these entities influence action and the likely feedback mechanisms connecting real choices to them.

According to the graphic representation proposed by the authors, these entities can all be located along a conceptual continuum where values are the most abstract elements and choices the most concrete, with norms and principles left to occupy more intermediate positions. Values influence policy choices through the definition of the norms which have to be followed to realise them and of the principles according to which those same norms have to be understood. Vice versa, policy choices impact on values through a feedback mechanism acting first on principles and then on norms. In this model,

> governors, public as well as private, would be obliged to make the origin of their ideas explicit: analytically, ethically and politically. When hard substantive governance choices are being made, it is inevitable that fundamental assumptions and worldviews are at stake. Interactive governance brings these notions to the surface so that they can be explained, discussed, defended and evaluated before they are allowed to underpin the choices made'. [As such] 'meta-governance can be considered the mortar that binds all attributes of governance and makes it a whole (*Kooiman and Jentoft 2009: 824.*).

The authors are keen to point out that their understanding of metagovernance is distinct from the ones put forward by Jessop (1998, 2003) and Sørensen and Torfing (2009; Sørensen 2006) – as discussed below. For them, metagovernance is not necessarily linked to state action, nor is it dependent on the notion of governance failure. As they put it, 'we do not see meta-governance primarily as related to the state (as most others do), for example, governments formulating sets of ground rules for all those active in governance, that is, public, private and mixed types such as networks. We see it as a major governance activity of public and private actors together and interactively, responsible as they are for societal meta-governance' (Kooiman and Jentoft 2009: 822–23). If for Kooiman metagovernance is the roofing structure of a governance complex with an inner unity and logic, in Jessop's and Sørensen and Torfing's accounts it is depicted as a possible normative solution to the failure of governance arrangements. The label originates with Jessop's critical analysis of the limitations of network forms of organisations and is used to support hybrid institutional solutions which can combine networks, hierarchies and markets. Given the limitations affecting any pure form of organisation, be it hierarchy, market or network, Jessop (1998: 42) opines that 'metagovernance involves instead the design of institutions and generation of visions which can facilitate not only self-organization in different fields but also the relative coherence of the diverse objectives, spatial and temporal horizons, actions, and outcomes of various self-organizing arrangements'. As such, it combines two dimensions: an *institutional* one that 'provides mechanisms for collective learning about the functional linkages and the material interdependencies among different sites and spheres of action', and a *strategic* dimension that 'promotes the development of shared visions which might encourage new institutional arrangements and/or new activities to be pursued to supplement and/or complement existing patterns of governance' (*ibid.*). Of these dimensions only the second overlaps with Kooiman's model.

In 2003, Jessop develops his notion of metagovernance by restricting his attention only to the institutional dimension, and thus stretching the distance with Kooiman's understanding of it. Here, after stressing the various objections against any ideal form of organisation, and in particular the limitation of network forms of organisation, Jessop suggests adopting the cybernetic principle of 'necessary variety' as an institutional social insurance against the failure of governance. As he puts it,

> metagovernance involves managing the complexity, plurality, and tangled hierarchies found in prevailing modes of co-ordination. It is the organisation of the conditions for governance and involves the judicious mixing of market, hierarchy, and networks to achieve the best possible outcomes from the viewpoint of those engaged in metagovernance. In this sense it also means the organisation of the conditions of governance in terms of their structurally inscribed strategic selectivity, i.e., in terms of their asymmetrical privileging of some outcomes over others (Jessop 2003: 108).[5]

However, he still retains that 'this idea should not be confused with a super-ordinate level of government to which all governance arrangements are subordinated' (*ibid.*), and to this extent his notion of metagovernance needs to be distinguished from the one advanced by Sørensen and Torfing.

Jointly or as single authors, Sørensen and Torfing advance a 'political' reading of metagovernance that relies on the intervention of state institutions to solve the problems brought about by the decentralised interaction of societal agents operating within governance regimes, especially the problems concerning the democratic legitimacy of the latter. In their view, 'one of the most central tasks in promoting democratic governance is to develop a toolkit that equips politicians with the best possible means to exercise democratic metagovernance' (Sørensen 2006: 105). Underpinning this view are two main concerns derived from governance failure studies. The first has to do with the alleged lack of confidence affecting the political class in its ability to steer governance networks within the fragmented institutional landscape brought about by three decades of neoliberal reforms. As Sørensen (2006: 99) explains, 'what stands in the way for a strong representative democracy under conditions of governance is first and foremost the way many politicians perceive the politician's role. Because of these role perceptions, metagovernance tends to be exercised by other actors and not least by public administrators, at severe costs for democracy'. The second has to do with a wholesome sceptical attitude towards the notion of beneficial unintended consequences that inspired the first generation's faith in network governance, and is still detectable (in a weakened form) in the theory of decentred governance advanced by Bevir and Rhodes (2006).

If nothing can guarantee that the decentralised interaction of embedded societal agents could cause the emergence of effective and legitimate forms of joined-up government, then there is the need to reassess the role of state institutions and democratic politics in steering governance regimes in the right direction. Likewise can be said about democratic experimentalism. Dialogical interaction and deliberative forms of policy making cannot operate as free-standing institutions and need to be weaved back into representative democracy, if a further aggravation of the democratic deficit affecting OECD countries (and the EU in particular) is to be avoided.

> There are no guarantees that the democratic potentials of governance networks are realized. Nor is there any guarantee that governance networks are democratically anchored. The democratic impact and quality of governance networks depends on their particular form and functioning. This in turn depends on how these are designed and managed. The conclusion is that effective and democratic network governance depends on how the relatively self-regulating governance networks are metagoverned by public authorities or other legitimate and resourceful agents or networks (Sørensen and Torfing 2009: 245).

Metagovernance entails, therefore, a re-evaluation of traditional political forms by attributing to them new functions and purpose:

> (1) the production and dissemination of hegemonic norms and ideas about how to govern and be governed; (2) political, normative and context-dependent choices among different mechanisms of governance, or among different combinations of governance mechanisms; and (3) the strategic development of particular institutional forms of governance in order to prevent dysfunctions and advance particular political goals (*ibid.*: 246).

6.3. Network society and non-institutional modes of governance

The three readings just discussed can be considered as part of a research archipelago with well established channels of communication; they take part in a common debate and represent distinct elements of an evolving narrative of governance. This cannot be said about the perspectives included in the other sectors of our conceptual map. Despite the fact that all these readings also reach back to a common sociological tradition, they belong to worldviews which identify themselves, in a Wittgensteinian fashion, with specialised languages which cannot be fully translated into one another. Thus, (i) communication between these worldviews is both difficult and transient, (ii) they often fail to recognise/appreciate each other's contribution to this field of research, and (iii) they tend to develop independently.

The perspectives included in the bottom left part of our map (*see* Figure 6.2) are connected by the fact that they all conceive governance as a dynamic process of interaction, rather than an institutional form of organisation. This dynamicity is not due to the introduction in their theoretical models of temporal variables, but to the ongoing stress on notions like, 'information flow', 'speed of transmission', 'flexibility', 'adaptive ability', 'boundary crossing', etc. That is to say, a vocabulary in which institutions represent static heuristic categories too well-defined to convey the novelty and radicalism of current processes of change. Unlike the postmodern and systemic approaches located to the right (*see* Figures 6.3 and 6.4), the perspectives discussed here share an instrumental attitude that makes them more attuned to issues of efficiency and effectiveness, but that also blunt their critical edge, making them too celebratory, if not downright complacent. In analysing this conceptual area, my starting point will be several attempts which suggest a dynamic version of the notion of 'network governance' labelled, somewhat confusingly, 'governance network'. In putting the stress on networking activities, this body of literature has an elective affinity with a parallel body discussing the broad relevance of recent developments in ICT for promoting the rise of the network society. I shall therefore engage with this body of literature as well by considering the contribution of Castells (2005, 2010, 2012). The section will finally consider Dunsire's (1990, 1993, 1996) systemic analysis of what he calls 'collibration' mechanisms – a class of policy instruments often underrated by neo-institutional accounts of governance.

Figure 6.2: Instrumental approaches to governance as process

	Instrumental approach	*Reflexive approach*
Institution		
Process	Governance networks Network society Collibration	

6.3.1. From the Networked Polity to a Networking Politeia?

Neo-institutional and processual readings of governance develop almost simultaneously and have thus ended up sharing similar labels to indicate different understandings of the phenomena associated with them. Dissatisfaction with this state of affairs has pushed several authors to adopt a diverse vocabulary to avoid conceptual and theoretical ambiguities. Obviously, this attempt carries the risk, mentioned earlier, of increasing the complexity and terminological confusion of a field already beset with definition problems. A case in point is the attempt to substitute the expression 'governance network' for the better known 'network governance'. The reasons for doing this are explained by Klijn and Skelcher (2007: 587):

> we use the term 'governance network' to describe public policy-making and implementation through a web of relationships between government, business and civil society actors. The order of the words 'governance' and 'network' is important here. Our usage – governance network – emphasizes that the network relationships we are considering are specifically those concerned with governance, that is the articulation, resolution and realisation of public values in society. The alternative (and more usual) word order – network governance – we see as being a higher level concept associated with a particular mode of societal organisation, which is usually contrasted with market and hierarchy.

According to my understanding of this passage, the authors wish to use the expression *governance network* to identify 'sets of relations' whose aim is to realise public values, and reserve the more common expression *network governance* to indicate a form of social organisation distinct from both markets and hierarchies.

While appreciating their wish to improve analytical clarity, this attempt seems to me doubly problematic: first, because it is always difficult to change linguistic habits; second, because the new word order suggested by Klijn and Skelcher does not convey the more dynamic and processual vision of governance they wish to – if this is indeed the aim of the authors.[6] At present, the main effect seems to have been that of adding a further variant in a field already riddled with linguistic controversies especially difficult to settle, since governance is still used in literature as a synonym of government, and network governance is also vying with multilevel governance within fields like European Studies and International Relations. The risk of conceptual confusion is thus real; evident in the collection of essays edited by Sørensen and Torfing (2006) where the word order between 'governance' and 'network' keeps shifting for no detectable reason.[7]

Putting aside nominalist questions, it is clear that we deal here with an important attempt to switch the analytical focus from the notion of 'network' to that of 'networking'; that is to say, from a crystallised system of relations to the relations in themselves. 'in this view, governance is emphasised as dynamic and processual, and the institutions are regarded as increasingly destabilised by their changing boundaries' (Sand 1998: 272). For, as noted by Heclo (2002: 694), 'interactions with the world are more participles than nouns'. In many ways, this could be seen as an effort to re-propose the original epistemic aim of network analysis before the neo-institutional turn promoted in the Anglo-American sphere by Powell (1990) and strongly supported by Thompson (2003). With the interesting twist that, whereas traditional network analysis was occupied with the networking of individual agents operating within institutional contexts, governance theorists also apply it to the interaction of collectives, organisations and networks. Their aim is, in fact, to identify the patterns of interactions established by embedded individual and collective agents alike; a task that entails: (i) the definition of the environment wherein interaction occurs, (ii) the identification of the media through which it is carried out, (iii) the understanding of the standards and benchmarks used to assess its beneficial effects, and (iv) the mechanisms of inclusion and exclusion which make networking a viable practice.

These elements are discussed as parts of narratives describing momentous passages from: 'government' to 'governance' (at the polity level), 'hierarchy' to 'eterarchy' (concerning social relationships), 'aggregation' to 'deliberation' (in relation to politics), 'hard law' to 'soft law' (at the policy level), 'top-down' to 'bottom-up' (concerning implementation), 'vertical' to 'horizontal' (in relation to accountability mechanisms). The theoretical emphasis put on crossing traditional boundaries, separating the public from the private, the internal from the external, top from bottom levels, and the appreciation for hybrids which combine territorial and functional criteria, rational and relational features, concrete and symbolic aspects are meant to convey the sense of dynamics implicit in the transition between these binary categories. Compared to the neo-institutionalist narrative discussed above, the main difference lies in the assumption that new modes of governance must be considered not as transitional forms that will, eventually, crystallise into a new social and political order. Rather, their claim is that order and change can actually coexist. From this perspective, the Networking politeia is a dynamic entity changing continuously as it seamlessly moves from a steady state to another. However, I shall contend that such an allegedly dynamic picture of the Networking politeia creates the suspicion that we are indeed dealing with a sociological version of the spontaneous order theory underpinning neoliberal accounts of the Regulatory State. That is, a version of the catallactic order where an embedded notion of agency replaces the individual entrepreneur exalted by political economists old and new (Hayek 1982; Moldofsky 1989), and immortalised by Ayn Rand in the figure of John Galt. As in political economy, the criticisms moved against homeostatic notions of equilibrium and the feasibility of traditional forms of organisation are not meant to undermine functional and instrumental account of change altogether, but to advance more plausible revisions.

Recalling the distinctions suggested earlier by March and Olsen, we can then argue that these perspectives keep perceiving social dynamics in functional terms; that is, as directed at the achievement of unique optimal solutions (point d), and consider politics as a merely instrumental activity whose objective is to solve social problems through the authoritative allocation of scarce resources (point e).

6.3.2. Social networks and virtual interaction

This dynamic picture of governance arrangements find inspiration and support in the body of sociological literature that have tried to unravel the social implications of the communication revolution and digitisation in particular. Here, the appreciation of change promoted by technological innovations often debouches into a celebration of the post-modern information society, producing a genre of cyber-utopianism in the process. This body of work applauds change and speed in ways uncannily similar to those used a century ago in Marinetti's futuristic manifesto to praise technological innovations of the time: electricity, telegraph, internal combustion engine and radio. As a result, the scientific value of this endeavour raises doubts similar to those raised by Marinetti's literary skills, whose manifestos are often thought to be far superior to his own poetry. My intent in this section is neither to do an implausible survey of this body of literature, nor to single out the most celebratory examples to mock them. The discussion will consider only works that can make a contribution to the normative analysis of governance I am keen to develop here, and shall, therefore, focus on an author whose scientific credentials are unimpeachable. Castells (2005, 2010, 2012) is in my opinion the most emblematic figure in this field, if nothing else because his notions of 'network society' and 'network state' embody the qualities attributed to the Networked Polity in governance studies.[8]

Before engaging with Castells' notion of the network state, a preliminary clarification about the notion of network society needs to be made. At a semantic level, the definition of the network society supplied is twofold. First, the label is employed to refer to the people and groups who are actively engaged in creating and linking virtual communities (Smith and Kollock 1999). These virtual communities are composed of 'prosumers', a word coined, as seen earlier, by Ritzer to identify the new type of agency interacting within the multimedia networks which have emerged since the 1990s (chiefly Web 2.0 and 3.0). To this technical definition must be added a second and more speculative use of the expression network society. This additional definition endeavours to identify the ideal type of society that will eventually take shape once existing virtual communities will expand so as to encompass the great majority of people on Earth. Despite the dramatic expansion of ICT since the turn of the new century, cyberspace is still a sociologically restricted phenomenon. The speculative definition of network society concerns a world that has (i) globalised the innovations made available by the communication revolution, (ii) reshaped social interaction across cultural boundaries according to a digital network logic and (iii) internalised interconnectivity within its value system. Of these two definitions, the one that has special relevance for political theory is undoubtedly the second and it is this speculative definition that is used by Castells. Hence the space given to this author here.

For Castells (2005: 3), the network society is 'a new form of social organisation based on networking, that is on the diffusion of networking in all realms of activity on the basis of digital communication networks'. As he explains, 'nowadays wealth, power, and knowledge generation are largely dependent on the ability to organize society to reap the benefits of the new technological system, rooted in microelectronics, computing, and digital communication, with its growing connection to the biological revolution and its derivative, genetic engineering' (*ibid.*). Although the author acknowledges that the network logic underpinning this new form of society is indeed an historical feature at work in past societies as well, he opines that only recent technical innovations (namely, digitisation) have made it a viable alternative to forms of social interaction dependent on command-and-control and market exchange.

> Digital networking technologies enable networks to overcome their historical limits. They can, at the same time, be flexible and adaptive thanks to their capacity to decentralize performance along a network of autonomous components, while still being able to coordinate all this decentralized activity on a shared purpose of decision making. Digital communication networks are the backbone of the network society [...] (*ibid.*: 4).

Castells also maintains that the changes which brought about the network society will undermine the political and cultural elements which still remain anchored to old models of the industrial society. If in the economic sector ICT caused a passage towards a post-Fordist mode of production, in politics we are witnessing 'the rise of a new form of state that gradually replaces the nation-states of the industrial era' (*ibid.*: 15). To distance himself from vulgar Marxist accounts of change, Castells clarifies, however, that this emerging network state 'is not the result of technological change, but the response to the structural contradiction between a global system and a national state' (*ibid.*). Furthermore, to distance himself from the catallactic sounding neo-institutional faith in mechanical resolution of social contradictions, Castells points out that

> the network society is not the future that we must reach [...] It is our society, in different degrees, and under different forms depending on countries and cultures. Any policy, any strategy, any human project, has to start from this basic fact. It is not our destination, but our point of departure to wherever "we" want to go, be it heaven, hell, or just a refurbished home (*ibid.* 16).

This means that, to replace 'the rational bureaucratic model of the state of the industrial era [that] is in complete contradiction to the demands and processes of the network society', we need the pro-active intervention of Marx's midwife in the form of the new networked social movements. It will be thanks to the latter that the obsolete institutions of the welfare state are going to be superseded with a multifarious system of: 'e-governance (a broader concept than e-government because it includes citizen participation and political decision-making); e-health; e-learning; e-security; and a system of dynamic regulation of the communication industry, adapting it to the values and needs of society' (*ibid.*: 17).

To stress the distance separating his notion of the network state from neoliberal visions of the Regulatory State, Castells also boldly maintains the need to reform the main social institutions inherited from the previous industrial age and, in particular, the legal structure governing corporations that makes them bearer of rights as if they were real people, and the liberal understanding of property rights as absolute and exclusive individual entitlements. As we will see later on (§6.5), the legal framework regulating corporate governance is affected by two shortcomings: it establishes a power structure that enthrones shareholders in a privileged position and denies the crucial contribution of various other stakeholders in the productive process, while at the same time failing to protect diffuse shareholding from the speculative manoeuvring of managerial boards (Ireland 2005). Also, the notion of property rights subscribed by liberal legal systems support the policy of enclosure of digital commons and the setting of artificial barriers on the information flow (Bollier 2003). Thus, it systematically interferes with the unfolding of the network logic and reduces both the speed of technical innovation and the ability to adapt of society at large. Consequently, Castells calls for the adoption of a radical model of democracy that can overcome the electoral conceptions hegemonic in the post-war.

> Accepting democracy of communication is accepting direct democracy, something no state has accepted in history. Accepting a debate to redefine property rights goes to the heart of the legitimacy of capitalism. Accepting that the users are the producers of technology challenges the power of the expert. So, an innovative, yet pragmatic policy will have to find a middle way between what is socially and politically feasible in each context, and the enhancement of the cultural and organizational conditions for creativity on which innovation, thus power, wealth, and culture, are based in the network society (*ibid.* 2005: 20–21).

Castells clearly thinks that the change set in motion by the communication revolution has opened a gap between social and political institutions that needs to be addressed collectively and intentionally. At an explanatory level, technological innovations are said to have supplied the means to solve the traditional problems faced by networks and made available a superior functional alternative to markets and hierarchies that society can already exploit in many domains. Unlike the neo-institutional accounts of governance discussed above, Castells maintains, however, that the shift towards a network state is unlikely to occur spontaneously as a side-effect of the decentralised networking of prosumers involved in the policy process, and remains unmoved by the allegedly deliberative achievements of actual existing governance regimes. In fact, he seems to think that the grip neoliberal thought has on the political agenda opposes any mechanical realignment (at least in the short run) and could either slow the pace of change or even undermine the progress of the network society. Moreover, Castells (2012) lends his heartfelt political support to the social movements engaged in direct action worldwide, rather than to the lofty aspirations of metagovernance theorists. While sharing Castells's appreciation for the direct action of social movements worldwide, I find myself unconvinced by both his account of change and his faith in information technology.

From my perspective, Castells's account of change on the one hand underrates the role of state institutions in promoting and directing the innovations that brought about the so-called network society and, on the other hand, overstates the ability of information technology to solve the collective action problems faced by individuals, groups and communities networking in a decentralised form. The social movements analysed by Castells in his 2012 book are cases in point. None of the alleged revolutions initiated by those movements has so far succeeded. In OECD countries, the challenge against the neoliberal consensus politics has repeatedly failed and the movements engaged in it have petered out notwithstanding the stubborn persistence of the economic depression and the legitimation crisis affecting their ruling elites. Outside OECD countries, the peaceful uprising of Arab and East European populations has been superseded by more violent forms of confrontation whose future developments are, at present, either unpredictable or seriously deleterious. A more balanced assessment of the role played by information technology in all these cases needs to discriminate between the ability of social media to (i) mobilise individual and groups politically, and their ability to (ii) lend them staying power and (iii) empower civil society. So far, the last two dimensions have been shown wanting; a fact that perhaps indicates the persistence of deeper theoretical questions which our author fails to analyse.

Some of these questions have been highlighted by Hassan (2004). Writing in the wake of the turn of the century dotcom crash, Hassan (2004: 17) contends that,

> the network society [...] is embedded with the military–industrial logics of control, rationalisation, instrumentalisation and domination. [...] We tend to notice only the 'utility' and 'aesthetics' of ICTs because, in the main, the media (much of it operating on the same logic and with the same technologies) tell us that this is what is important. What is not overtly disclosed in the technology is that the underlying embedded logic of the on–off, yes–no, binary language of computerization tends, like the military itself, to be rigid, to foreclose other ways of seeing, other ways of thinking and other ways of being. So powerful is the ideology that masks this, however, we (mostly) are willing to adapt ourselves to it.

Upon this understanding, Hassan erects, what I think is, a more plausible assessment of future developments:

> Reading the development of capitalism historically leads to the conclusion that what is happening in the wake of the dotcom crash is the classic 'shake-out' of the capitalist economy; and in true social-Darwinist style, the strongest will survive and some will in fact thrive. Moreover we can expect the drivers of the network society to become fewer in number and to begin to resemble globalized oligopolies. A few mega-corporations in media, entertainment, IT, telecommunications and so on will dominate and help shape how we live, think and organize our lives [...]. Lots of money has been wasted, but a lot can still be made and so electronic networks will continue to have the technological momentum to shape society in ways that many of us will have little choice in (*ibid*.: 22).[9]

6.3.3. Collibration and non-institutional policy instruments

Within this sector, another approach to governance that I find particularly interesting is Dunsire's (1990, 1993, 1996) 'collibration'. This label is used by the author to refer to interventions directed at re-balancing the power between contending individual or collective societal agents by imposing external handicaps on some of them. In Dunsire's (1990: 10) words, collibration is supposed 'to mean "to join in the process of equilibration: to manage isostasy"'.[10] Despite its translation into a novel jargon, collibration refers to a class of strategic actions employed by governments from time immemorial which are often summarised by maxims like *dividi et impera*, balance of powers, equilibrium of terror, mutual destruction, etc. For sometime now, these strategic actions, and the equilibrium solutions they yield, have also been at the centre of developments in evolutionary game theory, in their attempt to replace the homeostatic notions of equilibrium still dominating rational choice theory with more dynamic notions. Dunsire approaches the topic through system theoretic analysis, though, and connects it with Luhmann's binary coding categories to assess the steering power of distinct types of public intervention.

In this systemic framework, collibration identifies interventions which do not advocate structural changes but rely on less demanding interferences with interacting societal agents; and which also are alternative to other policy instruments widely used in the post-war years, like financial subsidies, neo-corporative agreements and self-regulation – in policy study lingo: the carrot, the stick and the sermon (Bemelmans-Videc *et al.* 1998). For instance, economic policies directed at managing the aggregate demand, indirect industrial development through the building of public infrastructure and central bank manipulation of interest rates were part and parcel of the strategies composing the Keynesian collibration toolbox. Dunsire focuses his attention on three policy instruments less discussed but which, he maintains, are extremely important: fixing taxation rates, preferential credit streams and reducing information asymmetries. The author explains that this type of collibration techniques,

> makes use of the built-in checks and balances of a particular social subsystem or action arena wherein the determining binary distinctions or coding (government/opposition, employer/employee, buyer/seller, prosecution/ defence, and so on) is institutionalized in separate organizations, which are then self-referential in meaning only as a pair. A relative small use of power, as stick, carrot, or sermon, may then tip the balance of the self-policing tensions already manifest in the pair system (Dunsire 1996: 320–21).

Following Luhmann, Dunsire conceives society as composed of several autopoietic subsystems. Being self-referential, those subsystems create their own language and establish boundaries which reinforce their internal cohesion and help differentiate one subsystem from all the others. An environment composed of self-referential entities of this sort poses problems to the political subsystem. The latter could influence another subsystem only if it is able to understand that subsystem's language and communicate by using it; otherwise it will be shut down by counter-mechanisms attempting to preserve the subsystem's integrity. However, learning a subsystem's language carries the risk of creating some sort of identification with its value-system; something that could bias the actions of the political subsystem in deleterious ways. Within this systemic worldview, the political represents only one of the many subsystems populating a given environment and has very limited possibility to steer society in a specific direction having overall beneficial effects. This is the reason why to avoid egregious government failures authors like Teubner (1983, 1984) – who I shall discuss later on (*see* §6.4.2) – propose the development of reflexive legal tools based on self-regulation.

The logic behind this reflexive turn is as follows. Since subsystems tend to connect with each other, forming second order autopoietic systems, it is upon the latter that the political subsystem should exercise some form of indirect influence. Operating at this second order level entails exploiting the binary relational mechanisms established for inter-subsystemic connectivity such as, for instance, the distinctions between true/false, legal/illegal, good/bad, superior/inferior, etc. As Brans and Rossbach (1997: 425, emphasis removed) clarify:

> binary codes are qualitative, asymmetric schemes which discriminate irritations picked up from the environment. [...] The system 'science' consists precisely of those communications which refer to the code true/false; the system of law is characterized by the code legal/illegal; and the economic system draws on the code have/have not. The system of politics [...] employs the codes government/opposition as well as conservative/progressive in order to process information.

The political subsystem intervenes upon these binary codes by issuing interferences aimed at altering an existing balance and moving the system towards a new steady state. Calibrated interferences of this type could yield the changes wanted while avoiding the costs required by a more direct form of public intervention. As Dunsire (1996: 320) puts it: 'an administrator does not have to think about actually administering them [subsystems], only of finding a way of tapping into their self-governance, harnessing it to public purposes by using the familiar tools of governance: economic, legal and informational'.

To clarify what sounds like very abstract reasoning using a hermetic language, I would like to suggest two very diverse real life examples of collibration. The first is the establishment of the UN-backed no-fly zone in Libya during the 2011 uprising against Ghaddafi's regime. Briefly, the no-fly zone was imposed to redress the balance of power between government forces, who had air power, and opposition forces, who lacked it. In turn, this would protect civilian populations from government retaliatory tactics without committing the UN forces to a much more costly and unpredictable ground invasion (like those undertaken in Afghanistan and Iraq almost a decade before – a problem that is currently re-proposed by the Syrian civil war and its fallout in neighbouring countries). The second example pertains to the anti-union strategy pursued by Thatcher in Britain in the 1980s (*see* Chapter Two, §2.3). In this case, we have the passing of legislation imposing upon trade unions forms of internal democracy which raised the collective action problems faced by those organisations *vis-à-vis* their industrial counterparts limiting, in this way, their collective bargaining power. In so doing, the balance of power was altered in favour of the employer organisations and, since then, all successive British governments have resisted calls for similar legislation directed at democratising corporate governance or defining tougher standards for corporate social responsibility, preferring instead to conveniently consider those issues a matter for self-regulation.

Although I believe that what Dunsire calls collibration refers to strategic forms of interventions which antedate the development of new modes of governance, and that their translation in systems-theory language is not that forthcoming, their relevance for understanding the political and institutional changes of the last three decades is very important indeed. As said, collibration attempts to alter the existing balance of power between interacting societal agents so as to favour one against the other. Domestically, it could therefore be used for undermining the effectiveness of opposition forces while sustaining those which support government policy. Likewise can be said about international relations, where regional and global superpowers systemically use double standards in relation to perceived enemies and allies. In my opinion, this kind of strategic intervention has accompanied the construction of the neoliberal consensus at national and global levels since the beginning, and has not been limited to the field of industrial relations and trade-union bargaining power alone. As I argued in the previous chapter, the European negative integration process represents a macro policy area where collibration has been deployed in a sustained way in all its variety of forms. By using the 'bad-cop/good-cop' role play in turn, national and European decision makers have (i) distributed financial resources so as to benefit concentrated interests and penalise weak stakeholders, (ii) removed legislative barriers which favour export-oriented corporations against medium and small enterprises producing for the internal market, (iii) reinforced the grip of financial institutions on the economy to the detriment of small savers, consumers and even producers, (iv) rewarded the predatory activities of lobbies, top managers and consultants and criminalised those of grass-root opposition movements, marginal local constituencies and dissidents in general.

Dunsire (1996: 327) claims that, 'the main attractiveness to government of collibratory methods where applicable is that compared with the other three autopoiesis-compatible strategies of intervention discussed here, they are a cheap, noncommitting and unobtrusive form of intervention, with possibly greater steering capability'. And indeed, collibration has shown to be remarkably effective in shifting implementation costs and political responsibilities away from central government onto a variety of policy networks and PPPs having little or no decision power at all. The dark side of governance, seldom researched by the first generation of analysts, concerns the way in which national and transnational governments have exploited for-profit and not-for-profit organisations, local communities, charities and NGOs upon whom the burden of public services delivery has progressively fallen. To meet the standards and benchmarks imposed centrally and avoid blame for policy failure, these societal agents have been forced to adopt forms of corporate governance which have distorted their humanitarian and mutualistic values (Dauvergne and LeBaron 2014; Eikenberry 2009; Sandberg 2013). Organisationally, outsourcing, performance-related pay and the panoply of managerial techniques introduced by the NPM has worked the same magic in freeing top managers from political and administrative responsibilities, passing the buck onto street-level bureaucrats and prosumers, who now have to take part in a growing number of verification rituals and meet countless and periodically changing targets (Power 1997b). The outcome has been the generalised increase of regulation and red-tape noted previously, with the noticeable difference that its overwhelming objective is the micro-regulation of daily life, rather than the Keynesian macro-regulation of the economy. In disagreement with the narratives presenting governance as a shift away from the 1980s neoliberal heavy restructuring of the public sector towards a more managerial approach seeking to establish forms of joined-up government (*see* Chapter Four), I see collibration as a complimentary strategic form of intervention whose aim is either to prepare the ground for further rounds of neoliberal restructuring and/or for consolidating the terrain once this restructuring has been accomplished.

6.4. Governance as an autopoietic and reflexive system

The study of reflexive approaches to governance adds further difficulties to those encountered so far. A first additional difficulty concerns the identification of the sociological traditions to which the perspectives located on the right side of our map belong. This is due primarily to the fact that the perspectives included in these sectors define themselves by contrast with the instrumental approaches located to the left; that is, their identity is defined in negative terms: as the total sum of what those other approaches tend to exclude. A further difficulty consists in that there is here an underlying tension between critique and prescription; in the sense that, although these perspectives are not meant to be mere critique, it is never clear when their critical focus turns into an indication of alternative courses of action to follow. A problem compounded by the way in which descriptive, heuristic and normative levels of analysis are seamlessly combined. The overall result is that, whilst in their critical mode these approaches support theoretical perspectives antithetical to the ones already analysed, in their propositive mode they tend to introduce a number of qualifications which end up blunting supposedly crucial theoretical differences.

My entry point into the set of theoretical positions in Figure 6.3 is, once again, a distinction introduced by March and Olsen (2006), concerning this time what they call the 'logic of appropriateness'. According to our authors, social actions can be viewed (and analysed) from two distinct standpoints. Rational approaches are based on a consequentialist logic focusing on the 'calculus' of expected utilities derivable from alternative courses of action and suggesting the selection of the one that 'maximises' the total sum. By contrast, reflexive approaches are based on a logic focusing on the 'correspondence' between behaviour and rules

Figure 6.3: Reflexive approaches to governance as system of rules

	Instrumental approach	*Reflexive approach*
Institution		Appropriateness Autopoiesis Neo-evolutionism
Process		

of action, and suggesting the selection of the course of action thought to be more 'appropriate' in a given context of choice. As seen in the previous chapter, the most sophisticated refinements of rational choice theory redefine the consequentialist logic by reference to rules. So, it is no longer the notion of rule in itself which is the crucial element separating the two, but the role rules play within these two distinct standpoints. Whereas rational choice theory is concerned with the rationality of rules (rules must help maximise the total sum of expected utilities), reflexive social theory is drawn towards explanations affirming the rationality of following rules (even if this conformity does not maximise anything at all).[11] Since this anti-consequentialist stance opposes both a direct interest in problem-solving and functional types of explanation, the logic of appropriateness leads us beyond traditional debates in the social sciences between individualists and holists and is at odds with the positivist outlook these two methodological perspectives jointly introduced in political science. For March and Olsen (2006a: 691, references removed), 'The logic of appropriateness, in contrast, harks back to an older conception that sees politics as rule driven and brands the use of public institutions and power for private purposes as the corruption and degeneration of politics.'

6.4.1. Reflexive action, social rules and democratic legitimacy

Prima facie, the idea of rule-based behaviour and related logic of appropriateness seems to be derived from Wittgenstein's (1958) *Philosophical Explanations*– in particular those parts dedicated to the epistemic implications of following a rule and the relevance of the notion of forms of life (Winch 1990). However, no mention of the Anglo-Austrian philosopher (or of his British follower) is contained in March and Olsen's work. Moreover, they propose a very Weberian reading of those expressions, whose aim is to stress: (i) the links between roles occupied and behavioural regularities, (ii) the larger social expectations connected to those links and (iii) the normative questions concerning the social legitimacy lent by those expectations. As they put it,

> humans maintain a repertoire of roles and identities, each providing rules of appropriate behavior in situations for which they are relevant. Following rules of a role or identity is a relatively complicated cognitive process involving

thoughtful, reasoning behavior; but the processes of reasoning are not primarily connected to the anticipation of future consequences as they are in most contemporary conceptions of rationality. Actors use criteria of similarity and congruence, rather than likelihood and value. To act appropriately is to proceed according to the institutionalized practices of a collectivity, based on mutual, and often tacit understandings of what is true, reasonable, natural, right, and good (March and Olsen 2006: 690).

Unlike Weber though, they are committed to disconnect their notion of rule-based behaviour from any efficientist notion, even the one that for the German sociologist was crucial for understanding the development of modern bureaucratic forms. Thus, Weber's instrumental rationality, what he thought to be the hallmark of modernity, is replaced by more existentialist philosophical elements which insist upon both post-modernity theory and the exponents of the so-called second modernity (Bauman 1991; Beck 1992). For, March and Olsen (2006: 690, references removed) assume that, 'most of the time humans take reasoned action by trying to answer three elementary questions: What kind of a situation is this? What kind of a person am I? What does a person such as I do in a situation such as this [...]?' Hence their conclusion that, 'democratic governance, then, is more than an instrument for implementing predetermined preferences and rights. Identities are assumed to be reflexive and political, not inherited and pre-political, and institutions are imagined to provide a framework for fashioning democrats by developing and transmitting democratic beliefs' (*ibid.*: 692). In so doing, they end up blessing a second holy union (after the one between governance and neo-institutionalism discussed earlier) that has shaped both the research agenda and the (not always clearly stated) values system of governance theory – the one between new modes of governance and deliberative democracy to be discussed below (§6.5.2).

The departure from Weber's underlying efficientist account of bureaucratic forms is, however, due more to the emphatic way in which the authors juxtapose the two contrasting logics of action than to some irreducible substantive disagreement. Thus, the distinction is instantly qualified in ways that make it pretty inconsequential. In fact, March and Olsen's objective is not to point out, as in Wittgeinstein's (1958: 223e, 226e), the radical differences separating distinct forms of life and the corresponding impossibility to fully translate one's language unto another's. On the contrary, they seem keen to reach some kind of theoretical reconciliation between the two logics, and hasten to add that a pure logic of appropriateness – namely one lacking any interest in the rationality of rules – would be incomplete and open to criticism. Accordingly, they propose an evolutionary account of rules that sounds uncannily similar to the one advanced by Hayek (1982):

a conception of human behavior as rule and identity based invites a conception of the mechanisms by which rules and identities evolve and become legitimized, reproduced, modified, and replaced. Key behavioral mechanisms are history-dependent processes of adaptation such as learning or selection. Rules of appropriateness are seen as carriers of lessons from experience as those lessons are encoded either by individuals and collectivities drawing inferences from their own and others' experiences, or by differential survival and reproduction of institutions [...] roles, and identities based on particular rules. Rule-driven behavior associated with successes or survival is likely to be repeated. Rules associated with failures are not (March and Olsen 2006: 696 and 7).

Far from denying the possibility of an instrumental evaluation of rules, March and Olsen seem to subscribe to some sort of moderate agnosticism. In the end, their real objective is not to resolve knotty epistemic questions (as in Hayek's case), but to employ the analytical distinction between these two separate logics for highlighting the existence of theoretical cycles between them and for supplying an explanation of political and institutional change based upon this underlying cyclicity.

Compared to the *Rechtsstaat*, with its traditions and rhetoric tied to the logic of appropriateness, twentieth-century democracies (particularly the welfare states of Europe) embraced practices and rhetoric that were more tied to the logic of consequentiality. Consequence-oriented professions replaced process-oriented ones, and effectiveness and substantive results were emphasized more than the principles and procedures to be followed. Governance came to assume a community of shared objectives rather than a community of shared rules, principles, and procedures (*ibid.*: 701).

· According to them, new modes of governance could break these cyclic dynamics if they are used coherently with a new resolution principle: prescriptive clarity. 'An unsatisfactory approach is to *subsume* one logic as a special case of the other. [...] An alternative is to assume a *hierarchy* between logics. [...] A more promising route may be to differentiate logics of action in terms of their *prescriptive clarity* and hypothesize that a clear logic will dominate a less clear logic.' (*ibid.*: 703, italics in original). The Networked Polity is thus viewed and defended as a political enterprise committed to engender the prescriptive clarity advocated by our authors.

6.4.2. Reflexivity or self-referentiality? The autopoietic nature of the Networking Polity

A clear interest in the resolution of the epistemic issues on which March and Olsen wish to keep a Wittgensteinian silence is shown by autopoietic and neo-evolutionary approaches to governance – here I shall treat them jointly and will not attempt to investigate possible differences between the two. Given the relevance the German Sociology of Law professor, Günter Teubner, has had for these approaches, my discussion will be limited to his account of reflexive law only (Teubner 1983, 1984, 1997). In order to simplify things further, I will not consider either the likely divergences between Luhmann's (2008) attempt to import the notion of autopoiesis into the social sciences and Teubner's use of this same notion in support of his account of reflexive law either.[12]

Teubner's starting point is the crisis of regulatory systems, and public law in particular, first pointed out by Nonet and Selznick (1978) – a question I previously broached (*see* Chapter Three, §3.2 and Chapter Four, §4.3.1). For them, the crisis is affecting not only the more formalistic European legal systems but also those belonging to the common law tradition where 'autonomy is rooted in the network of precedents and the concomitant methods of *stare decisis*, distinguishing and overruling.' (Teubner 1984: 296). The deep causes of this crisis can be explained, according to Teubner, by the tendency of autopoietic social subsystems to preserve their autonomy by shutting out external interference: 'due to their self-referential circularity, autopoietic systems cannot interact directly with each other. Self-referentially closed systems only interact internally with their own elements' (*ibid.*). In the second post-war period, autopoietic closure was reinforced by legal developments promoted by the welfare state and liberal thought. The welfare state has forced a switch from procedural to substantive conceptions of law which have eventually turned out to be unable to manage the complex interaction between subsystems. These shortcomings were then compounded by the intellectual hegemony acquired by liberal thought in the legal field. 'Guided by the liberal, individualistic philosophy of freedom, the law is reduced to general rules of social interaction, thus contributing to the further development and stabilization of self-organizing subsystems in society' (*ibid.*: 297–8).

In developing his solution to the regulatory conundrum – his reflexive conception of law – Teubner is led to pursue two distinct objectives. First, he endeavours to define an analytical framework that can clarify the dynamic of autopoietic closure. Second, he also wishes to arrive at the definition of a justificatory framework that can indicate a viable solution to this problem. To this end, the argument develops in contrast to Nonet and Selznick's idea of responsive law, presented as an unstable evolutionary solution. According to Teubner (1983: 246), 'even if responsive law accurately describes the current situation in law, the amalgam it describes is unlikely to hold together. Indeed, reflexive law, now just an element in a complicated mixture of legal orientations, may emerge as the dominant form of post-modern law.' The unfolding of legal and social change will, for Teubner, bring about a new evolutionary stage that will, in turn, reinforce the reflexive dimension of law. 'This stage, in which law becomes a system for the coordination of action within and between semi-autonomous social subsystems, can be seen as an emerging but as yet unrealized possibility, and the process of transition to a truly "reflexive" law can be analyzed' (*ibid.*: 242). In his systems-theoretic account, reflexive law is presented as, '[a] post-instrumental law [with which] to construct internal models of social reality that can explicitly take into account the autopoietic structure of social subsystems' (Teubner 1984: 293).

Teubner's analytical framework is based on a neo-evolutionary reading of legal systems that adopts and builds upon Luhmann's attempt to extend the notion of autopoiesis to the social sciences – an attempt that is still pretty contentious even between the biologists who first suggested this notion (Kickert 1993). For Teubner (1984: 294–6, references removed):

> socio-legal evolution should not be understood as a developmental universal that necessarily unfolds to reveal higher and higher stages of law and society. Rather, we have to see it both as the product of the interaction among a number of mechanisms of variation, selection, and retention that can be identified within the legal system and as the product of the interaction of these mechanisms with similar mechanisms in other social subsystems.

Teubner's account is based on the idea that the legal subsystem is self-referential. 'The legal system is autonomous if its elements – legal acts – are components in the sense that their interaction is operatively closed with respect to legal acts and recursively reproduces legal acts' (*ibid.*: 295). In turn, self-referentiality and autonomy entail 'the circular relation between legal decisions and normative rules: decisions refer to rules and rules to decisions' (*ibid.*). This means that the broader environment wherein the legal subsystem operates can influence it only indirectly, through pressures exercised on its internal mechanisms. The upshot is the one mentioned earlier in relation to Dunsire's collibration: the difficulty underlying intersystemic interaction due to the offset of defensive closure mechanisms, and thus, the impossibility for the legal subsystem (as opposed to the political subsystem analysed by Dunsire) to regulate other subsystems from without.

The dynamics of autopoietic closure explains, as seen, the regulatory crises arisen in the twentieth century as well as the dysfunctional side-effects shown by various endogenous solutions – legal formalism, welfare state instrumentalism, liberal autonomism. Compared to the systemic models offered by Parson and Easton, the novelty introduced by Teubner's autopoietic approach lies in its focus on the internal working of societal subsystems (elements previously left unexplained and graphically represented as simple black-boxes); for, it is through those internal mechanisms that a subsystem communicates with, and reacts against, the other subsystems surrounding it. From this perspective, the biological metaphor (systems as organisms) seems to better capture the dynamics of social interaction than the mechanistic models employed by the Parsonians. This attention to the internal dynamics of subsystems is also crucial to Teubner for the definition of the post-instrumental justificatory framework he is committed to advance. In attempting to establish external connections, the legal subsystem builds virtual representations of the communication mechanisms of those it wishes to connect with – the introduction of foreign languages within national curricula is to me a good mental picture. Of course, those virtual representations could be of very different quality – exactly like the teaching of foreign languages tends to vary across public education systems. For Teubner, virtual representations employed by Western legal subsystems in the twentieth century have proved to be defective (like the teaching of foreign languages in some European countries – Italy and Britain come to mind – has been fairly poor compared to other continental countries). To improve the verisimilitude of faulty representational mechanisms, Teubner suggests moving towards post-instrumental legal arrangements operating through soft-law tools and indirect forms of governance.

The logic underlying Teubner's reflexive legal system depends on what the German sociologist labels black-box techniques:

> self-referential systems – social systems like law, politics, and regulated subsystems – are 'black boxes' in the sense of mutual inaccessibility. Each knows the input and the output of the other, but the internal processes that convert inputs to outputs remain obscure. 'Black-box techniques' do not try to shed light on the obscure internal processes but attempt to circumvent the problems posed by this obscurity through an indirect 'procedural' route. When the actions of black boxes must be coordinated, each focuses not on the unseen internal workings of the other but on the interrelations between them. The experience gained from observing patterns of behavior is increasingly valuable even though internal causal processes remain unknown. Thus, interacting 'black boxes' become mutually 'whitened' in the sense that the interaction relation that develops between them achieves transparency in its regularities (Teubner 1984: 299–300).

In other words, interaction between subsystems is possible because these subsystems are able to converge on joint courses of action, even when they are unable to understand the causal relations which lead their counterparts to adopt that course of action as well. This is so because *the experience acquired by each subsystem through the mutual observation of behavioural regularities yields*, for Teubner, *enough conceptual clarity to indicate what course of action a subsystem should adopt*. Is the analytical structure of Teubner's black-box techniques convincing? Does it supply a plausible resolution to the problem posed by autopoietic interaction as he describes it?

In mocking Parson's theories, C. Wright Mills (1959) suggested that these mainly rest on linguistic obfuscation. Thus, by re-translating them into a nonsystemic idiom, Mills arrived at the conclusion that they were based on trivial sets of statements which did not shed any new light on the issues at hand, let alone open up new vistas or leading to a scientific breakthrough. This is exactly my impression concerning the black-box techniques employed by Teubner. I contend that, rather than solving the question of subsystems interaction, what we have here is a mere translation in systems-theoretic jargon of the structure underpinning collective action problems amply studied by game theory; a translation that leaves those problems unaffected. The black-box techniques in particular seem to re-propose, in a systemic frame, some controversial solution concepts proposed by game theorists to solve the paradoxes posed by strategic interaction of self-seeking individual agents in prisoner's dilemma contests – above all Gauthier's (1986) 'constrained maximisation' with which it shares surprising terminological affinities.

Briefly, Gauthier's game theoretic approach to cooperation within a Prisoner's Dilemma contest faces two main logical problems, of which it is only the second that has relevance for us in this context. The first concerns the reasoning that justifies constrained maximisation as the best 'joint' strategy among all available. By shifting the theoretical emphasis from 'individual' to 'joint' strategies, Gauthier is in effect introducing a notion of social optimality that is inconsistent with game theory's microfoundations. The second problem concerns the reasoning that leads the agents to adopt the strategy of constrained maximisation. In fact, even if it were proved that the strategy of constrained maximisation is the only optimal solution in the game, an agent is rationally compelled to adopt it only if there is a high likelihood that his/her counterpart will do likewise. This, in turn, depends on (i) the characteristics of the population of interacting agents, (ii) the overall probability of meeting other agents disposed to adopt such a strategy of constraint maximisation, and (iii) the agents's belief system concerning the specific type of agent with whom he/she interacts in each round. Obviously, given the fact that it is impossible to know accurately the various agents's belief systems, (iii) amounts to a sort of guesswork supporting cooperation only by chance. It is at this point that Gauthier introduces the notion of 'translucency'. According to this, the agents who are somehow committed to the strategy of constrained maximisation are not like black boxes, namely completely unintelligible from without, but translucent in a way that enables them to recognise each other.

It is worth noting here the terminological affinity between Gauthier's *translucency* and Teubner's *whitened* and the crucial role both play in resolving the interaction problem as well as their questionable epistemic standing. Indeed, both look like *deus ex machina* sent down by a benevolent external observer wishing to rescue the players caught in troublesome strategic reasoning. In Gauthier's case, there are translucent behavioural traits that make cooperators able to interact only with those who are similarly predisposed and avoid any free-riders even when the latter try their level best to disguise themselves. In Teubner's case, there are already established and unambiguous behavioural regularities which make the internal models of reality of autopoietic subsystems readable from without and easy to establish perfectly matching replicas. In both cases, the solutions arrived at seem to rest on either a conceptual sleight-of-hand, a logical inconsistency, or a circular reasoning, or on all of the above.[13]

6.5. Discursive governance vs. governmentality

All the warnings expressed so far need to be kept in mind when approaching the theoretical perspectives located in this final sector of the map (*see* Figure 6.4). This is a battleground where the followers of two heavyweights of continental social theory, Foucault and Habermas, face each other. The difficulty here is due not only to the hermeneutic problems posed by the sophisticated philosophical positions held by these two masters of social and political thought, but also to the heroic attempt to use these philosophical systems to make sense of specific political and institutional phenomena which brought about the alleged shift from

Figure 6.4: Discursive governance and governmentality

	Instrumental approach	*Reflexive approach*
Institution		
Process		Dialogical networks Deliberative theories Governmentality

'government' to 'governance'. At times, this double hermeneutic endeavour turns into a triple somersault, as a result of the felt need to move beyond mere critique and stress more practical possibilities. A case in point is Habermas himself, who drifted away from critical theory towards a rationalism arguably stronger than the one proposed by Rawls. But similar theoretical shifts can also be found within the Foucauldian camp where, at the hands of some analysts (e.g. Rose and Miller 1992), the notion of governmentality was hollowed out of the radical critical stance the French philosopher attributed to it. In this sector, another remarkable theoretical 'holy union' has taken place: that between governance theory and deliberative democratic thought – a union that has revealed to be strong enough to rival the one between governance and neo-institutionalism discussed above. Although I very much approve of it, I also believe that this union is based on misunderstandings which can undo it as tragically as the plot of Romeo and Juliet so artfully devised by Shakespeare.

6.5.1. Communicative process and dialogical networks

While accepting the idea that new modes of governance are alternative solutions to both statist command-and-control strategies and market-based competitive mechanisms, dialogical approaches to governance studies develop accounts of change at odds with the systems-theoretic models just outlined. Politically, these approaches pursue distinct objectives. First, they attempt to overcome the traditional liberal distinction between state and civil society. Second, they support thicker conceptions of democracy than those which used to dominate liberal democratic thought and practise in the post-war period. The first objective is clearly stated by Bang (2003a: 8):

> political society comprises all those processes of authoritative decision and action that go on within its domain and terrain, which frames the play of difference. It concerns every activity, however remotely related to differences and struggles over the making and implementing of decisions that require acceptance and recognition if they are to be settled or to reach a desired purpose or outcome. It cuts across the sphere of state and civil society, system and life world, national and international, and local and global. Political society is everywhere as a dimension of what is going on within any socially constructed domain.

Concerning the second point, Bang (*ibid.*: 9) observes that 'political authority is no longer associated with relations of subordination and one-way control only but also with a set of flatly operating networks of political communication, where institutions and individuals are locked in multiple, reciprocal relations of autonomy and dependence.' My discussion here is restricted to briefly analysing two main notions employed in this context: the idea of 'communicative rationality' and the concept of 'stakeholder democracy'.

Concerning the idea of communicative rationality, a work that in my opinion helps understand its relevance for governance theory is Sanderson (1999), where this idea is juxtaposed to the competing notion of instrumental rationality. Sanderson's analysis develops within a broader context with which we are already familiar. For him,

> the debate of 'state versus market' is losing its validity as traditional boundaries and divisions are becoming more fluid; much of the cultural homogeneity which bound together interests in the past is being lost; the role of the state and its legitimacy and competence are being widely questioned; the increasing currency of the notion of 'stakeholding' emphasises the legitimate interest of citizens in issues around the development and delivery of public services and places the focus on how citizens should be involved in debate and decisions about such services (Sanderson 1999: 326).

Accordingly, the author discusses what are for him three underlying implications: (i) the shift from a 'technocratic' to a 'constructive' perspective, (ii) a switch from an 'instrumental' to a 'communicative' conception of rationality, and (iii) the rebalancing of power relations between state and citizens, empowering the latter. By and large, they re-propose and support the distinction between output-oriented legitimacy and input-oriented legitimacy already discussed in regard to the Regulatory State (*see* Chapter Five, §5.3.1). Unlike the latter, for Sanderson the switch towards a communicative notion of rationality, and the attendant need to re-politicise policy choice, demands the adoption of an input-oriented mode of legitimacy. In his words, '[...] an "instrumental" focus on means deflects attention from the nature of desired welfare outcomes. [...] However, if we shift the focus from means to desired outcomes then debate can be opened up beyond the "instrumental domain" of professional experts to address the "practical domain" of deciding what the desired ends and outcomes should be, a domain in which power can be shifted decisively in favour of citizens' (*ibid.*: 327). And again,

> the discursive model of practical discourse provides the best hope of moving forward towards an enhanced rationality of policy making – towards more responsible and effective government – not through the application by experts of objective knowledge achieved through scientific enquiry to identify 'correct action', but rather institutionalised discourse – the open debate of alternative interpretations and perspectives which recognises their moral basis and seeks a consensus on what would constitute 'appropriate action' supported by 'good reasons' (*ibid.*: 331).

I shall deal with the question of how the communicative form of rationality advocated could contribute to the more open process of evaluation below. For the moment, I would like to consider a second element that in Sanderson's work contributes to reinforce the social acceptance of policy choices (and in so doing distinguishes his approach from other liberal accounts of input-oriented legitimacy mentioned in Chapter One), the relevance he attributes to the notion of stakeholdership. As for the term governance, the expression stakeholdership is also derived from the managerial theories which appeared in the late 1970s (Freeman 1984). Against traditional conceptions of corporate governance which put an exclusive stress on shareholder value, managerial theories influenced by Rawls's theory of justice started to underscore the relevance other societal and economic agents had for the overall performance of business enterprises. As a result, it was argued that economic efficiency could not simply be viewed as a technical matter to be resolved by scientific means, but that it crucially depended upon the fairness of the rules regulating intra- and inter-industrial relations. As for any other cooperative enterprise, good corporate governance needed, therefore, to be based upon principles of justice which took into consideration all affected interests and treated them equally. This was the starting point of a managerial approach to corporate governance which eventually caused the rising of Business Ethics as an autonomous managerial discipline within business schools (Donaldson 1982).

In governance studies, the notion of stakeholding is developed in two further directions. First, it is applied so as to include all societal individual and collective agents now involved in policy networks, PPPs and prosumer activities. Second, the governance of public affairs is meant to purposefully develop a model of active citizenship through extended forms of democratic participation – the latter being an element that is not always appreciated in business ethics, where democracy is sidelined in favour of abstract mission statements, worked out by professionally appointed personnel, which are supposed to reflect hypothetical rational agreements (Palumbo 2009). For governance theorists who subscribe to a communicative type of rationality, the norms, values and principles which ought to regulate the decentralised interaction of embedded societal agents, and guarantee some form of horizontal coordination, cannot be demanded of specially-appointed professional experts. Rather, they contend that ground rules must be the outcome of social deliberations reached democratically. That is, by applying new modes of governance reflexively to the governance process itself. For Sanderson (1999: 331) this means, 'forsaking the illusion of certainty in modernist-rationalist "order" for a postmodern "messiness" based upon the "overwhelming sense of the contingency of existence"'. It must be noted, though, that this overwhelming sense of the contingency of existence is much more constrained than the one subscribed to by radical postmodernists like Foucault. The dialogical agreements reached by societal agents are always assumed to be based on the 'forceless force of the best argument', rather than disciplinary practices reifying asymmetric relations of power. As we shall see below, this is an ideal shared by various models of deliberative democracy. But it also is an ideal that raises awkward questions concerning both the feasibility and desirability of these dialogical policy solutions.

6.5.2. Governance and democratic deliberation

The dialogical policy perspective advocated by Sanderson has indeed had an impact upon the new modes of governance adopted at various institutional levels. The most remarkable example, on which much has been written over the years, is the 2001 White Paper on European Governance produced by the European Commission. 'The White Paper proposes opening up the policy-making process to get more people and organisations involved in shaping and delivering EU policy. It promotes greater openness, accountability and responsibility for all those involved. This should help people to see how Member States, by acting together within the Union, are able to tackle their concerns more effectively' (CEC 2001: 3). According to this document, all relevant stakeholders have to be involved in both decision making and the implementation processes through periodical consultation, inclusion in the comitology system and specifically established PPPs. Such an involvement pursues a double political objective: to introduce forms of functional representation that can somehow complement traditional forms of territorial representation, and to develop models of deliberative democracy which go beyond Schumpeter's CLM that used to dominate within real existing liberal democracies. The latter obviously refers to a conception of democracy developed in political theory and responsible for what is often called the deliberative turn. The features that characterise it *vis-à-vis* Schumpeter's CLM can be clarified by using three conceptual juxtapositions often encountered in academic debates on the topic: (a) aggregation vs. deliberation, (b) representation vs. participation, (c) polity legitimacy vs. policy legitimacy (*see* Chapter Eight, §8.4).

However, the academic debates which brought about the deliberative turn also suggest that there are several ways in which the notion of deliberative democracy can be modelled, some of which are not fully compatible with the dialogical policy perspective advocated by Sanderson and other governance theorists. As I shall explain later on (*see* Chapter Eight), the most philosophical strands of this democratic movement view deliberation as a truth-oriented procedure aiming at reaching a universal rational consensus of the type sought by Habermas and Rawls. The communicative process intends, therefore, either to identify a notion of public reason that could help define the principles of justice the Networked Polity must abide by, or to simulate the ideal speech situation from which to derive the right solutions for the policy problems that the Networked Polity is called to solve. In both instances, voting, the paramount democratic decision-making procedure, is rejected, and the deliberative process has to remain operative until a unanimous consensus is reached. In governance studies, these philosophical readings of deliberative democracy would, undoubtedly, raise questions concerning both their feasibility and desirability. Indeed, I suspect that any epistemic conception of this kind would remain within the 'modernist camp' and re-propose the 'medical' model that Sanderson retains utterly unsuitable in a postmodern and reflexive policy environment. As I will try to show (*see* Chapter Eight), at best these epistemic conceptions could support the technocratic solutions advocated by the theorists of the Regulatory State.

But no less problematic are, in my opinion, the non-epistemic models of deliberative democracy proposed in literature. The latter consider public deliberation as an institutional mechanism able to stimulate the participation of all 'affected interests' in policy making and policy implementation from the bottom up. The only epistemic role attributed to deliberation here is that of laundering the irreflexive preferences held by some of the stakeholders involved, without ever aspiring to arrive at reasons which no one could reasonably reject (Palumbo 2012). Being a not truth-oriented process, this type of public deliberation presupposes time-limits and requires voting mechanisms and majority rules for reaching political decisions. According to those who support readings of deliberative democracy like this, the idea of universal rational consent is not just unrealistic, but also undesirable. It reflects the antipolitical biases of modern philosophical liberalism; a system of thought that has unfortunately become, in the colourful words used by Dryzek (2000: 27) to explain Habermas's shifting position on this issue, 'the most effective vacuum cleaner in the history of political thought, capable of sucking up all the doctrines that appear to challenge it, be they critical theory, environmentalism, feminism, or socialism'. From my perspective, these political versions of deliberative democracy also fail to support the notion of stakeholder democracy advocated by the governance theorists discussed here. The latter, as seen above, wish to engender forms of governance without government that blur traditional political distinctions – between state and civil society, domestic and international politics, public and private spheres – which these democratic theorists are keen to retain. Hence the claim I made earlier that the celebrated union between governance theory and deliberative democracy ultimately rests on misunderstandings which could easily unravel it.

6.5.3. Governmentality, genealogy, governance

Foucault's (1978) notion of governmentality poses difficulties similar to those we confronted in analysing autopoietic approaches to governance. It is therefore worth keeping in mind that my intention is not to do a (more or less exhaustive) survey of this literature, but to discuss the theoretical relevance this notion has for governance studies. In so doing, I shall be exclusively concerned with the work of Rose and his collaborators (Rose and Miller 1992; Miller and Rose 1995; Rose et al. 2006), whose idea of 'governing at a distance' has had a major impact on governance theory. As is well known, Rose's 'governing at a distance' builds upon Latour's reading of Foucault's work and in particular on the idea of 'action at a distance'. However, I am not interested in investigating the accuracy of the readings of Foucault and Latour proposed by Rose, or related hermeneutic issues of this type.

The theoretical elements I shall ponder upon are three. The first two concern the analytical framework within which the notion of 'governing at a distance' unfolds – framework that structures the overall research programme. Underlying this notion is a liberal form of political rationality wishing to tackle the government failures affecting centralised political systems and the welfare state in particular – a preoccupation that is re-proposed by the side-effects imputed to neoliberal reforms of big government. This type of political rationality is analysed through empirical studies of government technologies (budgets, audits, standards, and benchmarks) developed for 'the operationalisation of programs of governing at a distance that characterized the forms of new public management taking shape under rationalities of advanced liberalism' (Rose *et al.* 2006: 95). Rose's empirical approach to governmentality has a peculiar British character that plays down the superstructural aspects found in Foucault, and is therefore at odds with both the continental Foucauldian school of thought and the discourse theory popular in US universities. This is why our authors hasten to clarify that, 'the aim of such studies is critical, but not critique – to identify and describe differences and hence to help make criticism possible' (Rose *et al.* 2006: 101). In concluding, I shall explain what type of genealogical approach Rose appeals to and express some critical remarks on the matter.

The idea of 'governing at a distance' is developed in reaction to two main lines of thinking: (i) the representations of the state advanced by historical political sociology, which Rose and Miller (1992) blame for being unduly concerned with realism, and (ii) the systems-theoretic accounts of the state suggested by Dunsire and Teubner, and those influenced by French superstructural perspectives: that is, those which blend systemic analysis and Marx's notion of superstructure (Harland 1987). The criticisms levelled against the first are of a kind that can basically be subscribed by all the theoretical approaches to governance encountered so far:

> the political vocabulary structured by oppositions between state and civil society, public and private, government and market, coercion and consent, sovereignty and autonomy and the like, does not adequately characterise the diverse ways in which rule is exercised in advanced liberal democracies. Political power is exercised today through a profusion of shifting alliances between diverse authorities in projects to govern a multitude of facets of economic activity, social life and individual conduct. Power is not so much a matter of imposing constraints upon citizens as of 'making up' citizens capable of bearing a kind of regulated freedom. Personal autonomy is not the antithesis of political power, but a key term in its exercise, the more so because most individuals are not merely the subjects of power but play a part in its operations (Rose and Miller 1992: 174).

However, doubts are also raised against the rationalisations of political and institutional change advanced by systemic and superstructural approaches:

> to understand how we are governed in the present, [...] requires us to turn away from grand theory, the state, globalization, reflexive individualization, and the like. Instead, we need to investigate the role of the gray sciences, the minor professions, the accountants and insurers, the managers and psychologists, in the mundane business of governing everyday economic and social life, in the

shaping of governable domains and governable persons, in the new forms of power, authority, and subjectivity being formed within these mundane practices (Rose *et al.* 2006: 101).

As an alternative, Rose and colleagues affirm the need to engage in the empirical study of restricted and apparently marginal social contexts – study of a prevalent descriptive character aimed at emphasising the contingency of the phenomena under investigation and the role played by the techniques used to identify failures and suggest proper solutions.

To understand the nature of this analytical framework, I think it useful to employ the distinction between hardware and software commonly used in computer sciences. According to this perspective, historical sociology and its systemic and superstructural counterparts pay too much attention to the hardware (i.e. the institutional framework), when the most significant element is instead its software (i.e. the managerial strategies employed within). Hence the attention given to programmes, the languages developed for programming, the techniques used during programming and the solutions arrived at to translate programmes into actions.

Government is a domain of strategies, techniques and procedures through which different forces seek to render programmes operable, and by means of which a multitude of connections are established between the aspirations of authorities and the activities of individuals and groups. [...] It is through technologies that political rationalities and the programmes of government that articulate them become capable of deployment (Rose and Miller 1992: 183).

This is why it is suggested that to analyse entities like power we need abandon the realist attitude of previous sociological traditions and adopt a constructivist outlook able to conceive political categories dynamically.

'Power' is the outcome of the affiliation of persons, spaces, communications and inscriptions into a durable form. [...] mobile and 'thixotropic' associations are established between a variety of agents, in which each seeks to enhance their powers by 'translating' the resources provided by the association so that they may function to their own advantage. Loose and flexible linkages are made between those who are separated spatially and temporally, and between events in spheres that remain formally distinct and autonomous. When each can translate the values of others into its own terms, such that they provide norms and standards for their own ambitions, judgments and conduct, a network has been composed that enables rule 'at a distance'. [...] centres of government are multiple: it is not a question of the power of the centralised state, but of how, in relation to what mentalities and devices, by means of what intrigues, alliances and flows – is this locale or that able to act as a centre (*ibid.*: 184 and 185).

The third element upon which I wish to dwell here is related to the (not always explicitly stated) justificatory framework underpinning this reading of the Networked Polity. Right from the start, I would like to make clear that, in principle, I have no objections to pure descriptive phenomenological inquiries which refuse to engage in the type of foundational disputes dear to philosophers. From my perspective, it is possible (and sometimes even healthy) to put to one side all ontological and epistemic questions pertaining to the existence of a reality independent from the observer, the referential or nominalist nature of languages used to describe it, the distinction between cause and effect, and the relation between action and structure, etc. Freed from these concerns, the social sciences could be left to develop empirical inquiries able to shed light on the complex relational tangles composing all social phenomena, the hermeneutic circles yielded by any attempt to study them, and the contingent and relational nature of our social knowledge. Unlike Habermas (1985: 185ss), I also believe that literature and philosophy could be combined together without demeaning any of them. I have thus no methodological reservations against the microanalysis of marginal social ambits and grey sciences. Nor do I have any hermeneutic objection about laundering Foucault's governamentality in the waters of the Thames in order to wash away supposed superstructural elements or tune down its radicalism. My claim instead is that these types of empirical micro-studies must still satisfy some epistemic criteria of evaluation that the notion of 'governing at a distance', and the suggested accounts of the passages from liberal programmes of government to neoliberalism via the welfare state underpinning it, fail to do.

One of these criteria concerns the gestalt-like power of the proposed rationalisations of political and institutional change. Are these rationalisations able to restructure the knowledge and experience of those affected by these changes, giving them more insight into their nature and rationale? In other words, are those micro-studies illuminating or not?[14] As an individual who is both personally affected by many of those changes and professionally engaged in studying them, my answer is negative. The first element I find particularly contentious is the narrative underpinning the model of governance without government subscribed by all the accounts of the Networked Polity analysed in this chapter, Rose's 'government at a distance' included. To repeat myself, the idea that governance develops as the unintended outcome of the decentralised interaction of societal agents facing coordination problems is empirically unfounded. At best, this thesis rests on an improper generalisation of very restricted (and controversial) empirical evidence; at worst, it is just wishful thinking. The various waves of reform occurred in the last three decades have clear political origins and rationale. They are the outcome of sustained political attempts to strengthen the power of central government *vis-à-vis* other representative institutions (parliaments, local government, neocorporative arrangements) and ambits of civil society that the welfare state did not manage to colonise (liberal professions, journalism, third sector, trade unions) or even unwittingly emancipate (Civil Service, NHS, public education).

As I tried to explain in Chapter Two, the template originally developed by Thatcher's government to reign in the British Civil Service (NPM) has been progressively refined, extended to other ambits of the public and third sectors, and exported to other national and transnational contexts by means of policy transfer. In OECD countries, the strategy of political centralisation and administrative decongestion at the core of this model of governance has been adopted by all main liberal and social democratic parties, and enforced through the undemocratic logic of TINA and the deployment of sophisticated forms of collibration. Rather than engendering a new type of stakeholder democracy or deliberative policy environment, its success has been based on empty consultations, the exploitation of artificially created grass-roots groups and the biased restructuring of social incentives. This is a theoretical conclusion corroborated by my personal experience, first as a student in British higher education from 1994 to 2001, and since then as an academic working in Italy – two very distinct educational systems where the same policy template is currently being implemented with disciplinary zeal, despite the opposition of many stakeholders and accumulating negative empirical evidence concerning its outcomes in related policy areas.

Although I share many of the doubts about the way in which Foucault uses the notion of governmentality (as power techniques deployed by total institutions to discipline individual personalities from the inside to subordinate them willingly – Harland 1987: ch. 12), I do believe that his dystopic picture has more gestalt-like power than the tamed anglicised version supplied by Rose. The latter looks to me so much like the cultural evolutionism of Hayek (1982) that it can aspire to be a constructivist reworking of the notion of catallaxy. This is a genetically engineered constructivism that, with a sleight-of-hand, throws any burdensome superstructural features out of the door to reintroduce them stealthily from the window. For instance, despite his stress on contingency and opposition towards deterministic explanations, Rose views neoliberal political rationality as a means for realigning politics (as a superstructural element) with the transformation of subjectivity which occurred at societal level (the basic structural element) in the 1960s and 1970s.

> [neo-liberalism] should be seen as a re-organization of political rationalities that brings them into a kind of alignment with contemporary technologies of government. [...] Neo-liberalism forges a kind of alignment between political rationalities and the technologies for the regulation of the self that took shape in Britain during the decades of the 1960s and 1970s. [...] These reorganized programmes of government utilise and instrumentalise the multitude of experts of management, of family life, of lifestyle who have proliferated at the points of intersection of socio-political aspirations and private desires for self-advancement. Through this loose assemblage of agents, calculations, techniques, images and commodities, individuals can be governed through their freedom to choose (Rose and Miller 1992: 199 and 201).

Moreover, if for Foucault these processes could always be dangerous and require critical attention, Rose seems ready to embrace them unconditionally, given that 'for neo-liberalism the political subject is [...] an individual whose citizenship is active' (Rose and Miller 1992: 199 and 201).[15] This begs the question concerning the kind of genealogy inspiring Rose's research programme and its normative role. On this point I find a 1996 essay by Lottenbach quite perceptive, in which two distinct genealogical traditions, Hume's and Nietzsche's, are analysed and compared. For Lottenbach, in both traditions of thought, genealogical analysis has clear normative objectives. In Hume's case, the objective remains very conservative: to show that although our morals rest on rules of justice of a conventional nature, they are not at all arbitrary. They shape our moral sentiments, define the ethical benchmarks we commonly employ, and are thus vital in achieving a commonwealth. Attempts to tinker with them for egotistical or partisan reasons could end up undermining individual compliance and thus unravel the social fabric altogether. Genealogical analysis plays a rather reverse role in Nietzsche. Here it is used to unmask the origins of extant moral rules and reject the (utilitarian) justifications supplied by the (British) moral philosophers. It represents an attempt to show that what was for Hume the cement of society (to use Elster's words) is in reality nothing more than a reified set of relations of power based on resentment. Now, if his political radicalism pushes Foucault to adopt a Nietzschean genealogical outlook, Rose's attempt to expunge any superstructural element from this very notion leads him to espouse a Humean genealogical outlook. In my opinion, this explains the similarities between Rose's notion of 'governing at a distance' and Hayek's idea of catallactic order. However, if I am right, the justificatory framework employed by Rose is vulnerable, *mutati mutandis*, to the same type of objections raised against the rule-utilitarianism subscribed to by Hume, Hayek and their neoliberal followers.

6.6. Conclusions

In this chapter I have presented several lines of research that, independently from each other, end up proposing similar accounts of the Networked Polity. In doing this, I wanted to highlight the existence of a rich plurality of sociological perspectives influencing governance studies, and offer a conceptual map that could help systematise them while shedding light on the epistemic and normative presuppositions underpinning the analytical and justificatory frameworks they yield. This has given me the possibility to substantiate some remarks I made earlier, concerning the feeling of *déjà vu* felt by many who approach this field of inquiry from without and the limitations of governance theory itself. Their epoch-making claims notwithstanding, many of the accounts of the Networked Polity considered here engage in re-appraisals of phenomena already identified and studied by political science in the past. The treatment of known phenomena using novel methodologies often results in translating old categories into a new scientific jargon, an operation that risks increasing the proliferation of definitions and theories without bringing genuine new knowledge. In this chapter I have insisted on two questions. The first pertains to the attempt to arrive at analytical frameworks based on thicker notions of agency than those used by the theorists of the Regulatory State. While appreciating and welcoming this attempt wholeheartedly, I find the end result pretty disappointing. Rather than arriving at an approach to policy analysis capable of fulfilling the political aspirations stated by March and Olsen, the adoption of sociological perspectives and methods has ended up supporting rationalisations of change that systematically dissolve the political into the social, and/or even undermine the very notion of agency. Hence the emphasis I posed on the similarities between catallactic readings of the Regulatory State and the systemic and superstructuralist accounts of the Networked Polity. The impression I derive from this is that of having swapped one methodological imperialism with another, an economic version of the spontaneous order thesis with a new, but no less troublesome, sociological variant.

The second question I have been keen to explore concerns the justificatory frameworks supplied by the theoretical perspectives examined. I have insisted on the fact that what is very often presented as an empirical trend that is going to be realised in the near future is, in reality, not so; it rather resembles a political aspiration. Were this the case, the Networked Polity (the deliberate and self-reflexive policy environment involving stakeholders and prosumers at all stages of the political process) would turn out to be a normative ideal. As such, it needs to be justified accordingly. The myriads of case studies on new modes of governance produced in the last two decades could be used to show that this normative ideal is a viable alternative to statist and market-based worldviews. In itself, however, the empirical evidence collected so far is not enough, and not strong enough, to support the confidence of governance theorists in the spontaneous realisation of the Networked Polity. In developing a proper normative justification of the Networked Polity, my suggestion is that particular attention should be given to two contentious categories: output-oriented legitimacy and deliberative democracy. Governance theories often take for granted that Networked Polity strives to overcome the procedural forms of legitimation sought by liberal democratic theories of the welfare state.[16] I have, however, shown that an output-oriented approach could easily lead to a neoliberal justification of foot-voting models of democracy (*see* Chapters Five and Eight), rather than the deliberative policy environment characterising the Networked Polity. Obviously, this would be inconsistent with the participatory aspirations of deliberative democratic theorists, for a great deal of their claims have a procedural value: (i) the involvement of all affected interests in the policy process, (ii) their ability to take part in the discussion on equal terms, (iii) their right to cast a vote for reaching political decisions. The epistemic claim that deliberation also ought to select the best outcome is far too contentious to be relied upon. Theoretical incomprehension of this sort needs to be detected and clarified to make the 'holy union' between governance theory and deliberative democracy a lasting and prolific one. This is indeed the task I set to myself in the third part of the book.

End Notes

1. The narrative based on diverse generations of studies is suggested by Sørensen and Torfing (2006). It is in this spirit that I use it too (*see* Chapter Three, §3.4).

2. On methodological individualism and related debates, the essential reader is still the one edited by John O'Neill (1973).

3. For instance, although Bang and Sørensen (1999: 334) claim that political activity 'has shifted from formal organizing to more informal *network*ing', they maintain that the task of the 'Everyday Maker [prosumer] is to produce concrete outcomes' (*ibid*: 332). Likewise can be said about the interactive governance approach discussed below. Here *governance* is tightly connected to the notion of 'governability', defined as, 'the overall capacity for governance of any societal entity or system' (Kooiman *et al.* 2008: 3).

4. It is in this attempt to combine action (Scharpf) and structure (Luhmann) that I find the similarities with Parsons (1968), of whom Kooiman makes no mention. For here we confront a problem similar to that undertaken by Parsons to combine Weber (to whom Scharpf is intellectually indebted) and Durkheim (whose influence on Luhmann is noticeable). On these genealogies see Ritzer and Goodman (2003).

5. Two things need to be noted on this point. First, as seen before, Kooiman also considers mixed forms. However, in his model they operate at the second order level (governance), rather than at the third order level (metagovernance). Second, in the passage just quoted Jessop claims that he now (2003) intends metagovernance as part of Dunsire's collibration, rather than as he claimed previously (1998). Given the reading of Dunsire's collibration I propose below, this means stressing the strategic dimension of metagovernance *vis-à-vis* its institutional dimension. My understanding of Jessop's revision is, however, the reverse. I believe that in 2003 Jessop actually stresses more the institutional elements of metagovernance than the strategic features proposed by Dunsire. Hence, to me his notion metagovernance is conceptually distinct from Dunsire's collibration. Perhaps, the main difference is due to the way in which we understand the adjective 'strategic', with Jessop using it to refer to institutional arrangements, while I consider it as a more processual element. Whatever the case, my reading of Dunsire's collibration is at odds with my understanding of Jessop's 'law of requisite variety'.

6. Stoker (2006) seems to me engaged in a similar operation and, to this end, he uses the expression 'networked governance'. Although this sounds (to my non-native ear) more apt than the one proposed by Klijn and Skelcher, the risk of increasing definitional confusion would, for me, advise otherwise even in this case. In fact, Ansell (2000) uses the expression 'Networked Polity' in a neo-institutionalist sense, whereas Castells uses 'network society' and 'network state' in a more processual sense. Thus, adopting Stoker's solution would leave us with a similar problem in cases like these.

7. In subsequent works, Sørensen and Torfing (2009) seem to have opted for a more consistent use of the word order solution suggested by Klijn and Skelcher 'governance network'. However, I have been unable to track down any explanation for this choice.

8. In the new preface to the third edition of the second volume of his trilogy *The Information Age*, the author acknowledges the contribution of governance studies to the corroboration of the hypothesis he himself made two decades earlier about the network state:

> over time, a new form of state emerged in practice: a state made of ad hoc networking in the practice of government between nation-states, European institutions, global institutions of governance, regional and local governments, and civil society organizations. While the core of the political process remained in the nation-states, their actual decision-making process became characterized by a variable geometry of co-sovereignty, involving a plurality of actors and institutions depending on the issue and the context of each decision to be made. [...] the process of governance became increasingly characterized by networks of cooperation (not exempt from competition) between nation-states and international institutions (Castells 2010: xxx).

9. This pessimistic conclusion is shared by Wu (2011). The latter is particularly concerned about the notion of 'net neutrality' (the ideological neutrality of the internet as technological platform) and maintains that the Internet will most likely follow in the footsteps of the communication technology revolutions which preceded it. Then as now, the democratic hopes raised by the new technologies faded away and radio/TV broadcasting either remained under strict governmental control or became dominated by a small number of commercially-minded private networks (or both, as the Italian case shows).

10. 'Isostasy' is an ideal theoretical balance between the crust of the Earth (lithosphere) and the denser top layer of the Earth's mantle (asthenosphere). Another author who employs a somewhat similar systems-theoretic approach to governance is Andersen (2005).

11. I owe this insight to Lorenzo Sacconi, who introduced me to game theory. It was reiterated to me some years later by Bob Sudgen to clarify the differences between his theory of social norms and Elster's.

12. It is a moot point whether Teubner's reflexive approach is at all consistent with Luhmann's, for the latter is much more pessimistic concerning the possibility of bypassing autopoietic closure. According to Brans and Rossbach (1997: 436) Luhmann's approach has Wittgenstenian implications: 'The role of "science" is therapeutic rather than prescriptive'. On these differences see Hernes and Bakken (2003) and Kickert (1993).

13. Since governance theorists are concerned with the coordination failures brought about by institutional fragmentation, it could be objected that the correct contexts of choice to take into account are mixed and pure coordination games and not prisoner's dilemmas. Indeed, developments in game theory have attempted to bypass the strategic problems created by noncooperative games of this kind by appealing to Humean and Darwinian solutions for coordination games. In Palumbo 2000, I deal at length with these attempts to show that they also are conceptually flawed. So, even if we relate Teubner's problem as due to an underlying coordination game, his reasoning would still be faulty.

14. To my knowledge, the most interesting (even if somewhat hermetic) statement of this criterion of evaluation comes from the German film director Werner Herzog (2010): 'we must ask of reality: how important is it, really? And: how important, really, is the factual? Of course, we can't disregard the factual; it has normative power. But it can never give us the kind of illumination, the ecstatic flash, from which Truth emerges'.

15. 'My point is not that everything is bad, but that everything is dangerous, which is not exactly the same as bad. If everything is dangerous, then we always have something to do. So my position leads not to apathy but to a hyper- and pessimistic activism' (Foucault 1984: 343). More in line with this critical spirit is the reading of governamentality proposed by Dean (2010: 200), for whom, 'government, if one likes, has becone more multiple, diffuse, facilitative and empowering. It is also, however, strangely more disciplinary, stringent and punitive.' More recent, Rose and Miller have qualified somewhat their earlier statements. Thus they now affirm that,

> The 'freedom' programmed by these reconfigurations of power and expertise was certainly so simple liberation of subjects from their dreary confinement by the shackles of political power into the sunny uplands of liberty and community. But neither was merely an ideological fiction or a rhetorical flourish. [...] This is not to say that our freedom is a sham. It is to say that the agonistic relation between liberty and government is an intrinsic part of what we have come to know as freedom (Rose and Miller 2008: 216).

I leave to the reader to judge how much this qualification affects my assessment. However, I would like to thanks Peter Triantafillou for the (very) friendly observations moved to an earlier draft of this work in which he raised the question concerning these late developments.

16. As seen in the first section, this claim is unwarranted and leads the authors discussed in this chapter to hold contradictory positions on the issue.

PART III

CRITIQUE

Chapter Seven

State, Globalisation and Governance: Rhetoric, Contradictions, Paradoxes

7.1. Introduction

Governance studies have interacted with and are built upon an even more flourishing literature on globalisation that has engulfed turn-of-the-century social sciences like bush fire. At the core of both bodies of work it is possible to find two main theoretical claims upon which I have tried to cast doubts in the previous chapters. The first has to do with the declining relevance of the nation state and the set of policy instruments used by this political actor in the past. The second claim is related to the rationales advanced to explain the declining relevance of the state form in domestic and international domains; rationales based on explanatory frameworks which (i) locate the roots of change in domains external to the political one and (ii) reframe the dynamics of change as the outcome of unintended consequences. As Shaw (2000: 11) notes, 'the global quality of social relations, in both these accounts, is seen as the result of cumulative changes in people's relations with each other and their physical environment. In essence, society has been globalised not because human beings thought or acted globally, but because in pursuit of other ends – profit, power, communication – worldwide connectedness has developed'. Those, like Shaw, who are not fully satisfied with the rationales advanced by globalisation and governance theory have tried to qualify the various accounts of change proposed without fully questioning the structure of the explanatory frameworks employed. Thus, it is sometimes claimed that the thesis about the demise of the state needs to be replaced by a more nuanced account of its transformations which does not challenge its non-political origins (Sørensen 2004), while at other times the political origins of current change are acknowledged but in ways which reaffirm the validity of the unintended consequences thesis (Rhodes 2007).

I have previously noted the rise of a second generation of policy analysts that is challenging these two core assumptions. The picture of political and institutional change emerging from this reappraisal of globalisation and governance theory is one that stresses both its political origins and rationale, and in doing so, it questions the validity of the explanatory frameworks used to date. The present chapter builds upon, and wishes to contribute to, this more critical line of inquiry by showing that the empirical evidence used to support the momentous transformation of state-based sovereignty, and the resulting passage from 'government' to 'governance', could be read in a diametrically opposed manner. Since I have maintained that, at the core of the various attempts to reshape the political and institutional landscape brought about by *les trente glorieuses,* is a twin strategy of political centralisation-cum-administrative decongestion, my task here is to substantiate this claim. I shall explain that the adoption of this strategy across OECD countries and beyond was meant to strengthen the governability of these societies by undermining the value-system established by liberal and social democratic forces in the post-war period, as well as the constitutional mechanisms engendered to support it. Thus, rather than undermining state sovereignty and empowering civil society, the transformations we are witnessing aim at reconfiguring the domestic and international balance of power in ways which are unremittingly hollowing out liberal democratic institutions. I will do this by questioning three main theoretical antinomies used in these fields: the idea that there is an inevitable trade-off between the state and the market (§7.3); the identification of the state with public hierarchies that are being inexorably supplanted by network forms of organisation (§7.4); the allegedly terminal implications that internationalisation is having on the Westphalian system of power relations (§7.5). Before delving into those issues, I wish to propose a genealogical analysis of the nation state that could clarify the reasons behind its historical ascendancy and the principles of action which used to guide its governing activities.

7.2. The nation state between narratives of modernity and the rhetoric of globalisation

The state is at the centre of all the narratives of modernity proposed by Western social sciences. Its irresistible historical ascendancy has been the object of continuous scientific analysis, to the point of defining both the domain of inquiry and the field of vision of these same disciplines. For Jessop (2003: 102–3), this state-centric bias explains the academic interest in governance theory and its success as a novel paradigm:

> Traditional disciplines reflect the organization of nineteenth century modern industrial societies: economics focused on markets, political science on sovereign national states, international relations on inter-state Realpolitik, and sociology on civil society. Not only has the taken-for-grantedness of national economies, national states, and national societies as units of analysis been challenged by the dialectic of globalization-regionalization but conventional conceptual couplets (such as market vs. plan, state vs. civil society, bourgeois vs. citoyen) also appear less relevant. 'Governance' is being introduced to bridge disciplines and to provide alternative ways of understanding.

In past narratives of modernity, the state is depicted as a *sui generis* entity having not just power of agency, but also as playing a pivotal role in influencing the phenomena which brought about this historical turn in human affairs. Usually, these narratives cover a period that goes from the Peace of Westphalia (1648) to the establishment of the UN (1948), and use multiple pair-wise juxtapositions of pre-modern and modern features (Chernilo 2008; Dunn 2000: ch. 2; Gill 2003; Mann 1993: ch. 3; Poggi 1978, 1992; Skinner 2002).

According to these narratives, state-building processes have impacted in all spheres of human activity, transforming them radically. Economically, the state is viewed as having been mainly responsible for undermining the feudal system and its subsistence-oriented agricultural form of production, and setting off the processes of urbanisation and industrialisation which eventually led to a capitalist organisation of the economy. Socially, it is held responsible for promoting a double process of territorial consolidation and functional differentiation: the first leading to the integration of various sub-units within the same national context, and the second establishing the complex division of labour required by capitalist activities. Finally, the state is given the task of consolidating those economic and social changes by fostering processes of cultural, administrative and political homogenisation capable of creating strong national identities, coherent value-systems and unitary legal frameworks. Following Weber, it is also suggested that the mortar used to glue together the modern social fabric is no longer the blend of religious and traditional beliefs employed in the past. A new form of political legitimacy, based upon the instrumental rationality of the rules established to regulate social interaction and assure individual compliance, is established. Despite its aspiration for value-neutrality, classical social theory ends up attributing to the state and the processes of modernisation a positive, even if critical, endorsement. Thus, Durkheim (1950: 63) states that, 'On peut dire que c'est lui qui constitue la fonction essentielle. C'est lui qui a soustrait l'enfant à la dépendance patriarcale, à la tyrannie domestique, c'est lui qui a affranchi le citoyen des groupes féodaux, plus tard communaux, c'est lui qui a affranchi l'ouvrier et le patron de la tyrannie corporative'[1].

Besides its formative stage, the narratives of modernity have attempted to chronicle and rationalise the transformations undergone by the state form by highlighting the analytical features thought to distinguish one type from another. Among these transformations, those that, from my perspective, have arguably yielded the most prolific results are three: the one discussing the shift from the Absolutist State to the liberal constitutional state, another analysing the passage from the liberal state to the welfare state, and the third charting the shape of the state form emerging from *les trente furieuses*, for which a plethora of competing new labels are suggested, among them the two considered in this work: the Regulatory State and the Networked Polity.[2] Building upon Weber and Durkheim's accounts, past narratives support the idea that the state form which emerged in the West has systematically acted so as to acquire some form of absolute sovereignty (Palumbo and Scott 2003). The monopoly of the legitimate use of physical force within discreet territorial jurisdictions is, however, only the most evident part of a more diffuse process that has made the state one of the few surviving collective agencies able to mobilise all the material and immaterial resources available in a given territory and decide how to employ them properly. In the struggle to fulfil this ambition, the Western nation state has established permanent administrative systems having universal reach, and successfully deployed them to quash any organised resistance coming from either within or without. The tensions and conflicts generated by this absolutist and expansive logic have defined the problematic relations the state entertains with civil society and with other state and non-state actors, and has been the privileged object of study of the social sciences all along. As Skocpol (1985: 27) would put it, 'the meanings of public life and the collective forms through which groups become aware of political goals and work to attain them arise, not from societies alone, but at the meeting points of states and societies'.

The definition and imposition of discrete national boundaries has, for instance, started dynamics of inclusion and exclusion justifying the marginalisation and/or oppression of all minorities unable to identify with the newly established national entities (Macartney 1934). The creation of well-integrated national economies with a gradual more sophisticated functional division of labour promoted, in addition, massive migratory flows and forms of exploitation (within and between national boundaries) which would put at the centre of scientific attention the so-called social question (Arendt 1963). The atomisation and juridification of social relations would, in turn, heighten the interest of social and political theorists towards the anomic side-effects of modernity and the individual restless search for authenticity (de Grazia 1948). As a result, the widespread processes of democratisation which have accompanied the evolution of the state form in the twentieth century can all be analysed as the outcome of the various efforts to influence the direction of social and economic change and redistribute the benefits of social cooperation so as to resolve the most evident contradictions between state action and its moral and political justification (Durkheim 1950). The welfare state and embedded liberalism are the political solutions arrived at after World War II, as explained at length in the first chapter; solutions which, while helping in the task of post-war reconstruction, would eventually fail to resolve the contradictions they were designed to avoid, thus setting in motion the new cycle of change with which we are concerned here.

A parallel process of change was set off by the rising of the state form at the international level. There, the nation state tried to establish the most congenial environment for the exercise of the absolute form of sovereignty it sought to affirm domestically. Outstanding victims of these other sets of events would be two main collective actors who had dominated the political scene from time immemorial, but whose universal aspirations were incompatible with state sovereignty: church and empire. The church would first be forced to withdraw from interfering in state affairs, then solicited to recognise the state's secularity, and finally made to accept a distinction between public and private that turned faith into a mere individualistic experience (Breuilly 1993: ch. 3, Sec. 2). Thus, Mann (1993: 84) notes that 'across all states most active Catholics opposed state centralisation. The church retained [remained?] transnational while strengthening local-regional organisation' (and in the process helped develop the notion of subsidiarity that has now been adopted by across Western nation states). On their part, multinational empires either imploded, under the secessionary pressure of national groups trying to establish their own state – in line with the dictum 'a state for each nation, and a nation for each state', or they were defeated on the military battlefield. Nowadays, the only imperial forms we still have are those underpinned by a strong national base, something that makes them more a projection of state power than empires in the old sense.[3] And even in these cases, old imperial strategies are shown to be unsustainable and in need of being replaced by more sophisticated strategies of economic domination and cultural hegemony.[4] From the international field the nation state has also managed to drive out all other polities which were unwilling to adopt, or else incapable of affirming, an absolutist conception of sovereignty (Warner 1999). Hence, the international system has come to closely resemble the kind of anarchic society theorised in the field of international relations (Aron 1995; Bull 1977): a context populated by nation states having (a) absolute sovereignty upon discrete geographical areas and (b) exclusive representative authority of the populations living in those areas, and where (c) the norms regulating interstate activities (i) have a consensual nature and (ii) rest on the voluntary compliance of those subscribing to them. Even if, as Mann (1993: 69) reminds us, diplomacy and geopolitics always remain rule-governed activities.

Globalisation and governance are said to have had a profound impact on the social and economic structures brought about by modernity, one that is rebounding upon the nation state causing its gradual unravelling (Hooghe and Marks 2003). Whilst globalisation is claimed to have undermined the external kind of sovereignty attributed to the nation state by the Westphalian system of international relations, new modes of governance are taken to have undermined its domestic sovereignty. As seen, both sets of phenomena are also imputed to impersonal social and economic forces creating a sort of feedback loop that is reinforcing their destructive effects and entrenching political and institutional change worldwide. Moreover, it is often, more or less forcefully, argued that compared to similar past events, the force, scope and reach of current changes are of a different kind and ushering in epochal transformations, which lead many social theorists to envisage some form of post-modernity (Bevir 2010). For them, the globalisation of markets has set the basis for a post-Fordist form of production, neutralising the Keynesian policy tools available to the welfare state and producing new forms of disembedded subjectivity (Bauman 2000). Similarly, they contend that the institutions of global governance emerged in the wake of globalisation are moving far beyond the regulatory regimes created by past intergovernmental activism, and are realising cosmopolitan ideals without the need of a global government called to enforce the rule of law and human rights by the sword (Rosenau 1995).

Within this reading, domestic and international changes reinforce each other seamlessly, making the unravelling of the state form an unstoppable force and causal explanations too simplistic to account for it. The globalisation of markets that allegedly deprived the nation state of its macroeconomic powers is tightly related to the set of changes that have in the meantime brought about the institutional fragmentation of the public sector: deregulation, privatisation and marketisation. Various defensive attempts to rein markets in through the empowerment of regional and transnational authorities like the EU have ended up aggravating the crisis of the nation state by draining from it more sovereign power. Their regulatory successes have not only amplified the sense of inadequacy of state institutions in a globalising world, but they have also weakened the exclusive ties connecting states to their citizens. In short, the nation state is being steadily hollowed-out of its governing capability while retaining its responsibilities for government failure (Howlett 2000; Rhodes 1994). My aim here is to contend that the demise of the nation state has been greatly exaggerated: not only many of the transformations mentioned above were initiated by state action,[5] but those changes have allowed the state to acquire new governing capacity (Jayasuriya 2001). I shall support this claim by showing, first, that the supposed trade-off between state and market is a red herring. Historically, the nation state has systematically utilised markets and market-based policies as instruments for expanding its sovereignty upon new realms; and the changes imposed in *les trente furieuses* support this thesis. I will then argue that it is not the state *per se* that is being unravelled, but the configuration of the constitutional set-up established by the post-war settlement. To put it bluntly, what we are witnessing is not the erosion of the state but the structural crisis of the representative model of democracy engendered during *les trente glorieuses*.

7.2.1. Peeking inside the state: heuristic and methodological problems

The idea that the state is a *sui generis* entity with agency power is at the root of debates and controversies which have kept social scientists busy across the years. Obviously, my aim here is not to summarise the terms of those debates, let alone restart one.[6] Rather, my objective is the far less ambitious one of outlining the reading of political and institutional change supported in the course of the work as clearly as possible to avoid eventual misunderstandings, even if I am aware that in doing so I tend to repeat myself. The distinction upon which I insisted above between the unravelling of the state and the reshaping of its democratic configuration overlaps, to some extent, with the one proposed by du Gay and Scott (2010). In adopting a Weberian perspective, du Gay and Scott contend that debates on the topic are often marred by claims confusing changes affecting the constitutional arrangements of the state with those affecting the political relevance of the state itself. Thus, they suggest the need to distinguish between 'state' and 'regime', and support the thesis that globalisation and governance are changing the regime form rather than the state form. While agreeing with their suggestion, I would, however, like to point out some methodological differences separating their endeavour from mine.

Du Gay and Scott's distinction between state and regime rests on the identification of two sets of elements: those that, according to them, are 'essential' to the state, in that they do not vary with the regime form, and 'additional' elements which reflect instead the specific configuration of each regime.

> Whereas the state is disembedded, the particular institutional arrangement via which the struggle for access to the power that the state lends social actors is conducted is deeply socially – and culturally – rooted. It is these institutional

arrangements, the coalitions between social groups and their associated beliefs and patterns of behaviour that we shall label 'regime.' [...] Regimes are shaped by the 'problems' and 'tasks' that they have to address. Their chief task is to preserve 'national unity' in the face of the inevitable competition between social groups for the distribution not only of power, but also of national wealth' (du Gay and Scott 2010).

From my perspective, such an underlying assumption is not only highly problematic (for it seems committed to some form of essentialism), but it is also redundant, in that it is not required by the Skinnerian (1989, 2002) account of the modern state they are keen to rely upon. In summarising the overall account proposed by the Cambridge historical school, Dunn (2000: 68) explains why this is so:

The state was a structural relation between three elements: a ruling power, a historically given set of human subjects, and a particular territory [...]. It was not a government. It was not a people. It was not a country or homeland (a *patria*). Rather, it was the structure which related together all three at any point in time, and, because it did so, could outlast quite drastic alterations over time in any, or even in all three, of them (a point repeated by the author later on, pp. 80–81).

The relational identity of the state proposed by Dunn does not rest on essentialist features and this makes it compatible with deep transformations affecting supposed core elements like territory, population, ruling power and even the structure of patriotic identification itself.

Using a horticultural metaphor, we can say that the picture of the state advanced by du Gay and Scott resembles closely that of an artichoke, with a solid 'core' that gives it a specific identity and an external 'cover' composed of leaves having diverse colour and variable dimensions that serve to distinguish among the varieties internal to the same species. By contrast, the picture of the state proposed by Dunn is more like that of an onion, where the mere stratification of layers confers to it a distinctive identity despite the lack of a solid core. My understanding of the state attributes to it the relational type of identity suggested by Dunn and is sceptical about using essentialist assumptions in general. Deeper questions separate my reading from the justificatory framework du Gay and Scott build in parallel with their analytical distinction – an aspect upon which I cannot unfortunately delve in detail. Briefly, besides my scepticism concerning essentialism, I find the Hobbesian justification of the state sought by du Gay and Scott far too crude and controversial to be useful. Here I wish to note only that similar defences of state sovereignty were put forward recently by the Libyan and Syrian leaderships in their (uncannily Hobbesian) attempt to warn their opposition about the risk of an all-out civil war if their regimes were challenged. An appeal that, as we know, was in both cases unable to change the course of events – a fact this that must surely appeal to the sociological sensibility of du Gay and Scott, for it underscores the practical limitations of the abstract instrumental justifications often offered by political philosophers. Finally, I find that the overall argument put forward by du Gay and Scott keeps oscillating, in a somewhat contradictory way, between the sociological antipolitical stance I detect in the accounts of the Networked Polity discussed before (Chapter Six), and a perspective more receptive of the epistemic intimations launched by March and Olsen (1984) concerning the relative autonomy of the political from the social.

In discussing the rationalisations of political and institutional change put forward by governance theorists, I have insisted on two things: that the political and institutional changes which occurred during the last three decades were initiated by the state and that they followed a political logic fulfilled to a remarkably large extent. In so doing, I keep attributing agency power to the nation state even if I am well aware of the epistemic and methodological objections raised against previous attempts to do so – above all by NPE theorists of whom I am particularly critical for being inconsistent with the methodological tenets they preach to others (Palumbo 2001). My objective, however, is not to arrive at a general explanatory model of social change that can be applied universally and a-temporally but to propose a genealogical account of very restricted sets of phenomena: those which occurred in the six decades up to the 2008 financial crisis and which have brought about the shift between two different types of consensus politics and the consequent alleged passage from 'government' to 'governance'. Thus, after showing that there is no theoretical or practical trade-off between the state and the market, I will disaggregate these collective entities and try to identify which actors have been at the forefront of the attempt to reconfigure the state by shifting from one 'regime form' to another.

To this end, we need to bear in mind the various elements used so far to explain the passage from the 'welfarist' consensus politics established after WWII to the 'neoliberal' consensus politics we find ourselves in at present. First, the current neoliberal consensus politics is much more restricted than its predecessor, and its diffusion across the political spectrum is due more to the implosion of the social and political coalition supporting the welfare state than to its inner ideological appeal or overall practical achievements. Second, the strength of the current neoliberal consensus politics depends on both the benefits the social and political coalition supporting it is able to muster, and the collective action problems faced by the social and political forces which are penalised by it (Polanyi's counter-movements). Third, both the dominant neoliberal coalition and the counter-movements opposing it are neither static nor homogeneous, but are shaped by internal and external competitive dynamics promoting the periodic consolidation of their institutional structures and the renewal of their forms of identification. Fourth, these competitive dynamics always unfold within contexts which are structured by sets of norms yielded by the interplay between regulators and meta-regulators at the national and international levels. Fifth, the benefits enjoyed by the dominant neoliberal coalition are not simply material but they also entail the exercise of power in various domains and are thus strictly dependent on questions concerning its political legitimacy.

In Mann's (1993: 80) words, 'powerful political actors pursue most of the multiple functions of state pragmatically, according to particular traditions and present pressures, reacting pragmatically and hastily to crises concerning them'. In doing this, I maintain that they pursue their own (broadly defined) interests,[7] keeping one eye on the way in which their actions are presented and justified to the general public, and the other eye looking for the most likely partners which can help them endorse their policy goals.

7.3. Market ideology as public policy

As seen in the previous part, the theorists of the Regulatory State and of the Networked Polity alike base their rationalisations of political and institutional change on socio-centric perspectives which (i) view non-political factors as independent variables in the unravelling of the state and (ii) support the idea that there is an inevitable trade-off between states and markets. The globalisations of markets, the technologies brought about by the information revolution and the feasibility acquired, as a result, by network forms of organisation are periodically taken to be the underlying reasons pushing for the radical restructuring of state institutions and changing of styles of governing. In the mid-1980s, the debate was kick-started by those interested in accounting for the changes then occurring in the manufacturing industry as a result of de-localisation. The literature on post-Fordism purported to show that production based on Tayloristic managerial principles was becoming obsolete (Amin 1994). By combining the efforts of a multiplicity of small producers located in different parts of the globe through ICT technology, a second industrial (or post-industrial) revolution was taking place (Piore and Sabel 1984).[8] In addition, similar arguments were used to explain the evolution of traditional corporations into either conglomerates with diversified productive activities, or managerial financial centres able to invest in, or pull out from, industries and markets at a moment's notice (Mann 2013). With the advent of the new economy at the end of the 1990s, those arguments were deployed to account for the spreading of Western patterns of consumption and styles of life (Barber 2007; Keohane and Nye 2000; Ritzer 2004). According to these explanations, cultures were loosing their specificity and insularity as people were able move across boundaries freely, virtually if not physically. The nation state was, therefore, called to compete with newly emerging global trends and actors to retain its socialising function and cultural role.

To use the successful metaphor suggested by Bauman (2000), social relations were assuming a liquid form undermining the state's ability to define social identities and retain the loyalty of its citizens. The term 'liquidity' also became pivotal in the body of literature dealing with the financialisation of economic activities. In this context, it is however used literally, rather than metaphorically, to refer to the predominance acquired by financial institutions and speculative financial activities *vis-à-vis* the 'real' economy; that is, the one dealing with the production of material goods and socially useful services. In developing a bleaker picture of the post-Fordist global economy than that put forward by Piore and

Sabel, and economists like Mishkin (2006), post-modern social and political theorists used that vocabulary to explain the limits faced by traditional Keynesian macroeconomic policies and the consequent decline of embedded liberalism (Ruggie 1998).

In these accounts, the broad changes caused by global impersonal social and economic forces have formidable negative implications for the post-war welfare state – an expression used to identify the ideal type of state from which to gauge the transformations in progress. In the hands of analysts like Majone, the Regulatory State undergoes a remarkable conceptual transmutation and from an American variant of the welfare state becomes its nemesis (*see* Chapter Five). Accordingly, it starts to be now used to indicate a changed political attitude towards public intervention and redistribution as such. First, in contrast to the welfare state, the Regulatory State is said to be characterised by an awareness of the limits and costs of state action that leads it to restrain itself to the regulation of economic activities, rather than attempting to make the national economy grow (let alone setting a specific annual growth rate, as Majone likes to remind us using France's *dirigisme* as a paradigmatic example). This means to abandon the Keynesian stabilisation tool-kit amply used in the past for reducing the effects of economic cycles. Second, the Regulatory State also intends to avoid getting involved in the redistributive policies which, according to Majone, were at the root of the unsustainable social expectations undermining the governability of real existing liberal democracies. This means to jettison the model of social citizenship responsible for the development of a parasitic entitlement culture and, to a large extent, even the regional development programmes with which the nation state was historically associated. Of the old welfarist mindset, the Regulatory State retains only the goal of regulating the market through the negative integration of economic activities approach favoured by Roosevelt; a negative integration policy that is supposed to be implemented through the system of independent regulatory agencies devised during the New Deal.[9]

Developed under the spell of NPE, the theory of the Regulatory State supports the idea that there is an inevitable trade-off between the state and the market – a trade-off that often even assumes the form of a zero-sum game. Given that the traditional structural limits faced by the nation state are gradually being reinforced by the changes brought about by globalisation, the state should only play an ancillary role to markets. This role requires a drastic rescaling of state sovereignty (so as to strengthen the authority of sub- and transnational entities and attribute to them clear responsibilities) and of the public sector *vis-à-vis* the private sector. Given the strict correlation discovered by public choice theorists between democratisation and bureaucratic growth, this rescaling also entails the depoliticisation of various policy areas and the selective review of the policy instruments available. In Moran's (2003: 36) words,

> The dominant scholarly orthodoxy of recent years has linked the regulatory state to images of retreat and dissolution: to the rise of modes of 'governance' that are concerned with the management of self-steering networks transcending

conventional public/private boundaries; to the rise of new systems of 'soft' bureaucracy that dispense with the hierarchies of Weberian administration; to the rise of soft law as a successor to command law; and to the displacement of the ambitious projects of economic and social control that are the characteristic product of high modernity by more modest projects of strategic steering.

For this dominant scholarly orthodoxy, globalisation and governance no longer represent rationalisations of political and institutional change whose plausibility is to be proved. Rather, they are turned into powerful rhetorical elements whose task is to justify and direct change – a task carried out by TINA, the rhetorical strategy profusely employed by Thatcher and Regan against their internal enemies (Douglas 1997).

In passing, I have mentioned analysts who have tried to contrast this dominant scholarly orthodoxy by qualifying various claims put forward and showing that the changes brought about by neoliberal reforms have transformed the state without necessarily eroding its policy capacity. However, as Levy (2006: 10) has forcefully argued,

> for the most part, they leave unchallenged the presumption that contemporary change pushes in a single direction, toward the reduction of state intervention. They differ mainly in their assessment of the strength of these pressures and of the capacity for political and institutional resistance, adopting a more sanguine position than the first camp on the possibilities for state persistence. They also tend to accept the first camp's metric of change as the decline of traditional forms of economic and social coordination, thereby confining politics and institutions to a kind of rearguard action. The logic of economic, technological, social, and ideological change is that state intervention should shrink, while national political and institutional forces resist this logic. Thus, politics is destined to defend an ever smaller, less relevant, and embattled sphere of state activity over time.

My aim here is to move a step forward by bringing to light and connecting together more radical critical perspectives, emerging with the second generation of governance studies, which challenge those common presumptions and, in so doing, sets the ground for an alternative Polanyian counter-narrative.

The context in which these lines of inquiry are sprouting up is particularly complex to chart. First, most of the authors I would include in the Polanyian camp do not always engage with the Hungarian social theorist directly, but share with him what I think is a clear intellectual affinity. Second, they encompass works blending historical, socio-economic and political issues and moving across the explicative and prescriptive analytical divide. They all agree in rejecting the spontaneist socio-centric analyses of globalisation and governance outlined above. Far from being the outcome of a Hayekian catallactic social order, globalisation of markets and the current neoliberal consensus politics are seen, in fact, as the result of state planning. As in the past, the markets composing the new economy still require: (i) legal authorities and systems of courts able to establish and enforce property rights and contractual agreements, (ii) centrally coordinated political action that can effectively neutralise the reaction of the defensive counter-movements opposing those changes, and (iii) the continuous state interference directed at turning socially embedded people into disembedded prosumers and stabilising markets through corporate welfare policies. A volume collecting various contributions charting the evolution of the state form in a post-statist policy environment, edited by the above-mentioned Levy (2006), painstakingly reconstructs the role played by various state actors, operating in distinct policy areas at national, transnational and international levels, in starting the market-based reforms at the root of both globalisation and governance. In particular, it shows that,

- trade liberalisation is often an instrument of power politics[10]
- state authorities have played a central role in expanding labour market flexibility and decentralising bargaining
- the shift towards soft-regulation in national contexts like Britain has a genuinely political rationale – to replace club government self-regulation
- de-*dirigisation* is above all an exercise in state redeployment, rather than simply rollback
- even in countries where neocorporate arrangements made internal changes look like consensual (Holland and Germany), they were actually carried out in the dark 'shadow of hierarchy' – threats to engage in Thatcher-style direct political confrontation with trade unions and other corporate bodies.

Among the many case studies discussed in that volume, the policy area that perhaps shows the closest resemblance to Polanyi's analysis is the field of intellectual property rights. Here state action has been pivotal in the various attempts to establish a system of absolute and exclusive property rights for intangible resources which digitisation has made both reproducible and transmittable at almost zero cost. In order to enforce this system of intellectual rights, a plethora of hard rules has been passed to outlaw an entire gift economy that had emerged in the meantime; even if the latter pertained to non-commercial activities and peer-to-peer forms of exchange, and its legal banning inevitably encroached on individual privacy and freedom of expression. The similarities with the eighteenth century movement of enclosure analysed by Polanyi are not only striking but repeatedly noted (Palumbo and Scott 2005). Then as now, parliamentary acts and state coercion have been crucial in bringing about a state of affairs that would not have otherwise occurred. It also would not have had the worldwide diffusion witnessed without the self-serving intervention of the dominant geopolitical powers – the British Empire in the nineteenth century, the USA now. A point that finds further corroboration in the work of Djelic and Sahlin-Andersson (2009: 193, but also 2006):

> in many governance stories, an endorsement by states and/or administrative units gives much greater clout and strength to a set of rules, particularly when it comes to local and national adoption and implementation. [...] the threat

of coercion undeniably remains a resource in the hands of states even in times so clearly characterized by soft and interactive forms of regulation and governance.

The Polanyian spirit pervading this literature contrasts markedly with Marxist readings of those very phenomena. The state here is not a 'sovrastructural' entity reacting to economic pressures, but an active agent pursuing specific political goals. Market based reforms are presented as directed at undermining intermediate social institutions and non-state organisations which could question the internal and external legitimacy of states, threatening the power enjoyed by their ruling elites. Once again, the point has been grasped by Djelic and Sahlin-Andersson (2009: 195 and 196),

> This means that a lot of what, at first sight, seems to be regulatory competition should ultimately be reinterpreted as many steps pushing in a parallel, if not the same, direction. Competition in the short term contributes, in other words, to the emergence of collective stabilization in the longer term. [...] intense competition at an apparent and superficial level tends to blind both actors themselves and most observers to the profound ordering and stabilization associated with meta-rules of the game.[11]

Many of the political and institutional changes brought about by the neoliberal reforms of the last thirty years are linked to the commodification of new commons and the recommodification of those nationalised by the welfare state and to the process of depoliticisation of state activities and deresponsibilisation of state actors mentioned earlier (*see* Chapter Two, §2.3). On the one hand, the policy of market building/expansion has allowed the state to gradually demote decisions from (a) the governmental to the public sphere, (b) the public sphere to the private sphere and (c) the private sphere to the realm of necessity (Hay 2007: 80). Thus, a great deal of what were political decisions were turned into questions of a technical or contractual nature, even if in reality it is still the state that retains full meta-ruling power in those areas (*see* Chapter Five). On the other hand,

> With the multiplication of regulatory and governance activities, responsibilities get diffused and dispersed. The movement towards soft regulation has a tendency to reroute, furthermore, responsibility away from rule-setters and towards rule-followers. Voluntary rules that are open to translation mean that those who choose to follow the rules and to follow them in certain ways are held responsible (Djelic and Sahlin-Andersson 2009: 182).

That the state is not eroded by the market is made evident by its ability to intervene when the search for corporate profits causes systemic shocks. In those instances, the nation state suddenly and miraculously manages to recover the strength needed to preserve the (financial) market from imploding – and allows unremarkable political figures like Gordon Brown to claim that he saved the world!

Have three decades of relentless reform of big government reduced state expenditure significantly? The general answer found in the bodies of literature under scrutiny seems to be: not really; although the causes for this alleged failure remain a moot point. If social welfare is supposed to have flat-lined (if not reversed its course downwards), in this same time frame corporate welfare seems to have increased. To quantify this increase is particularly arduous though. First because the state financial involvement in the general economy has differentiated and becomes progressively more indirect. For instance, within the EU negative integration policies have outlawed many forms of direct state support and thus member states are constantly seeking indirect ways to prop up their economies. Likewise can be said at the global level under the pressures of the liberalisation programmes enforced by the Bretton Woods institutions. Second because there is a dearth of available official data that makes any direct assessment simply impossible. As Farnsworth (2012: 2) explains,

> the key problem with the official data is that, where these are collected, this is not for the purpose of gauging levels of support for businesses, nor to increase transparency or the effectiveness or efficiency of state programmes. Rather, data are aggregated and collated for general accounting purposes (which hide specific forms of support) and/or to comply with international regulations on business support that are in place to identify unfair trade advantage, which tends, as a result, to focus primarily on direct subsidies. The problem here is that international regulations are weak and/or extremely narrow in their coverage. As a result, the extent of public and parliamentary scrutiny of cash and in-kind support provided by the state to corporations lags far behind other areas, thus making it impossible to assess the full and relative costs and benefits to business and society more generally.

The general perception is, however, that it is not only increasing in magnitude but that it has also become as ubiquitous as in pre-modern political systems based on royal patronage. To the point that the qualification 'neoliberal' referring to the current consensus politics is highly misleading and should be dropped altogether, if was not for the libertarian language with which these policies are justified.

Besides direct subsidies, currently state side-payments to its corporate partners follow at least four different streams:

- fire-sale privatisation of tangible and intangible public assets and commons
- outsource practices and private finance initiatives (PFI) imposed by central government across the public sector
- soft-touch regulation of financial activities and one-sided loopholes in tax legislation[12]
- supporting services supplied through the centrally-imposed subservience of public and social agents to businesses in the form of:

    i.   research and development
    ii.   flotation of pension funds and other liquid assets
   iii. workfare programmes
   iv. gambling activities
    v.   voluntary activism.

These funding streams are available in normal times and are therefore not inclusive of the emergency measures established by the state during the systemic shocks the state has to deal with periodically. The amounts of money distributed to corporate agents during these emergencies are so staggering that they defy my limited computational powers. They are, however, at the centre of estimates carried out by the flourishing industry of books published immediately after any of these natural or man-made catastrophes occur. As many critics from the left and the right often point out, corporate welfare on this scale tends to compete with social welfare and is responsible for entrenching social inequalities (another theme engaging a parallel and similarly flourishing industry). It also interferes with the free-market in the worst of Keynesian traditions and creates forms of corporate risk-taking which worry the most orthodox of libertarian ideologues (Posner 2010).

Current empirical research on corporate welfare has tried, with mixed fortune, to test and corroborate the existence of macro-trends yielded by *les trente furieuses* (Farnsworth 2013). In addition to a possible trade-off between corporate and social welfare, other trends concern the shift in state financial and in-kind support from:

- businesses operating for domestic markets to those working for the export markets;
- traditional manufacture to post-industrial services (especially the financial and insurance services operating in secondary and tertiary markets);
- industries sourcing standardised mass markets to those catering for specialised and exclusive markets (including the military and security sectors).

Taken together, the picture derived from this sectoral research is far from that of the Madisonian system of government suggested by the theorists of the Regulatory State, let alone the hollowed-out state inspiring the theorists of Networked Polity discussed next. The state is not only alive and kicking, as it were, but is as committed as ever to support a version of the modernisation project that can preserve its sovereignty throughout what look like epochal geopolitical and social transformations. And in doing so, it is permanently engaged in establishing strategic alliances with the economic forces willing to share both the costs and benefits brought about by any such a meta-PPP. The scale of corporate welfare thus helps explain the readiness of economic forces to assume risky public functions on behalf of the state; the macro-trends investigated within this body of literature are therefore useful to understand (if and when they are empirically supported) the constellation of forces composing the current neoliberal meta-PPP, as well as the changing internal balance of powers any time the terms of the (collusive) partnership are renegotiated.

7.4. Governance as a means to rework the separation of powers

Governance theorists supporting the Networked Polity paradigm supply a distinctive reading of change proposed by those working within the Regulatory State paradigm. First of all, they view the erosion of states by the market not as a process of the individual's liberation from governmental oppression, but rather as a process inducing institutional fragmentation and, therefore, increasing the risk of coordination failure. This point is positively emphasised by Bevir (2010: 31): 'when social scientists study neoliberal reforms of the public sector, they often conclude that these reforms have scarcely rolled back the state at all. They draw attention instead to the unintended consequences of the reforms. [...] the neoliberal reforms fragmented the service delivery and weakened central control without establishing proper markets'. In addition, these same social scientists advance a reading of the alleged passage from 'government' to 'governance' where the Networked Polity assumes the form of the unintended outcome of repeated attempts to solve the coordination problems caused by institutional fragmentation in a decentralised manner. Bevir (*ibid.*: 29, n. 15) is, once again, keen to stress the general theoretical implications of this attempt: 'by analogy, governance also can be used to describe any pattern of rule that arises either when the state is dependent upon others or when the state plays little or no role. [...] So understood, governance expresses a growing awareness of the ways in which diffuse forms of power and authority can secure order even in the absence of state activity'.

The abstract features that identify this new entity *vis-à-vis* its hierarchical predecessor are reported in neat, synoptic form by Hooghe and Marks (2003) (*see* Figure 7.1, emphasis in original). In it, the authors identify and compare two types of governance systems. One, identified as Type I, defines the salient characters of the ideal type hierarchical government yielded by the post-war welfare state, whereas the other, identified as Type II, sketches the outline of the horizontal post-statal authority gradually replacing it – the Networked Polity.

Figure 7.1: Types of multilevel governance

Type I	Type II
General-purpose *jurisdictions*	Task-specific *jurisdictions*
Nonintersecting *memberships*	Intersecting *memberships*
Jurisdictions at a *limited number of levels*	*No limit* to the number of jurisdictional levels
Systemwide architecture	*Flexible design*

According to Hooghe and Marks (2003: 236),

Type II multi-level governance is distinctly different. It is composed of specialized jurisdictions. Type II governance is fragmented into functionally specific pieces [...]. The number of such jurisdictions is potentially huge, and the scales at which they operate vary finely. There is no great fixity in their existence. They tend to be lean and flexible – they come and go as demands for governance change.

In Chapter Six, I explained that a similar picture of the Networked Polity and its associated style of governing can also be derived from neo-functional approaches, even if here processual elements are emphasised above neo-institutional aspects. And before that (Chapter Four), I spelled out the crucial divergence separating these two types of governance: those concerned with implementation issues (top down for Type I and bottom up for Type II), those pertaining to democratic politics (Schumpeterian for Type I and deliberative for Type II), and those related to accountability (vertical for Type I and horizontal for Type II). I shall come back to the last two issues in the following chapters. Here, I wish to focus instead on some shortcomings imputed to this reading of change, and thus complement the analysis developed in the previous section. Is the Networked Polity the outcome of deep social changes which are impacting on the political system reshaping it accordingly? Or is it the outcome of a genuine power game taking place within liberal democracies following the implosion of the consensus politics supporting the post-war welfare state?

A way to start looking for an answer to these complex questions would entail: (i) disassembling the narratives used to explain recent political and institutional change in sets of hypotheses to be accurately analysed and compared among themselves and with the available evidence; (ii) disaggregating complex collective entities like the state into more elementary and discrete parts and then studying what sort of changes have occurred, where exactly they have done so and the implications those changes are having; (iii) confronting the results of (i) and (ii) so as to assess the relative plausibility of the various hypotheses at the centre of competing rationalisations of those changes. Obviously, such an undertaking is so vast and complex that it defies many of the limited approaches used in political science and is susceptible to end up fuelling endless epistemic and methodological debates. There are, however, authors (and works) who have attempted just that in a more or less extended form. Sassen (2006) is a case in point, and a very ambitious one at that.[13] Sassen starts from the presupposition that globalisation affects distinct aspects of the state differently, and is therefore convinced that to understand its political implications we need to study its impact on three main elements: territory, authority and rights. Limiting ourselves to the changes affecting authority, Sassen (2008: 198, references removed) notes that in the USA one of the main salient events since the late 1970s is the shift in the balance of power from the legislative to the executive branch of government:

'privatisation, deregulation and marketisation have reduced the role of Congress but added to the role of the executive through the setting up of specialised commissions and the power they have assumed. In addition, this is a shift that is beyond party politics'.

The supposed erosion has not concerned the state *per se*, but its democratic configuration. In the first place, national parliament and other elected legislative bodies who have ceded decision-making power to their executive arms, and supervising functions to the judiciary branch. Sassen also points out that to this internal redistribution of power must be added the parallel rescaling of the public sphere that has caused a growing exercise of private power by economic and social corporate actors. Since this rescaling has been carried out by soft law and authoritative re-interpretations of extant laws and statutes, and since it has bolstered the regulatory and meta-regulatory powers of executive authorities, Sassen claims that the magnitude of the changes which occurred in *les trente furieuses* makes the shift qualitatively different from similar dynamics noted about the 1930s New Deal. The concentration of power in the executive happens contextually with a generalised reduction of the democratic control on the whole administrative process caused by the development of horizontal forms of accountability which are replacing (rather than complementing, *see* Chapter Nine) traditional democratic channels of supervision. Finally, Sassen explains how the emergent institutions of a similarly structured global governance (not to mention the emergency measures required by the never-ending *war on terror* launched by G.W. Bush Jr a decade ago now) are contributing to reinforcing this trend. For parliaments are constitutionally excluded from the international scene and have a voice in foreign policy only when summoned to ratify formal intergovernmental agreements; that is, regulatory tools which are gradually being marginalised by soft law instruments, as we will see in the next section.

The trend noted by Sassen is in no way confined to the USA, but affects, by and large, all advanced Western democracies (Poguntke and Webb 2005). For the UK, where the process originated and has reached its most comprehensive realisation thanks to its peculiarly flexible constitutional arrangements, I reckon it is enough to quote a single remark made by Mount (2012: 181), a privileged witness of British political developments from inside: 'the House of Commons has lost control of time, which is the Parliamentarian's greatest weapon. [...] Without mastery of time, Parliament is nothing – a fig leaf, a rubber stump, a ghost of past glories, just as many parliaments in other countries already are'. Indeed, as I argued some time ago in another work (Palumbo 2004), short of an extra-parliamentary *coup d'état* by the leading party heavyweights, there are in the British system no other constitutional safeguards left to get rid of unwanted policies and/or prime ministers. And the situation has deteriorated further in the last decade. Marinetto (2007) has collected the various strands of recent research on the British core executive to mount an all-out attack on what he calls the Anglo-governance school. According to him, this research shows that

Networking has been flourishing at the local level. But is does not resemble the autonomous system of governance which Rhodes argues has been ushered in by the transformation of government. One of the main reasons for this is that the central state, contrary to the exhortations of the Anglo-governance school, still places exacting political controls on local policy networks and institutions [...] the position of the centre in relation to local policy networks and actors was in many respects strengthened rather than weakened by public management reforms. Financial controls were not merely augmented to compensate for the loss of control to policy networks, as Rhodes argues. The central state also amassed greater political and administrative control during the course of the 1980s (Marinetto 2007: 67).

The above-mentioned Mount is also right in noticing the similarity between the British political condition and the one existing in other liberal democracies worldwide, as Webb and Poguntke try to demonstrate in their volume. The literature on the presidentialisation of parliamentary democracies is, in fact, flourishing and complementing nicely the parallel literature on the presidential administration produced on the other side of Atlantic by legal theorists and social scientists alike. The unfailing methodological debates emerging in their wake rather than questioning the existence of the alleged trend, seem instead preoccupied with how to label this phenomenon, suggesting that the expression *personalisation* of democratic politics is analytically more accurate than *presidentialisation* (see vol. 66 of *Parliamentary Affairs*).[14] This is however only one aspect of a more general phenomenon brought about by the logic of political centralisation-cum-administrative decongestion underpinning, in my opinion, the various processes of change. It quite clearly explains the horizontal process of diffusion followed by the governance template, fully developed and deployed in the UK since the late 1980s, and afterwards worldwide; that is, once various other political and societal agents operating in distinct constitutional settings came to realise the potential that template could have in bridging the governability gaps opened by the disintegration of the consensus politics dominating *les trente glorieuses* (Goetz 2008). In fact, Benz and Papadopoulus (2006: 3) list the undermining of representative institutions as one of the characterising features of governance as such:

> Elected politicians are deemed to play a secondary role. [...] governance usually leads to less formal modes of decision making within structure that are hardly visible to the public and that are not congruent with the official institutions of representative democracy. [...] In governance the initiative and control functions of parliaments are expected to be weak, with parliaments instead being confined to the role of ratifying bodies.

As seen in Chapter Two, equally important (and serious) are, from my perspective, the effects set in motion by the re-configuration of democratic politics within each specific constitutional setting. The strategy of political centralisation and administrative decongestion is permeating the political fabric. For those whom have been made responsible for the delivery of public services are likewise trying to pass responsibility on others. Democratic politics at the local level is thus being hollowed out not only by the direct acquisition of power by central governments, but also by the political activism of local authorities attempting to copy the governance template in order to shed acquired public responsibility either downwards to other political actors or sideways to private business companies and voluntary organisations. Stakeholdership and prosumerism gradually develop, in this way, into powerful instruments not for empowering civil society, but for privatising risks and relieving the political system, at its various jurisdictional levels, of the public commitments imposed by the model of social citizenship endorsed earlier. The overall effects of the deepening and entrenching of the governance template across various domains and jurisdictional levels are, as noted throughout,

- the attribution of growing political burdens upon middle and street-level bureaucrats and local communities with no decision-making power left;
- the perversion of voluntarism and the third sector under the relentless pressure to corporatise themselves or be subservient to other corporate actors;
- the subjugation of the individual to myriad of private, semi-public and public corporate actors operating in highly segmented markets and proxy markets; and
- the intensifying of localised social conflicts and inequalities among a mass of powerless denizens forced to assume growing responsibility for unwanted structural risks.

In other words, the outcome is a massive process of de-democratisation engendering what, following Crouch (2004), several authors have come to identify as a post-democratic condition. This body of work has emerged, as Blühdorn (2007) correctly notes, at the intersection of several research streams that either include or overlap with the ones making up governance studies. They are: (i) research about de-parliamentarisation and post-parliamentary democracy; (ii) the above-mentioned inquiries on presidentialisation and personalisation of democratic politics; (iii) studies of the politics of regulation and delegation; (iv) those concerned with the transition from the politics of decision to those of presentation. According to Blühdorn (2007: 300), 'while these debates are all taking different perspectives and are focusing on different aspects, they are ultimately concerned with exploring [...] the post-parliamentary and post-representative form of politics towards which the ongoing transformation is taking late-modern democracy'. In this post-democratic environment, new modes of governance have come to represent a set of 'solutions looking for a problem to solve', rather than the other way round. Sadly, given the dominance of the approaches discussed so far, this larger, and decidedly paradoxical, picture of political and institutional change finds it very difficult to emerge in governance studies. The power to supply some gestalt-like illumination seems to remain, as always, with fiction, and its uncanny ability to shed light on reality, as in the remarkable description of daily life in multicultural London supplied by John Lanchester (2012) and used as an epigram to this work.[15]

7.5. Westphalian order, regulatory regimes and diffuse global governance

In eroding the sovereignty of the nation state, globalisation has brought about a new form of government of international relations as well, global governance (Weiss 2013). As for the new modes of governance which have emerged within the nation state, the novelties introduced by diffuse forms of global governance are commonly explained by contrasting its ideal typical features with those taken to characterise its predecessor, identified as the Westphalian Order. As already mentioned, the Westphalian Order depicts the international system as the outcome of the balance of power between nation states, to which well-defined and self-regarding utility functions are attributed. The result, as said, is an anarchic order, where international rules and agreements can only rely upon the willingness of those who are supposed to abide by them. As Aron (1995: 28) puts it,

> the society of sovereign states is in essence asocial, since it does not outlaw the recourse to force among the 'collective persons' that are its members. Order, if there be one, in this society of states is anarchical in that it rejects the authority of law, of morality, or of collective force.

Obviously, the alleged erosion of the state means the unravelling of the Westphalian Order. However, governance theorists believe that, rather than fostering extant cosmopolitan institutions and the idealist paradigm supporting them, diffuse forms of global governance are in reality engendering an ideal typical form of governing alternative to the ones supplied by contending neo-realist and idealist theories of international relations (Desai 1995; Finkelstein 1995; Hewson and Sinclair 1999; Rosenau 1995; Weiss 2013). From this abstract perspective, Westphalian Order and global governance are said to identify two distinct types of anarchic order. The first is the type of balance of power created by the equilibrium solutions reached by nation states having a unitary and well-defined utility function that they strive to maximise. The second is instead the overall order arrived at by the more dynamic equilibrium solutions established by post-statal Networked Polities. In the first case, interaction takes place between the diplomatic branches of unitary and centralised nation states, the only institutions having the legitimate power of representation of national communities on the international stage. In the second case, we have multiple intermestic forms of interaction which bypass the intermediation of the political centre. Within a Westphalian system, international rules are the exclusive domain of public actors who are ultimately accountable to elected political principals, while global governance entails the involvement of a variety of societal actors, thus blurring the public/private divide.

This epochal passage is neatly summarised by Brühl and Rittberger (2002: 2, references removed), who suggest the need to distinguish between current 'global' governance from past forms of 'international' governance:

> International governance is the output of a non-hierarchical network of interlocking international (mostly, but not exclusively, governmental) institutions which regulate the behaviour of states and other international actors in different issue areas of world politics [...]. Global governance is the output of a non-hierarchical network of international and transnational institutions: not only IGOs and international regimes but also transnational regimes are regulating actors' behaviour. In contrast to international governance, global governance is characterized by the decreased salience of states and the increased involvement of non-state actors in norm- and rule-setting processes and compliance monitoring. In addition, global governance is equated with multilevel governance, meaning that governance takes place not only at the national and the international level (such as in international governance) but also at the subnational, regional, and local levels. Whereas, in international governance, the addressees and the makers of norms and rules are states and other intergovernmental institutions, non-state actors (in addition to states and intergovernmental institutions) are both the addressees and the makers of norms and rules in global governance.

Changing the protagonists of the political game played at the international level also means revising the policy instruments those actors can rely upon. In this new setting, intergovernmental agreements and international treatises are gradually replaced by a plethora of soft law tools: standards and benchmarks, guidelines and recommendations, ethical codes and Human Rights charters (Berman 2007). As Scholte (2005: 201) explains,

> Whereas interstate cooperation of the past normally took formal shape in treaties, much of contemporary transstate *governance* has no basis in conventional international law. At most, the collaboration is set down in memoranda of understanding among the officials concerned. In contrast to treaties, these MOUs do not require ratification by legislative bodies, so that transstate relations can easily become technocratic *networks* that operate outside democratic oversight.

The manifesto of global governance was made public in 1995 by UN Commission on Global Governance (CGG) in a document, *Our Global Neighbourhood*, that predates and anticipates many of the suggestions which will be contained in the 2001 White Paper on EU Governance discussed earlier (*see* Chapter Four, §4.3.2). The outline of global governance contained in that document is the following:

> At the global level, *governance* has been viewed primarily as intergovernmental relationships, but it must now be understood as also involving non-governmental organizations (NGOs), citizens's movements, multinational corporations, and

the global capital market. Interacting with these are global mass media of dramatically enlarged influence. [...] There is no single model or form of global *governance*, nor is there a single structure or set of structures. It is a broad, dynamic, complex process of interactive decision-making that is constantly evolving and responding to changing circumstances. [...] *governance* must take an integrated approach to questions of survival and prosperity. Recognizing the systemic nature of these issues, it must promote systemic approaches in dealing with them. Effective global decision-making thus needs to build upon and influence decisions taken locally, nationally, and regionally, and to draw on the skills and resources of a diversity of people and institutions at many levels. It must build partnerships – *networks* of institutions and processes – that enable global actors to pool information, knowledge, and capacities and to develop joint policies and practices on issues of common concern. In some cases, *governance* will rely primarily on markets and market instruments, perhaps with some institutional oversight. It may depend heavily on the coordinated energies of civil organizations and state agencies. The relevance and roles of regulation, legal enforcement, and centralized decision-making will vary. In appropriate cases, there will be scope for principles such as subsidiarity, in which decisions are taken as close as possible to the level at which they can be effectively implemented. [...] It will require the articulation of a collaborative ethos based on the principles of consultation, transparency, and *accountability*. [...] it will strive to subject the rule of arbitrary power – economic, political, or military – to the rule of law within global society. [...] global *governance* can only flourish, however, if it is based on a strong commitment to principles of equity and democracy grounded in civil society (CGG 1995: 2–6).

Global governance is used to mean several things: (i) a cluster of phenomena emerged since the 1970s, but magnified by the end of cold war bipolarism; (ii) rationalisations of political and institutional changes which attempt to understand international relations by means of a new explanatory paradigm; (iii) sets of more or less explicit normative judgements concerning the possibilities open to political actors operating in the international sphere. These issues are often discussed by using and comparing analytical models extremely controversial, to say the least. Within the Westphalian model, for example, state sovereignty is defined as a set of absolute and exclusive collective rights: the right of non-interference in domestic affairs, the right of representation of the national community on the international stage, and the right to use military force in self-defence and for affirming internal and external forms of national sovereignty. International governance, to use the distinction proposed by Brühl and Rittberger, is thus attributed the task to assure universal compliance with these collective rights.

Westphalian sovereignty held that each state would exercise supreme, comprehensive, unqualified and exclusive rule over its territorial jurisdiction. With supreme rule, the Westphalian sovereign state would answer to no other authority; it always had the final say in respect of its territorial realm and its cross-border relations with other countries. With comprehensive rule, the Westphalian sovereign state governed all areas of social life. With unqualified and absolute rule, the Westphalian sovereign state respected a norm of non-intervention in one another's territorial jurisdictions. With exclusive and unilateral rule, the Westphalian sovereign state did not share *governance* over its realm with any other party (Scholte 2005: 188).

This idealisation is then contrasted with a similarly idealised account of global governance as a decentred, mutual cooperative enterprise involving the main stakeholders of an emerging global civil society committed to solve collective action problems by dialogical means. Thus, the CGG (1995: 37) writes that,

Many people expect more from democracy. Two minutes in a voting booth every few years does not satisfy their desire for participation. Many resent politicians who, having won the elections in democratic systems, neglect large sectors of the community – sometimes even a majority of the electorate – who have voted for the 'losers'. The widening sign of alienation from the political process call for the reform of *governance* within societies, for decentralization, for new forms of participation, and for the wider involvement of people than traditional systems have allowed.

In allegedly attempting to satisfy this need, global governance becomes a superior functional solution for questions having global reach and relevance; one that is attributing political priority to human rights rather than to the rights of states (Buchanan 2013).[16] Simplifications of this sort are very misleading and undermine the heuristic power of the ideal types employed. A long-standing historiography stretching from Gross (1948) to Teschke (2004) has shown that the Westphalian Order has had the normative force attributed to it only for the nation states whose internal political cohesion, economic resourcefulness and military strength was capable of deterring effectively those statal and non-statal entities intent on pursuing expansive imperial policies. For the rest of the community of states, the principles underpinning the Westphalian Order have never represented any safeguard at all. The international balance of power has thus always had a precarious and very iniquitous nature, fomenting recriminations and endless calls for renegotiations.

Furthermore, these contrasting idealisations seem to have left out of their visual field the clichéd elephant in the room; that is, the existence of hegemonic political blocks into which less powerful nation states were dragooned. During *les trente glorieuses*, embedded liberalism reflected the polarisation caused by the Cold War and the need of Western states to diffuse the risks of the power politics responsible for two world wars and the revolutionary upheavals produced in their wake. Since the end of the Cold War, and in parallel with the development of global governance, we have also witnessed the strengthening of the worldwide hegemony of the sole remaining superpower and its regional allies, who keep using unremittingly the new flexible forms of regulation associated with global governance to impose their vision and interests upon the rest of the international community. As Wade (2003: 87) eloquently argues: 'this is the paradox of economic globalization – it looks like "powerless" expansion of markets but it works to enhance the ability of the United States to harness the rest of the world and fortify its empire-like power. And since it is occurring in a world of "sovereign" states its costs can be made the responsibility of each state to handle, not that of the prime beneficiary'. Thus, the good governance programme launched originally by the World Bank (and soon adopted by the rest of the Bretton Woods Holy Trinity) has represented a formidable instrument for perpetuating the economic and political dependence of developing countries from Western metropolitan centres by imposing ruthless shock therapies all over Africa, Asia and Latin America. Solutions which, since the turn of the century, have been deployed within OECD countries as well; an explanation that, if nothing else, clarify why 'while much of the world sees globalization as the new face of Western capitalism and imperialism, citizens of the Western democracies nonetheless feel themselves terribly aggrieved by it' (Goodhart 2001: 528).

An alternative and, in my opinion, more compelling explanatory framework has been supplied by Wolf (1999a, 1999b), for whom diffuse forms of global governance are ushering in a 'new *raison d'état*'. As the author explains,

> The term 'new *raison d'état*' describes a pattern of intergovernmental interaction triggered by transborder interdependence, transnational society-formation and growing domestic pressures. It involves not only self-assertion *vis-à-vis* other states, but also, at the same time and in complex interconnection with this, a search for external support in securing internal room for manoeuvre (Wolf 1999b: 347).

According to Wolf, in the past nation states used the threat coming from without as a means to impose their authority upon the myriad of societal agents clustered within national borders and extract from them the resources needed to fuel the state apparatus. Now the elites ruling nation states use their role in the manifold forms of intergovernmental cooperation to resist the pressures coming from their own civil societies by redesigning their constitutional settings in a self-serving manner. Wolf's explanatory framework gets its inspiration from the two-level game originally suggested by Putnam (1988). In the suitably revised version proposed by Wolf, the first level coincides with the intergovernmental cooperation established for dealing with global issues, one that is escaping the supervision of national institutions and supplying political credibility to the actors involved in it. The second level of Wolf's game is connected with the way in which the political credibility acquired on the international stage is then exploited at the national level to displace the challenges coming from domestic opposition forces. Unlike Putnam, Wolf employs the two-level game not to show why national representatives are led to defend their national interests within intergovernmental settings, but how these representative bodies use their international credentials to strengthen their hegemonic position at the national level. Within this explanatory framework, soft law instruments, epistemic communities, policy networks, PPPs and the consensual policy environment promoted by novel conceptions of stakeholder democracy are part and parcel of the strategies deployed by some state actors to reinforce their grasp on power while shedding public responsibilities on others, thus diffusing the risk of legitimation crises.

Is this alternative explanatory framework plausible? Has it more heuristic power than the one supplied by global governance theorists? Is there any empirical evidence supporting it? Starting with the last question, an attempt to test Wolf's 'new *raison d'état*' model that I believe is worth reporting is the one carried out by Koening-Archibugi (2002; 2004). Taking the EU as a case study, Koening Archibugi sought to see whether developments in the fields of security and foreign policy at community level could be explained by using Wolf's two-level game. It is renowned that these fields, belonging to the so-called second and third pillars, are much less integrated at the EU level than those which compose the first pillar (socio-economic) and the object of fierce resistance by some member states. The aim of the testing was therefore about the nature and form of this domestic resistance to extend EU authority in those fields as well. To do so, Koening-Archibugi (2004: 158) derives from Wolf's conceptual scheme two working hypotheses:

1. In any particular policy area, an executive that is comparatively less autonomous from parliamentary and other domestic coalitions will be more inclined to support the internationalization of governance than an executive that is more autonomous, *ceteris paribus*.
2. The same government will be more inclined to support the internationalization of the governance of a policy area over which it has relatively little control than a policy area where it has a relatively high degree of internal autonomy, *ceteris paribus*.

The results of the empirical test were then summarised by the author as such, 'the collusive delegation hypothesis states that the French and British executives' demand for supranationalism was low because their structural position *vis-à-vis* parliaments did not create incentives for delegation. Insofar as this expectation was borne out, it reinforces the finding of the correlation analysis of the previous section' (*ibid.*: 174). Koening-Archibugi also spells out the more general implications of the case study:

> When seen in this perspective, the much discussed 'democratic deficit' of European governance no longer appears as an unfortunate by-product of the integration process, but one of its purposes. This is because the design of international institutions is generally decided by national governments, which do it in a way that furthers their specific interests (*ibid.*: 148).

This conclusion corroborates the claims I made in the previous sections of this chapter (and other chapters as well). What I find really compelling about Wolf's explanatory framework and Koening-Archibugi's empirical test is the possibility of using it to further explain what is usually referred to in European studies as the end of the 'permissive consensus' and the large-scale developments of anti-European sentiments and movements. In spite of the systematic and concerted denigration mounted by mass-media and social scientists alike against these forms of populism, it seems to me that the growing opposition against European negative integration policies reflects some form of diffuse intuitive public awareness of the collusive delegation hypothesis indicated by Koening-Archibugi. As mentioned at the end of Chapter Five, some of these strategies used to accomplish the negative integration policy closely resemble the role-play used in TV fictions, with national and communitarian authorities play the role of 'good cops' and 'bad cops' in turn. Thus, sometimes unwanted changes are imposed by faceless Eurocrats against whom national authority are powerless, while at other times those very same changes are required by the recklessness and lassitude of member states and their representative institutions. In replacing (rather than complementing) traditional policy tools and mechanisms of accountability, new modes of governance end up supporting this strategic behaviour and, in the process, have actively contributed to the hollowing-out of democratic politics within and beyond national borders. Anti-European feelings and movements cannot simply be dismissed as the last refuge of narrow-minded populist forces but are symptomatic of a genuine popular discontent with the neoliberal consensus politics dominating European public affairs at both domestic and communitarian levels. Racism and xenophobia are the unwanted messy results of a widespread social discontent that is not addressed politically, but it is marginalised and criminalised by governmental strategies devised to displace it. The really surprising reaction is that of countless analysts and practitioners who, in the footsteps of Habermas (2012) find themselves dismayed about the brinkmanship between national and communitarian authorities and disappointed at the ease with which they move from 'intergovernmentalism' to 'multilevel governance' and back again. Even after, that is, governance studies had certified the death of intergovernmentalism and the closing down of all the ontological debates about the EU (Hix 1998).

7.6. Conclusions

Is the nation state affected by an irreversible and terminal crisis? Or is it the instigator of the current process of political and institutional change? Since the end of the Cold War, globalisation and governance theorists have put forward rationalisations supporting the idea of a progressive erosion of the state form and its gradual replacement by new modes of governance at both the domestic and the transnational levels. In the process, a growing mass of empirical case studies have been collected to corroborate those rationalisations empirically. An emerging new generation of governance theorists is casting doubts on these rationalisations and on the relevance of the empirical case studies used to support them. In emphasising the activism of national governments and in challenging the unintended explanatory dynamics responsible for the alleged unravelling of the state, this new generation is contributing to the development of a Polanyian counter-narrative. The chapter has tried to connect the dots outlining this counter-narrative and defend its overall plausibility. To this end, I have argued that the thesis concerning the unravelling of the nation state seems to be based on a theoretical confusion between state-form and regime-form and is assuming that changes in the latter necessarily entail equivalent changes in the former. By contrast, I have maintained that the changes occurred during *les trente furieuses* have reconfigured the regime-form without affecting the state-form. In other words, I claimed that those changes have hollowed out liberal democratic institutions rather than the state *per se*. In a Polanyian spirit, I have thus endeavoured to show that markets and states keep working in symbiotic ways to strengthen their power upon civil society.

How is it then possible to explain the delegation of sovereignty authority downwards to the subnational level, upwards to the transnational level and sideways to various societal agents blurring traditional internal/external and public/private divides? Is not this manifold process of delegation an indication of the reduced policy capability of the nation state? By recalling several attempts to disaggregate states and markets in their more elementary parts and investigating the overall effects of their interaction, I have tried to outline an alternative explanation focusing on the gradual shifting of the internal balance of powers within states and markets alike. On the one hand, the globalisation of markets has rewarded large corporations working across national boundaries, and penalised small and medium enterprises dependent on domestic markets. In turn, this has promoted the financialisation of economic activities to the detriment of the real economy. On the other hand, the introduction of new modes of governance has started a twin process of political centralisation and administrative decongestion reinforcing the hegemony of the executive branch of government on their legislative counterparts, the institutions of local government and the peripheral articulations of public administrations. According to this Polanyian perspective, the reference to impersonal social forces imposing their systemic logic on the political is part of the rhetorical armoury deployed to obscure the distinction between 'inevitable' and 'desirable' and overcome the opposition of large sectors of society against unwanted changes. By undermining traditional constitutional safeguards, the adoption of soft law instruments and flexible mechanisms of implementation has augmented the steering powers of central government while freeing it from democratic forms of accountability. Hence the current worries about the rising of post-democratic institutions and styles of governing.

Similar conclusions are reached by international relations theorists challenging parallel accounts of the evolution of a diffused global governance. These theorists start by noting that since the end of the Cold War bipolarism events on the global stage have caused an increase of multilateral cooperation together with the expansion and deepening of the hegemony of the last remaining superpower. Hence the suspicion that diffuse forms of global governance are creating the conditions for a redesigned balance of power at the global level, rather than for the rising and empowering of a global civil society and new forms of transnational democracy. Far from supplanting the extant Westphalian Order, multilateral cooperation can be used for supporting the development of a new *raison d'état*, thus contributing to the depoliticisation of public policy and the entrenchment of postdemocratic institutions worldwide. A paradigmatic case of collusive delegation brought to light by empirical attempts to test this hypothesis concerns the EU itself. The claim here is that there is a clear reverse relationship between the European integration of specific policy areas and the power enjoyed by the national executive in those areas. According to this result, the democratic deficit and accountability gap imputed to European governance is not the result of unintended side-effects of the policy of delegation, but the actual goal pursued by national executives engaged in redesigning the separation of power and systems of checks-and-balances imposed by the post-war settlement. The following two chapters will develop these points and in doing so they will try to separate and assess the contrasting explanatory and justificatory frameworks supplied by the theorists of the Regulatory State and the Networked Polity.

End Notes

1. Translated as 'We might say that in the State we have the prime mover. It is the state that has rescued the child from patriarchal domination and from family tyranny; it is the State that has freed the citizen from feudal groups and later from communal groups; it is the State that has liberated the craftsman and his master from guild tyranny.' (Durkheim 1957: 64).

2. Besides those using the prefix post- (modern, national, statist, etc.), we have the 'market-state' (Bobbit 2002), the 'competitive state' (Cerny 1997), the 'network state' (Castells 2005) the 'neoliberal state (Plant 2010), of course, the 'regulatory state' (King 2007) and even the 'disoriented state' (Arts and Lagendijk 2009). To which we must add, the 'multilevel polity' (Hooghe and Marks 2001), the 'differentiated polity' (Rhodes 1988) and, obviously, the 'networked polity' (Ansell 2000).

3. I would say that internal pacification leads systematically to the external projection of state power outwards, especially in capitalist economies where, besides social citizenship, historically colonial expansion has been the main strategy for neutralising the social question (Palumbo 2003).

4. The Iraqi and Afghan military campaigns are only the latest reminders of this more general point.

5. Against mainstream narratives, several authors have repeatedly pointed out that it was domestic reforms which kick-started globalisation of (financial) markets. Thus, Zysman (1996: 164) writes: 'National developments have [...] driven changes in the global economy; even more than a so-called "globalisation" has driven national evolutions. It is the success of particular countries, rather than some unfolding of a singular market logic, based on more and faster transactions, that has forced adaptations'. A similar position is held by Krippner (2011) and even Mann (2013) seems to lean in this direction.

6. Those interested in this would be advised to consult Abrams (1988) and Skocpol (1985).

7. 'Autonomous state actions will regularly take forms that attempt to reinforce the authority, political longevity, and social control of the state organizations whose incumbents generated the relevant policies or policy ideas' (Skocpol 1985: 15).

8. 'At the core of the globalization movement, however, are lightning-fast communication systems – especially the Internet – that have developed over the last decade. The communications revolution has made it possible to spread information around the world easily and cheaply. Not only has it fueled the 24-hour financial markets, it has, just as importantly, transformed *governance*. For the price of a local telephone call to connect to the Internet, organizations around the world can instantly exchange information' (Kettl 2000: 491).

9. Also, conveniently left out the picture are the non-Madisonian aspects of the New Deal, those which are at the root of the theory of regulation developed by the Chicago School. In fact, the New Deal was held responsible for 'the most significant expropriations of political power in American history' (Novak 2002: 270). In discussing this very issue, Sassen (2008: 175) clarifies that the 'expropriation' was carried out through formal parliamentary and presidential acts which preserved the democratic legitimacy of the overall process, and then contrasts it with the rise of the presidential administration since Ronald Reagan, where soft law instruments have been used to marginalise legislative institutions.

10. Something upon which earlier writers like Helleiner (1994: 21) expressed similar opinions, as already mentioned in note 4 above:

    advanced industrial states have played an important role in the globalization process since the late 1950s by (1) granting freedom to market operators, both through encouraging growth of the Euromarket in the 1960s and through liberalizing capital controls after the mid-1970s; (2) choosing not to implement more effective controls on capital movements in the early 1970s and in four instances in the late 1970s and early 1980s; and (3) preventing three major financial crises, in 1974, 1982, and 1987.

11. Similar conclusions were reached by Douglas (1997: 167): 'we are not witnessing the "evaporation of authority" but its reverse: the deeper embedding of order through marketisation, the rise of neoliberal orthodoxy and the reduction of the world to a single place. Globalisation (shorthand for each of these) must be questioned as a "rationality of government" and method of politics'. On this point also compelling is Hirschl's (2004: 9) analysis of juridification:

    Hegemonic élites and their political representatives are likely to initiate and carry out a delegation of power to the judiciary (a) when they find strategic drawbacks in adhering to majoritarian decision-making processes or when their worldviews and *policy* preferences are increasingly challenged in such arenas; (b) when the judiciary in that *polity* enjoys a better reputation than the political regime for its rectitude, professionalism, and impartiality; (c) when sociopolitical élites who delegate power to the courts enjoy general control over legal education and judicial appointment processes; and (d) when the courts in that *polity* are inclined to rule in accordance with secularist ideological and cultural propensities. [...] Such a strategic, counter-intuitive self-limitation may be beneficial from the point of view of threatened sociopolitical élites and power-holders when the limits imposed on rival elements within the body politic outweigh the limits imposed on themselves.

12. 'In most developing societies taxpaying remains unregulable and this has closed the door on credible state provision and state regulation. Of course it is more cost-effective to collect tax from one large corporation than ten small ones and most corporate tax is collected from the largest 1 percent of corporations in wealthy nations. But this is not the main reason that corporatization created a wealthy state. More fundamentally, corporatization assisted the collectability of other taxes [...]. As retailing organizations became larger corporate, as opposed to family-owned corner stores, the collection of indirect tax became more cost-effective' (Braithwaite 2006: 423).

13. A similar attempt that arrives, however, at divergent conclusions from Sassen's, is Leibfried and Zürn's (2005). The essay sums up the work of a research group based in Bremen (Germany) that has analysed changes affecting the state form in four distinct areas: resources, law, legitimacy and welfare. According to the authors, research in these areas shows that the state form, identified with the acronym TRUDI (*the Territorial State that secure the Rule of law is predicated on Democratic values and Intervenes actively in society*), is unravelling: 'the threads of the Golden-Age TRUDI are unravelling by different processes, at different speeds and in different directions throughout the OECD world, and they will not necessarily be rewoven into an attractive or even serviceable fabric. We cannot even predict whether TRUDI will *have* a follow-up model' (Leibfried and Zürn 2005: 26). Insofar as I'm concerned, the evidence reported in that volume does not support this conclusion. Ironically this comes up in the concluding section of Zürn and Leibfried's introduction, where the authors state that, in contradiction with what they said earlier, the current state of affairs is not like that of Heraclitus's *ta panta rei* (everything is in flux), but that it rather resembles the expression used by the Prince of Lampedusa, in the historical novel *The Leopard*: 'se vogliamo che tutto rimanga come è, bisogna che cambi tutto' ['if we want everything to stay the same, then we need to change everything']. So, I feel entitled to close with the standard QED.

14. In this debate, it would be analytically useful to distinguish two intertwining dynamics: the one pertaining to the transformations affecting executive offices (for instance, the overcoming of the cabinet system in the UK), and

the one pertaining to the way in which the re-configuration of the executive system re-defines the constitutional balance of power between the legislative and executive branches of government. Similarly, critics of governance theory like Goetz (2008) need to distinguish between the strengthening of state capacity and the re-balancing of powers within the state. Together with presidentialisation, new modes of governance are introducing within parliamentary democracies forms of spoils system by stealth. In the UK, this problem is often referred to as the 'quangoisation' of the British state. In Italy, the dynamics is at the roots of the transformation and extension of a phenomenon known as 'sottogoverno'. In both cases, appointed political personnel enjoy the benefits of the informal spoils system and gradually supplant both elected politicians and civil servants. This phenomenon is at the centre of Vibert's (2007) work, but the author welcomes it for reasons which blend together the arguments used to justify the Regulatory state on one side, and those used to advocate the Networked Polity on the other.

15. To my own surprise, the parking business was recently the issue of Channel 4 investigative programme 'Dispatches' broadcasted on 16 February 2015 under the title *Secrets of the Parking Wardens*, http://www.channel4.com/info/press/news/secrets-of-the-parking-wardens-channel-4-dispatches

16. On the role of global civil society in engendering a dialogical policy environment, see the articles included in the monographic issue of the journal *Development Dialogue* 49, November 2007.

Chapter Eight

Beyond Schumpeter: Delegation, Deliberation and Post-Democracy

8.1. Introduction

In this chapter, I discuss two distinct visions of democratic politics inspiring governance theory, both of which are in sharp contrast to the one endorsed in the post-war period: Schumpeter's CLM. The first of these advocates substantive solutions that oppose Schumpeter's faith in electoral moments and majority rule and views the Regulatory State as a multi-jurisdictional context capable of engendering a foot-voting form of democracy. Instead, the second vision invokes solutions derived from deliberative models of democracy developed in political theory and suggests seeing the Networked Polity as a multilevel, dialogical policy environment involving all affected interests. According to the genealogy of governance theory proposed so far and using the liberal democratic template established by the post-war settlement as a benchmark, we can say that the Regulatory State supports anti-democratic solutions aimed at depoliticising public policy and giving people the power to 'vote with their feet'. By contrast, the Networked Polity supports ultra-democratic solutions aiming to promote a more participatory model of democracy that can involve stakeholders at various stages of the policy process: agenda-setting, decision making, policy implementation. My aim here is to present the main features making up these two justificatory frameworks and to highlight their shortcomings. I argue that both sets of solutions are deeply problematic, although for diverse reasons, and try to show that the anti-democratic solutions suggested rest ultimately on disputed notions of social efficiency and contradictory appeals to pluralism. Moreover, their viability depends on a model of democracy which is not only unwarranted, but also at odds with the criteria of feasibility used in NPE to undermine the value of welfare policies and related ideals of social citizenship. I also maintain that the ultra-democratic solutions invoked by the theorists of the Networked Polity are, from a normative perspective, no less controversial. When understood as epistemic devices, deliberative models of democracy end up empowering deliberative polyarchies with unclear democratic credentials, thus undermining the value of political equality upon which their vision of democracy is grounded. Alternatively, when conceived as participatory tools supporting descriptive notions of representation whose goal is to supply restricted forms of policy legitimacy, they seem incapable of supporting the far-reaching claims associated with the idea of governing without government.

These shortcomings raise, in turn, a host of more difficult questions touching on a number of aspects of governance theory discussed earlier. Are we really dealing with attempts at what Warren (2009) calls 'governance-driven democratisation', or with what post-democratic critics see as a continuation of neoliberal efforts to depoliticise public policy? Is the front-line role acquired by policy and administration the outcome of bottom-up pressures to bypass political gridlock? Or is it rather an indication that lurking behind this reformist zeal are governmental attempts to undermine representative institutions in order to free themselves from the social and political responsibilities established by the post-war settlement and imposed through vertical mechanisms of accountability? In short, are we witnessing the rebirth of strongly democratic ideals, or the inception of a post-democratic order? I have already expressed my doubts on the explanatory power of the contrasting research programmes making up governance theory, affirming that the Regulatory State is a more powerful heuristic device for understanding the political and institutional changes brought about by neoliberal reforms of big government than the Networked Polity. I also claimed that, when we attempt to assess the justificatory frameworks supplied by these research programmes, the reverse turned out to be true: namely, that the Networked Polity is a more acceptable ideal than the Regulatory State. Here my main effort will be devoted to substantiate this normative judgment giving the reasons behind it. To do so, I shall employ three main criteria of evaluation used in political theory to carry this task forward – criteria related to the desirability, electability and feasibility of the justificatory claims put forward. As usual, conceptual analysis will be complemented with empirical considerations concerned with ability of the normative solutions implemented so far to reduce the risk of systemic legitimation crises similar to the one responsible for the unravelling of the welfare state. Throughout this chapter, the literature on EU governance and democratic experimentation will be used to highlight these questions but, as seen in the previous chapters, political and institutional changes taking place at the national level are having an equivalent impact and, therefore, give rise to similar normative perplexities.

8.2. The post-war settlement and its critics

Although neither liberalism nor democracy are logically dependent on welfare institutions, the post-war settlement derived its legitimacy from welfarist values and an expansive model of social citizenship attributing to the individual growing economic and social entitlements. As seen in Chapter One, politically it rested on the democratic foundations laid down by Schumpeter's CLM. Blending together procedural and aggregative features, the main tenets of CLM can be summarised as follows. First, it attributed full and exclusive sovereignty to the people. Second, it established that 'we, the people' can exercise this sovereignty only indirectly, through political representatives elected at regular intervals in general elections. Third, it defined a chain of delegation designed to transmit legitimacy downwards through the various institutional levels composing the body politic. Fourth, accountability mechanisms were reinforced by systems of checks and balances between elective and non-elective offices with well-defined monitoring powers. Finally, it imposed sets of formal constraints aimed at reducing the impact of majority rule on individual liberties: pre-political individual rights, the predominance of constitutional norms over statute laws, the rule of law as opposed to the rules of men. In this context, democracy becomes a 'method' for (i) aggregating individual interests into a social utility function and (ii) selecting the policies that could maximise it. To this end, what is needed is legitimate and responsible leadership, rather than the active participation of the *demos* in policy making. Hence, the endorsement of ample forms of delegation and competitive dynamics among those interested in acquiring delegated power. The democratic content of this form of government rests on the opportunity given to the *demos* to vote in the elite it would like to rule (Weber 1948), or, as Riker (1982) following Schumpeter puts it, to 'kick the rascals out'. During the post-war reconstruction, such a minimalist vision of democratic politics was able to put to rest liberal reservations, while its practical achievements deflated the appeals for a revolutionary overhaul of the social order. It eventually became what Warren (2009: 6) calls 'the standard model of democratic self-rule' – not only the most preeminent democratic template realised in OECD countries, but also the benchmark for gauging the democratic content of alternative political systems.

To a large extent, the post-war settlement was a compromise between two contrasting political visions: that of those who viewed democracy as a tool for emancipation and that of those who worried about the tyrannical tendencies of mass democracy. The former fought to bring down the class limitations imposed by the liberal state by granting universal suffrage and social and economic rights to the people (Kelsen 1945). The latter attempted to preserve individual liberty and social order by restricting the participatory role of the *demos* in the policy process (Hayek 1960). The complex structures of Western welfare states reflected this compromise. On the one hand, they recognised the *demos* as the only legitimate sovereign power and turned it into an assembly of citizens with growing rights and entitlements. On the other, they transferred real policy-making power to polyarchies, who were then given the task of defining both the needs and interests of 'we, the people', and to an administrative class seeking the means to maximise their satisfaction. This compromise was sealed by the acceptance of the mixed economy and Keynesian stabilisation policies as constituting the two economic pillars supporting post-war liberal democracy (Dahl and Lindblom 1953). Accordingly, individual needs and interests were translated into monetary terms and satisfied by macro-economic policies whose complexity was far beyond the comprehension of professional legislators (let alone common people) and became therefore the exclusive domain of welfare technocrats. Simultaneously, the set of commons, mutual institutions and self-help organisations comprising the pre-war social economy were progressively integrated into the welfare state through processes of vertical integration that handed their management over to anonymous national bureaucrats (Palumbo and Scott 2005). As explained in Chapter One, it was a consensus that promoted almost thirty years of continuous economic growth, producing both the post-war reconstruction and the industrialisation of OECD countries in the process. And it was duly celebrated as a managerial revolution capable of establishing a more humane 'third way' to modernity than those advocated by free marketeers and Soviet style planners (Polanyi 1944).

Right from the start, the Schumpeterian consensus was the object of fierce criticism from both the right and left wings of the political spectrum. On the right, the more systematic and rigorous critique was advanced by NPE, and the Public Choice school in particular. As explained before (*see* Chapter Two), the main objective of these economic approaches to politics was to highlight the likely perverse side-effects of unconstrained majority rule. These can be illustrated by using, albeit in a simplified form, Mueller's (1990: 59) graphic representation of the democracy game (*see* Figure 8.1).

In this graph, the vertical axis measures the utility of the rich class (Ur), the horizontal axis that of the poor class (Up), the curve XW represents the 'Pareto frontier' on which the actual society rests, and the point E indicates the *status quo* from which any collective choice is meant to depart. In E, the benefits reaped by the rich are S, while the slice of the social surplus which goes to the poor is T. Majority rule can lead the democracy game into any of the following situations:

- a state A (εXE) where democracy takes the form of a zero-sum game with a majority dominated by the rich and able to impose an upwards redistribution of social resources exploiting the poor;
- a state B (εEW) where the reverse happens and the poor redistribute the social resources downwards exploiting the rich;
- a state C (εX'Y) where democracy takes the form of a positive sum game, but where the public goods produced overwhelmingly favour the rich;
- a state D (εZW') very much like (iii), but where the public goods produced overwhelmingly favour the poor.[1]

Figure 8.1: Mueller's democracy game

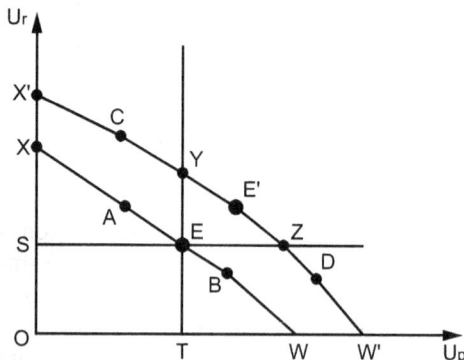

According to public choice theory, all these states of affair are socially inefficient and would, therefore, be unfeasible. They are inefficient because, in a world where the majority could only count on voluntary compliance, the only acceptable states would be those falling within the 'contract curve' (YZ) – namely, the outcomes upon which people would agree unanimously. They would be unfeasible because individual compliance would here require permanent external interference of the state with individual choices – something that is both costly and in need of justification (Coleman and Ferejohn 1986). To avoid inefficiency and waste – and the eventual conflict that could be generated as a result – public choice theory suggests establishing counter-majoritarian constitutional constraints capable of restricting the scope of democratic politics to those states lying along the 'contract curve' – namely, by imposing unanimity rules in crucial policy areas like taxation (Buchanan and Tullock 1962). In Chapter Two, I explained how this economic reading of the democracy game eventually acquired pre-eminence at both academic and governmental levels, helping replace in the process traditional concerns about the desirability of social outcomes with more modern and scientific-sounding criteria of feasibility. Since the 1970s, these economic approaches to politics have not only become a main academic subject taught across disciplinary boundaries (so-called PPE degree courses in the UK), but public choice models have been the reference point for most of the institutional reforms carried out in the 1980s and 1990s, and a major inspiration for the theorists of the Regulatory State.

Although no comparable analysis of this tradition of thought has been, nor can be, carried out in this work, on the left a long line of critics stretching from Arendt (1963) to Pateman (1970), from MacPherson (1977) to Barber (1984), and from Arblaster (1987) to Mouffe (2000) have insisted on the limits of representation and the minimalist politics of the ballot box supported by CLM. Although less homogeneous than those supplied by NPE, their analyses of liberal democracy share several overlapping themes. First, these critics advocate a thicker conception of 'the political' derived from classical political theory rather than political economy – namely one, 'which is first and foremost about preserving commonality while legitimating and reconciling differences' (Wolin 2008: 61). Political action is for them neither separable from other forms of social interaction, nor the outcome of unintended actions by self-seeking individual agents. Democracy, therefore, cannot be thought of as the exclusive domain of restricted elites, or merely as a 'method' for choosing those called to rule the masses. Second, the delegation of policy-making power to specialised administrative bodies is viewed as an abdication of sovereignty (Kuflik 1984). On the one hand, left-wing critics believe delegation leads to oligarchic and technocratic forms of government incompatible with the ideal of self-determination underpinning modern society. On the other, they claim that delegation exposes the body politic to anomy and the perverse influence of totalising populist ideologies aiming to regenerate it. Third, these critics highlight the corrupting influence the redefinition of democracy as a 'method' could have on the civic spirit (Sandel 1996). Far from being willing to sacrifice themselves for their countries, the private, self-seeking individuals idealised by liberal democrats are indifferent to the fate of the body politic and prone to harmful collective action problems.

If, as Schumpeter (1943: 295) clearly admits, liberal democracy presupposes a civic character it is unable to yield or even to sustain, participation for them becomes a way of (i) improving the quality of democratic deliberation; (ii) satisfying the individual's need for identification and recognition; (iii) fostering social learning and solidarity. Finally, these critics end up converging on a criterion of electability that rejects both traditional liberal concerns with the desirability of social and political change and modern liberal worries about its feasibility (Palumbo 2003). While the former are perceived as biased accounts of transformations that have in reality been largely exploitative and sometimes dysfunctional, the latter are shown to be self-serving strategies used for opposing any attempt to redress injustices and engender self-government.[2]

We saw that, despite its success, by the end of the 1960s the post-war settlement had entered an irreversible crisis of confidence, which eventually led to its unravelling and replacement by the alternative neoliberal consensus we are still part of. As argued in Chapter Two, the reason for this failure must be sought in the evident contradiction between the ideals of individual and social autonomy the post-war settlement preached, and the technocratic practices that CLM ended up endorsing in reality. From my perspective, this contradiction undermined the legitimacy upon which that settlement rested, eroded the social and political coalition supporting the welfare state in its various variants, and, paradoxically, allowed a minority and even more elitist neoliberal coalition to impose its worldview and political programs across OECD countries and beyond. Moreover, I argued that, although the neoliberal reforms of welfare institutions carried out in the last thirty years have left the political edifice established during *les trente glorieuses* formally intact, today liberal democracy is but an empty shell. The shift from 'welfare' to 'workfare' has redefined the model of social citizenship supporting it substantially and reversed the state's commitment to the rights-based process of democratisation described by Marshall (1950). Slowly but inexorably, the Keynesian policy tools box has been replaced by one derived from neo-classic thought, shifting government focus from macro-economics to micro-politics, from 'managed economy to managed democracy' (Wolin 2008). Finally, the alleged passage from 'government' to 'governance' is undermining public trust in the set of procedural values underpinning CLM in favour of alternative conceptions of democratic legitimacy. Consequently, I pointed out that the authors developing a more critical second generation of governance studies are rightly concerned about the fact that the changes underway are far from promoting the 'governance-driven democratisation' suggested by Warren (2009). Rather, they are overcoming the post-war settlement by ushering in a post-democratic age – one that is reintroducing pre-democratic elements in a post-modern setting, and where the unrestrained exercise of private power goes hand in hand with people's involvement in policy processes at local, regional, national and global levels.

The next section tries to clarify in what way the democratic visions at the heart of governance theory could have contributed to engendering a post-democratic political environment. In doing so, I shall analyse the arguments used to justify and support these emerging forms of diffuse governance.

8.3. Overcoming the post-war settlement I: anti-democratic strategies of exit

According to governance theory, the passage from 'government' to 'governance' represents a decentralised and bottom-up attempt to supply effective answers to the mounting political problems faced by liberal democracies since the mid 1970s. From the growing body of literature produced so far, I have discerned two main directions in the search for answers to the perceived legitimacy deficit of liberal democracies. As explained earlier (Chapter Four), the first adopts an economic outlook and attributes the difficulties of the post-war settlement to its reliance on the procedural values underpinning majority rule and on electoral politics. As an alternative, it suggests delegating decision and policy-making powers to either technical bodies independent of the political process (Majone 1998, 1999, 2003), or institutions requiring qualified majorities (Moravcsik 2002, 2004). Both anti- and counter-majoritarian solutions intend to move away from what Scharpf (2000) calls an 'input-oriented' mode of legitimacy and adopt in its stead an alternative 'output-oriented' mode of legitimacy – one concerned with the effective delivery of public goods and services mandated by the body politic. Given the post-war strict identification of democratic politics with majority rule and electoral and party politics, I shall refer to these approaches as anti-democratic. Indeed, I maintain that their overall goal is to replace formal channels of 'voice' with mechanisms of 'exit', giving people the possibility to 'vote with their feet', even if neither Majone nor Moravcsik do so explicitly. The adoption of a foot-voting model of democracy is, as argued above, a logical implication imposed by the need to avoid the otherwise insurmountable collective action problems faced by the substantive assessment of policy goals required by any 'output-oriented' mode of legitimacy. The aim of this section is to present the main features of this justificatory approach. In so doing, I shall endeavour to clarify both its continuities and discontinuities with the economic critiques of liberal democracy presented above, and then endeavour to show the theoretical limitations of this justificatory strategy and vision of democracy.

According to NPE influenced governance theorists, the neoliberal reforms of big government carried out in the last three decades of the twentieth century successfully dismantled the welfare (also called positive or dirigist) state established in the previous half and replaced it with a new political entity: the Regulatory State. In Majone's account, the rationale for this shift is related to the inefficiencies affecting the former on the one hand, and the latter's ability to find effective solutions for them on the other. Two weaknesses attributed to the welfare state are considered by Majone. First, the redistributive conflicts generated by governmental attempts to satisfy growing demands for the recognition of social and economic rights coming from the working classes led to increasing social instabilities and unreasonable expectations fuelling them. Second, the bureaucratic sclerosis promoted by the state's attempt to produce public goods and services directly, and be the employer of last resort, led to systemic overloading and one-size-fits-all managerial decisions creating public discontent. They both ended up producing the widespread rent-seeking attitudes – causing allocative inefficiencies and spiralling inflationary drives – upon which have insisted all sub-disciplinary fields making up NPE. Unlike the procedural constitutional devices advocated by NPE (Brenner and Buchanan 1985), Majone claims the solution to these problems requires the delegation of policy-making powers to non-majoritarian institutions – technical bodies independent from the electoral process and therefore able to resist majoritarian and sectoral pressures. According to Majone (1999: 19), 'Non-majoritarian institutions are important not only in federal-type systems, but in all "plural" societies'. In these contexts, delegation addresses four main issues. First, the cognitive limitations of elected representatives progressively more incapable of coping with the growing complexity of the policy process. Second, the need to cut decision-making costs by means of a division of labour which can free representatives from the nuts and bolts of policy making. Third, politicians' tendency to shift responsibility for policy failure onto public officials. Fourth, the endemic lack of credibility of representative institutions susceptible to cyclical majorities.

Above all, Majone believes credibility to be the crucial element explaining the trend towards delegation to independent technical bodies leading to the Regulatory State and the consolidation of regional transnational authorities like the EU, taken as a paradigmatic example of this emerging form of body politic. On this point, his explanation draws heavily on Riker's (1982) reading of Arrow's (im)possibility theorem, which attempted to work out the full implications of the problem of cyclical majorities for democratic politics. As is well known, cyclical majorities are reputed to be a problematic feature of democratic politics because of the wasteful allocation of social resources they bring about. For Majone, they are also at the root of the structural deficit of credibility witnessed in liberal democracies in the first half of the post-war period. Since democratically-mandated policy commitments can always be revised by alternative majorities, Majone argues that they can only be weakly credible. External rational agents can in fact replicate politicians' reasoning and realise that the validity of their policy commitments is, at best, limited to the duration of their electoral mandate. Given this limited time horizon, the outcome is a permanent sub-optimality problem, due to higher levels of transaction costs and the endemic shortage of long-term investments. Hence, the need to delegate policy making and regulatory power to independent technical bodies. Concerning delegation to regional transnational authorities such as the EU, Majone claims it to be justified for two additional reasons. In the first place, the presence of negative externalities that escape the power of control and sanction of limited jurisdictions like the nation state. Secondly, the clear ability of transnational authorities to tackle these externalities more effectively than traditional inter-governmental agreements. As for national regulatory agencies, the credibility of transnational authorities like the EU rests on: (a) their reliance on negative integration policies – i.e. policies that do not engage in redistributing social resources; and (b) their problem-solving expertise – i.e. their ability to deliver public goods and services mandated to them effectively, efficiently and economically.

A very similar account of current political and institutional change is put forward by Moravcsik, who uses the case of the EU as exemplary for understanding the rationale behind the development of a 'diffuse global governance system'. For Moravcsik (2004: 362, 2002: 622),

> The apparently 'counter-majoritarian' tendency of EU political institutions insulated from direct democratic contestation arises out of factors that themselves have normative integrity, notably efforts to compensate for the ignorance and non-participation of citizens, to make credible commitments to rights enforcement, and to offset the power of special interests.

This line of reasoning allows Moravcsik to contest the idea that the EU, and by extension other equivalent transnational authorities, 'suffer from a fundamental democratic deficit' (Moravcsik 2002: 621). On this point, his argument is twofold. To start with, Moravcsik contends that a proper assessment of the standing of transnational authorities requires sound empirical criteria of evaluation. For him, most of the current literature contesting their legitimacy rests in fact on normative ideals that many democratic countries would fail to meet. In addition, Moravcsik points out that many of the problems attributed to transnational authorities are, in reality, part of general trends affecting late twentieth century liberal democracies for which a recent phenomenon like global governance cannot be held responsible. Secondly, Moravcsik (2002: 614, emphasis in original) highlights both the normative and empirical benefits brought about by delegation to insulated institutions: 'First is *the need for greater attention, efficiency and expertise in areas where most citizens remain "rationally ignorant" or non-participatory.* [...] Second is *the need impartially to dispense justice, equality and rights for individuals and minority groups.* [...] Third is *the need to provide majorities with unbiased representation.*' Finally, Moravcsik agrees with Majone on the need to retain indirect forms of accountability capable of supplying transnational authorities with the democratic legitimacy they need to elicit the voluntary compliance of local societal agents.

Like NPE, from which their analyses derive, the defence of delegation to insulated regulatory agencies advanced by Majone and Moravcsik appeals to some form of guardianship. Left to itself, democratic politics (what Riker calls 'populist' democracy and Schumpeter before him the 'classic model' of democracy) is likely to end up promoting redistributive conflicts which will tear the body politic apart and majoritarian cycles which could misallocate precious social resources, while imposing the will of tyrannical majorities on hapless minorities. Hence, the need to establish external constitutional side-constraints that could channel the political process in the right direction. Classical liberal theory identifies individual rights as such a side-constraint. NPE tries to prop up these deontological barriers by suggesting a strict equivalence between citizen and consumer sovereignty that engenders further constitutional impediments to the exercise of majority rule. In this context, the 'contract curve' amounts to an additional trump card justifying the attribution of 'the power of veto' to wealthy minorities, allowing them either to block any maximisation of social utility likely to work against their own interests, or to slow down the democratic process and the democratisation of domains situated outside the public sphere. By contrast, the anti-democratic solutions advocated by theorists of the Regulatory State like Majone and Moravcsik are based on a conception of guardianship having a different goal in mind. Their overriding aim is not to slow down the political process by strengthening deontological and constitutional barriers. Rather, they wish to free the political process from the burdens imposed by formal mechanisms of accountability established in an age when core liberal values needed deontological protection in order to speed up the transition from the positive to the Regulatory State required by the current neoliberal consensus politics.

Part and parcel of this attempt to roll back the frontiers of liberal democracy (and not of the state as mistakenly assumed by many critics) are also various strategies of de-politicisation, the main aim of which is to (a) shield additional policy areas from majority rule (Hay 2007) and (b) refashion the political preferences of the electorate dependent on welfare policies (*see* Chapter Two, §2.3). Hence, the theoretical and political interest in switching from a procedural to a substantive form of legitimacy, and in extolling the virtues of indirect, horizontal and managerial forms of accountability above the supervisory role of traditional representative institutions and vertical mechanisms of accountability.

8.3.1. Limits of anti-democratic solutions and foot-voting forms of democracy

The short response to the alleged ability of the Regulatory State to foster its own legitimacy would be to point out that its impact on liberal democracy has, in fact, been devastating. In less than a decade the latter has gone from being hailed as the end of history (Fukuyama 1992), to being perceived as an exhausted experience, for reasons uncannily similar to those used by the Trilateral a quarter of a century earlier (*see* Chapter Two). A parallel parabola has, since the late 1990s, been traced by the EU, who has turned from being a net supplier of legitimacy to a net consumer – if not a political liability. As Offe and Preuss (2006: 184) state, 'virtually all students of the politics of European integration agree that the "permissive consensus" that used to generate passive and detached acceptance of EU decisions is wearing thin with the European citizenry, and that the EU has turned from a generator into a net consumer of generalized support'. The failure of the 2005 constitutional treaty confirmed the existence of a widespread resentment against the negative integration process. This resentment has somehow been contained because all member states, fearing negative outcomes, are carefully avoiding holding referenda, preferring instead the much safer parliamentary route, and have abandoned any reference to a European constitutional charter, preferring instead to present the new Lisbon Agreement signed in 2007 as a mere treaty – in other words, something that needed to be ratified rather than discussed by the legislative chambers. This tactic further undermines the already precarious legitimacy of national parliaments, which the fast disappearance of traditional mass parties is exposing as an unrepresentative, elitist institution more than ever disconnected from civil society (Mair 2008). If political legitimacy is inextricably connected to popular perception, as Majone (1997a: 142) seems to think, then we could turn against the Regulatory State the same line of reasoning he applies to the welfare state:

> That such criticisms are not always fair or empirically founded is immaterial; the fact is that an increasing number of voters [were] convinced by them and [were] willing to [oppose] a […] model of governance that included privatisation of many parts of the public sector, more competition throughout the economy, greater emphasis on supply-side economics, and far-reaching reforms of the welfare state.

My aim is, however to show that these popular perceptions are not the outcome of unrealistic expectations or of unappealing xenophobic sentiments, as often represented in mainstream mass media by progressist thinkers. Rather, in my opinion, it is due to clear shortcomings imputed to this model of governance many times in the past and worth restating here to sharpen the limitations of the justificatory framework supplied by Regulatory State theorists. The first of these limits concerns the economic reading of the democracy game presented above, and in particular the idea of the 'contract curve' supplied by it. According to Buchanan and Tullock (1962), from whom the idea is derived, the only legitimate outcomes are those lying along the contract curve YZ (*see* Figure 8.1), for they bring about Pareto improvements to which everyone would subscribe, thus justifying the constitutional side constraints imposed on democratic politics. The critique traditionally brought against this normative argument notes that its validity crucially depends on the acceptability of the distribution in E, the *status quo* (Gauthier 1986: ch. VII). Whenever E is deeply contested, the contract curve loses any political and moral import: attempts to resist redistribution beyond the contract curve by imposing unanimity rules will be perceived as a defence of the power relations system characterising the *status quo*, rendering any political agreement ultimately unstable.[3] As I see it, this criticism neatly applies to Majone's justification of the Regulatory State. The latter crucially depends on a seemingly neutral application of the notion of Pareto optimality against value-laden conceptions of social justice inspiring the redistributive policies of the welfare state – what Follesdal and Hix (2006) aptly call 'Pareto authoritarianism'. But is this really true? Is the Regulatory State neutral regarding the way social resources are redistributed?

To answer these questions, a simple analogy could be helpful. Past redistributive policies can be likened to a system of dams and locks built to control water flows to avoid cyclical flooding (i.e. economic crises) and promote the economic growth and social development of adjoining areas (i.e. full employment). Given the gravitational pull exercised by capitalist forces in OECD countries (and the world at large), the removal of these political barriers will have the predictable effect of letting economic resources converge freely towards the main basins of attraction (i.e. rich countries and dominant economic forces). Thus, far from supporting a neutral redistribution of social resources, by refraining to get involved the Regulatory State actively pursues market-based redistributive criteria while claiming no responsibility in the matter. Since its advocates seem uninterested in discussing the political acceptability and/or moral desirability of market distributive criteria, the justification of the Regulatory State supplied ends up in an obfuscation, making the validity of the whole reasoning depend on debatable elements about which they have nothing to say. The implications the perception of growing and unjustified social injustices can have on the legitimacy of the Regulatory State are thus either left unanalysed, or even dismissed as the complaints of self-serving and parasitic 'entrenched constituencies (the elderly, medical care consumers and the full-time unemployed)' (Moravcsik 2002: 618) unreasonably opposed to welfare reforms dictated by 'Pareto authoritarianism'.

This confirms the suspicion that the real objective of the Regulatory State is in reality to undermine procedures set up in the past to protect the diffuse interests of labour and consumer forces (majoritarian) in order to favour the concentrated (minority) interests of national and transnational corporations, the economic associations to which the latter belong and the financial centres backing them. A confirmation reinforced by the fact that the policy credibility sought by the Regulatory State seems exclusively interested in the acquisition/retention of the political support coming from this minority block. Similar considerations can be developed about the output-oriented mode of legitimation invoked as well. As I have already argued (*see* Chapter Five), this notion of legitimacy can work effectively only in political contexts where citizens are free and able to move across jurisdictions, and thus 'vote with their feet'. And indeed, by replacing hierarchical nested authorities with a multilevel system of governance, the EU negative integration process seems engaged in engendering such a democratic ideal: a milieu in which people, goods and money can move freely, and where 'exit' strategies are more meaningful and effective than alternative forms of 'voice'. Obviously, these changes empower those social and economic corporate forces that can easily disembed themselves and move across jurisdictional boundaries, but penalise those collective and individual actors who are geographically rooted, the social and economic forces catering for them and all individuals who lack the right transferable skills.

A second crucial feature that needs to be considered is the anti-democratic camp's celebration of expertise against political engagement. As Majone (1997a: 157) acknowledges: 'Regulation depends so heavily on scientific, engineering and economic knowledge that, […], expertise has always been an important source of legitimisation of regulatory agencies'. Expertise is not just the basis for assuring the credibility of policy commitments, but a crucial feature in the creation of non-majoritarian institutions 'best understood as mechanisms of cleavage management', particularly needed 'in all "plural" societies' (Majone 1999: 19). From this viewpoint, technical and impartial judgment represents the best antidote 'against the immediate "tyranny of the majority"' (Moravcsik 2002: 614). Dahl (1989: ch. 5) has illustrated the role expertise has played in supporting guardianship since Plato's attack on Athenian democracy in the fourth century BC. Anti-democratic arguments based on expertise traditionally rest on highly contentious scientific claims which turn out to be simply unacceptable in a post-positivistic age. Also, they tend to be deeply anti-pluralistic, for they support the idea that there exists a single and correct solution for any given policy issue. I argue that the same applies to the authors mentioned above, notwithstanding their attempt to connect expertise to pluralism and liberal values.

In discussing whether conferences of experts can arrive at the definition of an ideal democratic choice, D'Agostino (1998: 50) explains that, 'Expertise is compatible with self-government when, and only when, it "tracks" hypothetical courses of reasoning that "we, the people" could have performed for ourselves, whether individually or collectively, as the case may be.' However, D'Agostino claims that in societies that are genuinely pluralist this 'tracking condition' works only for trivial cases. It will not work in situations where genuine moral and political disagreement exists, 'because there are multiple argumentative pathways, leading, potentially, to different (and incompatible) solutions, each of which is nevertheless compatible with data *and with the demands of reason*' (*ibid.*). For D'Agostino, in genuinely pluralist societies,

> There are likely, in a variety of cases, to be (a) multiple independent dimensions for assessing the adequacy of any solution to the client's problem, which (b) are (partially) incommensurable, in the sense that (i) superiority on one dimension may not vary directly with superiority on other such dimensions, while (ii) there is no *given* rate of trading-off superiority along one dimension against superiority along others. In this case, of course, tracking the client's (hypothetical) course of reasoning requires much more than professional and ethical good conduct. At a minimum, it requires knowing how the client would resolve incommensurabilities to arrive at an overall scheme of assessment. However, since the client could resolve incommensurabilities, if at all, *only as a result of confronting the problem*, and since, ex hypothesis, the expert confronts the problem for the client, there may be no sense to the idea of the expert's tracking the client's course of reasoning. Crudely, there is, in the situation specified, no determinate course of reasoning for the expert to (try to) track (*ibid.*).

If reason is not able to dictate a single course of action, political and moral conflicts can be resolved only by rules and decision procedures that have a conventional basis. In this context, the relationship between citizens and experts takes the form of two contrasting sets of conventional decision procedures: those produced by democratic politics and those arrived at by professional organisations. In this case, choosing the latter over the former seems highly controversial.

This conclusion is reinforced by empirical observations of the way in which supposedly technical bodies actually operate. For instance, concerning judicial review, Waldron (1993: 471) points out that 'when justices disagree among themselves on matters of principle, they think it perfectly proper to settle the matter by simple majority voting. It is not majoritarianism, as such, that is at issue here; it is simply a question of whose votes are counted in the final analysis'. The same conclusion is reached unsurprisingly by Bellamy (2010) in relation to economic and environmental policy issues, policy areas where internal disagreement is routinely solved by majority voting. It is not clear, then, on what grounds we should restrain majority voting by representative institutions, and delegate policy-making powers to insulated institutions operating according to an equivalent decision procedure. In pluralist societies, such delegation is deeply controversial and, contrary to what defenders of the Regulatory State think, doomed to aggravate the popular perception of an increasing democratic deficit – especially so in constitutional settings which still attribute to 'We, the people', the ultimate sovereign authority.

The final issue that needs to be considered concerns the role of indirect accountability in keeping insulated institutions responsive and thus legitimate. Schumpeter's identification of democracy with electoral and party politics meant stressing the role of accountability above direct participation. While paying lip service to inherited formal lines of accountability, the Regulatory State is, in reality, actively hollowing them out (*see* Chapter Nine). Neither the autonomous administrative agencies created by NPM programmes nor transnational regulatory authorities like the EU are directly accountable to citizens, or even to elected representative institutions such as parliaments. Rather, they are often appointed by national executives and can be held to account only through these bodies, if at all (Scott 2000). As I shall argue in the next chapter, this practice has, in effect, amounted to the addition of new links to the already stressed accountability chain operating in liberal democracies, turning it into something resembling a daisy chain and raising growing concerns about a widening accountability gap. Supporters of the Regulatory State maintain these worries are unfounded. Moravcsik (2002: 605), for instance, believes a realistic assessment of the *modus operandi* of insulated institutions helps dispel worries about their accountability:

> if we adopt reasonable criteria for judging democratic governance, then the widespread criticism of the EU as democratically illegitimate is unsupported by the existing empirical evidence. [...]. Constitutional checks and balances, indirect democratic control via national governments, and the increasing powers of the European Parliament are sufficient to ensure that EU policy making is, in nearly all cases, clean, transparent, effective and politically responsive to the demands of European citizens.

The main weakness of this line of defence is the fact that its benchmark – the legitimacy of national governments upon which indirect accountability rests – is fast deteriorating and cannot be taken any longer for granted; something that Moravcsik intermittently acknowledges but accepts as 'a fact of life'. Moreover, it is possible to argue that the deteriorating legitimacy of national governments is, in part, the outcome of those selfsame policies that according to him have 'a great deal of normative and pragmatic justification' (Moravcsik 2002: 606); that is, the delegation of policy-making powers to insulated regulatory agencies and transnational authorities. As Offe and Preuss (2006: 177, emphasis in original) forcefully put it, 'the lack of democratic accountability at the European level penetrates into the domestic arena and affects the quality and credibility of the practice of national democracy. Thus the problem is not primarily that the *EU* must *become* democratic; it is that *member states* must *remain* democratic'. And so also does the reactive adoption of new modes of governance by sub-state authorities noted earlier (*see* Chapter Two, §2.4), a trickle-down process that to my eyes fully justifies the concerns expressed by post-democracy theorists.

8.4. Overcoming the post-war settlement II: ultra-democratic strategies of voice

A second perspective on legitimacy is derived from readings of governance influenced by political sociology which attempt instead to justify the Networked Polity:

a distinctive form of modern polity that is functionally and territorially disaggregated, but nevertheless linked together and linked to society through a web of inter-organizational and inter-governmental relationships (Ansell 2000: 303).

We already know that the latter is viewed as the outcome of spontaneous, decentralised and bottom-up processes capable of assuring horizontal coordination while reducing the problems related to both government and market failure. In this context, governing does not aim to impose central regulation of the economy, or to free economic institutions from political control. Rather, it is concerned with the management of societal networks through self-regulation, peer review systems and revised schemes of social incentives (*see* Chapter Six). As Sørensen and Torfing (2005: 196) clarify:

public authorities now aim to govern society by involving different kinds of citizens, professionals, voluntary organizations, labor-market organizations and private firms in self-regulating networks. The mobilisation and empowerment of active and responsible actors within self-regulating assemblages enables the state to 'govern at a distance'.

The legitimacy of the institutions making up the Networked Polity is here sought by actively involving all affected interests in the political process;

that is to say, 'compliance with collectively negotiated solutions is ensured neither by means of the legal sanctions of the state nor out of fear of economic loss on the market. Rather, it is ensured through the generation of generalized trust and political obligation, which are sustained by self-constituted rules and norms over time' (Torfing 2005: 309).

Theoretically, the reference point of these authors is not what Schumpeter identifies as the classical model, but is made up of models of deliberative democracy elaborated in political theory (Bohman 1998).[4] Thus, for Sørensen and Torfing (2005: 200) 'Governance networks might contribute to [...] enhance democratic legitimacy by facilitating political participation and influence on the output side of the political system [and] help to widen the scope for discursive contestation in society'. According to Hajer and Versteeg (2005), governance and democratic theory have converged by following a spontaneous trajectory very much like that of the Networked Polity itself. While policy analysts have come to view deliberative democracy as the apt theoretical underpinning for their empirically oriented accounts of governance networks, democratic theorists have found governance studies a fertile field of inquiry for testing the viability of their normative models of public deliberation. For those who have blessed this holy union (see Chapter Six, §6.5.2), the main weakness of the post-war settlement was the formation of technocratic forms of government which inevitably generated a growing chasm between political institutions and civil society (Goetz 2008; Müller 2006; Powell 2007). To reverse this tendency, the political process at its various levels needs to be opened up to the direct participation of all affected interests, thus promoting a more inclusive stakeholder democracy (Bingham *et al.*, 2005; Bovaird 2005; Fung and Wright 2001; Nabatchi 2010; Papadopoulos 2007). Given its misgivings on representation and its insistence on the direct involvement of citizens and civil society associations in the policy process, I shall refer to this approach as ultra-democratic.

As anticipated (see Chapter Six, §6.5.2), the differences between deliberative and Schumpeterian conceptions of democracy can be clarified by considering three main juxtapositions dominating current debate on the topic: (i) aggregation vs. deliberation, (ii) representation vs. participation and (iii) polity legitimacy vs. policy legitimacy. First, whereas Schumpeter depicts citizens as the bearers of preferences that are to be aggregated into a social utility function which the political system is expected to maximise, deliberative democrats view individual preferences as mere inputs that the political system has to process in order to arrive at a definition of the general will of the polity. Against the 'methodological fiction of an individual with an ordered set of coherent preferences', Benhabib (1996: 71) claims that 'the formation of coherent preferences cannot precede deliberation; it can only succeed it'. From this perspective, the scope of democratic politics is not that of aggregating pre-political preferences, but of setting in motion dialogical processes capable of creating common identities which can, in turn, give coherence to, and enhance the stability of, the body politic.

Second, Schumpeter's model of democracy applies to large territorial nation states and views direct involvement of the people in policy making is not only unfeasible but also undesirable; for it could expose the policy process to capture by factions and organised interests. By contrast, models of deliberative democracy emphasise the need to develop functional associations and actively involve them in policy making. 'Associative governance can provide a welcome alternative or complement to public regulatory efforts because of the distinctive capacity of associations to gather local information, monitor behavior and promote cooperation among private actors' (Cohen and Rogers 1992: 426). As such, deliberative democracy's aim is not to supersede representation, but to 'supplement nature with artifice: through politics, to secure an associative environment more conducive to democratic aims' (*ibid.*). Lastly, Schumpeter conceives democratic contestation in general elections as a means for periodically renewing the legitimacy of the polity. Deliberative models of democracy, instead, seek a bottom-up form of legitimation starting at the level of policy making. As Warren (2009: 8) writes, 'the strategy amounts to a functional compensation for the low global legitimacy of electoral democracy by generating legitimacy "locally" – issue by issue, policy by policy, and constituency by constituency'.

Once again, the research field where the union between network governance and deliberative democracy has been particularly prolific is EU governance studies. The EU is presented as the most remarkable instance of Networked Polity realised so far – a laboratory for democratic experimentalism and an example for other emerging global governance arrangements (Ansell 2000; Hooghe and Marks 2001; Sabel and Zeitlin 2008; Slaughter 2003; Yee 2004). As explained, a turning point for much of this literature is the 2001 White Paper on EU governance (Joerges *et al.* 2001). Following that White Paper, the EC has issued a string of similar documents dealing with more restricted policy areas and implemented ample institutional programmes aimed at increasing the transparency of EU policy-making procedures and the participation of EU citizens and their association in them.[5] Sabel and Zeitlin interpret these developments as a radical departure from the anti-democratic solutions envisioned by Majone and Moravcsik, and suggest seeing them as the embodiment of deliberative ideals. As

> a functioning novel polity without a state [the EU's] regulatory successes are possible because decision making is at least in part deliberative: actors' initial preferences are transformed through discussion by the force of the better argument. Deliberation in turn is said to depend on the socialisation of the deliberators (civil servants, scientific experts, representatives of interest groups) into epistemic communities, via their participation in 'comitological' committees: committees of experts and Member State representatives that advise the European Commission on new regulation and review its eventual regulatory proposals (Sabel and Zeitlin 2008: 272).

As a directly deliberative polyarchy, the EU is in their view engendering a two-step process of change: on the one hand, it is having a 'destabilisation effect on domestic politics, and through them, in return, on the EU itself' (*ibid.*: 277); on the other, it is 'prompting the emergence of new forms of dynamic accountability and peer review which discipline the state and protect the rights of citizens without freezing the institutions of decision making' (*ibid.*: 276).

A similar account is derived from the literature on deliberative supranationalism (Eriksen *et al.* 2003; Joerges 2002; Neyer 2006). According to this perspective, the evolution of the EU since Maastricht is at odds with both Majone's account of the EU as a Regulatory State and Moravcsik's inter-governmentalist perspective on EU integration. According to Joerges (2002: 141), at an institutional level,

> The most significant institutionalisation of the internal market [...] is not the new agencies, but the long-established comitology. Committees do not just have the so-called 'implementation' of Community framework provisions to deal with ('Comitology' proper), they also operate much more comprehensively as *fora* for political processes and as co-ordinating bodies between supranational and national, and governmental and social actors.

At a more political level, these innovations cannot be explained by focusing on the bargaining power of member states within the Council. Rather, a shift of emphasis from state to non-state agents and from bargaining to argumentation is required.

> Indeed, this is one of the most important functions of the myriad of comitology committees in the EU. They serve as political spaces which perpetuate the discourse about the meaning of shared rules, about acceptable ways of interpreting them, and about options to adapt them to changing scientific insights. Although formally equipped with the task of supporting and supervising the Commission in its implementation of European law, they have *de facto* developed into a decentralized political bureaucracy in which the EU is administered (Neyer 2006: 696).

Héritier (1999, 2003) has clarified the logic underpinning the deliberative turn in EU governance. Facing the growing erosion of popular consensus in attitudes to communitarian institutions and the opposition of member states to further developments along federal lines, the EC has viewed the deliberative approach as an alternative route to consensus building. First, it has attempted to reach those individuals, groups and communities more exposed to the effects of EU regulation by developing consultation programmes to elicit their opinions and suggestions. Second, it has implemented an open government policy to make all relevant information available to its stakeholders. Third, the EC has actively promoted the creation of supporting networks, involving them not only in policy making but also at the implementation stage as well. Hence the growing interest in developing new forms of democratic engagement along functional, rather than territorial, lines that go beyond the minimalist politics of the ballot box sought by supporters of CLM.

Even in this case, the differences between ultra-democratic solutions and the ideal of democracy appealed to by the left-wing critics of the post-war settlement recalled at the start of the chapter are worth exploring. As seen there, Schumpeter's definition of the classical model, with which these critics are often identified, collapses at least two distinct and opposed strands of democratic thought: the Rousseauian tradition based on the idea of a general will that cannot be delegated, and the Utilitarian tradition advocating a collective form of decision making based on majority rule compatible with delegation. Deliberative models depart from both traditions in significant ways. On the one hand, they reject aggregative procedures and minimise the relevance of voting (and therefore majority rule) *vis-à-vis* deliberation. Deliberation is presented as a reflexive and truth-oriented dialogical practice whose goal is to generate universal consensus, while voting and majority rule are seen as a contested, if not counterproductive, means to legitimate social choices. In this view, 'decisions taken by majority vote are democratically legitimate because they are *presumed* to be the *right* or the *most reasonable* policy proposal' (Geenens 2007: 360). This makes the epistemic quality of the reasons used, rather than majority opinion, the crucial legitimating element. On the other hand, deliberative democrats reject 'the fiction of a mass assembly carrying out its deliberations in public and collectively' (Benhabib 1996: 73). The endorsement of the people's participation in policy making does not amount to a rejection of representation as such, but only of versions of it that systematically exclude citizens from the policy process by delegating it to professional politicians and carrier civil servants. Against this 'liberal' conception of representation, deliberative democrats support the establishment of fora and juries with the power to decide specific policy issues. Given the restricted membership and limited scope of these fora, their democratic legitimacy does not rest on the value of participation *per se*, but on their descriptive representativeness and actual ability to express the general will. Hence the claim that 'there is no necessary connection between deliberation and "face to face" direct or participatory democracy' (Knight and Johnson 1994, n. 62: 295); a claim corroborated by analysis of actual deliberative practices: 'the contemporary ways in which citizens make these contributions […] assume neither the forms, purposes, nor rationales of classical participatory democracy' (Fung 2006: 74).

As I argue below, deliberative democracy, and the ultra-democratic solutions inspired by the deliberative turn, must be seen as attempts to combine: distinct notions of representation – liberal and descriptive; forms of communication – dialogical and strategic; and methods of social choice – majoritarian and consensual. Given the possible inconsistencies and shortcomings which are vitiating these attempts, a critical analysis of their limitations is required; a task I feel especially compelled to carry out because of my broadly sympathetic views and commitment to make them succeed in rejuvenating the democratic spirit that initially propelled the post-war settlement, but was eventually negated by the technocratic developments of Western welfare states.

8.4.1. Limits of ultra-democratic solutions and stakeholder democracy

Since ultra-democratic solutions are the offspring of the union between deliberative democrats and governance theorists, this section develops along two main lines. First, I consider the limitations that make deliberative democracy an unlikely theoretical framework for grounding empirically oriented accounts of governance, and in particular the ideal of 'governing without government' attributed to the Networked Polity. Then, I consider some shortcomings that make new modes of governance a less appealing field of inquiry for testing the viability of the normative models of public deliberation proposed in political theory.

Right from the start, we can identify (at least) two main readings of deliberative democracy with strikingly divergent implications (Palumbo 2012). The first, derived from liberal political philosophy, supports an epistemic reading of the deliberative process. It envisages deliberation as a means to replicate either Rawls's (1997) notion of public reason, or Habermas's (1995) ideal speech situation.[6] This perspective denies legitimating value to voting and majority opinion while stressing the force of the best argument in settling disagreement. As Habermas (2001b: 110) states,

> if we also ascribe an epistemic function to democratic will-formation [...] the democratic procedure no longer draws its legitimating force only, indeed even predominantly, from political participation and the expression of democratic will, but rather from the general accessibility of a deliberative process whose structure grounds an expectation of rationally acceptable results.

Politically, the substantive implications of strong epistemic versions of deliberative democracy are pretty indistinguishable from those of the anti-democratic solutions discussed above. As Geenens (2007: 357) explains: 'the reduction of democracy to a strictly epistemic ideal at the expense of other, equally important aspects of democratic legitimacy can easily lead to technocratic consequences'. Indeed, here deliberation seems not only unconnected to direct or participatory democracy, but could well be carried out without any actual democratic input (Newey 2002). It is a moot point whether the epistemic perspective goes beyond politics as well, for it seems to assume that there always is a correct answer to a policy problem that the deliberative process can duly uncover (King 2003).

Weaker versions, based on the idea of deliberation as 'reason-giving', have tried to make the search for rational consensus compatible with pluralism (Gutmann and Thompson 1996). However, they end up supporting a form of pluralism restricted to reasonable opinions only: those sharing fundamental liberal values like the principle of toleration and the public-private distinction. Radical democratic requests for the recognition of opinions that seek to permanently challenge dominant discourses, values and notions of reasonableness (thus turning democracy into an agonistic game, Mouffe 2000) would certainly be extremely difficult to accommodate within this framework. For governance theorists like King (2003: 43), deliberation as reason-giving also resolves into praise for the virtue of old-fashion forms of accountability: 'the reason-giving account insists that relevant representatives and experts answer directly to those affected by decisions, regardless of prior constituencies: the impact of their decisions creates a constituency that must be addressed in terms of sincere and informed reasons'. Thus, epistemic models fail to support governance's call for enhanced bottom-up participation and the overcoming of the state-civil-society divide, values upon which is premised the very idea of Networked Polity.

The second model of deliberative democracy views the dialogical process neither as an end in itself, nor as a rational problem-solving exercise, but as part of the ongoing struggle to improve the quality of social choice and democratic politics (Barber 1984; Christiano 2004; Waldron 1999). As Barber (1996: 248-9, emphasis in original) eloquently puts it

> it is the character of politics in general, and of democratic politics in particular, that it is precisely *not* a cognitive system concerned with what we know and how we know it but a system of conduct concerned with what we *will* together and *do* together and how we agree on what we will to do. It is practical not speculative, about action rather than truth. It yields but is not premised on an epistemology and in this sense is necessarily pragmatic. Where there is truth or certain knowledge there need be no politics [...] democratic politics begins where certainty ends.

Deliberation is here perceived in opposition to aggregation but not to voting; it is valued for the outcomes it produces and not just for the dialogical opportunities it creates. According to this perspective, democratic politics has to promote both ample discussion leading to confrontation and revision of diverging individual preferences, as well as decision moments where the participants are finally called to choose between policy alternatives by majority voting. Non-epistemic readings also consider deliberative democracy as a necessary complement to representative democracy, rather than a broad alternative to it.

> Mechanisms of direct participation are not (as commonly imagined) a strict alternative to political representation or expertise but instead complement them [...] public participation at its best operates in synergy with representation and administration to yield more desirable practices and outcomes of collective decision making and action (Fung 2006: 66).

While accepting traditional reservations about both the feasibility and desirability of Athenian-style forms of democratic politics, this perspective believes in establishing a variety of participatory opportunities for mini-publics that could strengthen the legitimacy and deliberative quality of democratic institutions (Goodin and Dryzek 2006). In so doing, its aim is threefold: (a) to challenge the stronghold politicians, bureaucrats and experts have on the definition and management of public opinion; (b) to set up public spaces where subsets of the citizenry can interact reflexively and decide matters of public concern; (c) to develop new forms of inclusion that could enhance the descriptive representativeness of public bodies structuring the policy process.

An emblematic instrument for participation is the randomly-selected deliberative forum suggested by Fishkin (1991) for the US presidential primaries. According to Fishkin, the creation of a deliberative 'National Caucus' as an opening for the primaries season could be the most effective solution for the latter's shortcoming – i.e. being 'front loaded'. The randomly-selected national mini-public making it up would be more representative than that of any state constituency; public debate could be more informative than the 'wholesale' and 'mass retail' politics with which the US electorate is routinely fed; and campaign contributions would play a much smaller role than they do in ads-driven national elections. In Fishkin's (1991: 9) words: 'In a deliberative opinion poll, the first evaluation of the candidates would have the thoughtfulness and depth of face-to-face politics, as well as the representative character of a national event that includes us all. [...] it permits the reflectiveness of small-scale interactions to replace the comparative superficialities of mass-retail and wholesale politics'. A second tool for engendering this type of reflexive participation are the citizens' juries discussed by Smith and Wales (2000: 55):

> A citizens' jury brings a group of randomly chosen citizens to deliberate on a particular issue [...] Over a number of days participants are exposed to information about an issue and hear a wide range of views of witnesses, who are selected on the basis of their expertise or on the grounds that they represent affected interests. [...] the jurors are given the opportunity to cross-examine the witnesses and, on occasion, call for additional witnesses and information. Following a process of deliberation among themselves, the jurors produce [...] a citizens' report [to which] the sponsoring body [...] is required to respond, either by acting on the report or by explaining why it disagrees with it.

Since these seminal contributions, the growing empirical literature on deliberative experiments has shown that the deliberations of randomly selected mini-publics can make a significant contribution to the resolution of policy issues that are too complex to be resolved by popular referenda, or too controversial to be left to the negotiating strategies of policy makers (Parkinson 2006; Smith 2005). However, that same literature has highlighted the limitations of these forms of participation. They can fail to (i) deliver better outcomes than those yielded by policy experts, (ii) select mini-publics whose descriptive representativeness is higher than that of elective assemblies, and (iii) supply stronger mechanisms of legitimation and more inclusive practices than popular referenda. Above all, given their restricted membership, limited scope and complementary status, deliberative assemblies can hardly engender a Networked Polity capable of 'governing without government' of the type advocated in governance theory.

What about new modes of governance themselves? Can governance studies be viewed as a research field suitable for testing the viability of deliberative democratic models? As repeatedly stated, governance theory represents a field of inquiry composed of two main reconstructive research programmes advancing several interconnected hypotheses about the (unintentional) outcomes of the reforms carried out in what I have labelled *les trente furieuses*. The first, supporting the notion of Networked Polity, 'consists of a diverse cluster of attempts to preserve mid-level analysis by emphasizing our social embeddedness and the role of social institutions as determinants of social life' (Bevir 2006: 427). This is in direct competition with the mid-level accounts put forward by the theorists of the Regulatory State, who propose alternative interpretations derived from a different epistemic outlook – NPE. The main implication I derive from this clarification is that the plausibility of these two research programmes is still a topic of public debate. Indeed, I argued that any evaluation has to distinguish between the explanatory and prescriptive sides of these research programmes. And in so doing, my personal conclusion was that the Networked Polity should be considered as a normative ideal wishing to be an influence for political and institutional change, rather than a reliable explanatory framework. I also pointed out that an emerging second wave of governance studies is increasingly questioning the alleged transition to a participative and dialogical policy environment and casting doubts on the various features composing the narrative of the Networked Polity, including the claims related to its democratic credentials (Benz and Papadopoulos 2006; Bogason and Musso 2006; Peters 2004; Skelcher 2010; Wälti *et al.* 2004).

A good example is Klijn and Skelcher's (2007) conjectural framework for analysis. Here the authors advance four conjectures concerning the effects governance networks have (or could have) on representative democracy, based on a review of the relevant empirical literature: (i) incompatible, (ii) complementary, (iii) transitional, and (iv) instrumental. Against the facile optimism shown by Networked Polity theorists, Klijn and Skelcher's work shows that only in some cases does it have complementary effects that could help strengthen the legitimacy of democratic arrangements; most of their findings point to a shift from representative government to the murky governance insisted upon by the post-democratic authors referred to in the course of this work.

All perspectives recognize that the significance of governance networks is in opening a new space for questions that were seen as being in the realm of elected politicians and for them to be relocated into arenas where politicians (if they are there at all) are likely to be in the minority, where managers play a greater role as policy entrepreneurs [...] This introduces problems of legitimacy that, to date, have not seriously been considered (Klijn and Skelcher, 2007: 604).

Possibly, even more interesting is the fact that Klijn and Skelcher's work highlights how the evidence collected so far could support diverse conjectures simultaneously, disputing the possibility to settle the question empirically.

As a reconstructive research programme, the Networked Polity seems no more convincing when it exalts the distinctive features of the participatory policy environment analysed *vis-à-vis* the neo-corporate solutions developed in the early 1970s. As suggested in Chapter One, the latter represent similar attempts to salvage the then crumbling post-war settlement by opening up the political process to institutional actors representing major social forces; attempts which, I pointed out, were ultimately unsuccessful. Generally (and rightly, in my opinion), governance theorists emphasise the fact that, unlike governance networks, neo-corporate solutions were restricted to organised labour and producer forces only, and also operated according to an aggregative logic that was incapable of promoting individual compliance with the various agreements signed to stop inflationary pressures. Governance networks, by contrast, 'move beyond the institutionalized peak bargaining of corporativism to more dispersed, flexible and, in some cases, transparent modes of agenda setting, policy making and implementation' (Klijn and Skelcher 2007: 604). However, governance theorists fail to discuss properly two crucial differences that made neo-corporate solutions normatively far less ambiguous than governance networks: their strong and permanent connection with the forces they claimed to represent; their formal and direct influence on policy making through the legislative ratification of the social compacts subscribed to. Governance networks are very often not only less representative than their neo-corporate counterparts, they also operate with soft law instruments which mean it is not always clear what their actual influence on policy is. Thus, for Smismans, new modes of governance 'may lack the more balanced representation of neo-corporatism, and in not providing real rights of participation it may also end up being a merely legitimating discourse without truly enhancing participation' (Smismans 2006: 618). An evaluation with which Bevir agrees:

> this 'democratic' turn is an elite project based on expert assertions that democratic innovations will promote efficient and effective governance. The result resembles neocorporatist incorporation more than a genuinely dialogic process. The state aims almost wholly at the involvement of organised groups of stakeholders and it retains control over which groups are involved. Further, the state restricts participation to consultation, for even those organized groups that the state recognizes as stakeholders are not themselves given decision-making powers (Bevir 2013: 11, also 2006: 429).

The point is important because it indicates the existence of two important weaknesses affecting the Networked Polity, both due to ambiguity pervading this approach concerning its reconstructive and prescriptive aspirations. By relying on functional reasonings which explain the evolution of new modes of governance as resting on their superior relative abilities *vis-à-vis* state and market solutions, governance theorists are led to overlook structural weaknesses that are no less serious than those vitiating past neo-corporate solutions, and which could well undermine any positive role governance networks could play in preserving liberal democratic arrangements from anti-systemic challenges – let alone promoting Warren's governance-driven democratisation. In failing to notice (and appreciate) the prescriptive aspects of the Networked Polity, governance theorists seem to be blind to the theoretical weaknesses of the justificatory framework employed and end up supporting a vulgar empiricism (producing what has become an unmanaged array of case studies) that undermines any attempt to shed some critical light on them – let alone attempt to find some plausible solution. Thus my previous remark (*see* Chapter Six, §6.5) that, under the mounting pressure of anti-systemic challenges brought about by those social and political movements dissatisfied with the current post-democratic shift observed in OECD countries, the holy union between democratic and governance theorists could eventually come to a premature and tragic end similar to the fictional one in Shakespeare's Romeo and Juliet.

8.5. Conclusions

The alleged passage from 'government' to 'governance' is, according to sympathetic observers like Warren (2009), not only redefining public policy but also reinventing democratic ideals and politics. In this chapter, I have considered two distinct ways in which this reinvention is being carried out. Theorists of the Regulatory State urge liberal democracies to abandon procedural conceptions of legitimacy in favour of substantive ones based on their actual ability to deliver the public goods and services wanted by citizens. Theorists of the Networked Polity instead suggest ways to reinforce the legitimacy of liberal democracies by bolstering their descriptive representativeness and people's involvement in policy making. Both oppose the CLM on which the post-war settlement rested. In the first case, because it puts too much emphasis on electoral politics and the majoritarian rules responsible for undermining the credibility of policy commitments while subjecting minorities to the whims of the majority. In the second case, because the competitive leadership model supports an aggregative conception of democracy incapable either of avoiding systemic overload or of resisting the paradoxes of disembedded social choice. These concerns lead supporters of the Regulatory State to justify extensive forms of delegation to non-majoritarian institutions, to attribute the power of veto to minorities and to restructure the democratic process so as to enable citizens to 'vote with their feet'. By contrast, it pushes supporters of the Networked Polity to invoke a stakeholder democracy willing to integrate those affected by public policy into the constellations of PPPs taking part in its definition and implementation.

I have attempted to expose the shortcomings of these two alternative accounts. Against the first, I have argued that their anti-democratic solutions rest ultimately on disputed notions of social efficiency, problematic denials of social justice claims, and contradictory appeals to pluralism. Against the latter, I have maintained that their ultra-democratic solutions are likely either to empower deliberative polyarchies, thus undermining political equality, or to prove incapable of supporting the far-reaching claims associated with the Networked Polity. I have also pointed out that, notwithstanding their differences, anti- and ultra-democratic solutions are having some curiously similar effects. Rather than promoting what Warren claims to be 'governance-driven democratisation', they could be held responsible for the large-scale process of de-democratisation affecting OECD countries noted by post-democracy theorists.

According to the latter, the interplay between these processes of change is not undermining the nation state as such, but its democratic basis, causing the development of a new 'reason of state' in the process (Wolf 1999a, 1999b). They also claim that the observed democratic retreat is, in turn, at the root of new forms of xenophobic populism cropping up all over the Western world (Mouffe 2005: ch. 4). Fuelled by the cat-and-mouse game played by a ruling meta-PPP that sees further negative integration policies and new modes of governance as the right policies to preserve their power on one side, and the counter-reaction of Polanyian movements unwilling to bear the burdens imposed by those policies and stakeholders affected by consultation fatigue on the other, democratic politics is exposed to a cultural backlash and anti-systemic sentiments that could have unpredictable outcomes. From this perspective, the troubles engulfing the EU are indicative of the fact that the 'strategy of functional compensation for low global legitimacy' that Warren imputes to governance is not working and could even be counterproductive. It is also clear that the solutions suggested by meta-governance theorists fall short of meeting the challenges posed by populist movements and anti-systemic forces. In my opinion, any effective solution needs to resolve the contradiction at the heart of the post-democratic condition – highly rhetorical appeals to deliberative ideals and a widespread functional support for neoliberal policies which deny any meaningful democratic participation. As I shall explain later in the Conclusion, resolving this contradiction requires two things. First, the awareness that although governance theory has shown the possibility of 'governing without government', in reality this largely remains an ideal to be endorsed rather than an already established practice. Second, a commitment to move beyond the democratic visions and functional analyses that justify the rule of restricted epistemic communities and to adopt a political programme whose goal is to really give politics back to the people, rather than offer the latter a token consultative role.

End Notes

1. Note that Buchanan and Tullock (1962), from which the representation is derived, believe that the democracy game will lead inexorably to the situations B and D that redistribute the cooperative surplus towards the poor. Mueller (1990), more correctly in my opinion, seems to think that all states of affairs have roughly the same probability to occur. For him, in fact, empirical

analyses of Western welfare states show the existence of multiple distributive flows rather than a single distributive flow towards those worst off. In confirming Mueller's findings, the literature on corporate welfare mentioned in Chapter Seven, §7.3.1 supports the idea that reforms of big government have reduced downwards redistributive streams while strengthening upward redistributive effects.

2. The distinction between three types of justification based on criteria of feasibility, electability and desirability is derived from Hamlin and Pettit (1989: 10). In my opinion, this is more sophisticated and heuristically interesting than the traditional binary distinction between desirability and feasibility discussed by Nelson (1980).

3. To drive the point home, Gauthier perceptively uses the example of an apartheid state like the then South Africa that decides to move towards a more democratic settlement; an example whose practical force can be appreciated by any disinterested observer of the development occurring in that part of world.

4. In both political theory and governance studies this distinction is not always forthcoming and therefore the source of many misunderstandings. I have tried to map the various traditions of thought responsible for the so-called deliberative turn in Palumbo (2012).

5. The most important are the following communications from the Commission: *Towards a Reinforced Culture of Consultation and Dialogue – General Principles and Minimum Standards for Consultation of Interested Parties by the Commission*, COM (2002) 704 final; *On the Collection and Use of Expertise by the Commission: Principles and Guidelines*, COM (2002) 713 final; *European Governance: Better Lawmaking*, COM (2002) 275 final; *Action Plan 'Simplifying and Improving the Regulatory Environment'*, COM (2002), 278 final; *Communication on Impact Assessment*, COM (2002) 276 final; *Framework for Regulatory Agencies*, COM (2002) 718 final; *Dialogue with Associations of Regional and Local Authorities on the Formulation of European Union Policy*, COM (2003) 811 final. For preliminary works on the White Paper: European Commission, *European Governance. Preparatory Work For The White Paper*. Office for Official Publications of the European Communities, Luxembourg, 2002. For an overview: Commission of the European Communities, *Report from the Commission on European Governance*. Office for Official Publications of the European Communities, Luxembourg, 2003; Commission Staff Working Document, *Report on European Governance* (2003-2004). SEC (2004) 1153. For a chronological overview and complete list of official documents cf. Almer and Rotkirch (2004).

6. Note that it is a moot point Rawls's compatibility with deliberative democracy and Habermas's relationship to liberalism. On these connections, the reconstruction proposed by Dryzek (2000: ch. 1) is instructive.

Chapter Nine

The Quest for Accountability: Democratic Politics in Neoliberal Times

9.1. Introduction

Political accountability is a cornerstone of liberal democracy. It represents the umbilical cord that connects citizens to their representatives and democratic politics to the common good. Its relevance is manifold. First, it establishes the channels of communication needed to legitimise the decision-making process and its outcomes. Second, it sets the side-constraints necessary for making representative institutions responsive to citizens' wishes. Third, it ensures the transmission of legitimate authority to the executive and administrative branches of government and helps maintain under scrutiny the activities of unelected officials and career civil servants. In short, accountability mechanisms are responsible for directing the political system towards the public interest and engendering the principles of social autonomy and political self-determination at the core of democratic politics.

Its theoretical relevance notwithstanding, in the twentieth century the evolution of actual existing liberal democracies with their large centralised governments and administrations, has conspired to gradually undermine the ability of their citizens to keep representatives accountable and political regimes responsive. The development of the welfare state in the post WWII period contributed to both by stressing its crucial role for the legitimacy of state institutions and hollowing out its real ability to deliver responsible and responsive government. Far from reversing this trend, the neoliberal reforms introduced since the 1980s have had the effect of reinforcing that tendency and yielding worrisome accountability gaps. Globalisation and the alleged transition from 'government' to 'governance' are thought to have further aggravated the problem, starting current debates about depoliticisation and the inception of a post-democratic age.

In this chapter, I endeavour to draw up a conceptual map of the issues raised in the various theoretical discussions on the state of accountability in representative political systems at both domestic and global levels. To make such a conceptual map intelligible, I start by clarifying the relevance accountability has for democratic politics (§9.2) and then describe the constitutional conventions devised over time to engender it (§9.3). Sections 9.4 and 9.5 subsequently discuss the erosion of accountability brought about by neoliberal reforms, globalisation of markets and new modes of governance. Following the arguments developed in the previous chapter, I contend that the managerial forms of accountability invoked by theorists of the Regulatory State and Networked Polity alike risk in effect to supply a theoretical justification for the policies of hollowing out of democratic institutions pursued by the ruling meta-PPP supporting the current neoliberal consensus politics. This is due to the fact that the new types of accountability proposed by the research programmes at the centre of governance theory view and present them as alternatives to traditional political and vertical mechanisms of accountability, rather than as complementary forms meant to make the latter more effective.

9.2. The formal and material elements of representation, delegation and responsibility

Political theory has advanced a double analysis of democratic politics (Dunn 1993; O'Donnell 1998). The first concerns the conception of democracy most appropriate for modern society. The outcome of this debate has been widespread support for a form of representative democracy that rejects radical participatory alternatives. As seen in Chapter One, political practice has followed a parallel course of action and caused the diffusion of this form of representative democracy worldwide, regardless of both geography and demography: it has become not only the hegemonic system of government in small and large countries alike, but it has also led to the adoption of the same basic institutional template (nested authorities) at federal, national, regional and local levels. Within this institutional template, political legitimacy rests on the effectiveness of the mechanisms devised to keep professional politicians and career civil servants accountable to the *demos*: (i) periodic elections which give people the possibility to punish the ruling elite that failed to govern properly; (ii) vertical mechanisms of accountability which give the representatives of the people supervisory power over the sprawling administration of the welfare state.

The second dominant issue that has preoccupied political theorists concerns the grounding of political authority (Christiano 2004; Dahl 1994). Theoretical debates have seen the confrontation between those who seek to ground it on substantive values and those who appeal instead to mere procedures. Notwithstanding the proceduralism that ended up dominating the post-war settlement, in this period political practice did not settle the issue one way or another, but combined procedural and substantive values together. The latter refers to the foundational role acquired by liberal rights as extra political limits on majority rule, while the former has to do with the practical defence of majority rule as the only viable criterion of decision making in the public sphere. To this end, what was needed was legitimate and responsible expertise, rather than the active participation of the *demos* in policy making. Consequently, real existing liberal democracies endorsed ample forms of delegation, periodically raising concerns about the accountability of those to whom authority was being delegated and/or the effectiveness of the mechanisms devised to enforce it properly.

To understand these concerns, the characteristics of the model of representative democracy established by the post-war settlements needs to be briefly clarified. Modern liberal democracy is characterised by a particular type of representation we can call 'political'. To understand it, a comparison with two other main forms is required. First, let us consider legal representation, from which it originally derives and which still inspires the analytical readings of political forms of representation proposed by NPE (Kelsen 1945). Here, an agent A delegates to another agent R the power to act on his behalf. Legal representation sets very strict limitations to R's discretion and leaves A free to dismiss R at a moment's notice. This is the basic form of representation used in business relationships, as well as in civil and criminal courts. It also had political relevance up to the French Revolution, when the ban on imperative mandates caused its demise in the public sphere altogether, making open mandates one of the main pillars of liberal constitutionalism. Second, we have the socio-graphic notions of representation developed by the social sciences since their inception; notions which have come to influence the vision of stakeholder democracy inspiring supporters of the Networked Polity. These notions refer to ways of constructing realistic social samples for the purpose of doing surveys and investigations which have scientific value. Usually, the representativeness of these samples is achieved by random selection mechanisms. In politics, lotteries were used in fourth century Athens to select those designated to occupy important public offices.[1] Today, they are employed to fill citizen juries operating in criminal courts, or in deliberative democratic experiments (Smith and Wales 2000).

Political representation differs from these two alternatives in two main ways. On the one hand, it attributes to representatives an open mandate in between elections. On the other, mandates rest on electoral mechanisms that are not even remotely attempting to bring about a sampled image of the *demos* – what Dahl (1989: 340) calls a 'minipopulus'. The hallmark of actual existing liberal democracy is the adoption of 'political' forms as the only valid form of representation. As a result, countless questions of legislative ethics arise from time to time concerning both the legitimacy of specific policy decisions taken by representative bodies and the effectiveness of the mechanisms devised to hold them (and their executive arms) accountable (Applbaum 1992; Thompson 1980).

We can distinguish four main links making up the chain of delegation established by actual existing liberal democracies in the course of the twentieth century. At the highest level operates a form of accountability we can also call 'political'. Elected representatives of diverse branches of government at various levels operate, as mentioned above, on the basis of an open mandate. As a result, their accountability relies on dialogical processes in which they endeavour to explain their actions to their electorates in order to acquire or retain consensus. According to normative political theory (Bellamy 2007a), it is on the basis of these dialogical processes that democratic politics has to clarify and develop the constitutional framework regulating the relationships between citizenry, the legislative and the executive. The outcome of these processes has to be not only the imputation of responsibilities, but also the definition of procedures for the revision of the institutions and norms which have somehow proved inadequate in practice. As an ideal and crucial element of democratic legitimacy, political accountability thus represents a persistent, self-reflexive and dynamic process through which democratic institutions constantly revise themselves in order to improve their popular appeal – and it is in this dynamic and self-reflective sense that it has been employed by those responsible for the deliberative turn (Dryzek 2000).

This understanding makes it significantly different from the vertical notion of accountability operating within the field of public administration (Deleon 1998). Delegation of authority to non-elected public officers and career civil servants takes place within an established and stable constitutional framework. Appointed and career public officers' duties and obligations are thus regulated by rules which have already democratic legitimacy and only need to be enforced and monitored impartially. Vertical accountability takes, therefore, a more legalistic aspect whose aim is to verify whether the right procedures have been followed correctly. Given this structure and nature, the actors to whom is entrusted the smooth working and effectiveness of vertical accountability mechanisms are two: the formal hierarchy operating within the administrative organisation, and the administrative courts and tribunals called to enforce the rule of law.

As seen in previous chapters, recent calls to overcome the governability problems experienced by liberal democracy in the 1970s caused the introduction of institutional flexibility and a more enterprising culture within public administrations. These measures have brought to an end the exclusivity that hierarchical forms of organisation and vertical systems of control used to enjoy in the public realm. The latter have been flanked, and sometimes even supplanted, by agencies, partnerships and networks operating according to managerial conceptions of accountability. These managerial conceptions rest on two contrasting features: (i) self-imposed restraints backed by peer-review systems, and (ii) the monitoring action of independent auditing agencies (*see* Chapter Four, §4.4.2). First, the dynamics of de- and re-regulation discussed in Chapter Five has promoted the development of soft-law instruments leading to the proliferation of intersecting and quasi-legal regulatory regimes. Second, neoliberal attempts to rule at a distance and thus reduce bureaucratic burdens have yielded the rising of semi-juridical systems of enforcement based on the monitoring work of semi-autonomous regulatory agencies and institutions of audit.

In Chapter Eight, I presented the justificatory frameworks used to support the shift towards managerialism and noted that it is based on notions of legitimacy and visions of democracy antithetical to the representative model underpinning the post-war settlement. The two perspectives analysed there arrive, in their distinct way, at different accounts of the problems affecting past systems of accountability and of the ways in which managerial forms can help solve them, thus strengthening the legitimacy of real existing liberal democracies (*see also* Chapter Two, §2.4). Here my goal is twofold. First, I wish to complement the normative analysis started there by clarifying the diverse features making up the notions of managerial accountability proposed by advocates of the Regulatory State and the Networked Polity respectively. Second, I shall discuss the side-effects produced in practice by current attempts to replace traditional mechanisms of accountability with more managerial forms. I argue that, given the doubts surrounding the democratic legitimacy of the institutions upon which these managerial solutions rest, the perception of a growing accountability gap affecting liberal democracies has become a persistent feature of public debate. Hence my conclusion that traditional and managerial mechanisms need to be integrated within a common democratic framework, rather than being treated as strict alternatives. I also maintain that any attempt to integrate these systems of accountability together needs to reconsider the notion of responsibility itself; that is, it needs to move beyond the individualist version advocated by neoliberal thinkers and the distinction between politics and administration used to ground the technocratic solutions advocated in support of the Regulatory State. It is to this question I shall now turn before discussing the accountability issues raised by the 1980s managerial turn.

9.2.1. Liberal vs. democratic conceptions of responsibility

Conventional debates between liberals and democrats have centred on the disputed shortcomings of political accountability *vis-à-vis* vertical accountability (Applbaum 1992). Old and neoliberals view the political process as too arbitrary to set effective side-constraints on majoritarian institutions and therefore push for a more legalistic reading of constitutional rules – which are, in turn, conceived as external side-constraints on political and policy processes (*see* Chapter Five). For them, proper accountability entails both the protection of individual entitlements, enforced through independent tribunals, and rigorous systems of checks and balances supervised by autonomous constitutional courts. By contrast, democrats advocate a notion of constitutionalism that views individual guarantees as the outcome of democratic politics itself, rather than external and/or pre-political side-constraints (Waldron 1999). According to this democratic perspective, accountability mechanisms originate as political self-restraints whose aim is that of preserving the integrity of the polity while improving its policy effectiveness. The managerial solutions introduced since the 1980s developed as an intriguing hybrid between these two contrasting perspectives. On the one hand, they operate outside hierarchical lines of authority and endorse dialogical forms of decision making (Sabel and Simon 2006). On the other hand, they are part of, and meant to carry further, the process of depoliticisation pursued by neoliberals (*see* Chapter Two). The constellation of regulatory agencies and networks involved in co-governance are thus taken to be technical bodies whose role is to strengthen the effectiveness of the policy process in an objective (rather than political) manner. Being apolitical, their legitimacy does not derive from their democratic credentials. Rather, it rests on their scientific status and independence from the electoral process. In short, managerial solutions are conceived and justified as being part of either (i) the anti- and non-majoritarian institutions established by the Regulatory State to reinforce its policy credibility, or (ii) the intricate web of interconnected and truth-oriented deliberative fora committed to engender the Networked Polity from the bottom up.

According to Schedler (1999), accountability rests on two main pillars: answerability and enforceability. In my opinion, a better reading would view these two elements as the opposite poles of a conceptual continuum including several intermediate types. Closer to the answerability pole, we find those mechanisms of accountability whose aim is to bring into the public domain information concerning intentions and actions needed to evaluate the policy process. This is a type of accountability whose main objective is to engender transparency, rather than attributing responsibilities or issuing sanctions. Moving towards the enforceability pole, we find a second type of accountability where the main goal is to explain someone's choices and actions. In addition to the release of relevant information, this undertaking also requires a full and explicit justification for the policy decisions taken. Next, we meet a conception of accountability whose aim is to assign responsibilities and establish some kind of redress for misadministration and the release of public 'bads'. These need not be formal sanctions, but could simply require a public apology. Closer to the enforceability pole is a form of accountability that entails issuing sanctions. These sanctions can be either of a political, legal or informal nature. Elections and votes of confidence are examples of the first kind; judicial review and internal disciplinary procedures are examples of the second kind; reputation costs are examples of the third kind. As Schedler (1999: 21) explains,

> the public nature of accountability serves all three aspects of accountability: information, reasoning, and punishing. It does more than bring the 'forceless force of the better argument' upon the conduct of the accountable party, it also involves an important form of sanction. It exposes cases of misconduct to public opinion, which often provokes highly damaging reputational consequences.

As I shall argue in the following sections, by replacing traditional mechanisms of accountability with managerial instruments of auditing, the reforms introduced since the 1980s have failed to engender a better system of accountability. At most, they have shifted the institutional emphasis from one type to another along the conceptual spectrum, and reinforced both pre-existing accountability gaps and their public perception. We need in addition to take into account the skewed and erratic way in which this shift to managerial systems has been carried out in practice. When this is done, we then get further corroboration for the theory supported throughout this work: that the ruling meta-PPP is in reality pursuing a strategy of political centralisation-cum-administrative decongestion that is not meant to address past accountability gaps but to bypass the restrictions constitutional conventions imposed on the executive branches of government. From this perspective, the spurious and somewhat arbitrary distinctions between policy and administration, and purchaser and provider, seem to have in fact reserved the most hard-hitting forms of accountability for middle- and street-level administrators with very little decision-making power.

By contrast, the political actors who now exercise ordinary and meta-regulatory powers find themselves having mere duties of answerability – something they discharge by employing ever more sophisticated and professionalised forms of political communication. Hence the growing public distrust towards politicians, and the spreading of very negative opinions which tend to perceive 'them' not just as a 'waste of time' (Blühdorn 2007: 299), but rather as a 'bunch of crooks' – a distrust 'they' share with other members of the ruling meta-PPP: bankers, financial authorities, corporations and mainstream press. Moreover, since the form of political representation adopted in liberal democracies establishes very limited channels of voice for expressing public discontent, any attempt to use electoral contests to 'kick the rascals out' rewards paradoxically antisystemic and antagonistic parties, further reducing the quality of deliberation of representative institutions and undermining their ability to control their executive branches.[2]

A final point of disagreement between liberals and democrats to which I wish to draw attention concerns the notion of responsibility itself. Liberals tend to support only personal forms of responsibility – and this is so even when they do not subscribe to the narrow, personalistic notion of coercion proposed by neoliberals like Hayek and Nozick (Brown *et al.* 2010). According to liberal thought (Paul, Miller and Paul 1999), we can meaningfully impute responsibility only to individual agents who have the power to choose freely between alternative courses of action. Conceptually, personal responsibility rests therefore on two crucial features: (i) a clear causal link between actions performed and some given states of the world; (ii) the agent's volition (or lack of) to bring about a given state of the world, to foresee its likelihood or to prevent it from happening. In practice, personal responsibility also requires (iii) the adoption of a retrospective outlook, in that it applies to past actions, and (iv) a commitment to identify ways to redress and compensate for abuses, misdeeds and wrongdoings that brought about a given state of the world. Democratic thought has highlighted the shortcomings this personalistic conception of responsibility shows when applied to the political realm. To start with, some states of the world are the outcome of collective actions for which it is difficult, if not impossible, to establish personal responsibilities. This has in part to do with the problem of many hands discussed by Thompson (1980), but also with the existence of structural conditions for which nobody can be held personally responsible (Young 2013). Moreover, contingencies, interferences and the self-reflexive nature of social action conspire to blur the boundaries between volitions and accidents as well as freedom and compulsion (Hardin 2000). Furthermore, even when personal responsibilities can be imputed, they could rest with previous generations or actors no longer able to make amends, thus making such attribution a mere academic or historical exercise. Finally, the attribution of responsibilities, and the issuing of sanctions to those who bear them (what goes under the name of compensatory justice), could fail to set in motion the processes of change needed to avoid those same abuses, misdeeds and wrong-doings from re-occurring in future. Given these limitations, democrats affirm the need to seek an alternative, more political conception of responsibility – suggestions that we know are routinely blamed for promoting the entitlement culture that allegedly caused the fiscal crisis of the welfare state (*see* Chapter Two, §2.2).

I contend that these liberal reservations often rest on some misrepresentation – to which third-way social democratic thinkers have unfortunately contributed (Giddens 2000). At a theoretical level, democratic thought is not logically dependent on the rights-based notion of social citizenship advocated by progressive thinkers in the post-war period. As I explained, this rights-based notion of social citizenship acquired acceptance and was functional with the defensive model of democracy imposed by the post-war settlement. Alternative participatory forms of democracy developed during the inter-war period. Far from attributing expanding sets of social and economic rights to the individual, these alternative forms established clear-cut responsibilities not only for various aspects of the citizen's personal condition, but also for the persistence of structural injustices it did not contribute to bring about directly. The political notion of responsibility proposed by the late Iris Marion Young (2013) arches back to this democratic tradition. In it, she develops an approach that attributes responsibility by 'structural' connection; that is, in ways which (i) do not try to 'isolate' those responsible, (ii) question the 'normal' background conditions where individual action takes place, (iii) are committed to look 'forward' rather than backward and (iv) can impute 'shared' forms of responsibility. Such an approach departs from liberal attempts to individualise responsibility by discounting the role played by environmental factors and contingencies. At the same time, her conception of political responsibility establishes a general obligation to refuse subjugation; one that (v) justifies revolt against exploitation by imposing on the citizen a duty to (a) 'organise' against social injustices, and (b) 'boycott' those involved in unjust practices.

Young's approach shows that within the democratic tradition there are the intellectual resources for re-conceptualising the question of responsibility which move beyond the sterile philosophical terrain into which neoliberal thought and third-way social democrats have driven it. Moreover, I contend that this re-conceptualisation is also needed for practical reasons. Under the pretence of connecting rights to responsibilities (Dwyer 2004), the reforms imposed by neoliberal policies in the last three decades have had, as I have noted several times so far, the curious effect of increasing the responsibilities of the powerless while removing those established in the past for directing the actions of the powerful towards the public good. In bringing this state of affairs about, the debates surrounding accountability have had a double political relevance. First, they have supplied the justificatory frameworks suitable for expanding the power of control of central government on (i) sectors of public administration which were made semi-independent by past welfare policies or (ii) realms of civil society which had somehow managed to escape the process of vertical integration carried by the welfare state in the post-war. Second, managerial mechanisms of accountability have supplied the practical means to actualise those disciplinarian projects in a deeply biased and self-serving manner. It must be noted, however, that the political re-conceptualisation sought by Young is likely to shift the theoretical focus of attention away from the 'poor' to the 'citizen', and from liberal notions of individual rights to the democratic category of public duties. In other words, it points in a direction contrary to the one advocated by T. H. Marshall and that still enjoys a hegemonic position within social and political theory (Somers 2008).

9.3. Mapping the accountability space: the four links of the delegation chain

As seen in Chapter One, in the post-war period real existing liberal democracies adopted a model of government (Schumpeter's CLM) where the *demos*, as the sovereign agent, had a very restricted or no real involvement in the policy process at all. By and large, CLM restricts the democratic input of citizens to choosing those who have to decide what constitutes the public interest and which means are most likely to accomplish this. The ban on imperative mandates also means that once elected, representatives are not legally bound to their voters and constituencies. Rather, they are required to pursue the policies that, according to them, achieve the common good of the polity as a whole. However, this represents only the first link of a long chain of delegation ending with the policy implementation carried out by street-level bureaucrats (Lipsky 1980). Here I shall consider the various links composing this chain and spell out both the problems they pose and the institutional mechanisms of accountability employed in the past to tackle them. Since, these mechanisms were arrived at under the spell of economic readings of the delegation process, in this section a great deal of attention will be reserved to the principal-agency theory, the analytical tool used to model the hypothetical issues this process is supposed to tackle.

The modern decoupling of popular sovereignty from people's involvement in actual policy decisions opens up a first critical area of analysis for issues of accountability. First-level accountability (L1A) raises the following questions: What sort of mechanisms can ensure that representatives will be responsive to people's wishes once elected? How is it possible to deter them from pursuing their own or sectoral interests, rather than the common good? Are there any means for redressing eventual public bads and apportion clear responsibilities for them? In dealing with questions like these, liberal democracies have endorsed three types of institutional arrangement. First, we have formal constitutional constraints on majoritarian decision making: the distinction between ordinary legislation and constitutional rules requiring qualified majorities; the division of power and systems of checks and balances between elected and non-elected public bodies; the rule of law as opposed to the rules of men. Second, there are periodic electoral moments when the citizens are called forth to evaluate their representatives and given the chance to vote them out for perceived past wrongs. Particularly contentious has been a third type of institutional arrangements devised to sanction representatives in between electoral intervals. Several political systems employ impeachment procedures designed to remove from office representatives who have committed crimes and misdemeanours. There have been few and very limited attempts to institute recall mechanisms to punish those who, in pursuing their free political judgment, betray the trust put in them by their own electors without violating any extant law. So far, recall mechanisms of this type are to be found mostly either at local level (or at state level in federal systems like the USA) or in newly-established democracies with dubious liberal credentials – the constitution of the Bolivarian Republic of Venezuela is, to my knowledge, the only charter that establishes this system of recall for all elective positions (art. 72), and was actually used in 2004 to try to unseat Hugo Chavez, the elected president at the time (Carter Center 2005).

However, recall mechanisms of this type have been at the forefront of liberal democratic attempts to tackle second-level questions of accountability (L2A): namely, those disciplining the relationships between legislative and executive branches of government. The issues raised at this level differ from those discussed above because they belong to a more remote link of the delegation chain: the one involving executive officers to whom representatives have passed on some of the powers delegated to them by the citizenry. Besides the constitutional norms establishing the division of power and systems of checks and balances mentioned above, at this level additional mechanisms of accountability depend on the institutional architecture of the body politic. In OECD countries, the main variants can be located along an institutional continuum, the ideal poles of which are pure parliamentary systems and pure presidential systems. Parliamentary systems attribute to the legislative an exclusive entitlement to define the public interest and the means needed to bring it about (Strøm 2000). Presidential systems, on the contrary, establish forms of co-government where both branches enjoy a shared constitutional right to define the public interest and the means to bring it about (Brown 1998). The implication for accountability is threefold. In parliamentary democracies, political accountability aims at reinforcing the sovereignty of parliament over the executive, whilst in presidential systems its goal is to preserve their respective autonomy. The existence of diverse constitutional architectures also explains why debates on accountability at this level overwhelmingly concern parliamentary systems with flexible constitutions (so-called Westminster systems), rather than presidential arrangements with formal constitutions and independent constitutional courts. Finally, the distinction is conceptually important because it clarifies why, in parliamentary systems, the alleged erosion of accountability concerns mainly L2A questions (e.g. the growing inability of UK Parliament to keep the Cabinet accountable), but refers to L1A issues in presidential systems (e.g. the unresponsiveness of the US presidential administration as a representative institution). A point that is very often obscured by current discussions about the accountability gap, but which has special theoretical relevance for locating the problems affecting the different forms of real existing liberal democracy, as well as for devising viable normative solutions.

L2A mechanisms rely on a variety of distinctive solutions. In parliamentary systems, the most direct way to keep the executive accountable to parliament is through votes of confidence. Since the authority of prime ministers and their cabinets derives from the trust of parliamentary majorities, a negative vote of confidence deprives them of any democratic legitimacy. In other words, votes of confidence at this level have the same political relevance elections have at L1A, which remains the only tool available to unseat an unresponsive presidential administration. Besides votes of confidence, parliaments are given the power to sanction national executives by activating formal procedures of impeachment. As in presidential systems, their role is however restricted to crimes and misdemeanours and thus they are not very useful instruments for checking the exercise of political discretion by national executives. Hence, their gradual institutional atrophy in OECD countries. A common means by which parliaments can keep governments in check is thus demanded of conventions regulating ministerial accountability. These conventions give parliaments the power to hold their governments, either as a whole or its individual ministers, to account and supervise in this way the activities of public offices and officials under ministerial jurisdiction as well. In Westminster systems, these conventions regulate three main aspects of the political process: parliamentary debates and sub-committees' powers of investigation; procedures established to share individual responsibilities; sets of sanctions applicable to those who have somehow failed to discharge their duties or abused the authority delegated to them. As mentioned above, these conventions are capable of supplying a spectrum of practical outcomes which can go from a simple public clarification of the type of activities undertaken (*informatory responsibility*), to an explanation of the reasons behind the choice of a particular course of action (*explanatory responsibility*), to the call for some public apology or form of redress for damages caused (*amendatory responsibility*), to the call for the resignation of those individuals held responsible for policy failure (*sacrificial responsibility*) (Woodhouse 1994: 28 ff.).

A third traditional critical area of inquiry concerns the activities of those officials filling the ranks of civil administrations in charge of implementing public policy (P3A). In modern nation states, policy has been traditionally implemented by large bureaucracies employing a vast number of people organised according to a complex, functional division of labour. Since the enforcement of public functions is backed by powers of sanction having ultimate democratic legitimacy, accountability mechanisms are meant to assure the transmission of legitimate power downwards from ministers to street-level bureaucrats and protect individual citizens from possible abuses. They also have to balance two potentially conflicting sets of civil servant loyalties: towards the ministers in charge of the various departments and towards the general public, of which the users of public services are only a subset. The first set of loyalties is enforced through the hierarchical organisation of public offices headed by ministers who are then politically accountable to parliament. The protection of individual entitlements is guaranteed by an independent system of administrative justice (i.e. judicial review, ombudsman, etc.) and is therefore part of a legal form of accountability distinct from the previous one. Vertical accountability aims to preserve the authority of sovereign power across the delegation chain operating within a representative political system. At the same time, its function is to keep in check possible abuses of power, sanction those responsible for outcomes incompatible with the common good, and establish both some form of redress and institutional learning. Thus, it represents a crucial complement to political accountability. Its replacement with horizontal mechanisms of accountability with semi-legal status and quasi-juridical value is therefore to be viewed as having necessarily perverse side-effects on political accountability as well – especially if, and when, these mechanisms are limited to financial matters and managerial questions having little or no political overall relevance. In failing to compensate for the loss of political supervision, this replacement opens troublesome accountability gaps which will increase the public perception of a democratic deficit.

Since the 1980s, public bureaucracies worldwide have lost political influence and administrative power in favour of market and quasi-market solutions (*see* Chapter Three). These innovations have brought to the forefront a fourth critical area of analysis: that concerning the authority and responsibilities of the growing number of appointed public managers, quangos and NGOs now involved in the delivery of public services in partnership with, or as subcontractors of, what is left of the old organisations which use to discharge those duties: P4A. Compared to P3A, P4A entails two major changes. First, hierarchical lines of authority are replaced by contractual relations and market incentives. Vertical accountability is consequently replaced by the supervision of a host of regulatory agencies and auditing institutions enjoying substantial autonomy and discretionary power (Power 1997b). As a result, parliaments have now only a remote influence on the regulatory process, while ministers operate by issuing general guidelines designed to make them govern at a distance. Second, managerial innovations of this type blur customary boundaries between public and private (beyond the domains of rule making and administrative justice noted above). Administrative personnel are now recruited from, and move freely across, distinct organisational realms and are also rewarded according to individual performance. Thus, market dynamics and profit motives come to dominate over traditional public values, loyalties and commitments. This process is compounded by the opening of national borders and the rising of the multilevel systems of governance analysed in Chapter Seven. In this context, public goods and services are increasingly supplied by myriads of agencies, partnerships and networks with a semi-public status and operating beyond the jurisdiction of representative institutions entitled to enforce accountability rules. Given that the overwhelming majority of activities carried out at this level concerns goods and services for which there is in reality no market alternative, competition turns out to be extremely limited, and with it the supposed benefits of market discipline. Hence, the doubts about the effectiveness of the new accountability system and rising concerns about another possible accountability gap reinforcing the one affecting P3A.

9.3.1. Squaring the circle: solving market failures by proxy markets

The traditional solutions outlined above were based on readings of the problems generated by the delegation process for whom only well thought-out constitutional side-constraints could supply an adequate answer. As seen in Chapter One, this reflected the intellectual division of labour at the root of the post-war settlement that justified state intervention for solving market failures. As for the market, the failures yielded by CLM required political, rule-based solutions aiming at regulating party competition and the temptations of power politics – what, according to Schumpeter, a long line of liberal thinkers came to call the 'pre-conditions' of a working democracy. With the rise of NPE's academic prestige, this intellectual division of labour was first undermined and then turned upside-down by the neoliberal insistence on the costs of government failure and red tape. According to the new economic orthodoxy that supplanted Keynesian macroeconomics (*see* Chapter Two), the overall relevance of market failures needs to be reassessed: the latter are presented either as (i) too irrelevant to justify state intervention (self-correcting markets thesis), or (ii) requiring political solutions whose costs offset their potential social benefits (negative cost-benefit analysis thesis), or else (iii) resolvable by more efficient proxy market-based managerial techniques (NPM thesis). Among the various heuristic models used to square the market failure circle, the one that has had more currency and strongly influenced the advocates of the Regulatory State is the principal-agent theory: an analytical tool that when applied to the study of the political delegation chain yields a set of simple representations of the issues liberal democracies need to tackle and of the most effective ways to tackle them (Tirole 1986). Since current debate on accountability has, to a large degree, adopted these analytical representations and is carried out under the shadow of the principal-agent theory (Strøm 2000), a brief presentation of the latter is required so as to ascertain its limitations when applied to the political realm.

In its basic form, a principal-agent model describes the strategic interaction between self-seeking parties linked by private contractual relations. Given the fact that information is distributed asymmetrically and tends to favour one of them (the agent) over the other (the principal), the former can maximise her self-interest by exploiting the latter. According to whether this information asymmetry is taken to pre-exist (*hidden information*) or follow (*hidden action*) the establishment of a contractual relation, we can have two main agency problems: (i) *adverse selection*, when the principal establishes contractual incentives which cause the selection of the wrong type of agent, or (ii) *moral hazard*, when the principal devises supervising procedures which make it easier for the agent to cheat him. Agency costs derive, in turn, from two kinds of behaviour: (a) *acts of omission*, when the agent does not fulfil his/her duties towards the principal, or (b) *acts of abuse*, when the agent goes beyond or against the limits imposed on his/her mandate. Applied to the various critical areas identified above (*see also* Chapter Two, §2.2), we derive four basic principal-agent situations formalising the accountability problems located along a four-link delegation chain:

- P1A describes a *democracy game* where political representatives can easily exploit the citizenry by pursuing their private or sectoral interests rather than the common good.
- P2A describes a *ministerial game* where the government is able to pursue policies that favour personal or party interests while shifting the blame for policy failure on the parliament.
- P3A describes a *bureau game* where career officers enjoy the benefits derived from delegated authority while making ministers pay for any government failure.
- P4A describes a *managerial game* where appointed managers and quangos maximise their profits regardless of the social and financial costs involved.

Within the neoliberal camp, the principal-agent theory was first used to explain the pathologies of big government and then to support market-based systems of incentives and proxy-market forms of competition (Miller 2005). I contend that its academic and political popularity notwithstanding, such a theory has shown to be controversial on both counts. First, at a more abstract theoretical level, principal-agent models very often fail to capture the logic of interaction unfolding in the public realm. According to them, the exploitation of political principals rests on the combined outcome of both the self-seeking attitude of agents and the existence of weak side-constraints on individual action. The latter are, in turn, due to the transaction costs caused by imperfect contracts and their legal enforcement. However, these explanatory devices overlook the fact that the interaction between state actors always takes place within highly structured and regulated constitutional settings and is therefore rule-bound. With the exception of P4A, all other levels of delegation mentioned above are far removed from the unconstrained market interaction employed in the basic model. Moreover, the rules of the games listed above cannot be viewed as equilibria solutions between the various contending actors, because their procedural and multilayered nature is doomed to persist over time and therefore shapes the pay-offs of the players themselves. Take, for instance, the bureau game, traditional public administrations rest on recruitment strategies, employment contracts and career prospects that seek to socialise officers into their roles and establish a strong public ethos. Those are solutions devised over time to protect those organisations from adverse selection and moral hazard, and this is why monetary incentives play an insignificant role and side-payments are always explicitly prohibited.

As I argued elsewhere (Palumbo 2001), whatever the practical effectiveness of these solutions, the players engaged in these games cannot change them – as individual agents reasoning and acting in isolation, they are rule-takers not rule-makers; informal agreements reached against the rule are not enforceable and inevitably produce free-riding opportunities undermining their viability.[3] The readings of the bureau game proposed by NPE authors rest, therefore, on a host of controversial theoretical claims, often inconsistent with the methodological tenets they affirm, about the players' motives, the plausibility of the beliefs upon which their strategies rest, and the collective action problems affecting the institutional players who are supposed to supervise them. If this was not enough, the normative predictions derived from those abstract models are either empirically unsupported, or have a very limited empirical support open to interpretation (Green and Shapiro 1994). I also claimed that, paradoxically, these weaknesses imply that while it is a far too simplistic analytical framework for understanding the pathologies of traditional public bureaucracies, the principal-agent theory can be viewed as a proper heuristic model for analysing the side-effects yielded by neoliberal reforms of big government, especially those raised by the managerial game at P4A. For, by removing previous institutional side-constraints, the managerial game tends to gradually resemble the competitive market setting congenial for the development of large-scale adverse selection and moral hazard opportunities which can be strategically exploited by the players.

Similar arguments can be developed, in a sort of theoretical domino effect, in relation to all other links of the delegation chain where similar institutional and political changes have been imposed, as I shall explain in the rest of this chapter. Particularly puzzling is, in this context, the role acquired by proxy-markets within the bureau game, thanks especially to the theoretical and practical efforts of Le Grand (2003, 2007, 2011) in the UK. Leaving aside the remarkable fact that these are the intellectual product of a market socialist tradition that the neoliberals who are currently re-evaluating them have supposedly refuted (Buchanan 1985: ch. 4; Le Grand and Estrin 1989), it is clear by now that these devises are not even remotely improving the independence of public managers in their daily activities or the efficiency of public services (Marquand 2004). As I argued in Chapter Five, their introduction has caused the super-imposition of an outcome-oriented logic upon a pre-existing procedural logic that leaves the government of the day free to strategically appeal to either one or the other as it sees fit. Accordingly, blends of the two logics are used in relation to middle- and street-level bureaucrats to strengthen or re-affirm the power of ministers on the peripheral branches of government, and to escape the power of control attributed to parliament by traditional conventions of accountability. Thus doing, a new separation of power is *de facto* established that allows executive bodies to acquire semi-presidential functions without the corresponding electoral burdens in parliamentary systems,[4] or presidential administrations to easily bypass the supervision of legislative institutions by falling back on soft-law tools in presidential systems. Given the fact that regulation inside government keeps on increasing the dissatisfaction of middle- and street-level bureaucrats forced to operate in worsening working conditions, public service users are facing deteriorating standards with no real power of exit, and the political discontent of taxpayers, who are ultimately called to foot the bill, finds itself channelled towards the democracy game currently unfolding in a political environment swamped by virulent populist movements and punitive electoral reactions. This set the stage, as said earlier (*see* Chapter Eight, §8.5), for the emergence of the opposed visions of democracy proposed by the theorists of the Regulatory State and Networked Polity at the centre of this work; visions which, in contributing to undermine the political and institutional basis upon which CLM was grounded, keep sustaining the post-democratic drift affecting all advanced real existing liberal democracies.

9.4. Political change and the erosion of accountability

So far, I have argued that current debate on accountability is fuelled by the widespread perception of a general and relentless erosion of accountability mechanisms and democratic values. Such an erosion is, in turn, imputed to a double process of political and institutional change: first, the restructuring of national democratic institutions brought about by neoliberal reforms of big government; second, the stretching of the delegation chain itself under the pressure of globalisation. In this section, I carry out a critical analysis of the first set of reasons put forward in support of this perception – I shall discuss the second set in §9.5. In doing this, I will raise three tricky issues. The first concerns the definition of the institutional landscape which current processes of change are allegedly eroding. The second deals with the ways in which neoliberal reforms are taken to have undermined traditional mechanisms of accountability. The last one considers the solutions put forward to counterbalance such an erosion and the side-effects produced by them. The aim is to support the critical remarks expressed in the previous chapter about the explanatory and justificatory frameworks of the Regulatory State and Networked Polity by considering the more restricted field of accountability. Although this analysis is carried out at a certain level of abstraction, it is based on a body of empirical literature concerned with the changes which have occurred in Westminster's political systems since the late 1970s (Stone 1995). The rationalisation I propose is meant to show that the magnitude of those changes in the theory and practice of accountability has repercussions which go beyond Westminster systems, in that they apply to other parliamentary regimes and to presidential systems as well.

Building on the discussion carried out in the first part of this book, I have indicated the various forms of delegation endorsed by real existing liberal democracies. Overall, we have a chain of delegation composed of four main institutional links describing both the problems arising at each level and the solutions devised over time to tackle these problems (to make the picture more realistic, each link could, in turn, be represented as a chain in itself rather than a solid tie). Thus, accountability defines two things: (a) the means by which legitimacy flows across institutional levels and (b) the ways in which the responsibilities of those entrusted with delegated power ought to be upheld. The previous sections of this chapter highlighted two of the main implications. First, different constitutional orders imply slightly different delegation regimes and stress the role of different accountability mechanisms. Second, constitutional orders, delegation regimes and accountability mechanisms are never static but evolve over time. Right from the outset, it is therefore clear that the identification of the institutional landscape subject to erosion is not an easy task. A constantly changing political coastline turns the idea of erosion into a rather complex and value-laden issue. Coherently with my general approach, I follow Goodin (2003) in attempting to bypass the problems besetting empirical analyses of delegation and accountability by employing ideal typical representations. To start with, I attempt to identify ideal typical features that characterise a specific model of representative democracy (say, parliamentary), and then go on to discuss whether the innovations brought about by neoliberal reforms of big government undermine them, leaving an accountability gap. This approach is repeated for each of the four accountability levels listed above.

Let us start with the democracy game and the problems that spring up at L1A. Here the delegation of power to political representatives allows them to pursue policy objectives that could systematically fail to reflect either the wishes of the electorate or the common good of the polity, or both. In the absence/impossibility of imperative mandates, the accountability of legislators rests therefore on the deterring power of periodic general elections. In the second post-war period, the ballot box came to represent not just the main tool for keeping elected politicians accountable, but, together with universal franchise, the very essence of democratic politics (*see* Chapter One). It must be stressed that even those who hold a realist conception of democracy similar to Weber's and Schumpeter's perceive general elections as something more than just the casting of votes. They also involve ample public debates where candidates and their sponsors have the opportunity to: (i) confront each other, (ii) present their political programmes and (iii) impute responsibility for past policy decisions. Thus, far from being merely sanctionatory devices (Schedler 1999), elections can satisfy the full spectrum of functions required from accountability: reporting, justification, apology and punishment. Analytically, it is therefore vital to distinguish between 'elections' and 'voting' on one side – a distinction akin to that used in deliberative democracy between 'deliberation' and 'decision' – and between 'voting' and 'acclamation' on the other. However, the evolving practice of actual existing liberal democracies has inexorably neutralised the real ability of general elections to keep representative institutions accountable and responsive. The electoral process has proved to be not only vulnerable to manipulation (of people's preferences, electoral systems and constituencies boundaries, to mention three main problem areas), but structurally incapable of fulfilling the electorate's desire for meaningful political choice. To quote a colourful remark made by Pettit (2008: 50) on the matter, 'The market in politics resembles the sort of department store that used to characterize communist regimes: most shelves are bare and empty; the well-stocked ones boast only the familiar, approved products; and ordering those products does not even guarantee getting them'. Hence, the growing disillusion with the politics of the ballot box, as evidenced by declining turn-outs all over OECD countries, and the search for the alternative visions of democracy embodied by the Regulatory State (foot-voting) and the Networked Polity (deliberative stakeholdership).

As clarified in Part I, this change seems however to be part of long-term trends that cannot be imputed to neoliberal reforms alone. By and large, the latter have left intact the formal institutions of liberal democracy inherited from the post-war settlement. Moreover, the political forces behind the current neoliberal consensus persist in having periodic elections, the rule of law and the formal division of power as the pillars of any process of democratisation, and emphasise their role in attempts to impose criteria of good governance worldwide (Williams and Young 1994). In my opinion, the most plausible criticism that can be levelled against the political forces supporting the current neoliberal consensus is that they not only failed to supply countervailing solutions to this long-term trend as rhetorically promised, but have actively contributed towards accelerating electoral impotence. For instance, it has been noted that the imposition of Compulsory Competitive Tendering rules in British local government has had the net effect of tying newly-elected local administrators to the satisfaction of private contractual agreements subscribed to by their predecessors, thereby creating a trade-off between democratic responsiveness and market liability (Parker 1991). Similar side-effects can be noted in relation to almost all political reforms aimed at making people 'vote with their feet', thus casting doubts on the market as an effective controlling mechanism for democratic politics (Goodin 2003; Pettit 2008). This sets serious limits to the notion of indirect accountability used by Regulatory State theorists to justify transnational authorities independent of the electoral process (as seen in Chapter Eight); for, there is a troublesome problem of democratic legitimacy at the core of national representative institutions that needs to be tackled first. And this is a problem that transnational authorities are actively aggravating with their attempts to impose external criteria of good governance upon those very metropolitan regimes that used to be taken as a benchmark for good governance, as the austerity policies imposed since the 2008 have amply proved (Mair 2013; Schäfer and Streeck 2013; Streeck 2014).

More direct and deeper are the implications of neoliberal reforms for the conventions of ministerial accountability (L2A). In dealing with this problem, analysts are first asked to clarify what mechanisms define political accountability in parliamentary systems. Briefly, the minimum common denominator between parliamentary democracies seems to be the supremacy of the legislative over the executive; a supremacy enforced through the formal attribution of a confidence vote. As Strøm (2000) accurately points out, very few constitutions give parliament the power to elect the executive. Some leave that question undetermined, whereas many others confer that prerogative to diverse constitutional bodies (Gallagher et al. 2006, Table 2.2, p. 46 for a survey). However, all of them recognise the power of parliaments to vote down an executive that the majority of their members feel they can no longer trust (a principle that the system of nested authorities characterising post-war liberal democracies has extended across the various levels of sub-national government). Sadly, we know that votes of confidence are plagued by the same ills as general elections: a systematic inability to keep national executives responsive and accountable to their own parliaments. For instance, in Britain the deterrent force of a vote of confidence is greatly diminished by both the control the Prime Minister has on backbenchers through the whip system and its exercise of the royal prerogative to dissolve Parliament itself. Another emblematic example is Italy. Since the 1980s, here the vote of confidence has routinely been employed by the government itself as a means to pass legislation likely to be opposed by factions of the governing coalition. By requiring an open ballot, the vote of confidence fulfils in fact several objectives. First, it forces individual MPs and parliamentary factions who oppose a specific policy to stand up and be identified. Second, it shifts onto them full responsibility for any defeat that could eventually lead to the dissolution of Parliament. Last but not least, a vote of confidence puts to an end parliamentary debate, and is therefore used to deprive the opposition of an opportunity to filibuster, thus achieving a Thatcherite form of *decisionismo*.[5]

Parliament's inability to enforce collective responsibility on the executive through a vote of confidence is symptomatic of the systemic shift in the balance of power between the two branches of government occurring in all parliamentary democracies. As seen earlier (Chapter Eight), in its attempt to assure governability by strengthening the role of national executives, the latter have slowly acquired features typical of presidential systems. However, this shift is occurring without any formal revision of constitutional conventions regulating accountability even when (as in Britain) this can be done by a simple act of Parliament and does not entail (as in Italy) complex constitutional reforms requiring qualified majorities. The upshot is a ministerial game where prime ministers act like presidents without any obligation to submit themselves to the electorate directly, thus lacking an explicit democratic mandate.[6] The accountability gap emerging at L2A has been compounded by two further changes amply discussed in relation to Westminster systems (Stone 1995), but affecting all other parliamentary systems as well. The first concerns the transformations shaping the core of central government itself, whereas the second has to do with the introduction of NPM in the civil service. National executives have evolved from collegial bodies, where the prime minister was a *primus inter pares* (first among peers), to cabinet structures, where the prime minister was the dominant figure, to premierships, where the prime minister is now the ultimate arbiter and decision maker. The process is neatly captured by the description of the working of Tony Blair's premiership, attributed to one of his former ministers. 'For Mo Mowlam, former Labour Cabinet minister, the "Cabinet is dead". No. 10 is now much like a law firm with Mr Blair as senior partner working with a small number of colleagues to filter ideas down through the business' (Gray and Jenkins 2003: 171). Similar remarks have been made in relation to George W. Bush's war presidency (Coglianese 2012). However, unlike the latter, the British premiership remains an unelected office. Hence the conclusion that, in the British system, the only way to oust an unpopular prime minister, government or policy is by extra-constitutional means: a party leadership contest – which will obviously end up with a new unelected Prime Minister, as the cases of John Major and Gordon Brown show. The extremely worrying developments of this process since the 2008 financial crisis in other European countries, particularly in Italy, are chronicled at length by Anderson (2014).

Individual ministerial responsibility has also undergone complex and troublesome changes. In Westminster systems of government, individual ministerial responsibility was traditionally a means through which Parliament carried out its supervising functions on civil servants as well. This was part of what I called vertical accountability. Given a hierarchical organisational structure, the acquisition of information on matters related to policy making and policy implementation was channelled to Parliament through the ministers in charge of departments. Civil servants who testified in front of parliamentary sub-committees spoke on behalf of their minister and had to comply with strict guidelines (restated in the Armstrong Memorandum, among other soft-law codes of discipline produced in the post-war period) aimed at protecting him or her from any embarrassment. A constitutional doctrine derived mainly from Dicey (1885) affirmed that the anonymity and facelessness of individual public officers was a means to preserve the political neutrality of the civil service. Responsibility for policy failures and administrative mismanagement thus rested with an individual minister and was punished by calling for his or her resignation. This reading of ministerial accountability was highly contentious even before the advent of neoliberal reforms (Turpin 1994). It was evident to anyone that the expansion in government activities which occurred in the twentieth century, and especially since the advent of the welfare state in 1945, made the very idea of ministerial responsibility for all acts carried out by civil servants untenable. Moreover, the alleged neutrality of the civil service rested on a heroic conception of public officers' ethos whose existence was questioned even by its top echelons since the 1968 Fulton Report doubted their professionalism. In post-war Britain, the relations between ministers and civil servants always had the strategic nature described in Chapter Two: ministers tended to shift the blame for policy failure onto civil servants, while the latter tried to influence policy making (imposing what was euphemistically called the 'departmental point of view') without assuming any direct responsibility (Dowding 1995: ch. 8). Hence, the periodic controversies when ministers were asked to resign for failures for which they were not responsible, or civil servants were punished for upholding the public interest against the machinations of their ministers.

As already remarked, rather than solving these underlying structural weaknesses, neoliberal reforms set in motion political and institutional changes that have aggravated them (Barberis 1998). First, administrative decentralisation policies have fragmented ministerial departments into myriads of autonomous agencies. These policies were based on a clear-cut distinction between policy and administration, and purchaser and supplier, underpinning the NPM philosophy which has been repeatedly shown to be deeply problematic, to say the least. In Britain, they failed to clarify to whom officers can be held accountable for maladministration, since ministers were no longer politically responsible for administrative matters and civil servants could not be held directly accountable to Parliament. Second, the introduction of NPM into the civil services of other OECD countries keen on copying the British template has transformed recruitment, tenure and managerial practices making departments and the constellations of administrative agencies gravitating around them more akin to privately-run companies. In so doing, NPM has attempted to boost the effectiveness and efficiency of administrative activities to the detriment of traditional values concerned with the neutrality, fairness and probity of the administrative process. The accountability gap is thus aggravated by the undermining of the ethos of public office in favour of market values, a move that has notoriously failed to unravel the problem of conflicting loyalties at the core of relations between ministers and civil servants (Polidano 1999). Obviously, with the adoption of the NPM philosophy by various other OECD countries committed to solve their governability problems along market lines, these problems are no longer confined to the British system where they first originated. They also characterise the ministerial game taking place not only in all Westminster systems but also in many other parliamentary democracies which have adopted similar managerial solutions. The response of national governments to the accountability concerns raised in the meantime has been almost uniformly the same: the creation of an increasingly large number of regulatory agencies to which they have attributed greater supervisory powers – the very institutional facts which are taken to explain and justify the rise of the Regulatory State. As I have insisted so far, and shall spell out below, the soundness of these solutions is, however, debatable, for they require further delegation of power to bodies whose nature and democratic credentials are themselves highly controversial (Scott 2000). In practice, this response has proved devastating, as democratic legitimacy goes. The features of the Regulatory State realised to date are in fact the object of growing discontent and the target of a number of populist movements which are polarising political confrontation in real existing liberal democracies from the bottom up.

9.5. Managerialism, governance and new forms of accountability

What currently goes under the name of managerial accountability actually comprises diverse forms of accountability conceptually distinct from the political and vertical types discussed above. In addition, the meaning attributed to these distinct forms tends to change according to the epistemic and normative tenets subscribed to by the analyst employing them. As anticipated (*see* Chapter Four, §4.4.2), Regulatory State theorists support two new forms of organisational control and supervision both derived from the principal-agent theory. The first, labelled 'performance accountability' (Bevir 2010: 33ff), is characterised by the definition of substantive standards of evaluations useful to indicate whether policy objectives were achieved effectively and efficiently. The features that characterise this form of accountability are the following. First, as mentioned several times, it shifts the emphasis from procedural standards of evaluations to substantive criteria of '*buon governo*'. Its goal is not that of assessing whether decisions were taken by legitimate agents or checking that they acted within their remit, but whether the indicated policy objectives were achieved effectively and efficiently. Second, it plays down individual loyalties towards superior authorities in favour of an enterprise culture and market-based values. Individual problem-solving abilities employed to bypass lines of authority and procedures which could obstruct or delay the accomplishment of given policy goals are thus viewed positively and rewarded accordingly by using performance-related pay schemes and production bonuses. Like public corporations characterised by the separation between ownership and supervision, the main goal of managers is consequently not to cultivate the values embodied in the public sphere, but to maximise shareholder value; something that even in this case tends to coincide with the (political) benefits enjoyed by the top managerial board of directors which happens to control the company at the time, i.e. the government of the day. Whether this also overlaps with the values of minority shareholders (those, that is, who are not included in the board of directors or who do not even have vote rights) is however a moot point that ultimately depends on the validity of a theoretical (political) market efficiency hypothesis. Even if it does, and this is a rather big if, we know from experience that it is very unlikely that it will satisfy the wishes of their patrons and other stakeholders.[7]

Neoliberal attempts to engender the validity of the (political) market efficiency hypothesis by giving people the real ability to 'vote with their feet' also insist on fostering 'horizontal' forms of accountability. To quote O'Donnell (1998: 117), 'This kind of accountability depends on the existence of state agencies that are legally empowered – and factually willing and able – to take actions ranging from routine oversight to criminal sanctions or impeachment in relation to possibly unlawful actions or omissions by other agents or agencies of the state.' Such a network is supplied by the myriad of quangos and regulatory agencies making up the Regulatory State: those charged with the supervision of privatised utilities and those operating within proxy markets (Scott 2002; Vincent-Jones 1999). To them, however, must be added two sets of agents not mentioned by O'Donnell: sovra- and transnational authorities (in particular the Bretton Woods holy trinity), and a variegated array of NGOs and non-profit organisations – ranging from the credit rating agencies, which failed to foresee the subprime crisis, to the various human rights watchdogs operating worldwide – who have acquired a growing public role in the definition of standards and benchmarks and the monitoring of their application (Held 2004; Scholte 2005). The qualifier 'horizontal' is justified on two grounds. First, accountability is enforced by regulatory agencies and authorities that are not hierarchically linked to the institutions under scrutiny. Indeed, this is a form of accountability that mimics the system of courts and tribunals employed in legal accountability. Unlike the latter, this constellation of regulatory entities operates in semi-juridical ways using quasi-legal means. As Ebrahim (2003: 196) explains: 'this view of accountability differs considerably from the legal perspective in that it relies not only on external regulation but also on the push and pull of constituent interests'. And this brings us to the second reason for calling it 'horizontal': the system of rules upheld by, and regulating, the agents involved. They are often not statute laws, but more flexible tools: orders in council, framework agreements, memoranda of understanding, guidelines, codes of ethics, charters of rights, criteria of good governance, professional standards, etc. In short, they are mostly soft-law rules unenforceable by traditional courts. Hence, the need to 'use benchmarks, indicators and peer review to ensure accountability' (Trubek and Trubek 2006: 541).

Together with the growing relevance of judicial review at the national level and the International Court of Justice at the international one, managerial forms of accountability are responsible for undermining the relevance of both political and vertical conceptions. As a result, the simple and linear (often simplistic and mythical) system of accountability enshrined in the constitutions of actually existing liberal democracies has given way to more fragmented and variegated practices. They involve multiple supervising agencies, plural lines of accountability and mixed standards of evaluation. In the process, the chain of delegation has been stretched by adding a new link, L4A, where: (a) clusters of autonomous agencies and networks with very remote formal links (if any) to the democratic process exercise power of control and sanction on (b) other clusters of agencies and authorities which have been granted normative and operational autonomy. For Goodin (2003), this amounts to a transformation of the delegation chain into something resembling a daisy chain. As such, it can easily break leading either to: (i) the unchecked exercise of power, or (ii) abuses of power, or (iii) collusive agreements between controllers and the controlled, or (iv) all of the above.

At the same time, these innovations have reinforced the shift in the balance of power towards national executives, who remain the ultimate arbiters when conflicts arise over interpretation and application. As noted earlier (Chapter Seven), transnational governance not only strengthens the role of national executives *vis-à-vis* parliaments, but also creates a regulatory environment that exalts their controlling functions while shielding them from parliamentary supervision. Hence the talk about the inception of a post-democratic era, to which the changes advocated by Regulatory State theorists are actively contributing. Since the two forms of managerial accountability advocated, performance-based and horizontal, are complementary and need to work simultaneously, and since their effective work depends on a host of background institutions which can only be realised piecemeal and are subjected to the vagaries of the equilibrium solutions reached in the set of interlocking games listed above, the attempt to use them as replacement for traditional systems of political and vertical accountability is doomed to generate accountability gaps. Moreover, since the logical conditions necessary for having the pure competitive (political) market, as described by general equilibrium theory, can never be fully realised in practice, accountability gaps will not be limited to a transition phase, but are likely to persist overtime.

What needs to be appreciated, however, is the way in which these uncertainties can be exploited at a more political level by the theorists and practitioners supporting the neoliberal consensus. The practical political difficulties afflicting the engendering of the Regulatory State can be used for making the theory immune from any empirical refutation and for supporting new and more extensive policies of negative integration. Similarly, the failures generated by an imperfect (political) market setting can be used to justify a permanent transition phase that leaves the ruling meta-PPP with ample discretionary powers and loose political responsibilities. A highly defective and exploitative neoliberal order could in this way manage to persist and reproduce itself in spite of the endless stream of case studies and research produced by the social sciences pointing out the inconsistencies, contradictions and unintended consequences yielded by it.

9.5.1. The mirage of civil society empowerment

Rejecting the analyses based on the principal-agency theory, theorists of the Networked Polity arrive at the conclusion that what in reality needs to be overcome is the traditional distinction between 'enactment' and 'enforcement' (Sabel and Simon 2006). This leads them to support only the second of the two new forms of managerial accountability sought by their counterpart, horizontal accountability, wishing to replace the first with what Scott (2000) calls 'downward accountability', to stress the inverted directional flow through which legitimacy is acquired and responsibility discharged. As anticipated (*see* Chapter Four, §4.4.2), the differences between 'downward' and 'performance-based' forms of accountability are subtle but considerable, for they reflect the diverse relevance attributed to competitive dynamics and dialogical cooperation by their respective advocates. According to the theorists of the Networked Polity, if those in charge of delivery need to be made accountable to all stakeholders whose interests are going to be affected, then engendering accountability means establishing channels of voice open to the latter, in particular those at the bottom for whom public goods and services are crucial, rather than to political sponsors only. Downward accountability thus reverses the institutional focus from the authorities above to the people below.

Limited forms of downward accountability were tried by various neoliberal governments during the 1990s. The main example comes again from the UK: the Citizen's Charter programme, that eventually served as the pioneer for all subsequent customers' rights charters issued by public utilities worldwide. It is worth noting that the reforms underpinning this type of downward accountability represent the only attempt to establish mechanisms of voice, rather than exit, that could empower people in their dealings with the monopolistic suppliers operating across the public and private sectors. So, to me they have a wider theoretical importance than the implemented empirical examples can convey. However, even a cursory review of the British Citizen's Charter programme is enough to highlight its structural shortcomings, especially when several background institutions vital for its effectiveness are lacking because they run against the foot-voting model of democracy underpinning the ideal Regulatory State (*see* Chapter Eight). The Networking Polity is supposed to bring about those background institutions by adopting the deliberative type of stakeholder democracy discussed previously (*see* Chapter Eight). Although I am very keen to explore the normative possibilities of this model, I shall use the following discussion to restate my claim that this is an ideal to engender rather than a tendency implicit in the current changes affecting accountability.

Launched by John Major in July 1991, the Citizen's Charter programme was eventually discontinued by the subsequent New Labour government before the end of its first ten-year term (Barron and Scott 1992; Drewry 2005; Hollingshead 2005; Taylor 1999). Its concrete realisations during the time it remained active were also very modest, due to a narrow consumerist understanding of its stated purposes. Rather than defining a framework of rights the citizen could employ against the newly privatised national utilities, the programme was composed of two parts: (i) a variegated list of standards of service private companies and franchisers were supposed to meet and (ii) a set of procedures establishing the systems of complaint and redress available to customers when those standards of service were not met. As Bellamy and Greenaway (1995) correctly note, the word citizens is a misnomer for the customer of those utilities and services. It is the actual consumer facing a host of private companies operating in very restricted and segmented markets who has a 'right' to some degree of quality for the services supplied; and it is only the actual consumer who can have access to the procedures of complaint and redress established. The citizen as such has in fact no voice in either the definition of the standards of service, or in the institutions evaluating individual complaints and establishing the means of redress. The only real voice left to the citizen is through its parliamentary representatives, to whom he or she can write to ask some form of political intervention in case of maladministration – a channel of voice that in the meantime has been undermined by the changes in the system of accountability at P1A and P2A mentioned above.

How were those standards of service arrived at? Those concerning the privatised utilities were often set by the same companies running the businesses; that is, through self-regulation. By contrast, those concerning the not yet privatised parts of the public sector operating at the time within proxy markets were either centrally imposed or established by centrally appointed regulatory authorities; that is, a matter left, in both cases, to Her Majesty Government's pleasure. Similar logic underpinned the complaint and redressment mechanisms: privatised utilities and services were left to devise them themselves, subject to the external lightweight regulation of anti-trust authorities, whereas those of public bureaucracies where, once again, centrally imposed and tightly regulated. That New Labour discontinued this only attempt to foster voice, rather than exit, in its attempt to implement the *Joining-Up Government* programme so much celebrated by governance theorists (*see* Chapter Four, §4.4.1), is the least paradoxical part of the story. During its lifetime, the Citizen's Charter programme served as a tool for deploying wide-ranging strategies of collibration (*see* Chapter Six, §6.3.3): the imposition of double standards and handicaps designed to undermine what was left of the public sector and reinforce its private counterpart, so as to prepare the ground either for further privatisation rounds or for bringing governmental discipline to peripheral branches of the public sector.[8]

Still, to my eyes, the logic behind downward accountability is normatively very interesting for two main reasons: first, it could be used as a feedback mechanism for disclosing hidden information that would otherwise be inaccessible to political principals and their supervisors (to use the principal-agent jargon);[9] second, customers and their associations could be included in the regulatory agencies used to establish standards of service and supervise their application, turning what are supposed to be anti- or counter-majoritarian institutions into fully fledged deliberative minipublics. And this lead us to the subtle diverse way in which the notion of horizontal accountability is understood by theorists of the Networked Polity. In a Networked Polity, its function is that of embedding regulatory authorities in civil society by transforming them into a multiform population of minipublics engaged in the constant revision and fleshing out of the constitutional framework of a pluralist society serially, dialogically and from the bottom up. This vision of stakeholder democracy is clearly expressed by Bevir (2006) when he juxtaposes system and radical governance perspectives. In Bevir's (2006: 432) words,

> whereas system governance often privileges a liberal agenda of constitutional and electoral reform, a pluralist vision encourages us to invent and establish yet other arenas in which citizens can deliberate and conduct themselves in relation to the state. Whereas system governance privileges the indirect representation of citizens and the incorporation of organised interests within the institutions of the state, a pluralist democracy seeks to assign aspects of governance to democratic associations other than the state. Similarly, whereas system governance promotes networks in which the state plays an active role, even seeking to regulate and control outcomes, a pluralist democracy hands aspects of governance over to associations other than the state. Whereas system governance adopts networks that aim to deliver services more effectively with little concern for the inner workings of the organisations with which the state cooperates, a pluralist democracy is committed to extending democratic principles to businesses, unions, and other groups within civil society.

A radical and pluralistic democratic governance pursues, in this vision, two interconnected tasks. In the first place, it is concerned with establishing (or constructing) dialogically the principles of action which have to orientate individual conduct at each level of government – a task to be accomplished by the creation of deliberative minipublics including all affected interests. Similar deliberative institutions are then supposed to enforce and supervise the actual application of those principles of action. The whole process has, finally, to be self-reflective in nature; that is to say, the two mechanisms have to somehow interact and revise principles and mechanisms of supervision and enforcement in turn, since principles are more flexible and open-ended than prescriptive rules, and enforcement and supervision cannot be a mere technical activity but requires the expression of judgments which are value-laden and therefore always political in nature.

This is indeed a normative vision of 'principled' governance to which I fully subscribe and have tried to articulate myself (Palumbo 2011: ch. 8). I shall briefly come back to this notion of principled governance in the Conclusion. I would like to close this one by stressing some reservations I have in relation to Bevir's and other radical accounts of democratic governance encountered so far, above all Warren's (2009) governance-driven democratisation. First of all, I maintain that this vision of principled governance has not been realised in practice through the decentralised model of governance suggested by Bevir and Rhodes (2006), and it is not at all implicit in the current forms of democratic experimentalism surveyed by various other authors (Fung and Wright 2003; Sabel and Zeitlin 2012). It is, and remains, a normative position that needs to be fully developed and justified before it has any chance to be engendered in practice; and so far I find that governance theory is too ambiguous, if not misleading, on this point. In addition, I also maintain that the bottom-up, governance-driven democratisation described by Warren will not be able to bring it about any time soon. If my reading of the post-democratic tendencies caused by new modes of governance has any plausibility at all, this normative aspiration risks remaining at the planning stage – another instance of utopian wishful thinking produced in reaction to modernisation.

Insofar as I am concerned, I see the present work as a mere launching pad for developing and articulating this vision of principled governance – a task that cannot be carried out here but will require a dedicated work where the steps which can bring us beyond governance are clearly spelt out. Part of this endeavour needs to understand the likely political alliances which can help bring this vision about; something that requires overcoming the reliance radical movements often put on mythological agents like the proletariat or the multitude or even the precariat, and the self-appointed vanguards able to divine their utterances and wishes. In turn, this means clarifying what sort of relation this vision of principled governance could entertain (or ought to entertain) with liberal democratic notions of representation. As argued earlier, governance theory is made up by various strands which want to replace traditional understandings of representation, and other strands which instead want to complement them; and it is neither clear what should eventually replace them, nor how new and old forms of representation could complement each other. The final step needs to consider the way in which the novel forms of accountability discussed in this chapter, downward and horizontal accountability, could help overcome the distinction between politics and administration that has been the hallmark of modern democracy in theory and practice alike.

9.6. Conclusions

In this chapter I have discussed the implications new modes of governance are having on traditional forms of accountability. First of all, I pointed out that they have added a fourth new problematic link to the chain of delegation established by real existing liberal democracies. This fourth link concerns the delegation of powers previously exercised by political and administrative actors to constellations of regulatory agencies independent from the electoral process. The managerial game yielded by the addition of this delegation link is characterised by competitive dynamics and sets of pay-offs which rewards self-seeking attitudes and strategic behaviour. To harness the latter and neutralise its likely side-effects, new managerial mechanisms of accountability have been devised and activated. I have tried to explain the nature and derivation of these managerial mechanisms of accountability. Theorists of the Regulatory State, deriving them from the principal-agent theory, advocate performance-based and horizontal systems of accountability aiming at reconciling individual self-interest with the public good. To this end, privatisation policies and proxy-markets have been employed to bring the discipline of the market within the public sector. By contrast, theorists of the Networked Polity suggest systems of downward and horizontal accountability which can engender a deliberative stakeholder democracy capable of making people, as prosumers, both self-regulators and self-administrators. Thus doing, a proliferation of notions of accountability has been generated. I maintain that, in principle, the multiplication of lines of accountability downward and sideways is not a negative development. On the contrary, I believe it could help bridge the accountability gaps left open by traditional delegation regimes. For instance, the involvement of consumers and consumer groups in the evaluation of public services could help offset the asymmetric information at the root of the agency costs faced either by parliament (in the ministerial game) or by the executive (in the bureau game). Similarly, third sector organisations when supplementing the provision of public goods by both markets and governments could advance a stronger conception of democracy than the minimalist one supported by the post-war settlement.

However, I have also argued that this democratic potential is mostly left unrealised and more often distorted to deflect responsibilities. Rather than complementing each other, managerial mechanisms are thought and used to replace traditional systems of accountability in ways which have magnified previous accountability gaps. By substituting political and vertical systems of accountability with performance-based and horizontal managerial solutions, the Regulatory State's attempt to resolve market failures by using centrally directed proxy-markets has eminently backfired. The 2008 financial crisis seems to be a perfect case in point. The crisis is largely imputed to a systemic failure of supervision resulting from the policies of financial liberalisation and soft-touch regulation pursued since the 1990s. I also argued that since such a replacement strategy has shifted responsibility for structural failures onto individual bureaucrats and societal agents with no actual decision-making power, it has effectively shielded the meta-PPPs ruling advanced liberal democracies from any democratic attempt to penalise them.

This explains, from my standpoint, why central governments seem more interested in pursuing policies aimed at bailing out the institutions responsible for the 2008 crisis and in imposing perverse conditions of austerity, rather than acknowledging such regulation failure and addressing it properly. Accordingly, warnings about the dangers implicit in substituting managerial mechanisms of accountability for traditional forms of supervision and enforcement are constantly being dismissed by using, once again, the Thatcherite rallying call of TINA. The intervention of transnational and global authorities has further exposed these suspicions and is having negative knock-on effects on the wobbly legitimacy of national representative bodies. This is epitomised by the growing anxieties about the democratic deficit of the EU and the populist backlash swiping the old continent.

End Notes

1. As Dunn (1993: 242) writes: 'Athenian military leaders were elected, since Athens was often at war, and its citizens understandably preferred to follow into battle individual generals in whom they had some confidence. But they fully recognized that election was an aristocratic method, which favoured the well-born, the prominent, and the wealthy, and they went to startling lengths to ensure that the great bulk of Athenian public roles were allocated instead by the incontestably democratic procedure of the casting of lots – by random selection from all eligible citizens rather than by the natural workings of social influence.'

2. The abysmal results of the 2014 European elections are the latest example of this perverse dynamics at work. By increasing the role of anti-European parties within the European Parliament, the electoral results are likely to increase the inability of the latter to challenge the power of the Council of Ministers in the appointment of the European Commission and subsequently the new rounds of negative market integration policies which will likely follow. Thus, electoral moments tend to start new cycles which will amplify and spread the democratic deficit to member states as well. Eventually, this increases the risk of a systemic legitimation crisis at a continental level – crisis that democratic experimentalism cannot neutralise as evinced by the fact that the expression 'consultation fatigue' is gaining currency in literature.

3. On this point, see Aghion and Tirole (1997), Laffont and Martimort (2002) and Tirole (1986, 1994).

4. From this perspective, the development of the so-called 'quango state' in Britain (Flinders and Skelcher 2012) is a successful attempt to import the US spoils system in a political context lacking the constitutional safeguards established by a formal constitution with a clear separation of powers and mechanisms of checks and balances. As already mentioned, an opposed and more optimistic reading of these events is proposed by Vibert (2007), *see* Chapter Seven, note 13.

5. The shift was in fact engineered by the late former Italian Prime Minister Bettino Craxi, an admirer of the then British Premier.

6. A democratic deficit brought to the fore by the coalition government formed after the 2010 general election. Electoral results punishing, in a Schumpeterian manner, all three main parties subsequently caused the formation of a Liberal-Conservative coalition unforeseen before the elections. Moreover, since the start this coalition engaged in wide-ranging austerity policies and political reforms unannounced in either party manifesto, and sometimes even against the political commitments stated therein. This record notwithstanding, the reforms introduced have been justified by using the same arguments used a few years earlier by New Labour: that is, a narrative that juxtaposes the coalition government's 'open, transparent and decentralized approach with

the top-down configuration of institutional power attributed to New Labour' (Painter 2013). As for the consensus politics established by the post-war settlement (Kavanagh and Morris 1989), within the current neoliberal consensus politics, the main differences between centre-right and centre-left political parties seems to be about the right way to manage it, rather than about its underlying principles. As a result, the insistence of social scientists and political analysts alike in distinguishing between shades of grey keeps missing the forest for the trees.

7. Current literature on inequalities and stalled social mobility is there to testify it, despite the inevitable debate it also tends to provoke. Piketty's (2014) is the latest and biggest tome on the matter that has come out so far. Within this literary genre, the precariat – a combination of disgruntled customers and impoverished stakeholders – is presented as the new historical actor who will carry on its shoulders the mantle of the old proletariat and redeem us from neoliberalism (Standing 2011).

8. NHS and public education have been the main victims of these strategies of collibration. In the NHS, central government has managed to impose five distinct levels of accountability for the services delivered, whereas in the private health sector customers are not even protected by the common law for mistakes and bad services (Pollock 2004). In the public education system, current reforms are on the brink of removing completely any power left to local government and making schools directly accountable to central government (Benn 2011).

9. This solution would be more effective than the introduction of third-party supervision, as suggested by Tirole (1986; Laffont & Tirole 1991). Here, the public nature of the information supplied by the voices of consumers would in principle block the formation of collusive agreements between coalitions of supervisors and agents.

Conclusion: Self-Service Politics or Self-Serving Policy?

In this conclusion my aim is to summarise the main issues raised in the previous chapters and then highlight what I take to be their normative implications. First, I endeavour to show that some of the difficulties encountered by liberal democracies worldwide are structurally related to governmental attempts to centralise political control by decentring managerial functions and shedding social responsibilities. Far from engendering a consumer-friendly Madisonian democracy, market-based solutions are sought, or so I argue, to bring under the control of central government a variety of local and peripheral branches of the apparatus of the state which welfarist policies had unwittingly emancipated by delegating to them policy-making and implementation powers. In presenting the overall outcomes of these attempts, I contend that, by making central governments less responsive to citizenry and less accountable to parliament, they are undermining the representative model of democracy established by the post-war settlement and ushering in a troublesome post-democratic age. Second, I discuss (some of) the normative shortcomings affecting the rationalisation of political and institutional change supplied by governance theory so far, and in particular the functional explanations used to account for the passage from 'government' to 'governance'. To the extent that the new modes of governance analysed by the theorists of the Regulatory State supply a more convincing heuristic of the changes undertaken during *les trente furieuses*, their normative justifications of this ideal typical entity are daily shown to be wanting. The Regulatory State has, in effect, failed to reinforce the output-oriented legitimacy of liberal democracies and is affected by accountability gaps and democratic deficits posing an increasing risk of system-wide legitimation crisis – on a par with the one experienced by the welfare state in the 1970s. By contrast, the accounts of change proposed by the theorists of the Networked Polity need to be viewed as an expression of normative aspirations. As such, a proper justificatory framework of the features they wish to engender ought to be developed. To this end, supporters of the Networked Polity have still to indicate how is it possible to turn what is clearly a self-serving neoliberal policy template into an instrument for realising a deliberative policy environment and a system of self-service policy.

C.1. The privatisation of political responsibilities and the hollowing out of liberal democracy

Political and institutional change is always the outcome of many factors which, by interacting among themselves, make any causal explanation unwarranted. Moreover, explanations are never neutral: they are arrived at from a particular perspective that makes them value-laden and interested in explaining change as much as influencing its pace and direction. This is especially evident to me when we focus on the various waves of reform carried out since 1979 by the governments working within neoliberal consensus politics. The point is well stated by Hibou (2004: 40–41) in a passage that is worth reporting here at length:

> Privatisation of the state arises not so much from a state strategy for survival or consolidation as from numerous actors or numerous logics of action. There are economic logics: the pursuit of profitability and efficiency in the productive sector and, still more, the search for new economic resources, for new opportunities for enrichment in a context of shrinking direct state revenues and, above all, of dwindling of rents and prebends available for distribution and indirect control over economic activity. Then there are political logics: management of opposed forces that are nonetheless indispensable to the state in a context of fragmentation of society and centres of power, renewal and reconversion of bureaucratic power as economic power dependent on the state, or a strategy of shifting responsibility in the face of social and political protests. And there are social logics: new relationships between states and citizens in a context of debureaucratisation. There are individual and collective logics of social mobility: upward mobility for a class associated with the state or a group of actors, but also possibilities of survival for marginalised groups. There are other logics as well: logics of creation of a new economic space for negotiation of social relations, even for bargaining over them; logics of insertion into the world economy with respect (or an appearance of respect) for conditionalities imposed by aid donors; logics of diversified management of dependence, notably to make the dependence less restrictive; administrative, financial and missionary logics of aid donors and, correspondingly, logics of resistance to those donors; logics of enrichment, logics of patronage, logics of war and conflict … and so on.

Well aware of this complexity, in opposing the narratives of change proposed by governance theorists, I have tried to develop a state-centric political perspective that is often actively rejected. Against the idea that the changes experienced during *les trente furieuses* are due to a reactive adaptation to impersonal social forces which have undermined the authority of the nation-state and fragmented state institutions, I have supplied an account that sees them as the outcome of state activism – one led by governmental attempts to either regain or affirm state control on institutional and social realms which had escaped it. In doing this, I have pointed out that neoliberal policies can be pursued for reasons other than those stated to justify them, and that the political actors supporting them could adopt them not for ideological conviction but as a mere expedient. I have argued that deregulation, privatisation and marketisation of state activities have not followed a principled neoliberal logic of conviction; rather they have been carried out by a systematic application of double standards. My next step has then been to understand whether underpinning this egregious application of double standards it was possible to detect something amounting to a well-defined political strategy, or was it instead due to the vagaries of electoral politics and political practice. In detecting a pattern of action showing a remarkable continuity and a curious process of (i) horizontal diffusion (across interconnected policy areas), (ii) vertical diffusion (across different levels of government) and (iii) international diffusion (across regions), my goal has been to propose what I called a genealogical account of the neoliberal policy template, confronting it with alternative accounts to test its plausibility. My conclusion is that the state is still alive and kicking and that it continues to represent a formidable political actor able to intervene at both national and international levels to affirm its internal and external sovereignty. In this sense, the globalisation thesis has been far too overstated, to the point that it has supported a flourishing of socio-centric perspectives which, in distinct ways, also deny autonomy to the political as such. The narratives of political and institutional change to be found in governance studies were chosen as the principal field of inquiry on which to concentrate in order to prove this claim.

In developing my counternarrative, I have taken issues with two analytical aspects of the accounts of change proposed in governance theory: their explanatory and their justificatory frameworks. Concerning the first aspect, I have pointed out the shortcomings of attempts to explain the alleged passage from 'government' to 'governance' by using functional explanations stressing the superiority of the latter over the former, and especially the theories combining functional claims and unintended consequences modes of explanation. Concerning the second aspect, I have been keen on stressing the 'performative' nature of the ideal types used and the shortcomings of the justificatory frameworks employed to engender them. To this end, a Humean genealogical reconstruction of the alleged passage from 'government' to 'governance' has been developed in parallel with a more Nietzschean assessment of recent political and institutional change. From this Nietzschean perspective, state activism is not considered a positive fact at all, nor are new modes of governance seen as pursuing the emancipatory goals often attributed to them. Rather, I pointed out that, by undermining features of the system of government built during *les trente glorieuses*, new modes of governance are in effect undermining the liberal democratic values upon which state institutions rested.

More than that in fact: I take the undermining of post-war liberal democratic values and institutions as the main goal of the reforms undertaken, not their unintended by-product.[1] Market-based policies are employed by central governments as a means to shed responsibilities acquired in the past and escape the mechanisms of accountability established by the post-war constitutional settlement. This is a point repeatedly noted in literature without, however, giving it the theoretical weight it deserves, and it is its relevance I want to establish with my counternarrative; for this has crucial normative implications to which I shall return later on. For instance, in what is often taken to be a seminal work in governance theory, Osborne and Gaebler (1992: 47) write: 'when governments contract with private businesses, both conservatives and liberals often talk as if they are shifting a fundamental public responsibility to the private sector. This is nonsense: they are shifting the delivery of services, not the responsibility for services.' The relevance of this distinction between 'shifting delivery' and 'shifting responsibility' and the reason why political actors of different hue try to play it down is unfortunately underrated by the authors themselves, who use that passage to affirm the need for 'more government, not less' (*ibid.*).

To me this passage indicates that politicians, political analysts and neoliberal ideologues could attribute different meanings to some policies, and that the tendency to conflate explanatory and justificatory levels of analysis could have perversed epistemic and normative consequences. Far from addressing government failures affecting the interventionist welfare state, new modes of governance could well be part of governmental attempts to shift the blame onto others (Hood 2010), thus setting in motion an informal redesign of the separation of powers and of the mechanisms of checks and balances established by liberal democratic constitutions that is, *pace* Vibert (2007), hollowing out representative democracy as we know it. Testing this hypothesis entails, in my opinion, seeing whether it could lead to better explanations of other sets of phenomena, like those pertaining to the increasing accountability gap noted in various national contexts and the general democratic deficit imputed to governance regime. Were this the case, appealing for more governance or for a more active role of the state in steering policy networks (metagovernance) could then turn out to be self-defeating. This is indeed the point I want to make in this work. To do it, I started with a reconstruction of the parabola of government; that is, the institutional set up yield by the post-war settlement and the logic of action that eventually led to the crisis of the welfare state in the mid-1970s.

I derive two main insights from this reconstruction of *les trente glorieuses*. First, that at the heart of the welfare state existed a deep cultural contradiction that slowly eroded the social and political support upon which that model of government rested. As an ideal type, the welfare state subscribed to progressive democratic values exalting notions of individual and social autonomy which committed public institutions to grant growing sets of social and economic rights (conception whose main theoretical figureheads were Kelsen and Marshall). At a more practical level, however, it adopted a minimalist conception of democracy and favoured technocratic institutional solutions which were in strident contrast with the values subscribed, practices endorsed and justified by distinguished figures like Schumpeter and Dahl, the differences between these two authors notwithstanding (*see* Chapter One). Growing dissatisfaction with the failure of welfare institutions to meet their newly acquired social and economic responsibilities ended up promoting pressures for an endogenous resolution of that contradiction along neocorporate lines. However, neocorporate forms of democratisation revealed to be both too cautious and too late to be able to withstand the shocks which rocked liberal democracies in the 1970s. Hence, towards the end of that decade the social and political coalition supporting the welfare state imploded, opening a void that was subsequently exploited by conservative forces.

Upon this rational reconstruction of what were, admittedly, messy social and political events, I base my second claim: that neoliberal consensus politics needs to be viewed as an attempt to rule the void left behind by the implosion of the post-war settlement. From this insight I then derive several hypotheses concerning the nature of current neoliberal consensus politics and the role new modes of governance play in it:

- that neoliberal consensus politics rests on a much more restricted basis than its welfarist counterpart and is affected by another cultural contradiction exposing it to periodic instabilities and legitimation crises
- that the neoliberal ideological apparatus has only a justificatory value that rests mainly on the academic prestige acquired by the new political economy in the 1970s and the opportunity its policy prescriptions are giving to powerful political actors to rewrite the rules of the liberal democratic game informally
- that in allowing the dominant neoliberal coalition of forces to do it, new modes of governance have actively contributed to further undermine both democratic values and representative institutions, ushering in a troublesome post-democratic age – hence the contested legitimacy of the Regulatory State noted above
- that the Networked Polity is in reality a normative ideal to be fought for in politically conscious ways, and that any illusion that it is implicit in the direction taken by the actual dynamic of change or as a by-product of networking activities needs to be abandoned, if we want to make sure that it will not suffer the fate of past neocorporate attempts

In the previous chapters I have defended at length the plausibility of the hypotheses used in developing my counternarrative of change. In the rest of this conclusion I will indicate in what direction a normative approach to policy analysis wishing to engender such an ideal needs to move.

C.2. The structural limitations of neoliberal governmentality

The counternarrative proposed in this work establishes two main starting points for those wishing to engage in further normative inquiries. The first has to do with the limitations of neoliberal governmentality, whereas the second concerns the limitations of the welfarist type of government that preceded it. Whilst the limitations of neoliberal governamentality tell us that it needs to be overcome because it is neither desirable nor feasible, the ones which affected its welfarist counterpart make it clear why a return to past policy solutions is also not desirable, even if this were still possible – and it is not. In Chapter Two, I claimed that the neoliberal consensus politics is highly exploitative and follows a perverse logic, fuelling wave after wave of Polanyian countermovements. There I also maintained that, in practice, the diffusion of market-based policies across OECD countries (and beyond) has undermined the restricted channels of 'voice' established by the post-war settlement, without actually establishing the mechanisms of 'exit' promised by neoliberal ideologues. Since those policies are, in my account, driven by an attempt to centralise decision-making power while shedding social responsibilities, it is evident to me that there is no reason to expect the realisation of some form of foot-voting democracy any time soon, even if this could somehow turn out to be feasible. The idea of being able to 'vote with one's feet' (and move across jurisdictions in ways which can help the individual to maximise its utility function) has only a rhetoric and strategic function, and will always be used as such by those who have the power to play the game of the rules (*see* Chapter Five). Rhetorically, its goal is to boost individual compliance with the (periodically changing) rules of the market game. Strategically, it aims at splitting any opposing social and political coalition by using patronage to redistribute social resources.

As noted in Chapter Two, three decades of privatisation, deregulation and marketisation seem to have created a two-tier system: a very large segment at the bottom of the social pyramid, where people are forced to compete against each other to get a shrinking share of the mythical social cake, and a very narrow segment at the top where a selected few are allowed to enjoy their riches without the need to compete and are shielded from major systemic risks. I also tried to make clear the reasons why many people in the lower segment feel compelled to play by the market, even if this takes the form of a chicken game that makes it very unlikely for the great majority of them to reach the top: (i) the absence of alternative individual strategies in a world where working conditions are fast deteriorating across the board, and (ii) the impossibility to switch from an individual to a social perspective in post-democratic settings where channels of voice are being muted. Hence the seemly irrational efforts of countless people to move up the social ladder in the hope of reaching what an aerial view would depict as a tropical socialist archipelago.

Here, however, I would like to point out the side effects of this two-tier system – the structural elements which make the neoliberal governmentality periodically open to challenges unmasking its vulnerability, like the 2008 financial crisis. The literature concerned with the latter has focused on the systemic risks generated by unregulated markets within the financial model of capitalism which emerged from *les trente furieuses*. By and large, the various accounts of the crisis rest on two main assumptions: the first concerns the basic soundness of the market failures theory that legions of neoliberal political economists have tried to undermine; the second follows instead the idea that governance and globalisation have reduced the regulatory powers of nation states and made them the pawns of impersonal systemic forces. Although I have not discussed the validity of the theory of market failures *per se*, I expressed reservations on the fact that a great deal of the economic analyses of politics undertaken since the 1970s have hijacked this very theory to show the inevitability and perverse nature of government failure – claims which are both theoretically inconsistent and empirically unwarranted (*see* Chapter Two). Throughout the book, I have also discussed the notions of unintended positive consequences underpinning the justificatory frameworks of the Regulatory State on one side, and the Networked Polity on the other. However, the assumptions upon which my counternarrative is based are clearly at odds with the claims supporting the current inability of nation states to regulate markets properly. In a bold Polanyian fashion, I maintain that the neoliberal consensus politics is the outcome of state planning, and that any dissent is due to the spontaneous activities of countermovements trying to oppose it in a decentralised manner. In turn, I attribute its weaknesses to a cultural contradiction at the heart of neoliberal governmentality, making any resulting social order highly susceptible to legitimation crises. Like the cultural contradiction noted about the post-war settlement, this depends, once again, on the strident contrast between the values subscribed to at a rhetorical level and the practices endorsed in reality. The values I am referring to are the meritocratic market values advocated by neoliberal ideologues, which the current consensus politics is satisfying only in a self-serving way to benefit a tiny global elite. The contradiction depends on the fact that the great majority of those who choose to follow this value-system will, in the end, find themselves unable to succeed for reasons for which they cannot be held personally responsible, inevitably fuelling feelings of disappointment and resentment. Let us see why.

Against the relevance governance theorists attribute to output-oriented modes of legitimacy, in Chapter Five I tried to show that in actual practice the Regulatory State employs both substantive and procedural criteria for assessing performance. The content of those criteria is, moreover, decided at governmental level in highly discretionary ways, and they are always enforced by using double standards. Private suppliers, especially the corporate agents running the now-privatised public utilities or operating in highly segmented markets, are often regulated by very broad legislative frameworks leaving them ample powers of self-regulation. In turn, those regulatory tools are supervised and enforced by independent authorities and audit institutions more than willing to apply those frameworks in a flexible and negotiated manner, if nothing else to minimise the legal costs due to litigation and judicial review. The public bodies operating within proxy-markets are, on the other hand, regulated by centrally established detailed regulation often applied in a very inflexible procedural manner. Since they lack independent sources of revenue from those established by the treasury, these public bodies have in fact only procedural means of judicial review available to them and therefore do not pose serious problems to their auditors and regulators.[2] The outcome is thus the coexistence of two opposed logics of action operating within the public sector: a utilitarian logic used by private corporate agents to decide whether, when and how to apply the rules they gave to themselves; and a deontological logic that attributes to public authorities and administrative agencies a duty of strict adherence to the law – even when this is made up of various contradictory instruments of soft law paying no attention to likely outcomes.

The same can be said about the internal modus operandi of public enterprises and administrative agencies at national and subnational levels. Within these industries only the top managerial layer seems able to enjoy the rewards made available by utilitarian market criteria, while the rest of the workforce is subjected to an intricate web of soft-law requirements giving them responsibility for structural elements beyond the reach of their limited personal powers (Brown *et al.* 2010). Application of the proxy market logic within universities is giving academic workers a taste of what other ambits of the public sector have experienced since the 1980s. As perceptively noted by Collini (2011: 19):

> the experience of being a senior academic now [...] may seem to more closely resemble that of being a middle-rank executive in a business organisation than it does that of being an independent scholar or freelance teacher, while the conditions of work of junior and temporary staff in some unfavoured institutions may [...] suggest comparisons with those of staff in a call centre.

Indeed, it is possible to argue that by adopting an organisational model and logic of action derived from the modern corporation, neoliberal reforms (and NPM in particular) have brought into the public domain its highly controversial system of governance as well. This system of governance supports a shareholder notion of democracy that formally attributes decision-making power to only a subset of the actors involved in the process of production while, in practice, depriving even this restricted subset of any actual voice in the management of public companies (Ireland 2005). The rest of the stakeholders who are crucial for the success of the productive process are thus left exposed to the vagaries of speculative activities carried out by the investors riding volatile stock markets. Individual and institutional investors are in turn left exposed to the strategic actions of the managerial boards controlling those companies, whose main goal is to influence their market value artificially. The pay-offs of managerial boards are finally dependent on market dynamics difficult to understand (let alone predict) but open to collusive manipulation. Hence, interaction between corporate stakeholders assumes the form of interlinked chicken-like games where cooperation depends on the institutional exploitation of those who have no real (1) power of exit, (2) possibility to diversify their investment portfolios, or (3) contractual clauses cushioning them from systemic risks (Palumbo 2009). In this highly competitive contest, weak stakeholders are structurally forced to play 'chicken' and made daily aware of it by the fact that: (i) rewards do not seem to be related to performance, (ii) individual performance depends anyway on structural conditions upon which they have no control and (iii) the rules of the game keep changing periodically in ways designed to defy their copying strategies.

All these facts have an underlying political rationale as they constitute governmental attempts to shift responsibilities onto middle-rank managers, street-level bureaucrats, private suppliers and prosumers to escape public accountability. As in the chicken games studied by game theorists, stable cooperation depends on mechanisms of coordination (systems of 'labelling' in economic jargon) which allow each player to (a) recognise the identity of its counterpart to avoid both destructive and inefficient mismatches, and (b) play different roles in turn with a theoretical probability of roughly 50 per cent.[3] Since these conditions are unlikely to be met as a by-product of individual rational choices, there is an inherent tendency for cooperation to periodically break down, forcing political institutions to make individual compliance compulsory. In these periods of crisis, questions related to the fairness of rules of the game and the legitimacy of those devising and imposing them come to the fore and open the possibility for a radical policy overhaul.

While this way of operating makes neoliberal governmentality quite unlike the total institutions described by Foucauldians, its power of resilience should not be underestimated either. To take a couple of examples which have occupied protest movements since 2008, the bonus culture pervading the private and public sectors alike and the tax-regime shopping strategies adopted by corporate and individual agents working across the public/private divide are phenomena far too entrenched to make any piecemeal reform effective. The same can be said about the escalation of managerial and political costs promoted by NPM in the public sector. If my counternarrative is at all plausible, these phenomena must be seen as parts of the interlocked mechanisms shielding national and global elites from systemic risks. In short, they are the very stepping stones leading upwards to the tropical socialist archipelago located beyond the reach of the competitive market struggle common people are expected to endure. Any piecemeal reform of these mechanisms of exit means upsetting the existing balance of power within the meta-PPPs sustaining the current neoliberal consensus politics in ways which can even help regenerate it. And this is indeed what events like the financial crisis of 2008 seem to produce: they pushed various components of the meta-PPPs engulfed by it to exploit these opportunities to renegotiate the terms of their partnership in the hope of maximising their positional power.

Caused by the burst of the real estate property bubble of the late 1990s (the so-called subprime crisis), the crisis led first to the sudden reactivation of allegedly powerless national political authorities called to save the world from financial meltdown. The upper hand gained by the public component of the dominant meta-PPPs pushed the private component to try to redress the balance by reframing the crisis discourse focusing attention on public budget deficits (the so-called sovereign debt crisis). Within these negotiating moves and countermoves, attempts at regulating bonus handouts to undeserving top managers were followed by scandals affecting the ruling classes concerning their systems of rewards (parliamentary expenses in Britain, budget boycotts in the USA, exorbitant costs of politics in Italy, etc.). Along such a renegotiation, sets of austerity policies and structural reforms are being carried out with the aim of shifting the final cost onto the taxpayer. In brief, the neoliberal consensus politics is underwritten by social and political coalitions engaged in a permanent renegotiation of the terms of their (collusive) partnership. If this attitude produces periodic fractures which could potentially undermine their legitimate claim to govern, the dynamic nature of the negotiating process also gives the various components of the partnership the opportunity to regenerate themselves. The 2008 financial crisis must, therefore, be viewed as a window of opportunity that will eventually shut down – until, that is, another crisis will give the next generation of activists a further opportunity to question the status quo.

C.3. The politics of fixing the ship at sea

Given that neoliberal governmentality is structurally unable to settle its inherent cultural contradiction once and for all, and that the latter is, of itself, incapable of bringing about the collapse of the current neoliberal consensus politics, the need arises for a concerted political action to establish acceptable principled forms of governance. Awareness of this need is far less trivial than it sounds and could even represent the major contribution of this study. To restrain ourselves to the field of governance studies, it would strike at the heart of many accounts of change presenting governance as a liberating process brought about in a decentred bottom-up fashion; that is, accounts which view politics essentially as a by-product of non-political activities. In addition, it would cast serious doubts on countless academic proposals invoking a more active role of the state through metagovernance. In this latter case, we confront indeed a paradox similar to the one often noted, with intellectual disdain, apropos the populist movements which have sprung up since the late 1990s. The populist paradox has been clearly stated by the American writer Thomas Frank (2004: 109), with the wicked irony that characterises his journalistic work:

> for decades Americans have experienced a populist uprising that only benefits the people it is supposed to be targeting. […] The angry workers, mighty in their numbers, are marching irresistibly against the arrogant. They are shaking their fists at the sons of privilege. […] and while the millionaires tremble in their mansions, they are bellowing out their terrifying demands. 'We are here' they scream, 'to cut your taxes'.

An even more ironical paradox affects the position of the legions of analysts, practitioners and opinion-makers inviting state actors, central governments and statesmen to assume a more active role and exercise leadership. Those calls seem impervious to the fact that these same agents have been highly active throughout the last thirty years exercising leadership in a resolute manner. They have employed the unyielding logic of TINA every so often to trample on dissent, electoral results and even on constitutional conventions and acquired rights retained by liberal democrats as their ultimate source of legitimacy.

Alas, since 2008 this paradoxical stance has also led to the mythologising of the welfare state and past Keynesian policies. The first intellectual enterprise has obfuscated the structural weaknesses which brought that model of government to collapse worldwide in the 1980s (Streeck 2014). The second attempt has turned Keynesian macroeconomics into a universal toolbox for fixing any crack that appears in the fabric of capitalist societies (Taylor 2010). The anti-normative attitude adopted by many analysts and practitioners thus ends up producing either a Panglossian embrace of new policy tools, or an even more Panglossian advocacy of past policy solutions. Given my personal dissatisfaction with the ethical perspectives which have come to dominate political philosophy since the 1970s (*see* Introduction), the development of a normative approach to policy analysis requires a radical change of perspective. If modern political philosophy and political science have had as their main goal the taming of democracy by imposing on it liberal values and institutions (Barber 1988), the task of the normative approach I endorse does exactly the opposite: it aims at democratising inherited liberal values and institutions.

In decreasing order of abstraction this means, first, the rejection of any normative approach that denies the value of politics as an autonomous domain and views ethical and metaethical analyses as a way to preempt political engagement and democratic deliberation. The definition of the constitutional framework of a well-ordered society is a collective practical endeavour requiring the participation of all affected interests. Thus, it is neither a philosophical exercise to be delegated to a professional class of academics endowed with the power of reason, or a revolutionary task for vanguards able to see beyond layers of false consciousness enveloping the rest of us, or even the historical fate of more or less restricted sectors of society who have nothing to lose but their chains (be it the proletariat or the precariat). It is also an ongoing activity that needs the full involvement of new generations called to periodically assess the mistakes made by their predecessors while trying to improve on them. Correcting defective constitutional arrangements is, thus, like the fixing-a-ship-at-sea metaphor evoked by Oakeshott (1962) – without necessarily accepting the conservative implications the British philosopher derives from it. As Barber (1984) shows, democracy is the best practical means devised by humans so far to accomplish this task. Liberal objections against democracy are often found to be either exaggerations or overstatements; they seem to depend on a blend of elitist distaste towards the uncouth, intellectual prejudice about the conventional and the tendency to use stark, binary analytical categories (Palumbo 2012). This is why democratically reached agreements and settlements are considered as mere *modus vivendi* having no moral authority and motivational force; established conventions are systematically treated as resting on utterly arbitrary policy choices; complex democratic practices are dissected into discrete and unconnected games yielding inevitably suboptimal equilibria. Liberal promises are likewise overstated and never fulfilled (Palumbo 2003). Values and rights thought to be fundamental are readily sacrificed on second thoughts for being either unfeasible or hubristic; externally imposed formal and substantive constraints receive a principled defence in spite of the privileges they manage to assure (or to the extent that they manage to do so); responsibilities are privatised and individualised when they have structural causes and are, vice versa, socialised when privileged minorities should bear the burden of bad judgment.

Democratic practices and common sense seem instead to be far less pretentious and more reliable than liberal musings and prescriptions. As McAfee (2009: 46) explains, deliberation can produce sound public judgment as well as public will. The results will be judged by how well they work, subject matter for future deliberation and choice. However it might disappoint the philosopher, there are no independent standards for judging; the standards or ends are developed within the deliberations themselves, and more broadly throughout the life world of a political community, and how well the policy choices work are also reflected upon and decided within the public life of the community. There is no getting outside of this.

A great deal of the governance literature discussed in this work shows that the liberal arguments in defence of leadership and expertise (used in the past to undermine the alleged classical model of democracy) need to be reconsidered in a new light. This has to do, in particular, not only with questions of 'high' politics, but also with those of 'low' politics as well; that is, those related to policy making and policy implementation – fields of activity which in the past were the exclusive domain of technocratic structures (governments, civil services, courts and tribunals) insulated from the democratic process. The shift from 'government' to 'governance' means that, in both ambits, the representative model of democracy realised in the post-war (but the various constitutive elements of which arch back to the revolutions of the eighteenth century) has exhausted its course and is in need of radical overhaul. The notions of Regulatory State and Networked Polity discussed in the previous chapters are predicated on distinct visions of democracy which are currently vying against each other (*see* Chapter Seven). These are, in turn, adopted by powerful political and social coalitions interested in exploiting them in self-serving ways.

Our normative task is, therefore, that of assessing these alternative visions properly and understanding how they can be integrated within our real existing constitutional settings. As I see it, this entails conscious concerted action on the part of progressive forces to make sure that the introduction of any policy innovation contributes to the further democratisation of our political systems, rather than to the current drift towards post-democracy. From this perspective, two things are clear (to me at least): first, that the model of shareholder (or Madisonian, or foot-voting) democracy advocated by Regulatory State theorists is unsuitable; second, that the model of stakeholder democracy jointly advocated by theorists of the Networked Polity and deliberative democrats needs to be reconsidered in a more critical spirit. Far from showing that it is possible to move beyond representation altogether, democratic experimentalism seems to stress the need to integrate 'territorial' organisational principles with 'functional' ones, and 'electoral' mechanisms of selection with 'non-electoral' ones (i.e. by lotteries). However, it is still to be seen how such an integration could be done without increasing current democratic deficits and accountability gaps.

A similar analytical and justificatory work needs to be done in relation to policy making and policy implementation. Far from showing that it is possible to dismiss expertise completely and turn apathetic citizens into active prosumers, new modes of governance have highlighted the existence of many administrative ambits which can be opened to the direct participation of qualified stakeholders. It is still to be seen how this can be done in ways which cause the empowerment of representative minipopulus, rather than the mere consultation of unrepresentative and easily manipulated minipublics (McAfee 2004). In revising the role expertise ought to play in public life, an issue that needs to be considered with special attention pertains to the likely redistribution of responsibilities such a task entails. In the previous chapters, I have suggested we need to consider the shifting of responsibilities as a key element for understanding the nature of recent political and institutional change. The politics of choice pursued by various neoliberal governments worldwide is, in reality, privatising public responsibilities under the pretence of liberating people from the one-size-fits-all logic of universal welfare services. In many fields of activities, this often means shifting on the individual responsibility for choices which are not amenable to neoclassic type cost-benefit analyses. First, they belong to public goods for which there are no market equivalents. Second, they concern non-standardised goods, the quality of which cannot be easily assessed. Third, the marketisation of those public goods creates countless distortions and negative externalities defying the computational abilities of many individuals. Education and health are instances in point. In these fields, 'consumers' find themselves overwhelmed by a growing amount of controversial information telling them very little, are exposed to the strategic actions of agents enjoying asymmetric information, are confronted with mechanisms of exit which are impracticable, and are unable to mount proper collective actions for the dearth of channels of voice.

In turn, those working within these sectors, the suppliers, face a similar predicament themselves. Their actions are dependent on structural conditions they cannot change, they are forced under growing pressure to conform to requirements laid down externally for specious reasons, and their rewards are either unrelated to their performance or at odds with the respect of ethical and professional standards. In the end, consumers and suppliers, individually and as prosumers, find themselves confronting a host of managerially engineered solutions which make their alleged freedom of choice a frustrating experience. Redressing this state of affairs means rethinking the way in which both responsibilities and social incentives are defined and attributed. The economic sociology that is at the root of network governance has pointed out the contribution of non-monetary sets of incentives to individual compliance through the process of identification and sharing (Granovetter and Swedberg 1992). A normative approach to policy analysis needs to be built on this insight in order to understand how monetary and non-monetary incentives ought to be combined together and who is ultimately qualified to do that. For me, this requires the adoption of a self-reflexive constructivist perspective that views normative policy analysis as a means for turning vicious circles in virtuous circles, rather than a theoretical enterprise for criticising circular reasoning or discovering unlikely ultimate truths. Finally, it entails to abandon justificatory strategies based on desirability and feasibility criteria to adopt less ambitious criteria of electability.

End Notes

1. In this sense I am more than happy to follow in Foucault's footsteps and claim that 'my point is not that everything is bad, but that everything is dangerous, which is not exactly the same as bad. If everything is dangerous, then we always have something to do. So my positions leads not to apathy but to a hyper- and pessimistic [and explicitly normative, in my case] activism' (Foucault 1984: 343).

2. A recent article reporting on the different treatment reserved in Britain to tax-dodgers *vis-à-vis* benefit fraudsters helps clarify this point.

> Richard Murphy, an economist and founder of the Tax Justice Network, said that tax authority figures suggest tax evasion costs the UK £34bn a year, while his own figures suggest it is much more than that, around £120bn. In comparison, figures from the Department of Work and Pensions suggest the total amount of money lost to fraud was around £2bn in 2011/12. Murphy said: 'The fact is there's an enormous difference in the amount of spend put into benefit fraud compared to tax loss, which is vastly higher. One of the things I did do was compare the amount of spend the DWP has on advertising about benefit fraud, and it is about 600 times [that of the spend for advertising tax evasion]. The reason is that it's easier to target benefit fraud than tax fraud. Benefit fraud happens within the system – they are just trying to find what's wrong in the data. With tax fraud, it's what's not in your data. I speak as someone who is an auditor – there's always a temptation to audit what's in front of you, not to see if the data is complete. The net benefit to society, however, obviously lies in chasing tax' (http://www.theguardian.com/news/2015/feb/14/tax-dodging-father-benefits-cheat-system).

3. This passage summarises a much longer and detailed critical analysis of game theoretical models of spontaneous order trying to supply theoretical foundations to neoliberal principles contained in Palumbo (2000). In that work I show that the stability of cooperation in this type of game crucially depends on the existence and observation of the provisos identified by Locke in the *Second Treatise On Government*, that no evolutionary theory has so far been able to naturalise Locke's provisos, and that in the absence of these conditions interaction reproduces a Hobbesian state of nature. Here I use those considerations to oppose the idea that neoliberal governmentality can be embedded and made to work by subliminal means alone.

Bibliography

Abrams, P. (1988) 'Notes on the difficulty of studying the state', *Journal of Historical Sociology*, 1(1): 58–89.

Aghion, P. and Tirole, J. (1997) 'Formal and real authority in organizations', *Journal of Political Economy*, 105(1): 1–29.

Albertazzi, D. and McDonnell, D. (eds) (2007) *Twenty-First Century Populism*, London: Palgrave Macmillan.

Allum, P. (1995) *State and Society in Western Europe*, Cambridge: Polity.

Almer, J. and Rotkirch, M. (2004) *European Governance*, Stockholm: Swedish Institute for European Policy Studies (Sieps).

Amin, A. (ed.) (1994) *Post-Fordism*, Oxford: Blackwell.

Andersen, S. C. (2005) 'How to improve the outcome of state welfare services: governance in a systems-theoretical perspective', *Public Administration*, 83(4): 891–907.

Anderson, M. (1978) *Welfare: Political Economy*, Stanford: Hoover Press.

Anderson, P. (2014) 'The Italian disaster', *London Review of Books*, 35 (22 May).

Ansell, C. (2000) 'The networked polity: regional development in Western Europe', *Governance* 13(3): 303–333.

—   (2006) 'Network institutionalism', in R. A. W. Rhodes, S. A. Binder and B. A. Rockman (eds) *The Oxford Handbook of Political Institutions*, Oxford: Oxford University Press pp. 75–89.

Applbaum, A. I. (1992) 'Democratic legitimacy and official discretion', *Philosophy and Public Affairs*, 21(3): 240–274.

Arblaster, A. (1987) *Democracy*, Buckingham: Open University Press.

Arendt, H. (1958a) *The Origins of Totalitarianism*, 2nd enl. ed., New York: Meridian Books.

—   (1958b) *The Human Condition*, Chicago: The University of Chicago Press.

—   (1963) *On Revolution*, Harmondsworth: Penguin.

Aron, R. (1995) 'The anarchical order of power', *Daedalus*, 124(3): 27–52.

Arrow, K. J. (1951) *Social Choice and Individual Values*, New York: Wiley.

Arts, B., Lagendijk, A., and van Houtum, H. (2009) *The Disoriented State: Shifts in Governmentality, Territoriality and Governance*, Dordrecht: Springer.

Atkinson, M. and Coleman, W. (1992) 'Policy networks, policy communities and the problems of governance', *Governance* 5(2): 154–180.

Bader, V. (2010) 'Complex legitimacy in compound polities: the EU as example', *Representation* 46(3): 261–279.

Ball, T. (1995) 'An ambivalent alliance: political science and American democracy', in J. Farr, J. S. Dryzek and S. T. Leonard (eds) *Political Science in History*, Cambridge: Cambridge University Press pp. 41–65.

Bang, H. P. (2003a) 'Governance as political communication', in H. P. Bang (ed.) *Governance as Social and Political Communication*, Manchester: Manchester University Press pp. 7–23.

— (2003b) 'A new ruler meeting a new citizen: culture governance and everyday making', in H. P. Bang (ed.) *Governance as Social and Political Communication*, Manchester: Manchester University Press pp. 241–265.

Bang, H. P. and Sørensen, E. (1999) 'The everyday maker: a new challenge to democratic governance', *Administrative Theory & Praxis*, 21(3): 325–341.

Barber, B. (1984) *Strong Democracy: Participatory Politics for a New Age*, Berkeley: University of California Press.

— (1988) *The Conquest of Politics: Liberal Philosophy in Democratic Times*, Princeton: Princeton University Press.

— (1996) 'Foundationalism and democracy', in S. Benhabib (ed.) *Democracy and Difference*, Princeton: Princeton University Press pp. 348–357.

— (2007) *Con$umed: How Markets Corrupt Children, Infantilize Adults, and Swallow Citizens Whole*, New York: W.W. Norton.

Barberis, P. (1998) 'The new public management and a new accountability', *Public Administration* 76(3): 451–470.

Barnett, C. and Low, M. (eds) (2004) *Spaces of Democracy: Geographical Perspectives on Citizenship, Participation and Representation*, London: Sage.

Barrett, S. M. (2004) 'Implementation studies: time for a revival? Personal reflections on 20 years of implementation studies', *Public Administration*, 82(2): 249–262.

Barron, A. and Scott, C. (1992) 'The Citizen's Charter programme', *The Modern Law Review*, 55(4), 526–546.

Bataille, G. (1985) 'The notion of expenditure', in G. Bataille *Visions of Excess: Selected Writings, 1927–1939*, Minneapolis: University of Minnesota Press pp. 116–129.

— (1997) 'The gift of rivalry "potlatch"', in F. Botting and S. Wilson (eds) *The Bataille Reader*, Oxford: Blackwell pp. 157–166.

Bauman, Z. (1991) 'A sociological theory of postmodernity', *Thesis Eleven*, 29: 33–46.

— (2000) *Liquid Modernity*, Cambridge: Polity.

Beck, U. (1992) *Risk Society*, London: Sage.

— (2000) *What Is Globalization?*, Cambridge: Polity.

Beito, D. T. (2000) *From Mutual Aid to the Welfare State: Fraternal Societies and Social Services, 1890–1967*, Chapel Hill: The University of North Carolina Press.

Bekkers, V., Dijkstra, G. and Edwards, A. (2007) *Governance and the Democratic Deficit: Assessing the Democratic Legitimacy of Governance Practices*, Aldershot: Ashgate.

Bell, S. and Hindmoor, A. (2009) *Rethinking Governance*, Port Melbourne, Vic.: Cambridge University Press.

Bellamy, R. (2007a) *Political Constitutionalism: A Republican Defence of the Constitutionality of Democracy*, Cambridge: Cambridge University Press.

— (2007b) *Citizenship*, Oxford: Oxford University Press.

— (2010) 'Democracy without democracy? Can the EU's democratic "outputs" be separated from the democratic "inputs" provided by competitive parties and majority rule?', *Journal of European Public Policy*, 17(1): 2–19.

Bellamy, R. and Greenaway J. (1995) 'The new right conception of citizenship and the citizen's charter', *Government and Opposition*, 30(4): 469–491.

Bemelmans-Videc, M. L., Rist, R. C. and Vedung, E. O. (1998) *Carrots, Sticks, and Sermons: Policy Instruments and Their Evaluation*, New Brunswick: Transaction Publishers.

Benhabib, S. (1996) 'Toward a deliberative model of democratic legitimacy', in S. Benhabib (ed.) *Democracy and Difference*, Princeton: Princeton University Press pp. 67–94.

Benn, M. (2011) *School Wars: The Battle for Britain's Education*, London: Verso.

Benz, A. and Papadopoulos, Y. (2006) 'Introduction: governance and democracy: concepts and key issues', in A. Benz and Y. Papadopoulos (eds) *Governance and Democracy: Comparing National, European and International Experiences*, London: Routledge pp. 1–26.

Berezin, M. (2009) *Illiberal Politics in Neoliberal Times*, Cambridge: Cambridge University Press.

Berle, A. A. and Means, G. C. (1932) *The Modern Corporation and Private Property*, New York: Macmillan.

Berlinski, C. (2008) *"There Is No Alternative": Why Margaret Thatcher Matters*, New York: Basic Books.

Berman, P. S. (2007) 'Global legal pluralism', *Southern California Law Review*, 80: 1155–1237.

Berman, S. (2006) *The Primacy of Politics: Social Democracy and the Making of Europe's Twentieth Century*, Cambridge: Cambridge University Press.

Bevir, M. (2006) 'Democratic governance: systems and radical perspectives', *Public Administration Review*, 66(3): 426–36.

— (2009) 'What is governance? Introduction', in M. Bevir (ed.) *Key Concepts in Governance*, London: Sage pp. 3–30.

— (2010) *Democratic Governance*, Princeton: Princeton University Press.

— (2013) *A Theory of Governance*, Berkeley: University of California Press.

Bevir, M. and Rhodes, R. A. W. (2006) 'Decentred theory, change and network governance', in E. Sørensen and J. Torfing (eds) *Theories of Democratic Network Governance*, Basingstoke: Palgrave Macmillan pp. 77–91.

— (2010) *The State as Cultural Practice*, Oxford: Oxford University Press.

Bingham, L. B., Nabatchi, T. and O'Leary, R. (2005) 'The new governance: practices and processes for stakeholder and citizen participation in the work of government', *Public Administration Review*, 65(5): 547–558.

Birch, A. H. (1993) *Concepts and Theories of Modern Democracy*, London: Routledge.

Bishop, M., Kay, J. and Mayer, C. (1995) *The Regulatory Challenge*, Oxford: Oxford University Press.

Blair, T. (1998) *The Third Way: New Politics for a New Century*, London: Fabian Society.

Blühdorn, I. (2007) 'The third transformation of democracy: on the efficient management of late-modern complexity', in I. Blühdorn and U. Jun (eds) *Economic Efficiency – Democratic Empowerment: Contested Modernisation in Britain and Germany*, Lanham: Rowman & Littlefield pp. 299–331.

— (2009) 'The participatory revolution: new social movements and civil society', in K. Larres (ed.) *A Companion to Europe since 1945*, New York: John Wiley & Sons pp. 407–430.

Bobbit, P. (2002) *The Shield of Achilles: War, Peace and the Course of History*, London: Penguin.

Boettke, P. (1998) 'Rational choice and human agency in economics and sociology: exploring the Weber-Austrian connection', in H. Giersch (ed.) *Merits and Limits of Markets*, Heidelberg: Springer Verlag-Berlin pp. 53–81.

Bogason, P. and Musso, J. A. (2006) 'The democratic prospects of network governance', *American Review of Public Administration*, 36(1): 3–18.

Bohman, J. (1998) 'The coming of age of deliberative democracy', *Journal of Political Philosophy*, 6(4): 400–435.

Bollier, D. (2003) *Silent Theft: The Private Plunder of Our Common Wealth*, London: Routledge.

Borrás, S. and Jacobsson, K. (2004) 'The open method of co-ordination and new governance patterns in the EU', *Journal of European Public Policy*, 11(2): 185–208.

Börzel, T. A. (2011), 'Networks: reified metaphor or governance panacea?', *Public Administration* 89(1), 49–63.

Bovaird, T. (2005) 'Public governance: balancing stakeholder power in a network society', *International Review of Administrative Sciences*, 71(2): 217–228.

Bowen, E. R. (1982) 'The Pressman-Wildavsky paradox: four addenda or why models based on probability theory can predict implementation success and suggest useful tactical advice for implementers', *Journal of Public Policy*, 2(1): 1–21.

Braithwaite, J. (2006) 'The regulatory state?', in R. A. W. Rhodes, S. A. Binder and B. A. Rockman (eds) *The Oxford Handbook of Political Institutions*, Oxford: Oxford University Press pp. 407–430.

—   (2008) *Regulatory Capitalism: How It Works, Ideas for Making It Work Better*, Cheltenham: Edward Elgar.

Brans, M. and Rossbach, S. (1997) 'The autopoiesis of administrative systems: Niklas Luhmann on public administration and public policy', *Public Administration*, 75(3): 417–439.

Brennan, G. and Buchanan, J. M. (1985) *The Reason of Rules*, Cambridge: Cambridge University Press.

Brenner, N. (2004) 'Urban governance and the production of new state spaces in Western Europe, 1960–2000', *Review of International Political Economy*, 11(3): 447–488.

Brenner, R. and Glick, M. (1991) 'The regulation approach: theory and history', *New Left Review*, 188: 45–119.

Breuilly, J. (1993) *Nationalism and the State*, Manchester: Manchester University Press.

Briggs, A. (1961) 'The welfare state in historical perspective', *European Journal of Sociology*, 2(2): 221–258.

Brinkley, A. (1985) 'Richard Hofstadter's *The Age of Reform*: a reconsideration', *American History*, 13(3): 462–480.

Brown, A. (2009) *Personal Responsibility: Why It Matters*, London: Continuum.

Brown, C., Eichengreen, B. J. and Reich, M. (2010) *Labour in the Era of Globalization*, Cambridge: Cambridge University Press.

Brown, J. (1995) *The British Welfare State*, Oxford: Blackwell.

Brown, R. L. (1998) 'Accountability, liberty, and the constitution', *Columbia Law Review*, 98(3): 531–79.

Brühl, T. and Rittberger, V. (2002) 'From international to global governance: actors, collective decision-making, and the United Nations in the world of the twenty-first century', in V. Rittberger (ed.) *Global Governance and the United Nations Systems*, Tokyo: UN University Press pp. 1–47.

Buchanan, A. (1985) *Ethics, Efficiency and the Market*, Oxford: Oxford University Press.

—   (2013) *The Heart of Human Rights*, Oxford: Oxford University Press.

Buchanan, J. M. (1972) 'Toward an analysis of closed behavioral systems', in J. M. Buchanan and R. D. Tollison (eds) *The Theory of Public Choice*, Ann Arbor: The University of Michigan Press pp. 11–23.

Buchanan, J. M. and Tullock, G. (1962) *The Calculus of Consent*, Ann Arbor: University of Michigan Press.

Buchanan, J. M., Rowley, C. K., Breton, A., *et al.* (1978) *The Economics of Politics*, London: IEA.

Bull, H. (1977) *The Anarchical Society*, London: Macmillan.

Burnham, J. (1941) *The Managerial Revolution*, New York: John Day.

Byrne, T. (2000) *Local Government in Britain*, 7th edn, London: Penguin.

Carpenter, D. and Moss, D. A. (eds) (2014) *Preventing Regulatory Capture: Special Interest Influence and How to Limit it*, Cambridge: Cambridge University Press.

Carter Center (2005) *Observing the Venezuela Presidential Recall Referendum: Comprehensive Report*, /www.cartercenter.org (accessed 16 October 2014).

Cashore, B. (2002) 'Legitimacy and the privatization of environmental governance: how non–state market–driven (NSMD) governance systems gain rule–making authority', *Governance*, 15(4): 503–529.

Castells, M. (2005) 'The network society: from knowledge to policy', in M. Castells and G. Cardoso (eds) *The Network Society: From Knowledge to Policy*, Washington: Johns Hopkins Center for Transatlantic Relations.

— (2010) *The Rise of the Network Society*, 2nd edn, with a new pref., Chichester: Wiley-Blackwell.

— (2012) *Networks of Outrage and Hope: Social Movements in the Internet Age*, Cambridge: Polity.

CEC (Commission of the European Communities) (2001) *European Governance: A White Paper*, COM(2001) 428 Brussels, 25.7.2001

Cerny, P. (1997) 'Paradoxes of the competition state: the dynamics of political globalization', *Government and Opposition*, 32(2): 251–274.

Chambers, S. and Kapstein, J. (2006) 'Civil society and the state', in J. S. Dryzek, B. Honig and A. Phillips (eds) *The Oxford Handbook of Political Theory*, Oxford: Oxford University Press pp. 363–381.

Chandler, A. D. (1977) *The Visible Hand: The Managerial Revolution in American Business*, Cambridge, Mass.: Belknap Press.

Chernilo, D. (2008) 'Classical sociology and the nation-state: a re-interpretation', *Journal of Classical Sociology*, 8(1): 27–43.

Chomsky, N. (1999) *Profit over People: Neoliberalism & Global Order*, New York: Seven Stories Press.

Christiansen, T. and Larsson, T. (eds) (2007) *The Role of Committees in the Policy-Process of the European Union: Legislation, Implementation and Deliberation*, Cheltenham: Edward Elgar.

Christiansen, T., Lie, A. and Lægreid, P. (2007) 'Still fragmented government or reassertion of the centre?', in P. Laegreid and T. Christensen (eds), *Transcending New Public Management: The Transformation of Public Sector Reforms*, Aldershot: Ashgate pp. 17–41.

Christiano, T. (2004) 'The authority of democracy', *Journal of Political Philosophy*, 12(3): 266–290.

Clarke, J., Newman, J., Smith, N. Vidler, E. and Westmarland, L. (2007) *Creating Citizen-Consumers: Changing Publics & Changing Public Services*, London: Sage.

Cockett, R. (1995) *Thinking the Unthinkable*, London: Fontana.

CGG (Commission on Global Governance) (1995) *Our Global Neighbourhood*, Oxford: Oxford University Press.

Coglianese, C. (2012) 'Presidential control of administrative agencies: a debate over law or politics?', *University of Pennsylvania Journal of Constitutional Law*, 12: 12–07.

Cohen, J. and Rogers, J. (1992) 'Secondary associations and democratic governance', *Politics Society*, 20(4): 393–472.

Cohen, J. L. (1996) 'Rights and citizenship, and the modern form of the social: dilemmas of Arendtian republicanism', *Constellations*, 3(2): 164–189.

Cohen, J. L. and Arato, A. (1994) *Civil Society and Political Theory*, Cambridge, Mass.: MIT Press.

Coleman, J. S. (1994) *Foundations of Social Theory*, Cambridge, Mass.: Belknap Press.

Coleman, J. S. and Ferejohn, J. (1986) 'Democracy and social choice', *Ethics*, 97(1): 6–25.

Collini, S. (2011) *What Are Universities For?*, London: Penguin.

Collins, R. (1998) *The Sociology of Philosophies: A Global Theory of Intellectual Change*, Cambridge, Mass.: Harvard University Press.

Crouch, C. (2004) *Postdemocracy*, Cambridge: Polity.

—— (2011) *The Strange Non-Death of Neo-Liberalism*, Cambridge: Polity.

Crozier, M., Huntington, S. P. and Watanuki, J. (1975) *The Crisis of Democracy*, New York: New York University Press.

Cuperus, R. (2004) 'The fate of European populism', *Dissent*, 2(Spring): 17–20.

D'Agostino, F. (1998) 'Expertise, democracy, and applied ethics', *Journal of Applied Philosophy*, 15(1): 49–55.

Dahl, R. A. (1956) *A Preface to Democratic Theory*, Chicago: University of Chicago Press.

—— (1961) *Who Governs? Democracy and Power in an American City*, New Haven: Yale University Press.

—— (1970) *Polyarchy, Participation and Democracy*, New Haven: Yale University Press.

—— (1979) 'Procedural Democracy', in P. Laslett and J. S. Fishkin (eds) *Philosophy, Politics and Society*, 5th ser., Oxford: Basil Blackwell pp. 97–133.

—— (1989) *Democracy and Its Critics*, New Haven: Yale University Press.

—— (1994) 'A democratic dilemma: system effectiveness versus citizen participation', *Political Science Quarterly*, 109(1): 23–34.

Dahl, R. A. and Lindblom, C. E. (1953; 1992) *Politics, Economics and Welfare*, London: Transaction Publishers.

Daniels, G. and McIlroy, J. (eds) (2009) *Trade Unions in a Neoliberal World: British Trade Unions under New Labour*, Abingdon, Oxon: Routledge.

Dauvergne, P. and LeBaron, G. (2014) *Protest Inc.: The Corporatization of Activism*, Bristol: Polity.

Davies, J. (2011) *Challenging Governance Theory*, Bristol: Policy Press.

Dean, M. M. (2010) *Governmentality: Power and Rule in Modern Society*, 2nd edn, London: Sage.

de Grazia, S. (1948) *The Political Community: A Study of Anomie*, Chicago: University of Chicago Press.

Deleon, L. (1998) 'Accountability in a "reinvented" government', *Public Administration*, 76(3): 539–558.

Desai, M. (1995) 'Global Governance', in M. Desai and P. Redfern (eds) *Global Governance: Ethics and Economics of the World Order*, London: Pinter pp. 6–21.

Dicey, A. V. (1885; 10th edn 1959) *Introduction to the Law of the Constitution*, London: Macmillan.

DiMaggio, P. (2003) 'Introduction. Making sense of the contemporary firm and prefiguring its future', in P. DiMaggio (ed.) *The Twenty-First Century Firm*, Princeton: Princeton University Press.

Djelic, M.-L. and Sahlin-Andersson K. (eds) (2006) *Transnational Governance*, Cambridge: Cambridge University Press.

— (2009) 'Governance and its transnational dynamics: towards a re-ordering of our world', in C. Chapman, D. Cooper and P. Miller (eds) *Accounting, Organizations and Institutions*, Oxford: Oxford University Press pp. 175–204.

Donaldson, T. (1982) *Corporations and Morality*, Englewood Cliffs, NJ: Prentice-Hall.

Douglas, I. R. (1997) 'Globalisation and the end of the state?', *New Political Economy*, 2(1): 165–177.

Dowding, K. (1995) *The Civil Service*, London: Routledge.

Downs, A. (1957) 'An economic theory of political action in a democracy', *Journal of Political Economy*, 65(2): 135–150.

Drewry, G. (2005) 'Citizen's charters: service quality chameleons', *Public Management Review*, 7(3): 321–340.

Dryzek, J. S. (2000) *Deliberative Democracy and Beyond*, Oxford: Oxford University Press.

du Gay, P. (2000) *In Praise of Bureaucracy*, London: Sage.

du Gay, P. and Scott, A. (2010) 'State transformation or regime shift? Addressing some confusions in the theory and sociology of the state', *Sociologica*, 4(2). http://www.rivisteweb.it/doi/10.2383/32707.

Duit, A. and Galaz, V. (2008) 'Governance and complexity—emerging issues for governance theory', *Governance*, 21(3): 311–335.

Duncan, G. and Lukes, S. (1963) 'The new democracy', *Political Studies*, 11(2): 156–177.

Dunn, J. (ed.) (1993) *Democracy*, Oxford: Oxford University Press

— (2000) *The Cunning of Unreason*, London: HarperCollins.

Dunsire, A. (1990) 'Holistic Governance', *Public Policy and Administration*, 5(1): 4–19.

— (1993) 'Manipulating social tensions: collibration as an alternative mode of government intervention', Max-Planck-Institut für Gesellschaftsforschung, discussion Paper 93/7. http://www.mpifg.de/pu/mpifg_dp/dp93–7.pdf (accessed 12 March 2007).

— (1996) 'Tipping the balance: autopoiesis and governance', *Administration and Society*, 28(3): 299–334.

Durkheim, E. (1950) *Leçons de sociologie: Physique des moeurs et du droit.* http://www.uqac.uquebec.ca/zone30/Classiques_des_sciences_sociales/index.html (accessed 20 March 2008).

— (1957) *Professional Ethics and Civic Morals*, trans. C. Brookfield, London: Routledge.

Dworkin, R. (1975) 'The original position', in N. Daniels (ed.) *Reading Rawls*, Oxford: Basil Blackwell pp. 16–53.

Dwyer, P. (2004) 'Creeping conditionality in the UK: from welfare rights to conditional entitlements?', *Canadian Journal of Sociology*, 29(2): 265–287.

Ebrahim, A. (2003) 'Making sense of accountability: conceptual perspectives for northern and southern nonprofits', *Nonprofit Management & Leadership*, 14(2): 191–212.

Eikenberry, A. M. (2009) *Giving Circles: Philanthropy, Voluntary Association, and Democracy*, Bloomington: Indiana University Press.

Elkins, Z. and Simmons, B. (2005) 'On waves, clusters, and diffusion: a conceptual framework', *Annals of the American Academy of Political and Social Science*, 598(1): 33–51.

Eriksen, E. O., Joerges, C. and Neyer, J. (eds) (2003) *European Governance, Deliberation and the Quest for Democratisation*, Oslo and Florence: ARENA and European University Institute.

Eriksson, K. (2012) 'Self-service society: participative politics and new forms of governance', *Public Administration*, 90(3): 685–698.

Evans, E. J. (2004) *Thatcher and Thatcherism*, London: Routledge.

Farnham, D. (1990) 'Trade union policy 1979–89: restriction or reform?', in S. P. Savage and L. Robins (eds) *Public Policy under Thatcher*, London: Macmillan pp. 60–74.

Farnsworth, K. (2012) *Social Versus Corporate Welfare: Competing Needs and Interests Within the Welfare State*, London: Palgrave Macmillan.

— (2013) 'Bringing corporate welfare in', *Journal of Social Policy*, 42(1): 1–22.

Farr, J. (1995) 'Remembering the revolution: behavioralism in American political science', in J. Farr, J. S. Dryzek and S. T. Leonard (eds), *Political Science in History*, Cambridge: Cambridge University Press pp. 198–224.

Finkelstein, L. S. (1995) 'What is global governance?', *Global Governance*, 1(3): 367–372.

Fishkin, J. (1991) *Democracy and Deliberation*, New Haven: Yale University Press.

Flew, A. (1981) *The Politics of Procrustes: Contradictions of Enforced Equality*, London: Temple Smith.

Flinders, M. and Skelcher, C. (2012) 'Shrinking the quango state: five challenges in reforming quangos', *Public Money & Management*, 32(5), 327–334.

Flora, P. and Heidenheimer, A. J. (eds) (1981) *The Development of Welfare States in Europe and America*, New Brunswick: Transaction Books.

Follesdal, A. and Hix, S. (2006) 'Why there is a democratic deficit in the EU: a response to Majone and Moravcsik', *Journal of Common Market Studies*, 44(3): 533–562.

Foster, C. (2005) *British Government in Crisis: Or The Third English Revolution*. Oxford: Hart.

Foucault, M. (1978) 'Governmentality', *Ideology & Consciousness* 6, 5–21.

— (1984) 'On the genealogy of ethics: an overview of work in progress', in P. Rabinow (ed.), *The Foucault Reader*, Harmondsworth: Penguin pp. 340–372.

— (1998) 'Nietzsche, genealogy, history', in J. D. Faubion (ed.), *Aesthetics, Method, and Epistemology: Essential Works of Foucault 1954–1984*, Volume two, New York: The New Press pp. 369–391.

— (2008) *The Birth of Biopolitics*, trans. G. Burchell, London: Palgrave Macmillan.

Fourastiè, J. (1979) *Les Trente Glorieuses, ou la révolution invisible de 1946 à 1975*, Paris: Fayard.

Fourcade, M. (2007) 'Theories of markets and theories of society', *American Behavioral Scientist*, 50(8): 1015–1034.

Frank, T. (2000) *One Market Under God*, London: Secker and Warburg.

— (2004) *What Is the Problem with Kansas? How Conservatives Won the Heart of America*, New York: Henry Holt and Co.

Freeman, R. E. (1984) *Strategic Management: A Stakeholder Approach*, Boston, MA: Pitman.

Friedman M. (1962) *Capitalism and Freedom*, Chicago: University of Chicago Press.

Fukuyama, F. (1992) *The End of History and the Last Man*, New York: Free Press.

Fung, A. (2006) 'Varieties of participation in complex governance', *Public Administration Review*, 66(s1): 66–75.

Fung, A. and Wright, E. O. (2001) 'Deepening democracy: innovations in empowered participatory governance', *Politics & Society*, 29(1): 5–41.

Gallagher, M., Laver, M. and Mair, P. (2006) *Representative Government in Western Europe*, New York: McGraw-Hill.

Gambetta, D. (1988) *Trust: Making and Breaking Cooperative Relations*, Oxford: Basil Blackwell.

Gauthier, D. (1986) *Morals by Agreement*, Oxford: Clarendon Press.

Geenens, R. (2007) 'The deliberative model of democracy: two critical remarks', *Ratio Juris*, 20(3): 355–377.

Giddens, A. (1998) *The Third Way*, Cambridge: Polity.

— (2000) *The Third Way and Its Critics*, Cambridge: Polity.

Gilardi, F. and Maggetti, M. (2011) 'The independence of regulatory authorities', in D. Levi-Faur (ed.) *Handbook on the Politics of Regulation*, Cheltenham: Edward Elgar pp. 201–214.

Gilbert, N. and Gilbert, B. (1989) *The Enabling State: Modern Welfare Capitalism in America*, Oxford: Oxford University Press.

Gill, G. (2003) *The Nature and Development of the Modern State*, London: Palgrave Macmillan.

Glaeser, E. L. and Shleifer, A. (2003) 'The rise of the regulatory state', *Journal of Economic Literature*, 41(2): 401–425.

Goetz, K. H. (2008) 'Governance as a path to government', *West European Politics*, 31(1–2), 258–279.

Goodhart, M. (2001) 'Democracy, globalisation and the problem of the state', *Polity*, 33(4): 527–546.

Goodin, R. E. (2003) 'Democratic accountability: the distinctiveness of the third sector', *European Journal of Sociology*, 44(3): 359–396.

Goodin, R. E. and Dryzek, J. S. (2006) 'Deliberative impacts: the macro-political uptake of mini-publics', *Politics & Society*, 34(2): 219–244.

Gospel, H. and Wood, S. (eds) (2003) *Representing Workers: Trade Union Recognition and Membership in Britain*, London: Routledge.

Gould, A. (1982) 'The salaried middle class and the welfare state in Sweden and Japan', *Policy & Politics*, 10(4), 417–437.

Granovetter, M. (1985) 'Economic action and social structure: the problem of embeddedness', *American Journal of Sociology*, 91(3): 481–510.

Granovetter, M. and Swedberg, R. (eds) (1992) *The Sociology of Economic Life*, Boulder: Westview Press.

Gray, A. and Jenkins, B. (2003) 'Government and administration: paradoxes of policy performance', *Parliamentary Affairs*, 56(2): 170–187.

Gray, J. (1998) *False Dawn: The Delusions of Global Capitalism*, London: Granta.

Green, D. L. (1993) *Reinventing Civil Society: The Rediscovery of Welfare Without Politics*, Choice in Welfare No. 49, London: Civitas.

— (1999) *An End to Welfare Rights: The Rediscovery of Independence*, Choice in Welfare No. 49, London: Civitas.

Green, D. and Shapiro, I. (1994) *Pathologies of Rational Choice*, New Haven, CT: Yale University Press.

Greene, F. J., Mole, K. F. D. and Storey, J. (2008) *Three Decades of Enterprise Culture*, Basingstoke: Palgrave Macmillan.

Gross, L. (1948) 'The peace of Westphalia, 1648–1948', *American Journal of International Law*, 42(1): 20–41.

Grugel, J. (2002) *Democratisation*, London: Palgrave Macmillan.

Gutman, A. and Thompson, D. (1996) *Democracy and Disagreement*, Cambridge, Mass: Harvard University Press.

Gyford, J. (1991) The enabling council—a third model, *Local Government Studies*, 17(1): 1–5.

Haakonssen, K. (1981) *The Science of a Legislator*, Cambridge: Cambridge University Press.

Habermas, J. (1976) *Legitimation Crisis*, London: Heinemann.

— (1985) *The Philosophical Discourse of Modernity*, Cambridge: Polity.

—   (1995) *Between Facts and Norms*, Cambridge: Polity.

—   (2001a) 'Why Europe needs a constitution', *New Left Review*, 11 (Sept–Oct): 5–26.

—   (2001b) *The Postnational Constellation*, Cambridge: Polity.

—   (2012) *The Crisis of the European Union: A Response*, Cambridge: Polity.

Hacker, J. S. (2006) *The Great Risk Shift*, Oxford: Oxford University Press.

Hailsham, Lord (1978) *The Dilemma of Democracy*, London: Collins.

Hajer, M. and Versteeg, W. (2005) 'Performing governance through networks', *European Political Science*, 4(3): 340–347.

Hajer, M. and Wagenaar, W. (eds) (2003) *Deliberative Policy Analysis*, Cambridge: Cambridge University Press.

Hall, P. A. and Taylor, R. R. (1996) 'Political science and the three new institutionalisms', *Political Studies*, 44(5): 936–957.

Hall, S. (1988) *The Hard Road to Renewal: Thatcherism and the Crisis of the Left*, London: Verso.

Ham, C. and Hill, M. (1984) *The Policy Process in the Modern Capitalist State*, London: Harvester Wheatsheaf.

Hamlin, A. and Pettit, P. (eds) (1989) *The Good Polity: Normative Analysis of the State*, Oxford: Blackwell.

Handler, J. F. (2003) 'Social citizenship and workfare in the U.S. and Western Europe: from status to contract', *Journal of European Social Policy*, 13(3): 229–243.

Hardin, R. (2000) 'Democratic epistemology and accountability', *Social Philosophy and Policy*, 17(1): 110–126.

Hargreaves-Heap, S. (1989) *Rationality in Economics*, Oxford: Blackwell.

Harland, R. (1987) *Superstructuralism: The Philosophy of Structuralism and Post-Structuralism*, London: Routledge.

Harris, J. (1992) 'Political thought and the welfare state 1870–1940: an intellectual framework for British social policy', *Past and Present*, 135 (May): 116–141.

—   (2006) 'Development of civil society', in R. A. W. Rhodes, S. A. Binder and B. A. Rockman (eds) *The Oxford Handbook of Political Institutions*, Oxford: Oxford University Press pp. 131–143.

—   (2010) 'Citizenship in Britain and Europe: some missing links' in T. H. Marshall's theory of rights, ZeS-Arbeitspapier, No. 02/2010. http://www.econstor.eu/bitstream/10419/43703/1/641427670.pdf

Hart, H. L. A. (1961) *The Concept of Law*, Oxford: Clarendon Press.

Hart, J. A. and Prakash, A. (1997) 'The decline of "embedded liberalism" and the rearticulation of the Keynesian welfare state', *New Political Economy*, 2(1): 65–78.

Harvey, D. (2001) *A Brief History of Neoliberalism*, Oxford: Oxford University Press.

Hasenclever, A., Mayer, P. and Rittberger, V. (1997) *Theories of International Regimes*, Cambridge: Cambridge University Press.

Hassan, R. (2004) *Media, Politics, and the Network Society*, Maidenhead: Open University Press.

Hay, C. (2006) (2007) *Why We Hate Politics*, Cambridge: Polity.

— (2014) 'Depoliticisation as process, governance as practice: what did the "first wave" get wrong and do we need a "second wave" to put it right?', *Policy & Politics*, 42(2): 293–311.

Hay, C. and Richards, D. (2000) 'The tangled webs of Westminster and Whitehall: the discourse, strategy and practice of networking within the British core executive', *Public Administration*, 78(1): 1–28.

Hayek, F. A. (1944) *The Road to Serfdom*, London: Routledge.

— (1955) *The Counter-Revolution of Science: Studies on the Abuse of Reason*, Glencoe: Free Press.

— (1960) *The Constitution of Liberty*, Chicago: University of Chicago Press.

— (1978) *New Studies in Philosophy, Politics, Economics and the History of Ideas*, London: Routledge.

— (1982) *Law, Legislation and Liberty*, London: Routledge.

— (1987) 'The rules of morality are not the conclusions of our reason', in G. Radnitzky (ed.) *Centripetal Forces in the Sciences*, New York: Paragon House pp. 227–235.

Heath, A. F., Jowell, R. M., Curtice, J. K. (2001) *The Rise of New Labour. Party Policies and Voter Choices*, New York: Oxford University Press.

Hechter, M. and Kanazawa, S. (1997) 'Sociological rational choice theory', *Annual Review of Sociology*, 23: 191–214.

Hechter, M. and Opp, K.-D. (2001) *Social Norms*, New York: Russell Sage Foundation.

Heclo, H. (2002) 'The spirit of public administration', *PS: Political Science and Politics*, 35(4): 689–694.

Held, D. (2004) 'Democratic accountability and political effectiveness from a cosmopolitan perspective', *Government and Opposition*, 39(2): 364–391.

— (2010) *Cosmopolitanism*, Cambridge: Polity.

Helleiner, E. (1994) *States and the Reemergence of Global Finance: From Bretton Woods to the 1990s*, Ithaca: Cornell University Press.

Henisz, W. J., Zelner, B. A. and Guillén, M. F. (2005) 'The worldwide diffusion of market-oriented infrastructure reform, 1977–1999', *American Sociological Review*, 70(6): 871–897.

Hennessy, P. (1990) *Whitehall*, London: Fontana Press.

Héritier, A. (1999) 'Elements of democratic legitimation in Europe: an alternative perspective', *Journal of European Public Policy*, 6(2): 269–282.

— (2003) 'Composite democracy in Europe: the role of transparency and access to information', *Journal of European Public Policy*, 10(5): 814–833.

Hernes, T. and Bakken, T. (2003) 'Implications of self-reference: Niklas Luhmann's autopoiesis and organization theory', *Organization Studies*, 24(9): 1511–1535.

Herzog, W. (2010) 'On the absolute, the sublime and ecstatic truth', *Arion*, 17(3) http://www.bu.edu/arion/archive/volume-17/ (accessed 23 May 2010).

Hewson, M. and Sinclair, T. (eds) (1999) *Approaches to Global Governance Theory*, Albany: State University of New York Press.

Hibou, B. (ed.) (2004) *Privatizing the State*, New York: Columbia University Press.

Hill, C. J. and Lynn, L. E. (2005) 'Is hierarchical governance in decline? Evidence from empirical research', *Journal of Public Administration Research and Theory*, 15(2): 173–195.

Hill, M. and Hupe, P. (2002) *Implementing Public Policy: Governance in Theory and in Practice*, London: Sage.

Hirschl, R. (2004) '"Juristocracy" – political, not juridical', *The Good Society*, 13(3): 6–11.

Hirschman, A. O. (1970) *Exit, Voice, and Loyalty*, Cambridge, Mass.: Harvard University Press.

Hix, S. (1998) 'The study of the European Union II: the "new governance" agenda and its rival', *Journal of European Public Policy* 5(1): 38–65.

Hodgson, G. (1998) 'The approach of institutional economics', *Journal of Economic Literature*, 36(1): 166–192.

— (2007) 'Institutions and individuals: interaction and evolution', *Organization Studies*, 28(1): 95–116.

Hodgson, P. (2006) 'The rise and rise of the regulatory state', *Political Quarterly*, 77(2): 247–254.

Hollingshead, I. (2005) 'Loose ends: Whatever happened to the Citizen's Charter?', *The Guardian*, 17 September.

Hollis, M. (1977) *Models of Man*, Cambridge: Cambridge University Press.

Honohan, I. (2002) *Civic Republicanism*, London: Routledge.

Honohan, I. and Jennings, J. (eds) (2006) *Republicanism in Theory and Practice*, London: Routledge.

Hood, C. (2010) *The Blame Game*, Princeton: Princeton University Press.

Hood, C., James, O. and Scott, C. (2000) 'Regulation in government: has it increased, is it increasing, should it be diminished?', *Public Administration*, 78(2): 283–304.

Hood, C., James, O., Jones, G., Scott, O. and Travers, T. (1998) 'Regulating inside government: where new public management meets the audit explosion', *Public Money & Management*, (April–June): 61–68.

— (1999) *Regulation Inside Government: Waste-Watchers, Quality Police, and Sleazebusters*, Oxford: Oxford University Press.

Hooghe, L. and Marks, G. (2001) *Multi-Level Governance and European Integration*, London: Rowman & Littlefield.

— (2003) 'Unraveling the central state, but how? Types of multi-level governance', *American Political Science Review*, 97(2): 233–243.

Horton, S. (1990) 'Local government 1979–89: a decade of change', in S. P. Savage and L. Robins (eds) *Public Policy under Thatcher*, London: Macmillan pp. 172–186.

Howlett, M. (2000) 'Managing the "hollow state": procedural policy instruments and modern governance', *Canadian Public Administration*, 43(4): 412–431.

Inman, R. P. (1987) 'Markets, governments, and the "new" political economy', in A. J. Auerbach and M. Feldstein (eds) *Handbook of Public Economics*, Vol. 2, Amsterdam: Elsevier pp. 647–777.

Ireland, P. (2005) 'Shareholder primacy and the distribution of wealth', *Modern Law Review*, 68(1): 49–81.

Jayasuriya, K. (2001) 'Globalization and the changing architecture of the state: the regulatory state and the politics of negative co-ordination', *Journal of European Public Policy*, 8(1): 101–123.

— (2003) '"Workfare for the global poor": anti-politics and the new governance', Asia Research Centre, Murdoch University, Working Paper 98.

— (2004) 'The new regulatory state and relational capacity', *Policy & Politics*, 32(4): 487–501.

— (2005a) 'Beyond institutional fetishism: from the developmental to the regulatory state', *New Political Economy*, 10(3): 381–387.

— (2005b) *Reconstituting the Global Liberal Order*, London: Routledge.

Jessop, R. (1997) 'Capitalism and its future: remarks on regulation, government and governance', *Review of International Political Economy*, 4(3): 561–581.

— (1998) 'The rise of governance and the risks of failure: the case of economic development', *International Social Science Journal*, 50(155): 29–45.

— (2003) 'Governance and metagovernance: on reflexivity, requisite variety, and requisite irony', in H. P. Bang (ed.) *Governance as Social and Political Communication*, Manchester: Manchester University Press pp. 101–116.

Joerges, C. (2002) 'Deliberative supranationalism - two defences', *European Law Journal*, 8(1): 133–151.

Joerges, C., Mény, Y. and Weiler, J. H. H. (eds) (2001) *Mountain or Molehill? A Critical Appraisal of the Commission White Paper on Governance*, Jean Monnet Working Paper 6/01.

Jones, O. (2014) *The Establishment and How They Get Away with It*, London: Penguin.

Jordana, J. and Levi-Faur, D. (eds) (2004) *The Politics of Regulation*, Cheltenham: Edward Elgar.

Judt, T. (2010) *Ill Fares the Land*, London: Allen Lane.

Kagan, E. (2001) 'Presidential administration', *Harvard Law Review*, 114(8): 2246–385.

Kajer, A. M. (2004) *Governance*, Cambridge: Polity.

Kant, I. (1787; 1998) *Critique of Pure Reason*, Cambridge: Cambridge University Press.

Kassim, H. and Le Galès, P. (2010) 'Exploring governance in a multi-level polity: a policy instruments approach', *West European Politics*, 33(1), 1–21.

Kavanagh, D. and Morris, P. (1989) *Consensus Politics*, Oxford: Blackwell.

Kelsen, H. (1945) *General Theory of Law and State*, trans. A. Wedberg, New York: Russell & Russell.

Keohane R. O. and Nye, J. S. Jr. (eds) (2000) *Governance in a Globalizing World*, Washington: Brookings Institution Press.

Kettl, D. F. (2000) 'The transformation of governance: globalization, devolution, and the role of government', *Public Administration Review*, 60(6): 488–497.

Kickert, W. J. M. (1993) 'Autopoiesis and the science of (public) administration: essence, sense and nonsense', *Organization Studies*, 14(2): 261–278.

King, A. (1975) 'Overload: problems of governing in the 1970s', *Political Studies*, 23(2–3): 284–296.

King, L. A. (2003) 'Deliberation, legitimacy, and multilateral democracy', *Governance*, 16(1): 23–50.

King, R. (2007) *The Regulatory State in an Age of Governance*, London: Palgrave Macmillan.

Kiser, E. and Hechter, M. (1998) 'The debate on historical sociology: rational choice theory and its critics', *American Journal of Sociology*, 104(3): 785–816.

Klijn, E. H. (2007) 'Managing complexity: achieving the impossible?', *Critical Policy Analysis*, 1(3): 252–277.

— (2008) 'Complexity theory and public administration: what's new? Key concepts in complexity theory compared to their counterparts in public administration research', *Public Management Review*, 10(3): 299–317.

Klijn, E. H. and Skelcher, C. (2007) 'Democracy and governance networks: compatible or not?', *Public Administration*, 85(3): 587–608.

Knight, J. and Johnson, J. (1994) 'Aggregation and deliberation: on the possibility of democratic legitimacy', *Political Theory*, 22(2): 277–296.

Koenig-Archibugi, M. (2002) 'The democratic deficit of EU foreign and security policy', *International Spectator*, 37(4): 61–73.

— (2004) 'International governance as new *raison d'état*? The case of the EU common foreign and security policy', *European Journal of International Relations*, 10(2): 147–188.

Kooiman, J. (1999) 'Social-political governance: overview, reflections and design', *Public Management Review*, 1(1): 67–92.

— (2000) 'Societal governance: levels, modes, and orders of social-political interaction', in J. Pierre (ed.) *Debating Governance*, Oxford: Oxford University Press pp. 138–164.

—   (2003) *Governing as Governance*, London: Sage.

Kooiman, J. and Jentoft, S. (2009) 'Meta-governance: values, norms and principles, and the making of hard choices', *Public Administration*, 87(4): 818–836.

Kooiman, J. and van Vliet, M. (1999) 'Self-governance as a mode of societal governance', *Public Management Review*, 1(1): 359–378.

Kooiman, J., Bavinck, M., Chuenpagdee, R., Mahon, R. and Pullin, R. (2008) 'Interactive governance and governability: an introduction', *Journal of Transdisciplinary Environmental Studies*, 7(1): 1–11.

Krippner, G. R. (2011) *Capitalizing on Crisis*, Cambridge, Mass.: Harvard University Press.

Kuflik, A. (1984) 'The inalienability of autonomy', *Philosophy and Public Affairs*, 13(4): 271–298.

Kymlicka, W. and Norman, W. (1994) 'Return of the citizen: a survey of recent work on citizenship theory', *Ethics*, 104(2): 352–381.

Laffont, J.-J. and Martimort, D. (2002) *The Theory of Incentives: The Principal-Agent Model*, Princeton: Princeton University Press.

Laffont, J.-J. and Tirole, J. (1991) 'The politics of government decision-making: a theory of regulatory capture', *Quarterly Journal of Economics*, 106(4), 1089–1127.

Lanchester, J. (2012) *Capital*, London: Faber and Faber.

Lascoumes, P. and Le Gales, P. (2007) 'Introduction: understanding public policy through its instruments--from the nature of instruments to the sociology of public policy instrumentation', *Governance* 20(1), 1–21.

La Spina, A. and Majone, G. (2000) *Lo stato regolatore*, Bologna: Il Mulino.

Law, M. T. and Kim, S. (2010) 'The rise of the American regulatory state: a view from the progressive era', Jerusalem Forum on Regulation & Governance, The Hebrew University, Paper No. 6, May.

Le Grand, J. (1991a), *Equity and Choice: An Essay in Economics and Applied Philosophy*, London: Routledge.

—   (1991b) 'The theory of government failure', *British Journal of Political Science*, 21(4): 423–442.

—   (2003) *Motivation, Agency, and Public Policy: Of Knights and Knaves, Pawns and Queens*, Oxford: Oxford University Press.

—   (2007) *The Other Invisible Hand: Delivering Public Services Through Choice and Competition*, Princeton: Princeton University Press.

—   (2011) 'Delivering Britain's public services through "quasi-markets": what we have achieved so far', Centre for Market and Public Organisation Research in Public Policy, winter. http://www.bristol.ac.uk/cmpo (accessed 4 November 2012).

Le Grand, J. and Estrin, S. (eds) (1989) *Market Socialism*, Oxford: Clarendon Press.

Leibfried, S. and Zürn, M. (2005) *Transformations of the State?*, Cambridge: Cambridge University Press.

Levi-Faur, D. (2012) 'From big government to big governance?', in D. Levi-Faur (ed.), *Oxford Handbook of Governance*, Oxford: Oxford University Press pp. 3–18.

—   (2013) 'The odyssey of the regulatory state: from a "thin" monomorphic concept to a "thick" and polymorphic concept', *Law & Policy*, 35(1–2): 29–50.

Levi-Faur, D. and Gilad, S. (2004) 'The rise of the British regulatory state: transcending the privatization debate', *Comparative Politics*, 37(1): 105–124.

Levy, J. D. (ed.) (2006) *The State after Statism: New State Activities in the Age of Liberalization*, Cambridge, Mass.: Harvard University Press.

Lipsky, M. (1980) *Street-Level Bureaucracy: Dilemma of the Individual in Public Services*, New York: Russell Sage Foundation.

Liska, T. F. (2007) 'The Liska model', *Society and Economy*, 29(3): 363–381.

Lobel, O. (2004) 'The renew deal: the fall of regulation and the rise of governance in contemporary legal thought', *Minnesota Law Review*, 89: 262–390.

Lottenbach, H. (1996) 'Monkish virtues, artificial lives: on Hume's genealogy of morals', *Canadian Journal of Philosophy*, 26(3): 367–88.

Loughlin, M. and Scott, C. (1997) 'The regulatory state', in P. Dunleavy, A. Gamble, I. Holliday and G. Peele (eds) *Developments in British Politics 5*, London: Palgrave Macmillan pp. 205–219.

Low, N. (2005) 'The discourse network: a way of understanding policy formation, stability, and change in the networked polity', in L. Albrechts and S. J. Mandelbaum (eds) *The Network Society: A New Context for Planning?*, London: Routledge.

Luhmann, N. (2008) 'The autopoiesis of social systems', *Journal of Sociocybernetics*, 6(2): 84–95.

Macartney, C. A. (1934) *National States and National Minorities*, Oxford: Oxford University Press.

Mackie, G. (2003) *Democracy Defended*, Cambridge: Cambridge University Press.

—   (2009) 'Schumpeter's leadership democracy', *Political Theory*, 37(1): 128–153.

Mackie, J. L. (1985) *Persons and Values: Selected Papers II*, Oxford: Clarendon Press pp. 152–169.

MacPherson, C. B. (1966) *The Real World of Democracy*, Oxford: Clarendon Press.

—   (1973) *Essays in Democratic Theory*, Oxford: Clarendon Press.

—   (1977) *The Life and Times of Liberal Democracy*, Oxford: Oxford University Press.

Maffettone, S. (2010) *Rawls: An Introduction*, Cambridge: Polity.

Mair, P. (2006) 'Ruling the void: the hollowing of western democracy', *New Left Review*, 42 (Nov–Dec): 25–51.

— (2008) 'The challenge to party government', *West European Politics*, 31(1): 211–234.

— (2013) *Ruling the Void: The Hollowing of Western Democracy*, London: Verso.

Majone, G. (1994) 'The rise of the regulatory state in Europe', *West European Politics*, 17(3): 77–101.

— (1997a) 'From the positive to the regulatory state: causes and consequences of changes in the mode of governance', *Journal of Public Policy*, 17(2): 139–167.

— (1997b) 'The agency model: the growth of regulation and regulatory institutions in the European Union', *Eipascope* 3: 9–14. /aei.pitt. edu/786/1/scop97_3_2.pdf (accessed 6 September 2007).

— (1998) 'Europe's democratic deficit: the question of standards', *European Law Journal*, 4(1): 5–28.

— (1999) 'The regulatory state and its legitimacy problems', *West European Politics*, 22(1): 1–24.

— (2003) 'Deficit democratico, istituzioni non-maggioritarie ed il paradosso dell'integrazione europea', *Stato and mercato*, 67(1): 3–38.

Mann, M. (1993) *The Sources of Social Power: Vol. 2, The Rise of Classes and Nation States, 1760–1914*, Cambridge: Cambridge University Press.

— (2013) *The Sources of Social Power: Vol. 4, Globalizations, 1945–2011*, Cambridge: Cambridge University Press.

March, J. G. and Olsen J. P. (1984) 'The new institutionalism: organizational factors in political life', *American Political Science Review*, 78(3): 734–749.

— (2006) 'The logic of appropriateness', in M. Moran, M. Rein and R. E. Goodin (eds) *The Oxford Handbook of Public Policy*, Oxford: Oxford University Press pp. 689–708.

Marinetto, M. (2007) *Social Theory, the State and Modern Society: The State in Contemporary Social Thought*, Maidenhead: Open University Press.

Marquand, D. (1988) *The Unprincipled Society*, London: Cape.

— (2004) *Decline of the Public*, Cambridge: Polity.

Marshall, T. H. (1950) *Citizenship and Social Class*, Cambridge: Cambridge University Press.

— (1961) 'The welfare state: a sociological interpretation', *European Journal of Sociology*, 2(2): 284–300.

Mauss, M. (1954) *The Gift*, London: Routledge.

Mayntz, R. (1993) 'Governing failures and the problem of governability: some comments on a theoretical paradigm', in J. Kooiman (ed.) *Modern Governance*, London: Sage pp. 9–20.

— (2003) 'From government to governance: political steering in modern societies', Summer Academy on IPP: Wuerzburg, September 7–11.

McAfee, N. (2004) 'Three models of democratic deliberation', *Journal of Speculative Philosophy* 18, 1: 44–59.

—   (2009) 'On democracy's epistemic value', *The Good Society* 18(2): 41–47.

McGowan, F. and Wallace, H. (1996) 'Towards a European regulatory state', *Journal of European Public Policy*, 3(4): 560–576.

Mead, L. M. (1986) *Beyond Entitlement*, New York: Free Press.

Meek, J. (2014) *Private Island: Why Britain Now Belongs to Someone Else*, London: Verso.

Mehde, V. (2006) 'Governance, administrative science, and the paradoxes of new public management', *Public Policy and Administration*, 21(4): 60–81.

Miller, G. J. (2005) 'The political evolution of principal-agent models', *Annual Review of Political Science*, 8: 203–225.

Miller, P. and Rose, N. (1995) 'Production, identity, and democracy', *Theory and Society*, 24(3): 427–467.

Mills, C. W. (1956) *The Power Elite*, New York: Oxford University Press.

—   (1959) *The Sociological Imagination*, New York: Oxford University Press.

Mirowski, P. (2013) *Never Let a Serious Crisis Go to Waste: How Neoliberalism Survived the Financial Meltdown*, London: Verso.

Mirowski, P. and Plehwe, D. (eds) (2009) *The Road from Mont Pèlerin: The Making of the Neoliberal Thought Collective*, Cambridge, Mass.: Harvard University Press.

Mishkin, F. S. (2006) *The Next Great Globalization: How Disadvantaged Nations Can Harness Their Financial Systems to Get Rich,* Princeton: Princeton University Press.

Mitchell, W. C. and Simmons, R. T. (1994) *Beyond Politics: Market Failures, and the Failure of Bureaucracy*, Boulder: Westview Press.

Moldofsky, N. (1989) *Order – With or Without Design?*, London: Centre for Research into Communist Economies.

Moran, M. (2002) 'Understanding the regulatory state', *British Journal of Political Science*, 32(2): 391–413.

—   (2003) *The British Regulatory State: High Modernism and Hyper-Innovation*, Oxford: Oxford University Press.

Moravcsik, A. (2002) 'In defense of the "democratic deficit": reassessing the legitimacy of the European Union', *Journal of Common Market Studies*, 40(4): 603–634.

—   (2004) 'Is there a "democratic deficit" in world politics? A framework for analysis', *Government and Opposition*, 39(2): 336–363.

Mörth, U. (ed.) (2004) *Soft Law in Governance and Regulation*, Cheltenham: Edward Elgar.

Mouffe, C. (2000) *The Democratic Paradox*, London: Verso.

—   (2005) *On the Political*, London: Routledge.

Mount, F. (2012) *The New Few: Or a Very British Oligarchy*, London: Simon & Schuster.

Mueller, D. (1990) *Public Choice II*, Cambridge: Cambridge University Press.

Müller, J.-W. (2006) 'On the origins of constitutional patriotism', *Contemporary Political Theory*, 5(3): 278–296.

— (2011) *Contesting Democracy: Political Ideas in Twentieth-Century Europe*, London: Yale University Press.

Munck, R. (2007) *Globalization and Contestation: The New Great Counter-Movement*, London: Routledge.

Murray, C. (1984) *Losing Ground*, New York: Basic Books.

— (1986) '*Losing Ground* two years later', *Cato Journal*, 6(1): 19–29.

Nabatchi, T. (2010) 'Addressing the citizenship and democratic deficits: the potential of deliberative democracy for public administration', *American Review of Public Administration*, 40 (May): 376–399.

Nelson, W. N. (1980) *On Justifying Democracy*, London: Routledge & Kegan Paul.

Newey, G. (2002) 'Discourse rights and the Drumcree marches: a reply to O'Neill', *British Journal of Politics and International Relations*, 4(1): 75–97.

Newman, J. and Clarke, J. (2009) *Publics, Politics and Power: Remaking the Public in Public Services*, London: Sage.

Neyer, J. (2006) 'The deliberative turn in integration theory', *Journal of European Public Policy*, 13(5): 779–791.

Niskanen, W. (1994) *Bureaucracy and Public Economics*, Cheltenham: Edward Elgar.

Nonet, P. and Selznick, P. (1978) *Law & Society in Transition: Toward Responsive Law*, New York: Octagon.

Novak, W. J. (2002) 'The legal origins of the modern American state', in A. Sarat, B. G. Garth and R. A. Kagan (eds) *Looking Back at Law's Century*, Ithaca: Cornell University Press pp. 249–286.

Nozick, R. (1974) *Anarchy, State, and Utopia*, Oxford: Blackwell.

Oakeshott, M. (1962) *Rationalism and Politics and other Essays*, London: Methuen & Co Ltd.

O'Donnell, G. A. (1998) 'Horizontal accountability in new democracies', *Journal of Democracy*, 9(3): 112–126.

OECD (2011) *Divided We Stand: Why Inequality Keeps Rising*, Paris: OECD.

Offe, C. (1987) 'Democracy against the welfare state? Structural foundations of neoconservative political opportunities', *Political Theory*, 15(4): 501–537.

— (2009) 'Governance: an "empty signifier"'?, *Constellations*, 16(4): 550–562.

Offe, C. and Preuss, U.K. (2006) 'The problem of legitimacy in the European polity: Is democratization the answer?' in C. Crouch and W. Streeck (eds) *The Diversity of Democracy*, Cheltenham: Edward Elgar pp. 175–204.

Olson M. (1965) *The Logic of Collective Action*, Cambridge, Mass.: Harvard University Press.

O'Neill, J. (ed.) (1973) *Modes of Individualism and Collectivism*, London: Heinemann.

O'Neill, O. (1989) *Constructions of Reason*, Cambridge: Cambridge University Press.

Osborne, D. and Gaebler, T. (1992) *Reinventing Government: How the Entrepreneurial Spirit is Transforming the Public Sector*, Reading, Mass.: Addison-Wesley.

Ostrom, E., Walker, J. and Gardner, R. (1992) 'Covenants with and without a sword: self-governance is possible', *American Political Science Review*, 86(02): 404–417.

O'Toole, B. (2006) *The Ideal of Public Service: Reflections on the Higher Civil Service in Britain*, London: Routledge.

O'Toole, L. J. (2004) 'The theory–practice issue in policy implementation research', *Public Administration*, 82(2): 309–329.

Painter, C. (2013) 'The UK coalition government: constructing public service reform narratives', *Public Policy and Administration*, 28(1): 3–20.

Palumbo, A. (2000) *The Evolution of Constitutional Contract*, unpublished PhD thesis, Norwich: University of East Anglia (https://www.academia.edu/913913/The_Evolution_of_Constitutional_Order._Spontaneous_Order_and_Analytical_Theories_of_the_State_in_a_Critical_Perspective).

—— (2001) 'Administration, civil service and bureaucracy', in K. Nash and A. Scott (eds) *Blackwell Companion to Political Sociology*, Oxford: Blackwell pp. 127–138.

—— (2003) 'Liberalism', in R. Axmann (ed.) *Understanding Democratic Politics*, Sage: London pp. 231–240.

—— (2004) 'From Thatcherism to Blairism: Britain's long march to the market', *Österreichische Zeitschrift für Soziologie*, 29(4): 5–29.

—— (2009) 'Due tipi di *corporate governance*: approcci manageriali ed etici a confronto, *Ragion pratica*, 33(2): 541–560.

—— (2010) 'Beyond the post-war Schumpeterian consensus: Governance, legitimacy and post-democracy', *Critical Policy Studies*, 4(4): 319–343.

—— (2011) *La polity reticolare: Analisi e critica della governance come teoria*, Roma: XL Edizioni.

—— (2012) 'Epistemic turn or democratic u-turn? On the tension between philosophical reasoning and political action in deliberative democracy', *Teoria politica*, NS Annali II: 269–291.

Palumbo, A. and Scott, A. (2003) 'Weber, Durkheim and the sociology of the modern state', in R. Bellamy and T. Ball (eds) *Cambridge History of Twentieth Century Political Thought*, Cambridge: Cambridge University Press pp. 368–391.

—— (2005) 'Bureaucracy, open access and social pluralism: returning the common to the goose', in P. du Gay (ed.) *The Values of Bureaucracy*, Oxford: Oxford University Press pp. 267–293.

Papadopoulos, Y. (2007) 'Problems of democratic accountability in network and multilevel governance', *European Law Journal*, 13(4): 469–486.

Parker, D. (1991) 'The 1988 Local Government Act and Compulsory Competitive Tendering', *Urban Studies*, 27(5): 653–667.

Parkinson, J. (2006) *Deliberating in the Real World*, Oxford: Oxford University Press.

Parsons, T. (1937; 1968) *The Structure of Social Action*, New York: Free Press.

Pateman, C. (1970) *Participation and Democratic Theory*, Cambridge: Cambridge University Press.

Paul, E. F., Miller, F. D. Jr, and Paul, J. (eds) (1999) *Responsibility*, Cambridge: Cambridge University Press.

Peacock, A. (1978) 'The economics of bureaucracy: an inside view', in J. M. Buchanan, C. K. Rowley, A. Breton, *et al. The Economics of Politics*, London: IEA pp. 117–128.

— (1992) *Public Choice Analysis in Historical Perspective*, Cambridge: Cambridge University Press.

Peters, B. G. (2002) 'Governance: a garbage can perspective', Institute for Advanced Studies, Vienna, Political Science Series 84.

— (2004) 'Governance and public bureaucracy: new forms of democracy or new forms of control?', *Asia Pacific Journal of Public Administration*, 26(1): 3–15.

— (2011) 'Governance as political theory', *Critical Policy Studies*, 5(1): 63–72.

Peters, B. G. and Pierre, J. (2002) 'Multilevel governance: A view from the garbage can', Manchester Papers in Politics: Epru Series 1/2002.

Peters, B. G. and Pierre, J. (eds) (2004) *Politicization of the Civil Service in Comparative Perspective: The Quest for Control*, London: Routledge.

Pettit, P. (1990) '*Virtus normativa*: rational choice perspectives', *Ethics*, 100(4): 725–755.

— (2008) 'Three conceptions of democratic control', *Constellations*, 15(1): 46–55.

Piattoni, S. (2009) 'Multi-level governance: a historical and conceptual analysis', *Journal of European Integration*, 31(2): 163–180.

Pierre, J. and Peters, B. G. (2000) *Governance, Politics and the State*, Basingstoke: Macmillan.

Piketty, T. (2014) *Capital in the Twenty-First Century*, trans. A. Goldhammer, Cambridge, Mass.: Belknap/Harvard University Press.

Piore, M. J. and Sabel, C. F. (1984) *The Second Industrial Divide: Possibilities for Prosperity*, New York: Basic Books.

Plant, R. (2010) *The Neo-Liberal State*, Oxford: Oxford University Press.

Podolny, J. and Page, K. (1998) 'Network forms of organization', *Annual Review of Sociology*, 24: 57–76.

Poggi, G. (1978) *The Development of the Modern State*, Stanford: Stanford University Press.

— (1992) *Lo stato*, Bologna: Il Mulino.

Poguntke, T. and Webb, P. (2005) *The Presidentialization of Politics*, Oxford: Oxford University Press.

Polanyi, K. (1944) *The Great Transformation*, Boston: Beacon Press.

Polidano, C. (1999) 'The bureaucrat who fell under a bus: ministerial responsibility, executive agencies and the Derek Lewis affair in Britain', *Governance*, 12(2): 201–229.

Pollock, A. M. (2004) *NHS Plc: The Privatisation of Our Health Care*, London: Verso.

Posner, R. A. (1974) 'Theories of economic regulation', *Bell Journal of Economics and Management Science* 5(2): 335–358.

— (2010) *The Crisis of Capitalist Democracy*, Cambridge, Mass.: Harvard University Press.

— (2014) 'The concept of regulatory capture: a short, inglorious history', in D. Carpenter and D. A. Moss (eds) *Preventing Regulatory Capture: Special Interest Influence and How to Limit it*, Cambridge: Cambridge University Press pp. 49–56.

Powell, F. (2007) *The Politics of Civil Society*, Bristol: Policy.

Powell, W. (1990) 'Neither market nor hierarchy: network forms of organization', *Research in Organizational Behavior*, 12: 295–336.

Power, M. (1997a) 'The audit explosion', in G. Mulgan (ed.) *Life after Politics*, London: Verso pp. 286–293.

— (1997b) *The Audit Society*, Oxford: Oxford University Press.

— (2003) 'Evaluating the audit explosion', *Law & Policy*, 25(3): 185–202.

Press Association (2014) 'Public sector cuts may last five more years, outgoing civil service head says', *The Guardian*, Friday 26 September. http://www.theguardian.com/society/2014/sep/26/public-sector-cuts-five-more-years-outgoing-civil-service-head-kerslake (accessed 27 September 2014).

Putnam, R. (1988) 'Diplomacy and domestic politics: the logic of two-level games', *International Organization*, 42(3): 427–460.

Rawls, J. (1955) 'Two concepts of rules', *The Philosophical Review*, 64(1): 3–32.

— (1971) *A Theory of Justice*, Cambridge, Mass.: Harvard University Press.

— (1993) *Political Liberalism*, New York: Columbia University Press.

— (1997) 'The idea of public reason revisited', *University of Chicago Law Review* 64, 765–808.

Reitan, E. A. (2003) *The Thatcher Revolution: Margaret Thatcher, John Major, Tony Blair, and the Transformation of Modern Britain, 1979–2001*, Lanham, Maryland: Rowman & Littlefield .

Rhodes, R. A. W. (1988) *Beyond Westminster and Whitehall*, London: Unwin Hyman.

— (1994) 'The hollowing out of the state: the changing nature of the public service in Britain', *Political Quarterly* 65(2): 138–151.

— (1997) *Understanding Governance*, Buckingham: Open University Press.

— (2000a) 'New Labour's Civil Service: summing-up joining-up', *Political Quarterly*, 71(2): 151–166.

— (2000b) 'The governance narrative: key findings and lessons from the ESRC's Whitehall Programme', *Public Administration*, 78(2): 345–363.

— (2006) 'Policy network analysis', in M. Moran, M. Rein and R.E. Goodin (eds) *The Oxford Handbook of Public Policy*, Oxford: Oxford University Press pp. 426–447.

— (2007) 'Understanding Governance: Ten Years On', *Organization Studies*, 8(28): 1243–1264.

Riker, W. H. (1982) *Liberalism against Populism: A Confrontation between the Theory of Democracy and the Theory of Social Choice*, San Francisco: W. H. Freemen.

Ritzer, G. (2004) *The McDonaldization of Society*, rev. new century edn, London: Sage.

Ritzer, G. and Goodman, D. J. (2003) *Sociological Theory*, 6th edn, New York: McGraw-Hill.

Ritzer, G. and Jurgenson, N. (2010) 'Production, consumption, prosumption: the nature of capitalism in the age of the digital "prosumer"', *Journal of Consumer Culture*, 10(1): 13–36.

Rose, N. and Miller, P. (1992) 'Political power beyond the state: problematics of government', *British Journal of Sociology*, 43(2): 173–205.

— (2008) *Governing the Present*, Cambridge: Polity.

Rose, N., O'Malley, P. and Valverde, M. (2006) 'Governmentality', *Annual Review of Law and Social Science*, 2: 83–104.

Rosenau, J. N. (1992) 'Governance, order, and change in world politics', in J. N. Rosenau and E-O. Czempiel (eds) *Governance without Government*, Cambridge: Cambridge University Press pp. 1–29.

— (1995) 'Governance in the Twenty-First Century', *Global Governance*, 1(1): 13–43.

Rothschild, K. W. (2008) 'Economic imperialism', *Analyse & Kritik*, 30(2): 723–733.

Rowe, N. (1989) *Rules and Institutions*, New York: Philip Allan.

Ruggie, J. (1993) 'Territoriality and beyond: problematizing modernity in international relations', *International Organization*, 47(1): 13–74.

— (1998) 'Globalization and the embedded liberalism compromise: the end of an era?', in W. Streeck (ed.), *Internationale Wirtschaft, nationale Demokratie*, Frankfurt: Campus pp. 79–98.

Runciman, W. G. (1963) *Social Science and Political Theory*, Cambridge: Cambridge University Press.

Ryan, A. (1991) 'The British, the Americans and rights', in M. J. Lacey and K. Haakonssen (eds) *A Culture of Rights*, Cambridge: Cambridge University Press pp. 366–439.

Saad-Filho, A. and Johnston, D. (eds) (2005) *Neoliberalism*, London: Pluto.

Sabel, C. (1995) 'Design, deliberation, and democracy: on the new pragmatism of firms and public institutions', paper presented at conference on *Liberal Institutions, Economic Constitutional Rights, and the Role of Organizations*, European University Institute, Florence December 15–16.

— (2004) 'Beyond principal-agent governance: experimentalist organizations, learning and accountability', in E. Engelen and M. Sie Dhian Ho (eds) *De Staat van de Democratie: Democratie voorbij de Staat. WRR Verkenning 3*, Amsterdam: Amsterdam University Press pp. 173–195.

Sabel, C. F. and Simon, W. H. (2006) 'Epilogue: accountability without sovereignty', in G. de Búrca and J. Scott (eds) *New Governance and Constitutionalism in Europe and the US*, Oxford: Hart pp. 395–412.

Sabel, C. F. and Zeitlin, J. (2008) 'Learning from difference: the new architecture of experimentalist governance in the European Union', *European Law Journal*, 14(3): 271–327.

— (2012) 'Experimentalist governance', in D. Levi-Faur (ed.) *Oxford Handbook of Governance*, Oxford: Oxford University Press pp. 169–183.

Sand, I.-J. (1998) 'Understanding the new forms of governance: mutually interdependent, reflexive, destabilised and competing institutions', *European Law Journal*, 4(3): 271–293.

Sandberg, B. (2013) 'The road to market', *Administrative Theory & Praxis*, 35(1): 28–45.

Sandel, M. (1996) *Democracy's Discontent: America in Search of a Public Philosophy*, Cambridge, Mass.: Harvard University Press.

Sanderson, I. (1999) 'Participation and democratic renewal: from "instrumental" to "communicative" rationality?', *Policy & Politics*, 27(3): 325–341.

Sassen, S. (2006) *Territory, Authority, Rights: From Medieval to Global Assemblages*, Princeton: Princeton University Press.

— (2008) 'Neither global nor national: novel assemblages of territory, authority and rights', *Ethics & Global Politics*, 1(1–2): 61–79.

Saville, J. (1957–8) 'The welfare state: an historical approach', *New Reasoner*, 3(1): 5–25.

Schäfer, A. and Streeck, W. (eds) (2013) *Politics in the Age of Austerity*, Cambridge: Polity.

Scharpf, F. (1994) 'Games real actors could play: positive and negative coordination in embedded negotiations', *Journal of Theoretical Politics*, 6(1): 27–53.

— (1997) *Games Real Actors Play*, Boulder, CO: Westview.

— (2000) 'Interdependence and democratic legitimation', in S. J. Pharr and R. D. Putnam (eds), *Disaffected Democracies: What's Troubling the Trilateral Countries?*, Princeton: Princeton University Press pp. 101–120.

— (2009) 'Legitimacy in the multilevel European polity', *European Political Science Review*, 1(2): 173–204.

Schattschneider, E. E. (1942) *Party Government*, Holt, NY: Reinhart & Winston.

— (1960) *The Semi-Sovereign People*, Holt, NY: Reinhart & Winston.

Schedler, A. (1999) 'Conceptualizing accountability', in A. Schedler, L. Diamond and M. F. Plattner (eds) *The Self-Restraining State: Power and Accountability in New Democracies*, Boulder, CO: Lynne Rienner Publishers pp. 13–28.

Schmidt, V. (2013) 'Democracy and legitimacy in the European Union revisited: input, output and "throughput"', *Political Studies*, 61(1): 2–22.

Schmitter, P. C. (1983) 'Democratic theory and neocorporatist practice', *Social Research*, 50(4): 885–928.

Schneiberg, M. and Bartley, T. (2008) 'Organizations, regulation, and economic behavior: regulatory dynamics and forms from the nineteenth to twenty-first century', *Annual Review of Law and Social Science*, 4: 31–61.

Scholte, J. A. (2005) *Globalization: A Critical Introduction*, 2nd edn, Basingstoke: Palgrave Macmillan.

Schotter, A. (1981) *The Economic Theory of Social Institutions*, Cambridge: Cambridge University Press.

Schumpeter, J. (1943) *Capitalism, Socialism and Democracy*, New York: Harper & Row.

Schwarzmantel, J. (2005) 'Challenging neoliberal hegemony', *Contemporary Politics*, 11(2–3): 85–98.

Scott, C. (2000) 'Accountability in the regulatory state', *Journal of Law and Society*, 27(1): 38–60.

— (2002) 'Private regulation of the public sector: a neglected facet of contemporary governance', *Journal of Law & Society*, 29(1): 56–76.

— (2003) 'Regulation in the age of governance: the rise of the post-regulatory state', National Europe Centre, Australian National University, Paper No. 100.

Searle, J. R. (1995) *The Construction of Social Reality*, New York: Free Press.

Self, P. (1993) *Government by the Market*, London: Palgrave Macmillan.

Shapiro, S. and Wright, R. (2011) 'The future of the administrative presidency: turning administrative law inside-out', *University of Miami Law Review*, 65(2): 577–620.

Shaw, M. (2000) *Theory of the Global State: Globality as an Unfinished Revolution*, Cambridge: Cambridge University Press.

Simon, H. A. (1944) 'Decision-making and administrative organization', *Public Administration Review*, 4(1): 16–30.

— (1946) 'The proverbs of administration', *Public Administration Review*, 6(1): 53–67.

— (1947; 3rd edn 1976) *Administrative Behaviour*, New York: Free Press.

Skelcher, C. (2010) 'Fishing in muddy waters: principals, agents, and democratic governance in Europe', *Journal of Public Administration Research and Theory*, 20(s1): i161-i175.

Skinner, Q. (1989) 'The state', in T. Ball, J. Farr and R. L. Hanson (eds) *Political Innovation and Conceptual Change*, Cambridge: Cambridge University Press pp. 90–131.

— (2002) 'From the state of princes to the person of the state', in Q. Skinner *Visions of Politics, 2: Renaissance Virtues*, Cambridge: Cambridge University Press pp. 368–413.

Skocpol, T. (1985) 'Bringing the state back in: strategies of analysis in current research', in B. Evans, P. D. Rueschemeyer, and T. Skocpol (eds) *Bringing the State Back In*, Cambridge: Cambridge University Press pp. 3–37.

Slaughter, A.-M. (2003) 'Global government networks, global information agencies, and disaggregated democracy', *Michigan Journal of International Law* 24: 1041–1075.

Smismans, S. (2006) 'Participation in new governance', *Columbia Journal of European Law*, 13(3): 595–622.

Smith, G. (2005) *Beyond the Ballot*, London: POWER Inquiry. http://www.soton. ac.uk/ccd/events/SuppMat/Beyond%20the%20Ballot.pdf (accessed 7 July 2008).

Smith, G. and Wales, C. (2000) 'Citizens' juries and deliberative democracy', *Political Studies*, 48(1): 51–65.

Smith, M. A. and Kollock, P. (1999) *Communities in Cyberspace*, London: Routledge.

Soederberg, S., Menz, G. and Cerny P. (eds) (2005) *Internalizing Globalization: The Rise of Neoliberalism and the Erosion of National Models of Capitalism*, New York: Palgrave Macmillan.

Somers, M. R. (2008) *Genealogies of Citizenship*, Cambridge: Cambridge University Press.

— (2011) 'Reply to the critics', *Trajectories* 22(2): 25–34, http://www. asanet.org/sectionchs/documents/newsletters/SCHSspring2011.pdf.

Somin, I. (2011) 'Foot voting, political ignorance, and constitutional design', *Social Philosophy & Policy*, 28(1): 202–227.

Sørensen, E. (2006) 'Metagovernance: the changing role of politicians in processes of democratic governance', *American Review of Public Administration*, 36(1): 98–114.

Sørensen, E. and Torfing, J. (2005) 'The democratic anchorage of governance networks', *Scandinavian Political Studies* 28(3): 195–218.

— (2006) 'Introduction: governance network research: towards a second generation', in E. Sørensen and J. Torfing (eds) *Theories of Democratic Network Governance*, Basingstoke: Palgrave Macmillan pp. 1–33.

— (2009) 'Making governance networks effective and democratic through metagovernance', *Public Administration*, 87(2): 234–258.

Sørensen, E. and Triantafillou, P. (eds) (2009) *The Politics of Self-governance*, Farnham: Ashgate.

Sørensen, G. (2004) *The Transformation of the State*, New York: Palgrave Macmillan.

Standing, G. (2011) *The Precariat: The New Dangerous Class*, London: A&C Black.

Stigler, G. J. (1971) 'The theory of economic regulation', *Bell Journal of Economics and Management Science*, 2(1): 3–21.

Stiglitz, J. (2008) 'Government failure vs. market failure: principles of regulation', paper for the Tobin Project's conference on *Government and Markets: Toward a New Theory of Regulation*, Yulee, Florida, 1–3 February http:// academiccommons.columbia.edu/download/fedora_content/download/ ac:126998/CONTENT/JES.Govt.Failure.Mkt.Failure.pdf (accessed 7 March 2010).

Stoker, G. (1998) 'Governance as theory: five propositions', *International Social Science Journal*, 50(155): 17–28.

— (2006) 'Public value management: a new narrative for networked governance?', *American Review of Public Administration*, 36(1): 41–57.

Stone, B. (1995) 'Administrative accountability in the "Westminster" democracies: towards a new conceptual framework', *Governance*, 8(4): 505–526.

Strange, S. (1995) 'The defective state', *Daedalus*, 124(2): 55–74.

— (1996) *The Retreat of the State*, Cambridge: Cambridge University Press.

Streeck, W. (2014) *Buying Time: The Delayed Crisis of Democratic Capitalism*, London: Verso.

Stringham, E. (ed.) (2005) *Anarchy, State and Public Choice*, Cheltenham: Edward Elgar.

Strøm, K. (2000) 'Delegation and accountability in parliamentary democracies', *European Journal of Political Research*, 37(3): 261–289.

Stuckler, D. and Basu, S. (2013) *The Body Economic – Why Austerity Kills: Recessions, Budget Battles, and the Politics of Life and Death*, New York: Basic Books.

Sugden, R. (1991) 'Rational choice: a survey of contributions from economics and philosophy', *Economic Journal*, 101(407): 751–785.

Tawney, R. H. (1952) *Equality*, 4th edn, London: G. Allen & Unwin Ltd.

Taylor, I. (1999) 'Raising the expectation interest: New Labour and the Citizen's Charter', *Public Policy and Administration*, 14(4): 29–38.

Taylor, L. (2010) *Maynard's Revenge: The Collapse of Free Market Macroeconomics*, Cambridge, Mass.: Harvard University Press.

Teschke, B. (2004) 'The origins and evolution of the European states-system', in W. Brown, S. Bromley and S. Athreye (eds) *Ordering the International: History, Change and Transformation*, London: Pluto pp. 21–65.

Teubner, G. (1983) 'Substantive and reflexive elements in modern law', *Law & Society Review*, 17(2): 239–286.

— (1984) 'Autopoiesis in law and society: a rejoinder to Blankenburg', *Law & Society Review*, 18(2): 291–301.

— (1997) 'The king's many bodies: the self-deconstruction of law's hierarchy', *Law & Society Review*, 31(4): 763–788.

Thompson, D. F. (1980) 'Moral responsibility of public officials: the problem of many hands', *American Political Science Review*, 74(4): 905–916.

Thompson, G. (2003) *Between Hierarchies and Markets*, Oxford: Oxford University Press.

Tiebout, C. M. (1956) 'A pure theory of local expenditures', *Journal of Political Economy*, 64(5): 416–424.

Tirole, J. (1986) 'Hierarchies and bureaucracies: on the role of collusion in organizations', *Journal of Law, Economics, & Organization*, 2(2): 181–214.

— (1994) 'The internal organization of government', *Oxford Economic Papers*, 46(1–1).

Titmuss, R. M. (1963) 'The welfare state: images and realities', *Social Service Review* pp. 1–11.

— (1976) *Essays on the Welfare State*, 6th edn, London: G. Allen & Unwin Ltd.

Torfing, J. (2005) 'Governance network theory: towards a second generation', *European Political Science*, 4(3): 305–315.

Torfing, J., Peters, B. G., Pierre, J. and Sorensen, E. (2012) *Interactive Governance: Advancing the Paradigm*, Oxford: Oxford University Press.

Torgerson, D. (1995) 'Policy analysis and public life: the restoration of *phronesis*', in J. Farr, J. S. Dryzek and S. T. Leonard (eds) *Political Science in History*, Cambridge: Cambridge University Press pp. 225–252.

Toye, R. (2003) *The Labour Party and the Planned Economy, 1931–1951*, Woodbridge: The Boydell Press.

Trattner, W. I. (1994) *From Poor Law to Welfare State: A History of Social Welfare in America*, 5th edn, New York: The Free Press.

Treib, O., Bähr, H. and Falkner, G. (2007) 'Modes of governance: towards a conceptual clarification', *Journal of European Public Policy*, 14(1): 1–20.

Trubek, D. and Trubek, L. (2006) 'New governance and legal regulation: complementarity, rivalry or transformation', *Columbia Journal of European Law*, 13(3): 539–564.

Tullock, G. (1972) 'Economic imperialism', in J. M. Buchanan and R. D. Tollison (eds) *The Theory of Public Choice: Political Applications of Economics*, Ann Arbor: The University of Michigan Press pp. 317–329.

— (1976) *The Vote Motive: An Essay in the Economics of Politics, with Applications to the British Economy*, London: IEA.

Turpin, C. (1994) 'Ministerial responsibility', in J. Jowell and D. Oliver (eds) *The Changing Constitution*, 3rd edn, Oxford: Clarendon pp. 109–151.

Turpin, C. and Tomkins, A. (2007) *British Government and the Constitution: Text and Materials*, 6th edn, Cambridge: Cambridge University Press.

Vanberg, V. (2000) 'Globalization, democracy, and citizens' sovereignty: can competition among governments enhance democracy?', *Constitutional Political Economy*, 11(1): 87–112.

Vernon, J. (2011) 'Canary in the coal mine', *Times Higher Education*, 1 December.

Vibert, F. (2007) *The Rise of the Unelected: Democracy and the New Separation of Powers*, Cambridge: Cambridge University Press.

Vincent-Jones, P. (1999) 'The regulation of contractualisation in quasi-markets for public services', *Public Law*, Summer: 304–327.

Wade, R. (2003) 'The invisible hand of the American empire', *Ethics and International Affairs*, 17(2): 77–88.

Waldron, J. (1993) *Liberal Rights*, Cambridge: Cambridge University Press.

— (1999) *Law and Disagreement*, Oxford: Oxford University Press.

Walker, J. L. (1966), 'A critique of the elitist theory of democracy', *American Political Science Review*, 60(2): 285–295.

Walker, N. and de Burca, G. (2006) 'Reconceiving law and new governance', *Columbia Journal of European Law*, 13(3): 519–537.

Wälti, S., Küjbler, D. and Papadopoulos, Y. (2004) 'How democratic is "governance"? Lessons from Swiss drug policy', *Governance*, 17(1): 83–113.

Waltz, K. (1999) 'Globalization and governance', *PS: Political Science and Politics*, 32(4): 693–700.

Warner, C. M. (1999) 'The political economy of "quasi-statehood" and the demise of 19th century African politics', *Review of International Studies*, 25(2): 233–255.

Warren, M. E. (2009) 'Governance-driven democratization', *Critical Policy Analysis*, 3(1): 3–13.

Watkins, S. (2013) 'Vanity and venality', *London Review of Books*, 35(16): 17–21.

Weale, A. (1992) '*Homo economicus, homo sociologicus*', in S. Hargreaves-Heap, M. Hollis, B. Lyons, R. Sugden and A. Weale *The Theory of Choice: A Critical Guide*, Oxford: Blackwell pp. 62–72.

Weber, M. (1948) *From Max Weber: Essays in Sociology*, H. Gerth and C. W. Mills (eds), London: Routledge.

Weinberg, J. (2013) 'The practicality of political philosophy', *Social Philosophy and Policy* 30(1–2): 330–351.

Weiss, T. G. (2013) *Global Governance: Why? What? Whither?*, Cambridge: Polity.

Whelan, R. (1996) *The Corrosion of Charity*, London: IEA.

Williams, B. A. O. (2002) *Truth & Truthfulness: An Essay in Genealogy*, Princeton: Princeton University Press.

Williams, D. and Young, T. (1994) 'Governance, the World Bank, and liberal theory', *Political Studies*, 42(1): 84–100.

Williamson, O. (2000) 'The new institutional economics: taking stock, looking ahead', *Journal of Economic Literature*, 38(3): 595–613.

Williamson, O. E. and Winter, S. G. (eds) (1993) *The Nature of the Firm*, Oxford: Oxford University Press.

Winch, P. (1990) *The Idea of Social Science and Its Relation to Philosophy*, London: Routledge.

Winston, C. (2006) *Government Failure versus Market Failure*, Washington, D.C.: AEI-Brookings Joint Center for Regulatory Studies.

Wittgenstein, L. (1958) *Philosophical Investigations*, 2nd edn, Oxford: Blackwell.

Wolf, K. D. (1999a) 'Defending state autonomy: intergovernmental governance in the European Union', in B. Kohler-Koch and R. Eising (eds) *The Transformation of Governance in the European Union*, London: Routledge pp. 231–248.

— (1999b) 'The new *raison d'état* as a problem for democracy in world society', *European Journal of International Relations*, 5(3): 333–363.

Wolin, S. (1960) *Politics and Vision: Continuity and Innovation in Western Political Thought*, 2004 expanded edition, Princeton: Princeton University Press.

— (1996) 'The liberal/democratic divide: on Rawls's *Political Liberalism*', *Political Theory*, 24: 97–142.

— (2008) *Democracy Incorporated: Managed Democracy and the Specter of Inverted Totalitarianism*, Princeton: Princeton University Press.

Woodhouse, D. (1994) *Ministers and Parliament: Accountability in Theory and Practice*, Oxford: Clarendon.

Wu, T. (2011) *The Master Switch: The Rise and Fall of Information Empires*, New York: Knopf.

Yee, A. (2004) 'Cross-national concepts in supranational governance: state-society relations and EU policy making', *Governance*, 17(4): 487–524.

Young, H. (1989) *One of Us: A Biography of Mrs. Thatcher*, London: Macmillan.

Young, I. M. (2013) *Responsibility for Justice*, Oxford: Oxford University Press.

Zysman, J. (1996) 'The myth of a "global" economy: enduring national foundations and emerging regional realities', *New Political Economy*, 1(2): 157–184.

Index

www.ingramcontent.com/pod-product-compliance
Lightning Source LLC
Chambersburg PA
CBHW072045020426
42334CB00017B/1400